CONCEPTS AND CASES IN

Retail and Merchandise Management

FAIRCHILD BOOKS
New York

CONCEPTS AND CASES IN
Retail and Merchandise Management

second edition

Nancy J. Rabolt
San Francisco State University

Judy K. Miler
Florida State University

Executive Editor: Olga T. Kontzias
Senior Associate Acquisitions Editor: Jaclyn Bergeron
Senior Development Editor: Jennifer Crane
Assistant Development Editor: Robert Phelps
Art Director: Adam B. Bohannon
Associate Art Director: Erin Fitzsimmons
Production Director: Ginger Hillman
Associate Production Editor: Andrew Fargnoli
Project Manager: Jeff Hoffman
Copyeditor: Joanne Slike
Cover Design: Adam B. Bohannon
Text Design: Nicola Ferguson

Library of Congress Catalog Card Number: 2008923 810
ISBN: 978-1-56367-600-0
GST R 133004424

Printed in the USA

TP09, CH13

Special appreciation to my parents, George and Anne Kuchler, and my San Francisco State University colleagues for their support—NJR

To my parents, who were with me for the first edition, for their many years of love and support—JKM

Contents

Extended Contents

FOUR: MERCHANDISE CHARACTERISTICS

EIGHT: SALES PROMOTION, ADVERTISING, AND VISUAL MERCHANDISING

NINE: PERSONAL SELLING AND CUSTOMER RELATIONS

Extended Contents

Extended Contents

Acknowledgments

We would like to thank the many friends and colleagues who are members of the American Collegiate Retailing Association and the International Textile and Apparel Association. From these two professional organizations we were able to draw support, as well as find the majority of the case authors. Without their active participation, we would not have a book at all. A listing of contributing authors (called "About the Authors"), along with short biographies and their professional affiliations may be found at the end of the book. We thank you all!

A special thank-you to Sidney Packard and Nathan Axelrod, for pioneering the predecessor to this book about 30 years ago.

To our Fairchild editors, Jaclyn Bergeron, Jennifer Crane, and Olga Kontzias, for their belief and support in this project, we wish to express our appreciation.

We would also like to thank our students, who were wonderful critics and willing case testers.

Preface

Merchandising is based on decision making; therefore, understanding the complexity of decision making and sharpening critical thinking skills is paramount in preparing students for their place in business management. Skills need to be developed to provide potential professionals the capability to successfully function in the increasingly complex world of retailing. Case study analysis is a proven means of sharpening critical thinking for effective decision making. Working in the industry has reinforced our belief that actual experience is the best teacher, and if this is not available, simulated experience, such as case studies, can be an excellent substitute. Analyzing case studies have proven to be a much better and more enjoyable way to learn about businesses and their problems and successes than just reading about them.

PURPOSE OF THIS BOOK

The major purpose of this book is to provide a merchandising-based casebook that identifies and presents critical management issues in contemporary retailing and related manufacturing. It should provide an aid in preparing and developing future retail executives to meet the many changes they will encounter in the next decade. Several benefits distinguish this casebook from other retail, marketing, or merchandising case books. First, the authors have attempted to present a comprehensive book that covers all aspects of retail and merchandise management from a conceptual and case perspective. Second, most of the cases have been selected to represent commonly encountered beginning and middle management business problems, such as those a beginning professional would encounter. Third, we have presented both qualitative and quantitative types of cases, because both arise in the business environment.

And last, because the manufacturer and retailer are becoming closer partners today than ever before, and in many cases the retailer is also a manufacturer or the manufacturer is also a retailer, the authors felt that it was important to present more manufacturing/retailing problems than other casebooks have in the past. As a result, quite a few of the cases stress the integrative nature of the manufacturer and retailer working to meet the consumer's needs and wants today. Additionally, almost all of the cases presented are customer service driven, which serves to emphasize the importance of satisfying the customer from both the manufacturing and retailing perspective, because the customer is the one who actually drives the business.

It was not our intention to rewrite a basic retail, merchandising, or management textbook, but to highlight and emphasize the major concepts and principles of retail and merchandising management, so that they may be used to analyze the cases we are presenting without the use of any other source. It was our intention, however, for our casebook to stand alone as a practical learning tool for merchandising management decision making. Some may wish to use the book as a supplement to a larger text, for example, in a merchandising management class, and others may use it alone in an upper-division case analysis class.

CONTENTS AND CHAPTER OBJECTIVES

In this second edition of the book, about a third of the cases are new in addition to many revised cases from our first edition, as well as some previously published cases that round out concepts we wanted to illustrate. Authors are from both the profession and academia, and they have written from retail, manufacturing, marketing, and merchandising perspectives. The book contains a total of 76 cases (including one two-part case). To ensure that we covered all the major topics that are vital to retailing and merchandising, a combination of real and simulated cases were used in this book. Propriety sometimes dictated that company and personal names used in the cases be changed. We are pleased that there is such a vast array of material covered in the cases. Many major companies are profiled, such as Gap, Wal-Mart, Nordstrom, Saks Fifth Avenue, Abercrombie & Fitch, Best Buy, Anthropologie, Target, eBay, and JCPenney.

For ease in using the numerous cases, we have compiled a list of case summaries that starts on page xxxix, which highlights the major concepts and/or principles contained in the cases, chapter by chapter. The case numbers and titles identify the cases for easy reference.

Multiple objectives are presented at the beginning of each of the 11 chapters in the book. They represent the major focus for each of the chapters. Additionally, the opening abstract-like paragraph to each chapter summarizes the concepts and principles that are contained in the text that appears before the cases.

Chapter 1 describes retail management's role and responsibilities. A discussion of the methods and importance of effective training and evaluation of retail management personnel along with an explanation of organizational structure, delegation of authority, and chain of command is also contained in this chapter.

Chapter 2 identifies the major types of retailers and their characteristics and differences, emphasizing the diversity and complexity of retail formats today. This chapter also describes retail ownership and retail format trends.

Chapter 3 relates image, identity, and retail positioning to companies and products. It stresses the importance of retail differentiation and successful merchandising. The relationship between competition, positioning, and target marketing in today's complex marketplace is also discussed.

Chapter 4 presents major merchandise characteristics, such as style, fashion, price, and quality, as related to image. Branded versus private-label merchandise is also discussed, in addition to the concepts of licensing, knockoffs, and counterfeiting.

The importance of merchandise planning and forecasting is highlighted in Chapter 5. In addition, the relationship of planning, pricing, productivity, and profit to buying is examined. Also considered is dollar, unit, and assortment planning and their importance in merchandise management, as well as the critical role of standards and controls in successful retail management.

Chapter 6 examines the challenges and opportunities of domestic and international sourcing. This chapter emphasizes the importance of careful merchandise source selection. Centralized and decentralized buying, along with other types of buying origination and ordering, are also presented. Lastly, an explanation of the use and importance of buying offices and markets to retailers is given.

The importance of good retail-vendor partnerships is stressed in Chapter 7, and the role of negotiation between buyer and seller is explored. Major problems between vendors and retailers and potential resolutions are also presented. Additionally, the types of orders that retailers utilize are discussed.

Chapter 8 presents methods of communication between retailers and customers and analyzes their effectiveness. Promotional mix is defined and related to media selection. Also, the types and importance of advertising, promotional planning, and budgeting are presented.

The importance of customer service and the role of personal selling at retail are emphasized in Chapter 9. The concepts of good customer service, compensation, selling incentives, and product knowledge are examined. The importance of product knowledge in the selling process is explained. The methods and importance of effective sales training and evaluation of retail sales personnel are also discussed.

Chapter 10 describes entrepreneurship and presents characteristics of successful entrepreneurs. The process and challenges of starting your own business are also explained, and the role of leadership is examined.

When this book was originally conceived, the authors debated whether or not ethics warranted its own chapter. As we received and reviewed cases, we found out that our first instincts had been correct. Ethics is such an important issue today in the business environment that we ended up having more cases that shared some ethical dimension than any other facet. Therefore, we concluded that a chapter focusing on ethics was indeed a good idea and remains so today. Chapter 11 explores ethics and social responsibility of retailers and manufacturers, while distinguishing between business and personal ethics. Ethics in sourcing and selling are explained, as are the legal considerations within which retailers and manufacturers operate.

Technology is an essential factor in today's business environment at all levels and is therefore incorporated into all chapters.

INSTRUCTOR'S GUIDE

An Instructor's Guide accompanies this book. To help direct the resolution to the cases, this instructor's manual gives a thorough analysis of the cases with alternative solutions, suggested answers to selected case study questions, and exercises for further student investigation. Some cases do not follow this format but require general discussion, and it has been stated to "do not use the alternative solutions format for this case." Some study questions from the cases can be answered with the alternative analysis presented for the major question or through the material in the case and/or from the introductory chapter text. Also provided is teaching strategy for using the recommended formats in the How to Use section. The instructor's guide is arranged by chapter and contains the following:

1. Teaching objectives
2. Case analyses
3. Study question answers and/or suggestions

HOW TO USE THIS BOOK

The challenges and opportunities facing retailers and manufacturers today are tremendous because of the rapidly moving business environment that surrounds all of us in this global marketplace. Because of this pace of change, students need to be prepared to meet these challenges and opportunities head-on. Preparation is necessary to think and act quickly and efficiently to be able to meet the changes that will be encountered in the workplace. Critical, innovative thinking is paramount, and case study analysis will help position you into lifelike business situations that simulate those that may be encountered in future careers.

An overview of today's retail merchandising and management concerns is provided through the concepts and issues examined in this book. Eleven major topical areas of concern to current and future retail professionals—like yourself—are presented in the chapter text and the related cases. The cases in this book are based on real business situations or amalgams of real situations. These involve both individuals and groups, independent and corporate businesses, retailers and their suppliers, along with domestic and international settings. The cases help exemplify to students the challenging and exciting nature of merchandising, from both a retail and a manufacturing perspective. They also support the reality that retailing and manufacturing are more interrelated (and more interdependent) today than ever before, as they must work together cooperatively toward success, particularly in the apparel manufacturing and retail industries.

CONCEPT OVERLAP

Business decisions are often complex, overlapping several areas and affecting more than one facet of business or industry. Problems can stem from a myriad of sources. Likewise, the cases presented in certain chapters could very well have been placed in other chapters or sections. It may be helpful to use the Case Summaries, which lists concepts and principles for each case. Concepts addressed in one case may appear in several chapters; therefore, this list shows the position of each case in its chapter in addition to secondary chapter usage. For example, *Case 23, The Knockoff* is discussed in Chapter 4, Merchandise Characteristics, under the concept of fashion image, but it also is related to the issues in Chapter 11, Ethics and Legal Behavior in Merchandise Management. The chapter text often makes reference to cases in other chapters with similar applications. This serves to emphasize the fact that decision-making related to a specific business function may be a more complex effort than it first appears, as well as to reinforce the interdependence and interrelationship of all aspects of retailing and manufacturing.

CHAPTER STRUCTURE

The 11 chapters in the book are arranged in six parts:

1. Chapter objectives
2. Chapter text with key terms in bold
3. Key terms listed
4. Chapter bibliographies
5. Cases with major question for analysis and additional study questions
6. Chapter discussion questions

Chapter objectives are those goals that the authors intended a particular chapter to accomplish.

Some information provided in the chapter text does not have an illustration in a case but has been included to provide a more complete overview of the major topic or concept.

Key terms are bolded and defined within the chapter text and are listed alphabetically before the start of the cases. These terms are important components in the overall understanding of the chapter topic and are highlighted to bring attention to them.

The 76 cases that appear in this book all contain a major problem for you to analyze. Each case also has several study questions and exercises that should stimulate further inquiry pertaining to the chapter concepts/principles and/or the specific problems presented in the cases themselves. Discussion of and investigation into these additional activities may also help lead you to an approach to use for the analysis of the cases.

The chapter discussion questions found at the end of each chapter may be used for debating and discussing a concept, which can incorporate several of the cases and concepts in the chapter. Additionally, they may be used to compare and contrast the various issues raised within all the chapters, as well as being helpful in formulating strategies to solve the cases.

Chapter bibliographies provide sources used in the text, in addition to other readings and information that might be helpful to prepare an analysis of individual cases. Tables and figures (including photographs and diagrams) are used to supplement and support material in the chapters. This supporting evidence either highlights and reinforces the concepts/principles and data explored in the chapter text or presents vital statistics and data that are actually necessary in understanding and solving the case.

WHAT IS A CASE?

A case is a written description of a business situation or problem. It generally provides factual information about a company's background, which often includes organizational or financial data related to the present situation. The use of case analysis in teaching was developed by the Harvard Business School in the 1920s with the purpose of introducing the highest possible level of realism into teaching management decision making. A case raises contemporary issues and provides information to analyze from a business perspective. Also, often included in a case is information that is outside of the immediate company, which is related to the sociocultural, political, legal, technological, and competitive environments. Data related to such industry sectors as apparel or fashion are described to give the reader a better understanding of the circumstances surrounding the situation. It is your job to propose solutions to the problems. In some circumstances, the case authors have purposely presented cases with no readily identifiable problem, just facts to sift through to arrive at the problem. In this book, however, each case poses at least one specific problem to be solved or analysis to be undertaken.

THE VALUE OF THE CASE METHOD OF INQUIRY

The case analysis method is different from other teaching/learning situations that you are probably more familiar with, such as lectures or demonstrations. There is no memorization of facts or other material presented by the instructor. The case study method is an active, problem-solving way of learning in which you have to think about the problem, use the facts provided in the case, and then decide on the most appropriate action to take. External environmental factors (those outside the company) should also be considered, along with the specific internal facts about the company and the situation. Analyses are reliant on critical thinking, logic, and sound integrative reasoning. A form of experience in handling a variety of problem situations can be gained through this process, providing preparation for the reality of the workplace.

The cases themselves can also help you to improve your reading, writing, and speaking abilities, which are vitally important for good communication in business. Additionally, exposure to others' thoughts and reasoning (such as those characters portrayed in the cases) can open your mind to other views. Most of the cases in this book are descriptions of real situations in a company; some, however, are an amalgam of several companies. In these cases, a name for the company has been created; therefore, you will not recognize the company name. In other cases, companies have requested that their firm's name not be used and because of this we have changed the names of their organizations. The facts are real, however, and you are to use them in your analysis. Primarily, this book focuses on cases about retailers and manufacturers of apparel; nevertheless, other related products available to the consumer today are also included.

CASE ANALYSIS

When analyzing a case, you should assume the role of the challenged individual in the case and react as you believe that person should to best remedy the problem. As in all problem situations, there never is a single solution, nor a right or wrong answer. Therefore, your fellow classmates may come up with different recommendations and devise other solutions than you. However, your recommended course of action (the best alternative) relies on a justification for that recommendation. It should be based on the facts contained within the case, along with the basic concepts and/or principles of retail and merchandise management provided in the chapter text.

Often it may seem that you don't have enough information to solve the case problem. Welcome to the real world of business! Often, decision makers do not have all the information needed for a "good" decision. But they must make a decision with the information available at the time. Later, when more information becomes available, it may appear that the decision was not the best. However, most of us do not have a crystal ball and we must do the best we can with the information and data we have at that time.

COMMON QUESTIONS AND DIFFICULTIES WITH CASES

Case analysis takes time. More time is required in doing cases properly than just answering questions. There are often numerous variables to consider within a case, and sometimes the solutions are not obvious. Sometimes there is more information offered than is necessary, and at other times it seems that there may not be enough data given. You may be assured, however, that there is enough information in all the cases in this book to propose viable solutions.

Frustration can occur when trying to solve a case because very often there is not just one answer to remedying the situation at hand. Here, a thorough analysis of the facts presented helps to determine the best solutions. You—the case analyst—must also realize that the more knowledge you bring to the solving of a case, the more thorough a job you can do. Just as in the real world, the more knowledge and information accumulated, the better a problem can be resolved or a decision made. Caution must also be taken because there is a definite difference between identification of the problem to be solved in the case and identification of the central or major issue raised by the problem. The problem is the specific situation to which a resolution must be identified. The major retailing concepts or principles involved in the problem are such issues as image, advertising, customer service, selling, or buying principles.

When a group approach to case analysis is used, students must understand that participation by everyone is absolutely necessary for this approach to be effective. Assuming that you are a part of a management team charged with a problem to solve may also help to motivate everyone in the group to participate.

It is also important to remember that using common sense may help you to realize what is relevant for solving a case. Logic is another tool you will find helpful. Used in tandem with management concepts and principles, logic will also assist you in formulating your plan of action and your arguments and justifications for the selection of the best alternative solution.

A RECOMMENDED APPROACH FOR STUDENTS

Not all case analyses can be approached exactly the same way, but generally we recommend the following approach to analysis of the cases found in this book:

- Read the case completely through, along with the major question.
- Reread the case and any accompanying illustrations or data carefully and do the following:
  1. Clearly *define the immediate problem* to be solved, if it is not already done for you.
  2. *Develop several alternative solutions* to the problem and that could be applied to the situation.
  3. *Evaluate each alternative* by listing its advantages and disadvantages. (This may include consistency with company mission or strategy, long-term implications, resources available, or impediments.)
  4. *Identify the recommended solution* along with any further justification.
  5. *Develop a recommended course of action* if needed.

There are two types of major questions used with the cases. In most instances, the major issue(s) of the case is incorporated into the major question. In some cases, however, these major issues have purposely not been identified in the major question. This was done so that you, the case analyst, can do so. One question type involves the use of a narrowly defined and specific question. The other question type uses a more general inquiry approach. For example, in Chapter 2, *Case 11, Creative Kids Wear's Short Run,* the major question asked is this: What could Suzanne have done differently in the planning, merchandising, and production of Creative Kids Wear to ensure more success? In Chapter 4, *Case 22, The Fabric Problem,* the major question presented is this: What should Robert do? In this book, the first type of specific question is used much more often; however, the generalized questions are also used.

Some cases present information about a business situation before any action has been taken in regard to a specific business problem. Other cases present a situation that needs some remedial action, or, rather, the major question asks you to recommend alternative action(s) that are different than what has already transpired in the case. Additionally, you should not judge the complexity of a case by its length. A case may be short, but the problem and issue(s) and subsequent analysis may be much more complex than those for a longer case.

As stated earlier, there is sufficient information within each case and each chapter for you to determine alternatives to case solutions and to choose the most appropriate course of action. You should be realistic and explicit when recommending alternatives. Specific action and outcomes should be identified.

The study questions might also be considered as a way of leading to the identification of issues or determining your approach to the analysis. Some of these queries might take you in a different direction than the main case question, but they also might raise some important issues that may be discussed either within the class or within your case analysis group.

An instructor's guide is available to teachers, which provides the authors' analysis and justification for the recommended alternative. Your analysis and recommendations may differ and can be justified if based on sound logic and use of the facts. Certainly, other analyses are warranted, particularly with the passage of time and changing environments that can (and often do) affect the situation. For example, the enactment of a law may change the circumstances of the described situation and a different decision may benefit customers, employees, or the company. Most of the analyses found in the instructor's guide are taken from the real circumstances and provide the actual decision and justification for it. Sometimes the actual decision is not the best, but this is pointed out with the author's recommended alternative solution.

THE ROLE OF THE STUDENT AND INSTRUCTOR IN CASE ANALYSIS

As indicated earlier, the case study method is probably different from other learning activities that you as a student have been involved in, for example, lecture and discussion. The case study method is student—not teacher—oriented. In a case analysis situation, the instructor's primary role is to guide students in the analysis process, keeping them on track, sometimes interjecting ideas, judging the quality of the discussion, and at times acting as a devil's advocate to provide a new viewpoint. The specific role of the student and instructor varies depending on the method used for "solving" the case study. The next section examines the various types of methods used for case analysis.

CASE STUDY METHODS

There are different structural approaches to accomplishing case analyses: (1) individual, (2) group or collaborative, (3) brainstorming, and (4) role playing. In addition to these methods, the actual case analysis can be presented either narratively (orally) or as a written paper. Students can do individual analyses on their own, with whatever resources are available (in this case, the teacher role above does not apply), or students can come together in small groups or one large group in which everyone participates in discussion. In this method, no one should just sit and listen. Everyone must prepare before the discussion for this collaborative method to work, and this preparation should include carefully reading the case and the chapter text for needed background. Then each student should outline an analysis, as suggested earlier, which will be presented to the group. Some of you may have more experience in the workplace than others from which to draw upon for further input, and all group members can learn from hearing about your experiences. As in most group situations, some individuals will be more productive than others. But group members should respect and consider each other's opinions and contributions. A group leader, recorder, and spokesperson can be assigned or elected, which automatically gives three members an active role, and perhaps some leadership experience. The leader should guide and direct the group's case analysis. The recorder should act as secretary, writing all information down, including the proposed solution. The spokesperson can then present the group's conclusions to the instructor and the remainder of the class or the other groups. Varying the roles of group members gives variety to the group dynamics and stimulates different perspectives. These variations can be initiated by the instructor or can be done voluntarily by the group itself.

In addition to these variations, a single case can be done by all the groups in a class, and then all solutions can be heard and a consensus reached for the best, most appropriate solution. Another possibility is that different groups solve different cases, so that more material and issues are covered during the class.

The brainstorming method of case analysis is another group method, which is based on oral discussion. It is unstructured and is the most informal. Here, the instructor or a student leader plays the role of the facilitator, who directs the group through the stages of analysis. Essentially, any input from all participants is used, and the consensus is reached for selection of the best alternative solution.

Role playing is another effective approach to case analysis. It also is a group method and can be fun and exciting. It is the dramatization of a structured case, which is enacted by members of a group who are chosen as actors. This method may not be suitable for all cases, but it could be quite practical and useful for those cases in which there is a situation that can be "played" out and in which there are not too many characters. In some instances, background information may have to be reviewed, and data could be presented as reports or charts. The actors would then proceed with solving the case, and the class would evaluate the recommendation(s) proposed.

A case study solutions form is given for use in helping to guide the analysis and ensure consistency and completeness in the evaluation of cases. In addition to this, a sample case and step-by-step analysis with solutions to the case problem are presented to help illustrate how to approach case study analysis.

Sample Case Study
The Classification Conundrum

Castle's Department Store, which has an annual sales volume of $120 million, is located in Atlanta, Georgia. The climate there usually ranges from mild to hot almost all year long, with a few cold days during the winter months. The average annual temperature is an ideal 70 degrees Fahrenheit. These conditions are perfect for most sports, and tennis in particular, which has become the number one sports activity among young professionals in Atlanta.

While much of the area surrounding Atlanta is still agricultural, such big industries as textiles, technology, paper, chemicals, pharmaceuticals, as well as all media-related industries, such as television, radio, and publishing, are becoming a larger part of the area's economy. All in all, the influx of a younger, more professional population and their growing families has been good for Castle's. This change in the demographics of the area has brought a younger, more affluent group of customers to the store and has required that the store's management "think fashion" somewhat differently than its competitors because Castle's has always been known as "the best apparel store in town."

Kate Butler has been Castle's women's sportswear buyer for the past three years. She is very happy at Castle's, is doing a good job, and is well thought of by upper management.

During the annual Atlanta Womenswear market, Kate bought something new for Castle's—an off-white tennis dress with lace details for non-tennis players—really an *après* tennis outfit. Previously, similar dresses had sold very well in smaller markets and had done especially well at the shops at private country clubs. Kate just knew that this dress would be a hit and so she bought it. When the merchandise arrived, she first called the visual merchandise department and arranged to have a mannequin display placed at the entrance to her department. When the display was in place, she and her assistant finished ticketing the goods and then they arranged a good-sized sample assortment on a T-stand next to the display. When Kate looked at the display and the assortment, she knew she would have a "hot" seller in no time. She was considering the possibility of advertising the dress, when Janice Reed, the junior dress department buyer, stormed into her office.

As it happened, the location of the display and the T-stand abutted one side of the junior dress department. Janice had practically fallen over the display and new merchandise, and after looking it over, strode into Kate's office.

"Hey, Kate, where do you come off selling those off-white dresses in the sportswear department? You're practically flaunting them in my face!" Janice said angrily.

Kate looked at Janice calmly. "If you'll look closely, you'll see that they are not really dresses at all. They are tennis dresses, as their labels clearly state. I bought them from Miss California, one of my key resources."

Janice persisted. "Well, it's bad enough that you're carrying them right next to my department, but they're also priced $10 lower than similar dresses that I'm overstocked with already!"

"Janice, you know that sportswear prices are generally lower than dress prices," Kate answered. "You know they have a lower cost and sportswear workmanship is not as costly as dresses are. Why don't you just sit down and I'll go get us both a—" Kate abruptly stopped when she saw that Janice's face was red with anger. She saw those tennis dresses as a potential threat to her department, especially because the numbers of tennis "buffs" were growing steadily and showing no signs of abating.

Accordingly, Janice sought Jessica Cunningham, the ready-to-wear merchandise manager, and discussed the full impact of Kate's purchase of the so-called tennis sportswear. Jessica listened carefully, and after Janice finished, she promised to check into the matter at once.

Jessica then called Kate into her office and listened to her side of the story, which included her reasons for buying the dress and the necessity of the display and T-stand.

Jessica is relatively new to Castle's, having come from New York City, where she had been the dress buyer for a large chain department store. Generally, she is regarded as an astute merchandiser, and she has not been known to play favorites among the buyers under her supervision.

MAJOR QUESTION

If you were in Jessica Cunningham's place, what would you do in regard to the sportswear buyer's purchase of the tennis "dresses" and the dress buyer's objections?

STUDY QUESTIONS

1. What classifies a dress as a "dress"? When would a dress be classified as something other than a dress?
2. Do you think the display and the T-stand of tennis dresses will negatively impact the junior dress department sales? Why or why not?

A STEP-BY-STEP SOLUTION TO THE SAMPLE CASE

(Using the "Case Study Analysis Form" sample, starting on p. xxxvii.)

Major Question and Immediate Problem

The junior dress buyer discovers that the neighboring sportswear department is selling a "tennis" dress at a lower price than similar dresses found in the junior dress department.

If you were in Jessica Cunningham's place, what would you do in regard to the sportswear buyer's purchase of the tennis "dresses" and the dress buyer's objections?

ALTERNATIVE SOLUTIONS

1. Leave the situation as it is now—status quo.

   ADVANTAGES
   - It is the easy way out—let it be.
   - A buyer should be able to use her own resources that provide merchandise for her department and/or classification.

   DISADVANTAGES
   - This provides unfair competition for the junior dress department.
   - Customer confusion may arise as to price and merchandise location.

2. Transfer the similar dresses from the junior dress department to the sportswear department, after the junior dress department takes a markdown of $10 to bring the merchandise in line with the sportswear department's price on the tennis dresses.

   ADVANTAGES
   - It is an easy, simple solution.
   - Customers get the best buys, building good customer relations. No more confusion because only one department is selling the like items.

   DISADVANTAGES
   - Dresses belong in a dress department—this is self-evident and customers generally look for dresses in a dress department.

- There is usually better quality in the dress market than in sportswear—so this would be lowering those standards and it is important to maintain quality standards.

3. Transfer the tennis outfits from the sportswear department to the junior dress department, but first taking a markup of $10 to bring the merchandise in line with the dress department's price on similar goods.

   ADVANTAGES
   - It is an easy, simple solution.
   - Customers will not be confused because the merchandise will be selling in one department only.
   - Dresses belong in a dress department.

   DISADVANTAGES
   - Customers are not receiving the best possible price.
   - It is a sportswear item and should be sold in the sportswear department.

4. Take the merchandise from both the junior dress and sportswear departments and sell it in the activewear department.

   ADVANTAGES
   - It is a natural place for such outfits to be sold.
   - It is neutral ground and avoids conflict between the two buyers.

   DISADVANTAGES
   - The activewear buyer is not the buyer who has the responsibility to buy such fashion merchandise.

- The sales associates in the activewear department are untrained to sell the level of fashion that sportswear does.
- The activewear department does not have the facilities, such as dressing rooms, for trying on these tennis dresses.

RECOMMENDED SOLUTION,
JUSTIFICATION, AND
COURSE OF ACTION

(Alternative 1) Leave the situation as it is now—status quo. These are the days of "scrambled merchandising" and customers are accustomed to competition within stores and departments. A buyer usually has the right to buy the offerings of what manufacturers consider a trend in their markets, particularly from their key vendors. This sets a precedent (knitted dresses, golf dresses, knitted suits, two-piece dresses, and so forth) that favors the maintenance of stock in both the sportswear and junior dress departments.

Bring both buyers into the merchandise manager's office and tell them of the decision to let the tennis dresses remain where they are. If need be, listen to both sides again, but remain firm in this decision, because it is the fairest way to go.

Case Study Analysis Form

Name _____

Date _____ Case Study Number _____

Case Study Title _____

Major Question _____
_____
_____
_____

Alternative Solution 1 _____
_____
_____
_____

   Advantages _____
_____
_____
_____

   Disadvantages _____
_____
_____
_____

Alternative Solution 2 _____
_____
_____
_____

   Advantages _____
_____
_____
_____

Disadvantages _____
_____
_____
_____

Alternative Solution 3 _____
_____
_____
_____

   Advantages _____
_____
_____
_____

   Disadvantages _____
_____
_____
_____

Alternative Solution 4 _____
_____
_____
_____

   Advantages _____
_____
_____
_____

   Disadvantages _____
_____
_____
_____

Recommended Solutions and Justification _____
_____
_____
_____
_____
_____
_____
_____
_____

Case Summaries

Chapter 2: Retailing Formats and Structures

Case Summaries

Chapter 4: Merchandise Characteristics

Chapter 5: Merchandise Planning, Buying, Control and Profitability

Case Summaries

Chapter 8: Sales Promotion, Advertising, and Visual Merchandising

Chapter 9: Personal Selling and Customer Relations

Case Summaries

Chapter 10: Entrepreneurship and Small Business Ownership

CONCEPTS AND CASES IN

Retail and Merchandise Management

one

Merchandise Management, Roles, and Responsibilities

CHAPTER OBJECTIVES

- Describe retail and merchandise management's roles and responsibilities.
- Emphasize the methods and importance of effective training and evaluation of retail management personnel.
- Explain organizational structure, delegation of authority, and chain of command.
- Emphasize the importance of technology at the management levels.

*T*he challenges and opportunities in merchandising are tremendous in our global econ-omy today. Retailers and manufacturers alike have to quickly react and adapt to change, and these business organizations must prepare and enable their management to do so in order to be successful. Additionally, many manufacturers are retailers and vice versa, so businesses are more diverse and complex than ever, needing more thorough and integra-tive management than in the past. Managers plan, organize, direct, and control businesses and should possess effective communication skills and leadership traits to do their jobs in the best possible manner. Successful and effective managers must be flexible, open-minded, and *visionary in order to lead their companies and employees. Organizational charts, tools used to clarify positional structure within an organization, help delineate authority and reporting associations, as well as organize the work functions. Through the proper training and evaluation methods, retail and manufacturing organizations can help ensure that management is prepared to succeed. Technology plays a key role in all aspects of merchandise at the manufacturing and retail levels, from product creation to sales and inventory management, marketing, and final distribution of merchandise to the consumer; technology is also an important tool in the management of employees of a business at each stage.*

MANAGERS AND MANAGEMENT

Management is the process of getting activities completed efficiently and effectively with and through other people. **Managers** are the people who have been given formal authority and power to direct, supervise, and motivate employees to complete those activities that ensure that a company's needs are met, essentially guiding and directing the organization. A business usually has at least three management aspects: (1) the business, (2) the employees, and (3) the operations. Managers may supervise one or more of these aspects. For example, a divisional merchandise manager directs the business within a specific domain but also supervises and directs the buyers who are under this position. Another example is that of a store manager who not only oversees the store employees but also runs the store operations and the company business. The organization of the business guides management toward realizing goals. Communication lies at the base of effective management from clarifying roles and responsibilities to the training and evaluation of personnel. Many companies have philosophies or missions that help to clarify and relay the objectives of the organization, as shown in Figure 1.1.

Merchandise management can be defined as planning, organizing, directing, and controlling products through people who are given formal authority to direct, supervise, and motivate employees to achieve the goals set by an individual or organization. It also involves the five "rights" of merchandising: obtaining the right merchandise, at the right time, in the right quantity, at the right price, and at the right place (see Chapter 4 for merchandise characteristics). In *Case 1, How Would You Fix the Gap?*, six retailing experts answered the question for *Advertising Age*. Most responses related to having the right merchandise for their target market and understanding what that customer wants.

MISSION STATEMENT

The mission of Belk stores is to be the leader in our markets in selling merchandise that meets customers' needs for fashion, quality, value and selection; to offer superior customer service; and to make a reasonable profit.

Reflecting the beliefs of our founders, we want all customers who shop at a Belk store to have a feeling of confidence that they will receive honest and fair treatment, that they will get full value for every dollar, and that they will be satisfied in every respect so that they will want to shop with us again.

Belk has a responsibility to the people who make its growth and success possible. We are committed to maintaining relationships of integrity, honesty, and fairness with our customers, our associates, our vendors, our other business partners, our stockholders, and with all people in every community we serve.

Figure 1.1 Belk's mission statement.

Today, many major retailers and manufacturers are **vertically integrated.** That is, they may play a role in more than one stage in the marketing channel, such as creating the product, as well as distributing through their own formats. These include designers such as Ralph Lauren, or original retailers such as the Gap, and American Apparel that began manufacturing and distributing their own products in their specialty stores. If a company is vertically integrated, management must control the activities and flow of goods (logistics) along with associated information between the channels.

The management of merchandise, either from the manufacturing/wholesale or retail level, is today very often dependent on the use of technology and computer software systems. These systems may be proprietary or turnkey. **Proprietary software** refers to systems that are designed specifically for a company and their needs, while **turnkey software** is ready-made and mass-marketed for use with personal computers. In *Case 2, Canine Computer Caper,* a decision has to be made whether or not to purchase a turnkey system. Finding the right cost-effective system is often a challenge, as there are so many available. **Management information systems (MIS)** are software programs utilized to plan, organize, and monitor a business and its employees. **Information technology (IT)** is a general term that describes all data that may be captured electronically.

ROLES AND RESPONSIBILITIES

There are a myriad of management positions in retailing and manufacturing today, and with these management positions come roles and responsibilities that must be adopted in order to achieve success. To be effective, however, managers must first understand the goals of the company and the role they play toward achieving this shared goal. The position of manager generally includes four basic functions:

1. Planning
2. Organizing
3. Directing
4. Controlling

Creating and/or maintaining company policies and procedures is another major role of management. Personnel decision making also lies at the base of a manager's position. The manager may undertake numerous specific duties and decisions while planning, organizing, directing, and controlling staff. These duties may include the following:

- Planning goals and such events as promotional sales
- Organizing, scheduling, and assigning work
- Leading, instructing, informing, training, and assisting employees
- Motivating, directing, and supervising staff
- Monitoring, disciplining, and counseling employees

Influencing people to act in a certain way or persuading them to do certain work is dependent on a stimulus—**motivation**—which is the drive to stimulate action. Managers are usually responsible for motivating others, based on the needs or goals of the company. Often motivation is tied to rewarding the employee. These rewards can be intrinsic or extrinsic, and sometimes management plays a role in determining what rewards are given and to whom. **Intrinsic rewards** are those personal rewards that fill an individual's need such as self-esteem.

Extrinsic rewards are those tied to material gain, for example, raises, promotions, and recognition within a company. Job roles and responsibilities are given to company employees to clarify what their jobs are and to help guide them. **Job roles** designate the part an employee plays for an employer. **Job descriptions** also clarify the objectives/tasks of the job. **Job titles** may also help to identify those roles and responsibilities that a particular position denotes. (See Chapter 9 for more discussion of nonmanagement job descriptions and roles.) For example, an operations manager would be responsible for the running of the company (operations) and a merchandise manager would be in charge of all merchandising functions. Unclear job expectations and poor communication between two managers is a problem in *Case 3, Learning to Document Performance at Gap*.

Repercussions of not clarifying roles are evident in *Case 66, Part 1, Many Tasks, Few People: Lullaby Begins* in Chapter 10. Here, family members, who are unsure of their roles and responsibilities at their store, are creating frustration, disagreement in decision making, crossover in management duties, and general confusion. Clarification of roles and the assignment of authority are necessary, but how to implement these amicably is the challenge.

The types and numbers of managers within an organization vary depending on the kind of company and the goals of that organization. In *Case 4, The Impossible Goals,* a buyer is making her sales goals but no profit, and she does not agree with the goals her supervisor has set. The problem is made more serious with miscommunication between levels of management. Management style, or the way in which managers conduct themselves while managing, also varies from one individual to another, reflecting the way individuals interact and manage others. Managers can be authoritative and dictatorial, or they can be caretaking, team builders. Some like to work alone, others as a team. Some are delegators, others are not. Many retail managers practice **management by walking around,** a technique that places the manager in the work site, interacting directly with employees. A good example of this is Nordstrom store managers who used to reward excellent customer service given by sales associates by distributing dollar bills to them on the spot while working the store. Some upper managers walk the floor calling out anything that is irregular, which requires department managers to give explanations for department conditions. Other retail managers do not spend much time on the selling floor, instead directing activities primarily from an office.

Although job titles may help describe the job an employee holds, often the job titles of managers vary from company to company, creating confusion as to roles. For example, at Bloomingdale's, all management personnel are called "executives," while at another similar organization, management personnel are referred to as "managers." Some retailers have assistant store managers, yet another may have "second keys." (This term refers to the fact that the store manager holds the first set of keys and the assistant holds the second set.) There may also be "merchandise managers" at one company, who oversee and manage a merchandise division at the store level, and are also involved with the day-to-day operations, merchandise presentation, and sales. However, at another company, a divisional merchandise manager, the buyers, and their assistants manage the merchandise at the corporate level. It is therefore not always easy to define a particular manager's job just by the title that has been given to that person.

Three major levels of management may exist within an organization. These, along with typical corresponding job positions, are as follows:

1. **First-line, entry-level managers,** which include supervisors and assistant managers.
2. **Middle managers,** which include department heads, managers, divisionals, and buyers.
3. **Top, upper-level managers,** which include officers and top executives, for example, the president and vice president of a company.

A **supervisor** is usually a first-line, entry-level manager and is any person who is responsible for the conduct of others in the accomplishment of a task. Supervisors can be managers or vice versa. A **leader** has qualities and/or abilities that emerge to influence and direct others. Leaders may not be managers within an organization, but it would be ideal if all managers were leaders. Unfortunately, this is not always the case. Types of managers and leaders vary from company and even within companies. (Leaders as entrepreneurs are discussed in Chapter 10.)

A RETAIL EXECUTIVE CHECKLIST			
Attributes Required	ability	desire	**In the Retailing Environment**
Analytical Skills; ability to solve problems; strong numerical ability for analysis of facts and data for planning, managing, and controlling			Retailing executives are problem solvers. Knowledge and understanding of past performance and present circumstances form the basis for action and planning.
Creativity: ability to generate and recognize imaginative ideas and solutions; ability to recognize the need for and to be responsive to change.			Retail executives are idea people. Successful buying results from sensitive, aware decisions, while merchandising requires imaginative, innovative techniques.
Decisiveness: ability to make quick decisions and render judgments, take action and commit oneself to completion.			Retail executives are action people. Whether it is new fashion trends or customer desires, decisions must be made quickly and confidently in this ever-changing environment.
Flexibility: ability to adjust to the ever-changing needs of the situation; ability to adapt to different people, places, and things; willingness to do whatever is necessary to get the task done.			Retail executives are flexible. Surprises in retailing never cease. Plans must be altered quickly to accommodate changes in trends, styles, and attitudes, while numerous ongoing activities cannot be ignored.
Initiative: ability to originate action rather than want to be told what to do and ability to act based on conviction.			Retail executives are doers. Sales volumes, trends, and buying opportunities mean continual action. Opportunities for action must be seized.
Leadership: ability to inspire others to trust and respect your judgment; ability to delegate and to guide and persuade others.			Retail executives are managers. Running a business means depending on others to get the work done. One person cannot do it all.
Organization: ability to establish priorities and courses of action for self and/or others; skill in planning and following up to achieve results.			Retail executives are jugglers. A variety of issues, functions, and projects are constantly in motion. To reach your goals, priorities must be set, work must be delegated to others.
Risk-Taking: willingness to take calculated risks based on thorough analysis and sound judgment and to accept responsibility for the results.			Retail executives are courageous. Success in retailing often comes from taking calculated risks and having the confidence to try something new before someone else does.
Stress Tolerance: ability to perform consistently under pressure, to thrive on constant change and challenge.			Retail executives are resilient. As the above description should suggest, retailing is fast-paced and demanding.

Figure 1.2 A checklist of ideal attributes for retail executives. Not all executives will have all of these attributes, but a majority of these qualities make for better managers/leaders.

Figure 1.2 presents a list of nine general attributes, which would be ideal if all executives possessed them. How these ideal attributes translate into a retail executive perspective is also presented. Often a manager becomes a role model to other employees, who then strive to emulate that manager. Consequently, if managers are helpful, encouraging, patient, and understanding to fellow employees and still achieve company goals, they are modeling positive attributes to those they supervise and are providing a good example of how to effectively manage. On the other hand, a poor management role model might be demanding, impatient, unkind, and un-motivating, and might not exemplify the best traits for a good manager to possess. Future managers can suffer if not exposed to a positive management role model. Therefore, the development of positive leadership traits is essential for successful, good management.

An organization is a systematic arrangement of people to accomplish some specific purpose. **Organizational structure** describes how a company is set up and directed. The organizational structure aids in monitoring and managing work to be done by assigning accountability for that work. This, in turn, facilitates companies to reach their objectives and goals. To aid in this, **organizational charts** are used by many retailers and manufacturers to model the structure of their companies. These charts depict the **hierarchical structure** (pecking order), **chain of command** (who reports to whom), and the relationship between the parts of the company and the whole through **line** (direct authority and responsibility) and **staff** (advisory and support) components. In *Case 4, The Impossible Goals,* chain of command is used in directing an employee to set goals that the company desires. Usually the divisions, departments, and even positions within an organization are pictured on a company's organizational chart along with who reports to whom. Paul Mazur (1927) is credited with introducing the four-function department store organizational chart, which is used as a basis for most retail organizational charts.

The **Mazur plan** divides retail activities into four divisional areas. The following are descriptions of the responsibilities of the four major **retail divisions.**

1. **Merchandising,** which is the buying and selling of goods and services for a profit. This includes the planning, pricing, and control of sales and inventory.
2. **Advertising and promotion,** which is concerned with promotion and advertising, display, special events, and public relations.
3. **Store (operations) management,** which involves the operations of the retail store, selling, customer service, and all physical concerns for the store, such as maintenance and receiving.
4. **Control/finance,** which is concerned with all the financial aspects of the business, including credit, collection, budgets, accounting, control, bookkeeping, and even security.

A fifth divisional area that most retailers include is **human resources** (or personnel). This division has the responsibility of monitoring employee concerns,

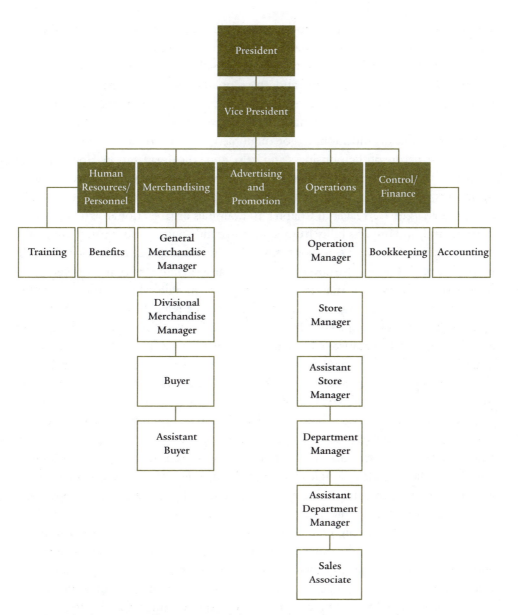

Figure 1.3 Five-function retail organizational chart.

such has hiring, training, benefits, firing, and sometimes payroll. A five-function organizational chart is depicted in Figure 1.3.

Retailers vary the configuration of their organizational charts from the four-function chart to accommodate the size and type of their company and how their company is structured. Specialty chains, for example, may differ from department stores in structure and composition. Some retailers may also have a sixth divisional area to account for and handle their branch stores. Yet others may be organized according to regions and/or divisions. All retailers, however, must have at least two functional areas—merchandising and store operations management—to run the business; by very definition, in a retail company, a product and/or service must be offered and a method of selling that offering is essential.

Like the retail organization, major manufacturers have organizational charts to depict the structure of their business and help guide the organization. However, since many manufacturers are also retailers, those companies may operate as two distinct operations, with separate charts, management, and staff. *Case 66, Part 2, Out of Control: Lullaby, Fifteen Years Later* in Chapter 10 examines organizational structure, chain of command, and responsibility from a private, family-owned and -operated specialty store perspective. Line and staff positions, roles, and responsibilities are clear, but employee morale is low and turnover is very high, and therefore a solution is sought to remedy the problems. The maintaining of employee morale, which is the responsibility of management, may take time and effort. **Morale** refers to the state of enthusiasm and happiness of employees. It is often very difficult—if not impossible—to keep all employees happy, because of the nature of individuality. Research shows, however, that high morale in a company contributes to happier employees, which translates to the customers, very often resulting in higher sales and greater profit. Conversely, low morale is rarely conducive to company success. A disappointed staff receives a new store manager from outside the company and morale immediately drops in *Case 5, The Outsider.* Not only have some employees been passed up for promotion, but their new, backroom manager doesn't seem to care about the customers or them. Morale is reflected in the attitude of employees, and this attitude is relayed to other employees and/or customers, creating a kind of chain reaction. A positive attitude helps create better customer service, which, in turn, helps retain customers. Managers can play a direct role in developing high morale within an organization. All people like to be appreciated and valued, and employees are no exception. A good manager can behave and act in ways that relay appreciation and value to those they supervise. Whether it is a pat on the back or a prize, there are many ways for management to help boost employee morale. Because employee morale can directly impact a business, it is an important issue for all managers to understand.

MANAGEMENT TRAINING

Generally, training prepares personnel to do a certain job. Management personnel often need to be trained, just as nonmanagement does in specific job tasks.

However, training other employees is often a major part of a manager's job. For example, a buyer who has an assistant buyer should be training that assistant to become a buyer at a later date. In *Case 6, Sell or Buy: What's Right?*, an assistant buyer is left in charge for a buyer and given instructions to make sure sales are met, and to only buy basic, special orders if necessary. However, the assistant purchases an immediate promotional order that does not sell, and the result is a serious inventory problem. Management training can also be directed by human resources, as is sales training. (For more on sales training and training in general see Chapter 9.) Training can be structured (formal) or unstructured (informal). **Informal management training** is the type in which managers are expected to learn their job "on the job," taking the initiative themselves. Informal training is used in *Case 56*, Apropos: *Managing a Multi-Aged Staff* in Chapter 9. **Formal management training** is usually supervised or directed, and follows a program that involves the accomplishment of certain set goals. Training can involve working with new employees or working with employees who are already a part of the company, but who may be changing positions. Employees are often promoted to new positions and need to learn skills that are associated with them. For example, those employees who have worked their way up to management or higher levels of management may not know what their new position entails specifically, as in *Case 3, Learning to Document Performance at Gap*.

Training can be new training, retraining, or even such specific forms of training as **management executive training** or buyer negotiations. Management training prepares managers for their job roles and varies from retailer to retailer just as sales training does. Some companies employ management training programs to prepare employees to become first-level managers. (See Figure 1.4 for an example of an exectuive training path.) Others believe that "working your way up through the ranks" is the best way to prepare for management. Nordstrom and *Apropos* are examples of retailers who believe that all managers should begin their professional careers on the sales floor whether they are going into operations or merchandising. (See *Case 56*, Apropos: *Managing a Multi-Aged Staff.*) Training challenges vary from large organizations to small, family-run retailers as in *Case 66, Parts 1 and 2*, in Chapter 10.

In *Case 6, Sell or Buy: What's Right?*, the buyers are ultimately responsible for sales. Most large department and specialty store chains, such as Macy's, as well as major manufacturers such as Liz Claiborne and Levi's, use structured executive training programs to ready recent college graduates for entry-level management positions. Some retailers even provide self-directed management training programs, although this occurs infrequently.

FOUR PHASES IN THE EXECUTIVE TRAINING DEVELOPMENT PROGRAM

(structured to provide an atmosphere that encourages the growth of an associate's talents, abilities, and success in Belk stores)

1 SELLING

Mastering the art of selling and understanding Belk customer service expectations are very important skills that all future Belk leadership must possess. In several weeks, the trainees will develop leadership skills in selling, enhance their customer interaction, and gain knowledge of company policies and procedures. Success in this phase is required before continuing in the program.

2 CLASSROOM

Executive Trainees are expected to participate in formal classroom instruction facilitated by expert leadership from within the Belk stores. These experts focus on such topics as:
• Leadership and Teamwork
• Merchandising
• Presentation Skills
• Productivity and Scheduling

3 BUYING AND SALES SUPPORT

Executive Trainee will gain hands-on experience in the Belk buying process, which will include such areas as: Inventory Management, Merchandise Selection, Marketing Analysis and Planning, and Vendor Relations. Also Executive Trainees will experience and understand the relationship the sales support areas have with the overall store and merchandising operations. They will be exposed to such areas as: Human Resources, Loss Prevention, Shipping and Receiving, and Customer Service.

4 SUPERVISORY EXPERIENCE

This assignment pairs the trainee with an experienced Area Sales Manager, giving them the opportunity to use the talents and skills they have been developing in the role of a manager. Their trainee's supervisory experience during this period is vital in determining their placement upon successful completion of the training program.

Figure 1.4 An example of a retail executive trainee development path.

Internships are another structured method of training employees to become managers while they are still enrolled in college. Management/executive training and internship training can take place in the classroom or on the job, at headquarters or at the retail-outlet level, and is often supplemented with technological training support. Additionally, **continuing (ongoing) education** and training is an effective way in which successful retailers help to motivate, refresh, and assist

Figure 1.5 Belk's management career paths.

management to advance into higher management levels. Continuing education can be in the form of a seminar or classes, which teach specific job skills or product knowledge. Usually, this type of ongoing training is done as the need arises.

Advancement and Promotion

Progressive management advancement is the most common way for employees to be promoted within a company. An employee moves through the management level ranks of a company to higher levels by phases and structured management training programs. These programs vary in design and scope but usually begin with the formal training of recruits who progress in position, stage-by-stage, through evaluation and promotion. *Case 1, How Would You Fix the Gap?* exemplifies this. Many times **career ladders** (or **career paths**) are utilized in which progression of rank and position is planned in stages. An example of two paths can be found in Figure 1.5.

Job promotion occurs when an employee is advanced into a higher-level position. It often presents unexpected challenges and circumstances for a manager to face that may not have been addressed before. A retail district manager must decide between promoting several internal candidates or bringing in an external one for store manager in *Case 5, The Outsider.* The new role can cause frustration and concern as it does in *Case 56,* Apropos: *Managing a Multi-Aged Staff.* Managers often encounter specific problems when supervising for the first time, balancing a professional and personal life, directing and delegating work, and evaluating others.

New managers often turn to others for help in large companies just as the manager does in *Case 59, A Story of Target Guest Services* in Chapter 9. A new store manager has to resolve a morale problem with inherited multi-age employees in *Case 56.* Luckily the manager can turn to her district manager for help in resolving the problem. In small, privately owned companies, the manager would have to resort to outside help if some is desired.

Effective communication between management and nonmanagement is crucial for an organization to succeed, and developing good communication skills should be a goal of all managers. The effectiveness is dependent on the clarity of the relayed message. Information can be communicated from management to employees in a number of ways. It may be written, oral, or nonverbal. Some of the most frequently used methods of communicating within an organization are (1) individual and/or group meetings, (2) memos and letters, (3) and e-mails. For communication to be effective, it should be two-way; there must be ways for nonmanagement to communicate back to management. In *Case 3, Learning to Document Performance at Gap,* an assistant manager undergoes an annual performance review by a new supervisor. Much to the surprise and disappointment of the assistant who thought he was doing an excellent job, his supervisor rates his performance below expectations. The assistant manager has no recourse, because he has not documented his work and performance.

Some methods instituted by companies to encourage communication are suggestion systems and open-door policies. In an **open-door policy,** a superior allows others to interact with him or her—as the need arises—as if his or her office door were always open. Even with the best efforts by management for open communication, there may be problems due to barriers of one kind or another that need to be overcome.

How to handle specific problems and/or difficult employees is a challenge many first-time managers encounter. Along with training, measures should be employed that ascertain whether or not a manager is effectively carrying out his or her job and responsibilities. One manner in which this can be done is through management evaluations.

MANAGEMENT EVALUATION

The **management evaluation** (or **review**) should be done by the manager's immediate supervisor as a means to communicate how that manager is performing. These can be **formal evaluations** (or structured) or **informal evaluations** (or unstructured) and should provide feedback on the work that is being completed. This evaluation may occur after a task is completed or after a specific period of time. Formal evaluations of employees are usually held annually or semiannually, and they are often tied to rewards and promotions, or are given after various training periods. Additionally, a probationary period may be used for a new employee evaluation.

The evaluation procedures and methods for management personnel may entail more than nonmanagement personnel evaluations. (See Chapter 9 for evaluations on selling staff.) For example, it is not unusual for managers to help set their own job goals that are used in their evaluations. The **management by objectives (MBO)** method of evaluation is a common way of involving management in monitoring their own progress and success on the job. In this method, managers play an active part in setting their own management goals.

SUMMARY

Because managers often supervise, train, and evaluate employees, it is essential that their roles and responsibilities be clearly defined in order for them to manage effectively. Proper training and evaluation methods also help ensure the success not only of management but also of their employees and the entire retail organization. Such tools as job descriptions, organizational charts, and career ladders can clarify management positions within an organization by delineating duties and responsibilities, as well as helping to organize the various functions being managed. Reward systems, either extrinsic or intrinsic, can also assist managers in providing incentives to the people that they manage, thereby helping a manager (or a department or a store) reach the goals set by the company. Additionally, personal management style plays a large part in the success or failure of a manager. Knowing whether or not to push to achieve goals, whether to rally or regroup, and whether to fire or retrain an employee are vital characteristics of an effective manager. Management is able to work smarter and faster with the technological applications afforded them today. From planning, organizing, directing, and controlling the business to managing merchandise and employees, technology is proving to be an invaluable aid in maintaining and managing a successful organization.

KEY TERMS

advertising and promotion	formal (structured) evaluation
career ladder	formal management training
career path	hierarchical structure
chain of command	human resources
continuing (ongoing) education	informal (unstructured) evaluation
control/finance	informal management training
extrinsic reward	information technology (IT)
first-line, entry-level manager	internship

intrinsic reward
job description
job promotion
job role
job title
leader
line
management
management executive training
management by objectives (MBO)
management by walking around
management evaluation (review)
management information systems
 (MIS)
management review
manager
Mazur plan

merchandise management
merchandising
middle manager
morale
motivation
open-door policy
organizational charts
organizational structure
progressive management advancement
proprietary software
retail divisions
staff
store (operations) management
supervisor
top, upper-level manager
turnkey software
vertical integration

BIBLIOGRAPHY

Anderson, C. H. (1993). *Retailing concepts, strategy, and information.* St. Paul, MN: West Publishing.

Berman, B., & Evans, J. R. (1998). *Retailing management: A strategic approach.* Englewood Cliffs, NJ: Prentice Hall.

Donnellan, J. (1996). Educational requirements for management level positions in major retail organizations. *Clothing and Textiles Research Journal, 14*(1), 16–21.

Donellan, J. (2007). *Merchandise buying and management.* New York: Fairchild Books.

Dunne, P. M., & Lusch, R. F. (2007). *Retailing.* Norman, OK: South-Western College Publishing.

Levy, M., & Weitz, B. A. (2009). *Retailing management.* New York: McGraw-Hill.

Mazur, P. (1927). *Principles of organization applied to modern retailing.* New York: Harper and Bros.

Poloian, L. G. (2003). *Retailing principles: A global outlook.* New York: Fairchild Books.

Robbins, S. P., & Coulter, M. (2008). *Management.* Upper Saddle River, NJ: Prentice Hall.

Seckler, V. (2006, April 26). The great shopping divide. *Women's Wear Daily*, p. 6.

Varley, R. (2005). *Retail product management.* London: Routledge.

Case 1

HOW WOULD YOU FIX THE GAP?[1]

Mya Frazier, Advertising Age, January 10, 2007

Can the ailing Gap brand be saved? Published reports that $16 billion The Gap Stores, Inc. might be on the block—and may consider a private-equity play or a breakup of its brand trio, Gap stores, Banana Republic, and Old Navy—prompted *Advertising Age* to ask the experts what they would do to repair the sales gulf at Gap.

Paco Underhill, author of *Why We Buy* and founder and CEO of behavioral research firm Envirosell, New York: "They have to stick with Monday through Friday, which is where America works and plays, and not be distracted by Saturday night. They have to be in the uniform business rather than the costume business. They have to follow their customers. I wouldn't compete with Abercrombie & Fitch and American Eagle. I would focus on Gen Xers and boomers."

Lee Peterson, VP-brand and creative services at WD Partners, a retail design and development firm in Columbus, Ohio: "I'd hire better merchants and close some stores and spin off Banana Republic. There is too

much similarity to the Gap and Old Navy, which goes back to the merchant problem. If you made a hard-core effort to hire some merchants, you could start to turn things around. They just have too many stores, and their fashion sense is just awful. If their target customer is really baby boomers and just below that cusp—something like 80 million people—they are just clueless to what those people like."

Joseph Beaulieu, retail analyst at Morningstar, Chicago: "They need to be less low-end at Old Navy. The store is starting to look like a cheap discount store. If you freed the Gap brand from having to avoid competing with Banana Republic at the high end and Old Navy at the low end, that could improve their target focus. They have these three segmented brands and don't want them to step on each other. It's more of positioning and merchandise issue."

Kerry Feuerman, creative director at Fallon, Minneapolis: "I'd live in the practical, and create campaigns for the next fashion season, but that's defensive. Offensively, I would have a team creating an image for them that is above and beyond clothing. If you can penetrate deeper, beyond 'Do I look cool?' and stand for something deeper, there's a long-term benefit to that. They are missing some form of reason to believe in the brand beyond the faded jeans and the new hoodie of the month."

Seth Godin, marketing guru and author of "Small Is the New Big and 183 Other

Riffs, Rants and Remarkable Business Ideas," via e-mail: "I don't think it can be done. The Gap represented a movement. It nationalized something regional at the same time they profited from the death of business dress. Both are over, quirkiness is back, and that's that."

Love Goel, a former Federated executive who heads Growth Ventures Group, a Minnesota-based investment firm: "I would work to really understand what customers want. You need people who understand the product, but the Gap has gotten so reliant on analytics and data, I would bring a balance to fashion merchandising and analytics. You can't let just data and analytics drive the business. You can't just have computer programming figuring out what the right assortment is for the season. I would also move into direct marketing and Internet advertising and shift away from mass advertising on TV, which is too expensive."

Major Question

If you were the CEO of Gap, what would you do to stop sagging sales?

Study Question

Do you agree or disagree with each of the retailing experts in this article?

Case 2

CANINE COMPUTER CAPER

Antigone Kotsiopulos and Molly Eckman, Colorado State University

Kara Jules owns a pet store that sells pet supplies and also provides animal grooming and training services. She loves animals, has worked for several kennels in the area, and is now the proud owner of her own business. She has a good location in a strip mall not far from a major city street. In addition to some already established local competition, she had also heard that a large chain pet store may be expanding into the area. However, she felt confident that her combination of products and services, along with a more personal touch, would attract a good following. Furthermore, she has a very supportive husband and family who can assist in times of crises and serve as a sounding board on business issues.

Kara was right—the business did grow. She expanded her training space and hired someone to handle client scheduling and retail sales. She now spent most of her time grooming and training dogs. Her new employee, Jane, is also her daughter. Jane is a young, aggressive college graduate, who is very enthusiastic about seeing the business grow.

At the close of her second year of business, Kara asked Jane to complete a physical inventory of all retail merchandise. Jane was not thrilled with the idea. After all, she had just completed a bachelor's degree and was capable of more than counting the number of bottles on a shelf. Furthermore, she used computers extensively and felt they should have a more efficient method of tracking merchandise. It was her first experience with taking a physical inventory and, while her mom had given her some tips and guidelines, she became even more frustrated with the process while still trying to serve customers. She decided to push her mom harder to use their computer for more than communication purposes.

Kara listened to Jane's recommendation to install a computer system for inventory control and discussed the idea more extensively with her husband. Kara's husband, a college professor, knew about computer applications but not in the area of retailing, and thought it was worth checking out the idea. The family sought input from a number of sources including local computer retailers, vendors at trade shows, Web sites, and a fellow college professor who taught merchandising.

Kara was now totally confused after hearing a variety of recommendations, while her husband and daughter remained excited about purchasing the turnkey system. At opposing ends of the spectrum were the trade show salesman and the merchandising professor. The trade show salesman had a turnkey system (hardware and software) that would do everything from point of sale to accounting at a cost of $12,000. The turnkey system was specialized for pet stores, but there was no local sales representative in the community. It would also be difficult to resell or use the turnkey system for anything but a pet store. The computer salesman was very thorough in pointing out all the benefits of computerization, including detailed reporting and business analyses, many of which contained data and terms that were not familiar to Kara or Jane. The salesman also reported that the accounting system typically made it possible to greatly reduce daily bookkeeping costs.

The merchandising professor argued that the business was too small for such an investment, as annual sales were less than $200,000. Kara also believed that good manual records, spreadsheets, or simple bookkeeping software would serve as a good preliminary way of analyzing the business. If they did want to purchase a turnkey system, the professor recommended a personal computer and printer at a cost of $2,500 to $3,000. This computer could serve other such business and personal needs as word processing, spreadsheets, development of a client list, and desktop publishing for advertising and mailings. There were several retailers in the area that sold and supported personal computers, and most knew of software that could be modified to generate customized reports. Because of the computer support offered by local vendors, this seemed to be a better option than purchasing hardware online.

Both the turnkey system and the personal computer would require some training, however, and Jane did know something about the latter from her college courses.

Lists of satisfied customers for both the turnkey system and the personal computer were available from the salesman and other retailers.

Major Question

What would you recommend to Kara in regard to computerization of her pet store?

Study Question

Are there any other items you believe should be considered by the Jules to help them make a decision about their computer needs?

Exercises

1. Investigate options for a turnkey system appropriate for small businesses. Provide a list of the criteria that could be used for decision making for selection of a system.

2. Investigate options for accounting packages appropriate for small businesses. List the criteria that could be used for decision making for selection of a system.

3. Interview small store owners to see who is using computer technology. Are they satisfied the system, support, training, and service offered? What additional needs do they have?

Case 3

LEARNING TO DOCUMENT PERFORMANCE AT GAP

Joseph H. Hancock, II, Drexel University

Joe was excited about his new job as an assistant manager for Gap at their Michigan Avenue location in Chicago. It had been his dream to work for the company ever since he started college four years ago. Gap does not usually place new managers in their high-volume locations; however, Joe was highly recommended by his district manager in Indiana. Even though Joe had just graduated college, it was his two years of previous retailing experience as a part-time sales associate for Gap and his degree in retail management that had truly helped him get this wonderful opportunity. Gap was Joe's favorite brand, and he knew he would be very successful at the company.

After one year, Gap conducts annual reviews of each employee's performance. Joe was very excited about this review because he had the impression his performance was spectacular. He had been in charge of the men's department, visual presentation, and had even led a store visit for upper management. Joe had bonded with his colleague, Jane, who had worked for Express ten years before coming to Gap. She told him to write down his accomplishments in a journal, as well as any comments or feedback from management. Being so busy and scrambled for time, Joe never felt that this was truly important. Besides, he felt that everyone *knew* how fabulous he was at the store.

Mona, the Michigan Avenue store's general manager, had been working with Joe for six months and was pleased with his performance. She knew Joe was new, so she had more experienced associate managers like Jane work with him. After her two years at the store, Mona received a promotion and went to the corporate office.

Richard, Joe's new general manager, was hired after his ten-year position as a buyer at Marshall Field's had been terminated due to the Macy's buyout. Richard had never been a store manager before; however, Gap felt his excellent track record as a buyer responsible for $25 million in revenue would make him an excellent GM for their Michigan Avenue location. Plus, Richard was the best friend of the district manager, Jim, who had worked with Richard at Marshall Field's.

Richard was used to managing product but not people. He took a superior tone with his managers and spent a lot of time sitting at his desk in the office, whereas Mona had always worked on the sales floor. While Richard was used to paperwork, he was not used to sales floor tasks and the amount of time needed to complete them. He created impossible workloads for employees to complete in the amount of time they needed to be done. He relied on his assistant managers like Joe to complete projects only to be disappointed when they were not done on time. However, Richard never told Joe or any managers that he was upset.

Joe often told Richard that his projects required more time and manpower. Richard informed Joe that payroll was tight and current sales did not accommodate for more employees. He commanded Joe to work with the manpower given and get the job done. Richard told Joe to practice better time management and "work smarter," not "harder."

As a new assistant manager, Joe thought Richard was the expert, so he followed his orders. Jane told Joe about her frustrations as well. She knew Richard was creating impossible workloads, and she had been documenting everything. She had discussed her issues with Richard only to be told the same things that he told Joe. When she suggested he work with them on the sales floor, Richard was insulted. Feeling the strain of the working relationship, Jane reiterated to Joe the importance of documenting his progress. Again, Joe told her he was busy and would get to it as soon as possible. Joe never did.

The time came for annual reviews of all assistant and associate managers in Joe's store. Each wondered who would evaluate their performance, since Richard was a new general manager and had not been there the entire year. The district manager informed everyone that Richard would conduct the performance appraisals. When it came time for their reviews, every assistant and associate manager had to challenge Richard with documentation as evidence in order to defend their exceptional performances. Joe was nervous because he had not documented anything.

When it came time for Joe's assessment, Richard informed him that his performance was below expectation. Joe would be placed on a 90-day corrective-action program and not receive a raise. Joe was very upset and distraught. None of the exceptional things he had done for Mona were on the review. Only his last six months of performance when Richard had been the GM were listed. When Joe challenged Richard, he asked Joe for documentation. Joe had none. He asked Joe to sign his review, but Joe refused. Joe left his review upset and felt that Gap had let him down, but he knew it was his fault.

Major Question

If you were Joe what would you do now?

Study Questions

1. Should retail and fashion companies educate employees on how to document their performance? Where should students learn about documenting their work performance?

2. Why is the store manager at fault? Why should all managers discuss performance expectations with their employees?

3. Is working "off the clock" illegal? Why?

Case 4

THE IMPOSSIBLE GOALS

Judy K. Miler, Florida State University
Nancy J. Rabolt, San Francisco State University

The Norris Department Store of Pittsburgh, Pennsylvania, has an illustrious background. Established a century ago, it has grown with the city and currently enjoys a fine reputation as one of the leading stores of the state, with a sales volume of over $50 million a year on moderately priced to better merchandise. Its advertising slogan—*A Complete Store for the Complete Family*—is more than a slogan. The assortment and depth of merchandise and range of prices are more than ample proof of the truth of the slogan.

Although competition gets tougher and tougher each year, Norris Department Store seems to pull through with a profit every year. During the last few years, though, some departments are not contributing much to the overall profit picture and a few departments are even realizing a loss. When one department in particular, the moderately priced dress department—the Miss Norris Department—did not yield a profit for the second consecutive year, management became concerned and scrutinized the department.

After promoting several associate buyers to the Miss Norris Department with no noted success, management finally went outside and hired a buyer from New York City. Cara Standard was 35 years old with a strong background in chain store moderately priced women's wear buying. She was given a handsome salary and a bonus arrangement based on a sales-volume goal. Cara would be the new kid on the block, as all the other buyers and upper management had been with Norris for years, moving up through the ranks. Cara came in knowing this and felt she had to prove herself to everyone.

From the beginning, it was apparent that Cara knew the market. She was able to add new resources and "hot" selling styles, build price ranges, and increase promotion. In the course of a year and a half, she was responsible for a 25 percent sales increase in business.

Management, at first, was exceedingly happy. The department was a flurry of activity on most days of the week. On Saturdays, the department looked like Grand Central Station at rush hour with customers everywhere.

After reviewing the financial records, however, the general merchandise manager, Hank Higgins, called Phil Forrester, the divisional merchandise manager, to his office and said, "Phil, department 345, the Miss Norris Department, is showing a healthy sales increase, but I'm concerned about the bottom line. Your buyer, Cara Standard, certainly has achieved the sales we've been looking for, but at what price? The advertising cost has doubled, the markdowns have gone from 12 to 17 percent, the cumulative markup from 43 to 38.2 percent, and the turnover rate from 5 to 8.5 times a year. It's true that the margin has also increased a little this year, which is good. I feel that expenses are going to be out of line again, and we still won't see any appreciable

profit. An increase in sales is good, but not at the cost of profit. I think we better put a brake on Cara before she goes haywire and we end up looking like a discount store."

Accordingly, Phil Forrester called Cara in for a meeting. He began by saying, "Cara, you've been here almost two years, and you've done a great job. I'm not going to give you the numbers; you're a merchant and can read them as well as I can. Sales are super, but we still haven't realized the needed profit. The time has come to pause and take a close look at where we're going. Let's start by reviewing the store, its customers, and the merchandising tactics that are good for the long run. Next, we'll look at your figures and all the expenses to try to get them in line."

Cara's immediate reaction was defensive, and she replied, "I'm confused. First you want sales volume; now that you have it, you're unhappy. That hurts because I've done what you wanted. You know that I'm trying to build a career in this store, and I want to eventually be promoted to divisional merchandise manager. I came in expecting praise, and I hear myself being damned."

"Hold on," Phil said. "I haven't uttered a word of criticism. All I've said is that we should review where we've been and where we're going. We need to take a hard look at your department." Phil continued, "We want a slower turnover, about six times; a higher initial markup; a higher cumulative and maintained markup; a lower markdown rate; and more controlled advertising expenses."

"And less volume," Cara added.

"If necessary," Phil replied, "because we must turn your business around."

The meeting continued, during which Phil assured Cara that she had a place in the store, that management was happy with her and the great sales increases, and that the meeting was designed to prepare plans to ensure future success.

When Cara went home that night, she was quite disturbed. She could not get it out of her mind that someone was trying to do her harm and that, in the long run, she had satisfied no one in higher management. One of her thoughts was that she had too high a salary for the store's comfort and, now that a cure for the department had been developed, she was being eased out. She had seen this happen before at other companies. Her greatest concern was that she was under the impression that she was doing an excellent job and she had been getting ready to request a promotion; now she felt that she was under pressure to try to hold her job.

She thought she had two alternatives: (1) move on and look for another job or (2) stay at Norris Department Store and, if possible, try to do the job as management requested.

Major Question

If you were Cara and selected the latter alternative, what could you do to try to obtain the goals of the general merchandise manager?

Study Questions

1. What can Phil Forrester, the divisional merchandise manager, do in the future to help Cara maintain the merchandise standards and goals he has set for her department?

2. How can a new buyer in a store prevent miscommunication in regard to what management expects and what the buyer thinks is reasonable to expect?

3. Do you feel that Cara, the buyer, was responsible for the overall state of her department? Why or why not?

Case 5

THE OUTSIDER

Berkeley K. Stone and Dee K. Knight, University of North Texas

The Cosmic Company is a value-driven company dedicated to the betterment of its employees and their families, and most importantly excellent service quality for customers to help build brand loyalty. Not Just Lotion, a division of the Cosmic Company, is a specialty retail shop with locations across the United States. This year Not Just Lotion reached exciting new sales revenues of $5.1 billion. This company attributed this dramatic increase in sales to their highly motivated employees and the relationships they have forged with their customers.

One of the company's top-performing stores is located in the Southeast. This store is one of the largest stores in the region and was promoted to an A+ volume store based on its profits of $2.2 million last year. Unfortunately, the store manager resigned in September to move to another part of the country, and many in the company, especially the store's employees, wondered who would be hired to lead this highly successful store. As a temporary measure, the district manager promoted two part-time associates to temporary sales leaders until the new store manager was chosen. This decision meant that the store would be temporarily managed by two co-managers and two new sales leaders. The employees had always worked well together, and they were confident they could meet their sales goals and keep their customers happy even in the absence of a store manager.

During the two-month period that the store was without a store manager, the store soared to its highest sales in the store's history, and the staff was recognized as the top store in their district. The entire staff was elated! Given the success at the height of the Christmas selling season, the employees assumed that the decision to select a store manager would be postponed until after the holiday season.

Store employees were well aware that corporate policy stated that management should first consider internal candidates when positions became available. The policy further stated that if an employee was a strong candidate for the job and ready for a promotion or a development opportunity, the employee should be considered before external applicants.

Possible Candidates

Several current employees were qualified for and interested in the position of store manager and were confident they would be considered based on company policy.

Kathy, a co-manager, had been with the company for seven years and had worked in the retail environment for 17 years. Prior to joining Not Just Lotion, Kathy had experience as a department store manager and as a buyer for a clothing company in Minnesota. While at Not Just Lotion, Kathy had been a co-manager or manager at stores ranked as C, B, and A stores. Kathy was an effective manager in coaching and developing associates and motivating them on the sales floor. She had a reputation as a professional with customers and received positive reviews from management teams.

Jaci, another co-manager, had been with Not Just Lotion for five years. After working as a part-time associate for three months, she was promoted to co-manager. She has exceptional insights in hiring and developing and promoting good relationships among associates. She was especially dedicated to ensuring that customers' needs were met by offering outstanding customer service. Jaci consistently receives high performance reviews and is eager to accept the challenges of the next level in her career development.

Pam, one of the temporary sales leaders, had been working part-time at Not Just Lotion for nine years without a promotion. Before working at Not Just Lotion, Pam was an assistant buyer at a department store for three years. While at Not Just Lotion, Pam used her abilities and experience to implement a new shipment processing system and had sole responsibility for all store inventories. She also took the initiative to see that all customers entering the store received the attention of sales associates. Just like Jaci and Kathy, Pam also had received good reviews and has been a respected associate among management and her peers.

Sarah is the final internal associate who was a candidate for promotion to the store manager's position. Sarah was a full-time student in a retail-related academic program at the local university. She had two years' tenure with Not Just Lotion, but over three years' experience with the Cosmic Company, during which she received several customer service awards. Sarah was goal-oriented and motivated to find ways to drive sales. During the last two years, she had implemented two successful strategies that helped the team surpass their sales goals: First, she began calling customers to inform them of new products in the store, and second, she called customers to let them know their special orders had arrived. The phone calls frequently resulted in sales. The creative product displays that were credited, at least in part, for the sales increase also were the work of Sarah. In fact, her visual presentations had been recognized by the district manager and called "exemplary." Sarah was liked and respected by management, peers, and customers. Last year, when the managers did their yearly part-time associate reviews, Sarah was one of two employees who received top scores and was awarded a higher hourly pay.

The district manager also was considering an external applicant. Susan had almost 12 years of retail experience, including five years' experience at a plus-size women's boutique where she progressed from sales associate to co-manager and finally to store manager. If hired as store manager at Not Just Lotion, Susan would be leaving a retail store where she functions as the merchandising manager, logistics manager, training logistics manager, and acting general manager. Her previous employer ranked her as a top performer in the areas of communication and staff development.

When Things Went Wrong

In mid-November on a conference call with their district manager, the employees of Not Just Lotion were informed that their new store manager would be arriving the last week in November, the busiest time of the retail year. This news was startling to the employees given their record sales and the fact that none of them had been interviewed for the open position. Not only was the new manager coming from outside of the state, but she was coming from outside of the company. The store staff could not help feeling disappointed and wondering how she would ever be ready to take on the tasks of learning about the company and the responsibilities of store manager during the height of the Christmas selling season.

When the leadership team met with the new store manager, she informed them that she was told to revamp the store from the bottom up. She also gave the impression that she was not there to make friends but just to get promoted to the next level, which would be district manager. Interestingly, the district manager also was hired from outside the company, contrary to company policy.

Problems began almost immediately. Associates became dissatisfied with their jobs and visited with members of the leadership team about leaving, but they did not say anything to the store manager. They complained that the store manager sat in the back room all day engrossed in paperwork, did not interact with them or consider their needs, and did not seem to be concerned about customers or what was occurring on the sales floor. While associates understood that paperwork responsibilities were part of the store manager's responsibilities, they felt that no consideration was given to them as people and that they were regarded as little more than hourly labor.

Kathy and Jaci, the two co-managers, felt that they were bypassed in the process of selecting a new store manager. They were frustrated with the fact that their district manager did not attempt to follow company policy by reviewing their records and qualifications and interviewing them for possible promotion. They also were frustrated because their responsibilities for coaching and developing employees, as well as operations, had been reduced to a minimum level under the new store manager. Most of all, employees were frustrated because the new store manager demonstrated no interest in learning about the Cosmic Company culture—building customer relations—a tradition that was important to each employee of Not Just Lotion.

Major Question

If you had been the district manager, how would you have ensured that you were hiring the best candidate as the new store manager?

Study Questions

1. Were any of the current employees qualified to be store manager?

2. What justification could there be for not following company policy when there was an opening?

3. If you were in the position of one of the employees who felt qualified to be the store manager, what would you have done when you learned of the open position?

4. What would you have done when the new store manager arrived?

Case 6

SELL OR BUY: WHAT'S RIGHT?

Judy K. Miler, Florida State University
Nancy J. Rabolt, San Francisco State University

Fred Marcus, the men's sportswear buyer of Brody's Department Store, which is located in Portland, Oregon, is going on his first long vacation in many years. Fred had arranged to take Georgette, his wife, on a three-week tour of China as a fifteenth wedding anniversary celebration. John Gross, the assistant buyer of the department (who, incidentally, is number one on the general merchandise manager's list for promotion to buyer) is being given last-minute instructions by Fred.

John is sharp, highly motivated, well educated, and very articulate. He has been at Brody's for four years, starting out as an executive trainee. As the assistant buyer of the men's sportswear department, he is in charge of selling and promotional activities but also buys several segments of the department's merchandise, including such active sportswear as skiwear and exercise clothing. Everyone—including Fred Marcus—has full confidence in John's ability to handle the department during the buyer's three-week absence.

"John, you have a relatively simple job," Fred was saying. "While you are in charge, all you have to do is make sales plan. You have lots of merchandise. The racks are full, and your last big shipment is due on Monday. Your stocks are at peak."

"Don't worry, Fred, selling is my middle name," John replied assuredly.

"Of course, you can always put through a special order or two for basics," Fred continued, "but, otherwise, stay away from buying anything. We want to maintain our stock-to-sales ratio just as it is, and our stock turn for the period will come out just as we planned. Remember—the big word is SELL!"

With that, Fred left the department in the care of John. Fred was only gone a few days when Bill Walker, the sales manager of Todd & Todd, a nationally known branded merchandise manufacturer, came in to see Fred, and unaware of Fred's absence, he found John in charge. Bill knew John quite well, however, because John had been buying the skiwear for the department and Todd &

Todd made a well-known, nationally advertised line of ski clothing.

Bill Walker greeted John, then got down to business immediately. "John, I have a sensational deal for you. I can offer you our Todd & Todd men's ski jackets in the latest colors and patterns and in a full size range. These jackets are our regular $150 retail sellers. I can give you a price on these jackets that will enable you to sell them for half price, and you can still get your regular markup."

When John inquired as to the reason for this great giveaway, Bill explained that Todd & Todd was having a temporary cash flow problem and that it had to convert a big part of its current stock to raise cash. To sweeten the deal, Bill further offered to pay the entire cost of an ad in two major newspapers of Brody's Department Store's choice.

Ernest Brenner, the divisional merchandise manager, listened attentively as John laid out the Todd & Todd offer. While he was not too familiar with the exact merchandise, he did know the firm well. "I'll say this to begin with, John," Ernest said, "I've known Todd & Todd for more than 25 years, and everything they do or make is on the up-and-up. I agree with your thinking that if we turn this deal down, one of our competitors will take it and seize our market. So, if you feel this merchandise is salable, buy it. I'll approve the purchase order and get you the open-to-buy. But remember, I'm not telling you to buy it. You must use your own judgment."

Burning with the fervor of a possible great merchandising coup, John bought the entire lot of 300 ski jackets. The merchandise was delivered in 24 hours, and the ads were rushed into print. Unfortunately, the promotion, despite the undeniable bargains offered, was a huge failure—for no apparent reason other than apathy on the part of the buying public.

Fred returned from his trip to China and plunged right into work, going over the department's sales and inventory reports and reviewing what had occurred during his absence. Within a few minutes, he was able to put his finger on the ski jacket problem immediately and called John into his office.

"John, you have made a serious error buying these jackets, as I had told you not to. This is unforgivable for someone who is supposed to be a seasoned fashion merchandiser and who is allegedly ready to become a buyer."

Major Question

What should John have done before placing the order?

Study Questions

1. Do you think special purchases should be made for a department even though the department is overstocked? Why or why not?

2. What are the problems with being overbought or underbought?

CHAPTER DISCUSSION QUESTIONS

1. What are some attributes that make a "good" retail management executive? Explain how these attributes would readily translate into specific job roles and responsibilities.

2. How are organizational charts beneficial to retail managers? What are the basic divisional areas and their functions?

3. Discuss why training and evaluation is such an important part of a manager's role. Incorporate some case examples (both good and poor) in your discussion.

4. Name and explain the four basic functions of a management position. Use a management case example to explain how the responsibilities of that particular position modeled those roles.

5. Explain the differences and similarities between supervisors, managers, and leaders. Categorize individuals from case examples into these various positions and relate how the person "fits" (or doesn't fit) the job.

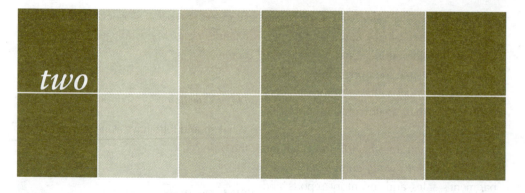

two

Retailing Formats and Structures

CHAPTER OBJECTIVES

- Identify major types of retailers and their characteristics and differences.
- Emphasize the diversity and complexity of retail formats today.
- Describe the differences in terms of retail ownership.
- Identify trends in retailing formats.

*B*usinesses have a myriad of formats in which to market their products and to own companies in today's complex, highly competitive business environment. Technology has created new formats that are challenging older formats. More and more apparel companies are mixing retailing and manufacturing, are becoming more vertically or horizontally integrated, and are streamlining operations. Retailers are merging and eliminating nonprofitable units. Only those formats that truly meet consumer needs in a profitable manner are surviving. The distinction between retailer types today seems harder to verbalize because of the blending of retail formats, and many standard definitions are no longer appropriate.

RETAILING CLASSIFICATIONS

The North American Industry Classification System (NAICS, pronounced "Nakes"), developed in 1997, is the industry classification system for classifying business establishments. NAICS replaces the Standard Industrial Classification (SIC) codes used in the past. These codes are used by the statistical agencies of the United States for reporting jobs and measuring productivity, unit labor costs, and other industry factors. NAICS was developed jointly by the United States, Canada, and Mexico to provide comparable statistics about business activity across North America. The 44–45 classification (the first two digits) is designated Retail Trade with breakdowns such as 448 (adding the third digit 8) Clothing and Clothing Accessories Stores, 454 Nonstore Retailers, and 452 General Merchandise Stores. Further breakdowns include subcategories (in 452) of department stores, discount department stores, superstores, variety stores, dollar stores, among others. The U.S. Census Bureau provides a wealth of information on these classifications on its Web site at http://www.census.gov/epcd/naics02.

Types of Ownership

A **sole proprietorship**, which is a company owned by one person, is fully controlled by the owner, and all benefits and costs accrue to that individual. A **partnership** is a firm owned by two or more persons, each of whom has a financial interest. A **corporation** is different because it allows capital to be raised through the sale of company stock and does not allow legal claims against individuals as in sole proprietorships and partnerships.

An **independent store** is a single unit owned by an individual. There are about one million retail establishments in the United States (www.360.org). The relative ease of entry into the marketplace of independent stores creates a great deal of competition, and today only the strong are surviving. The Small Business Administration (SBA) estimates that one-third of all new retail firms fail within the first year of business. The trend in ownership of department stores today is fewer and fewer independent stores, as they are being bought out by conglomerates. For our purposes here, independent means it is not owned by a large conglomerate, but the majority of stocks or holdings is owned by a family. For example, Nordstrom is a public corporation, but the majority of stock is owned by the original family and the corporation is still run by the family.

A **chain** is defined as multiple retail units under common ownership and usually has centralized buying and management that may be incorporated. The Limited, for example, is a chain. The parent company, Limited Brands, owns several chains including Victoria's Secret, Henri Bendel, Bath & Body Works, C.O. Bigelow, The White Barn Candle Company, and La Senza. Some define a chain as the same ownership having at least two stores; however, chains generally have more than two outlets. Department stores are often chains, for example, Macy's and Nordstrom; but they may not have the same degree of corporate control as such chains as Gap or The Limited. Macy's is organized in the "hen and chick" format, in which there is a flagship or main store. Macy's Herald Square in New York City is the flagship in this case, and it has many branches—or chicks—in other locations. The chicks may not receive the same merchandise as the hen. (See Chapter 6 for more on different types of buying arrangements.)

Retail concepts are sometimes licensed or franchised—for example, Benetton stores. In some instances, the company owns some, but not all, of the stores. This arrangement is known as franchising. A **franchise** is a contractual arrangement between a franchisor (the entity selling its name) and a franchisee (the owner). A franchise combines independent ownership with franchisor management assistance, which includes a well-known name and image. The franchisee pays royalties for the privilege of using the company name. This licensing (franchising) of stores is similar to a designer licensing his or her name to a manufacturer that produces a product and then places the designer's name on the product for an agreed-upon price and/or percentage of profit. The potential problems with lack of control over one's business that is franchised are shown in *Case 7, Corporate-Owned Stores versus Franchising for Comfort Cloud Shoes.*

Merchandise Mix/Service

Retailers are further defined by the type of product or merchandise mix and service level they provide their customers. Still another major delineation is that the retail format can be stored or non-stored. The next sections explore the many varieties of both stored and non-stored formats. See Figure 2.1 for the changes in the percentage of where women shop most often for apparel. These are data from a study by WSL Strategic Retail, market research consultants (Seckler, 2006).

Stored Retailers

Precise definitions of retail formats have blurred over time with the changes occurring in the retail and merchandise mix. For years *Stores Magazine*, published by the National Retail Federation, listed the Top 100 Department Stores and the Top 100 Specialty Stores. With so many formats, these categories became artificial. Now the magazine publishes the Top 100 Retailers and also the Top 100 Hot Retailers (www.nrf.com). The definition of a department store included the sale of furniture. Today we often use the term *department store* for large specialty stores that sell clothing for all members of the family but don't sell furniture. The meaning of the

WHERE WOMEN SHOP MOST OFTEN FOR APPAREL					
Type of Apparel Store	Share of Shoppers		Share of Shoppers by Age, 2006		
	2004	2006	18–34	35–54	55–70
Department stores	42%	32%	23%	32%	40%
Discount apparel	7%	19%	25%	17%	16%
Specialty apparel	21%	18%	27%	17%	11%
Supercenters with food	6%	10%	6%	11%	12%
Mass merchants	17%	7%	9%	7%	5%
Catalogues	2%	5%	2%	4%	10%
Online	1%	4%	6%	4%	1%
Dollar stores	0	1%	1%	0	0
Warehouse clubs	0	1%	1%	1%	0
Other	4%	3%	0	3%	4%

SOURCE: "HOW AMERICA SHOPS 2006," WSL STRATEGIC RETAIL

Figure 2.1 This chart shows department and specialty stores have had a decrease in share, while supermarkets, discount, catalog, and online have increased. (The survey instrument asked "where you most shop for apparel.") Department stores attract older shoppers while specialty and discount stores attract younger.

term *factory outlet* has also changed from its inception. Factory outlets used to be attached to the factory selling seconds and overruns. Today we see outlets far from production sites and often as part of mega outlet malls. Some manufacturers see the outlet as a venue to sell a full line of their merchandise to a specific target customer, and they produce extra inventory or special lines specifically to be sold in their outlets. Often, identical merchandise as that at retail is held in storerooms until a certain agreed-upon date for release onto the outlet floor. A similar concept is operative at the retail level. Nordstrom Rack—Nordstrom's clearance outlet—sells its own markdown merchandise, and more. The Rack has its own buyers who purchase comparably priced merchandise (to the markdown prices of Nordstrom products) from vendors that are different from those selling to the Nordstrom stores. They are appealing to the Rack customer who is looking for a "bargain."

The traditional retailing that we are most familiar with are stored brick-and-mortar retailers. The following is a listing of the most common types of **stored retailers**:

- **Department stores** are large units that carry an extensive assortment of merchandise organized into separate departments for different types of customer needs, such as accessories, women's and children's clothing, and furniture. Macy's, Bloomingdales, and JCPenney are classified as department stores.
- **Specialty** (or **limited assortment**) **stores** sell a limited type of merchandise, for example, shoes, electronics, or apparel that appeal to specific customers. Generally, this type of store provides the customer with special services not often seen in department or discount stores. Ann Taylor, Brooks Brothers, Diesel, Burberry, Abercrombie & Fitch, Gap, and Urban Outfitters are all examples of specialty apparel stores. Some specialty stores have become so successful at beating the competition in their specialized product that they are considered **category killers**, or some call them **big box stores.** These stores, such as Toys "R" Us, are specialty discounters that focus on one product and have the best selection at the best price, which effectively "kills" the competition. Variety and discount stores find it difficult to compete with Toys "R" Us because of their price and selection. Because of competition from category killers, small independents are closing in malls throughout the country, and big box stores are replacing them, for example, Lowes, Home Depot, Barnes & Noble, Ross, and so forth.
- **Boutiques** are small specialty stores, which are often owned or franchised by designers. These can offer both accessories and apparel.
- **Variety stores** sell a wide assortment of popularly priced goods. Woolworth and Ben Franklin are examples of this type of operation.
- **Mom-and-pop stores** are small, privately owned, independent stores that are owned and operated by the proprietor with perhaps a few employees. Often these stores are run by a husband and wife, hence "mom and pop."
- **Discount stores** sell merchandise at prices lower than other traditional department and specialty stores due to lower operating costs. Generally, they offer self-service and large-quantity purchases to lower costs. Kmart and Wal-Mart are considered discount stores. These are also often referred to as mass merchandisers.
- **Mass merchandisers** are large discount stores that serve the mass market. Discounters have begun to use the term in an effort to "trade up." Kmart, Wal-Mart, Target, and Sears are examples.
- **Off-price stores** sell brand-name merchandise at lower than department store prices due to low overhead and such special purchases as overruns or end-of-the-season merchandise. T.J. Maxx, Ross, and Marshall's are examples of this type of retailer.

Above: Herald Square at the turn of the 19th century. Corbett's Cafe was torn down to make way for Macy's. Here: Herald Square today.

Figure 2.2 Macy's, one of the early department stores, celebrates its 150th birthday, as shown in an extensive *Women's Wear Daily Milestones* publication.

- **Warehouse stores** are discounters that offer food and other items in a no-frills setting. They often concentrate on special purchases of brand-name goods. Generally they are characterized by a lack of such customer services as limited credit card usage or bagging. Many times these operations require a "membership fee," which the consumer must pay before being able to shop at the store. Costco and Sam's Club are considered warehouse stores.
- **Factory outlets** are manufacturer-owned stores that sell the manufacturer's closeouts, overruns, canceled orders, discontinued items, and irregulars. Today, there are many examples of this type of retailer, from Liz Claiborne to Hanes and Nike.

One of the challenges of retailers today is to become a **destination store,** which is a type of retailer that a customer shops because only it can provide the product or service that the customer wants. These are magnets for customers, distinguishing them from other retailers that customers also patronize. Customers make special efforts to go to destination stores. Because we are in such an over-stored environment, that is, there are more stores than the marketplace can support, consumers generally shop at whatever store is most convenient for them. Formerly, department stores were destinations; now, the mall often is the destination. *Women's Wear Daily* research has shown that women have decreased department store shopping because of the merchandise, location, confusing layout, and lack of service. However, there are some destination stores left—those that have some outstanding feature. Bloomingdale's flagship store in New York City is a good example, as it is one of the largest tourist attractions in New York. Customers and tourists alike shop Bloomingdale's because of the exciting atmosphere and the store's image of having the newest trendy merchandise. Other successful destination stores are Costco, Sam's Club, and other warehouse outlets because of their price advantage image and their (generally) convenient locations with ample parking facilities.

Non-stored Retailers

As technology and competition expand, we are seeing more nonconventional ways to sell merchandise. Following are some examples of **non-stored retailers.**

- **e-commerce** includes individual retail Web sites, such as www.macys.com and www.landsend.com, and Internet portals, such as www.fashionmall.com, which tie together a large variety of sites. E-commerce has exploded in the last decade, and with so many sites, it can become overwhelming to consumers. They can now comparison-shop with such sites as www.shopping.com or www.bizrate.com. Consumers use the Internet not only to buy but to search for information before going to the store. Internet auctions such as eBay have become highly successful. Despite its many advantages, such as convenience, e-commerce does have limitations; these include not being able to touch the merchandise and security. We hear horror stories of consumers whose credit cards and other identity information have been stolen. Nevertheless, online consumer sales totaled more than $50 billion in 2002 and are expected to reach over $300 billion by 2010 and retailers continue to debate the "bricks versus clicks" format of the future. See *Case 8, eBay,* for a look at eBay's phenomenal growth since its inception in 1995, and *Case 9, The Jumbo e-Retailers Continue to Innovate,* for innovative e-retailers.

- **Television shopping,** such as Home Shopping Network and QVC, continues to be a popular form of shopping from home. It shares the same problems as Internet and catalog shopping because customers cannot try on the merchandise and can be hesitant to buy. Additionally, colors and even styles look different at home than on the television, which can lead to a high level of returns. Many late-night TV watchers are "hooked" on TV home shopping and find it exciting as well as entertaining. See *Case 10, Home Shopping Dilemma,* for challenges of this type of retailing.

- **Mail order,** a conventional form of non-store retailing, continues to grow as busy two-income families are finding less and less time to shop the stores. However, as Internet retailing grows and the cost of paper and postage continue to increase, a slowing of mail order will probably occur. Mail order can be an extension of a store's business, for example, Williams-Sonoma and Bloomingdale's by Mail, or it can be such stand-alone operations as Spiegel and Lands' End. As the market becomes more and more specialized and targeted, successful mail order is serving the needs of specific niches. Because of this trend, such general-merchandise catalogs as Montgomery Ward and Sears are disappearing. Many mail-order specialists, such as J. Jill and Coldwater Creek, have found that a stored presence has helped build their business.

- **Direct marketing** is a broad term that includes many forms of nonpersonal communication, for example, mailed catalogs, flyers, radio, magazine, and newspapers. It also includes forms of personal communication, such as telemarketing and TV home shopping, in which customers call toll free numbers to order merchandise.

SINCE 1912

L.L.Bean

NO MINIMUM PURCHASE

FREE
Shipping

See inside for details

More styles, more colors,
more products at llbean.com

FAST, RELIABLE DELIVERY

Figure 2.3 Cover of L.L.Bean catalog, an example of direct marketing. The 95-year-old company headquarters are in Freeport, Maine. In addition to L.L.Bean's successful catalog, the company has retail stores and an active Web site.

- **Home parties** consist of merchandise showings in the home to "guests" or customers. Examples of successful home-party companies are the venerable Tupperware, Mary Kay Cosmetics, Sarah Coventry, and other accessories and clothing lines. See *Case 11, Creative Kids Wear's Short Run* for a clothing line example.
- **Kiosks** are small, stationary facilities that generally have the capability of customer ordering of merchandise through a computer.
- **Temporary retailers** are generally small vendors who periodically set up tables or carts and sell a variety of goods—often one-of-a-kind—made by the seller or artist. They usually set up on street sidewalks or walkways of malls. Some larger retailers are experimenting with temporary stores, often called **pop-up retail**. Like trends that come and go, these spaces come and go. Sometimes the purpose is to sell "fast fashion"; sometimes it's to start a buzz. Levi's opened a pop-up in Milan for four months. Swatch opened an instant store in London, Paris, Barcelona, Amsterdam, and Berlin. Comme des Garcons' opened 12-month-only stores in Berlin, Barcelona, and Singapore. Target opened up a temporary store in Rockefeller Center for two months to celebrate adding Mizrahi's lines, and housed a temporary floating store on the Hudson River for one Christmas season—pop-up retail at its best! Even Wal-Mart opened pop-up shops in Florida for its new Metro 7 line.

MALLS AND SHOPPING CENTERS

With the return of many veterans after World War II, the starting of families and the construction of suburban housing, regional shopping centers—or malls—were built by developers to serve consumers moving to suburban communities. Large department stores have traditionally served as **anchor stores** for the malls. These are large retail centers that attract considerable numbers of people and are located at the ends of the mall (hence the term "anchor"). Today, however, other formats are adopting the anchor role, for example, Borders Books, which is a "big box store." The remainder of the mall generally consists of specialty and/or chain stores. However, recently developers have experimented with non-anchored malls. As discussed in the previous section, the mall has become the shopping destination as people go to the mall, rather than to individual stores, to shop. The Mall of America outside Minneapolis is a good example of this because it includes not only Macy's, Bloomingdale's, Nordstrom, and Sears as anchor stores, plus many

Figure 2.4 Rendering of Dubai mall to open in 2009. It has over 1,200 stores, 120 food and beverage outlets, access to the Burj Dubai, the world's tallest tower, a SEGA indoor theme park, a world-class aquarium and educational discovery center, the world's largest indoor gold souk, fashion avenue dedicated to haute couture, an indoor olympic-size ice rink, and the region's first Galeries Lafayette and Bloomingdale's department stores.

Figure 2.5 The Shops at Columbus Circle, a vertical mall in Manhattan, encompasses upscale retail establishments, as well as other businesses and restaurants.

small retail stores, but also a full amusement park for the family. In urban settings, we are seeing more **vertical malls** that consist of multiple shopping levels. Examples are Water Tower Place in Chicago, San Francisco Center, and Trump Tower and Columbus Circle in New York.

The **factory outlet mall** is another concept. Outlet stores sell factory overruns, seconds and/or irregulars, and specially produced private-label merchandise.

Figure 2.6 Outlet malls, composed of factory outlets of many well-known manufacturers such as Bass and Ferragamo, have become popular throughout the United States. This highly successful outlet mall (Woodbury Common) is located 30 minutes outside of New York City and is designed with stand-alone buildings, which give the effect of a small village. Along with the many outlet stores, there are also restaurants and other services, including a bank with ATMs.

Malls and shopping centers have similar concerns and problems to retailers in attracting a certain target market and the need for appropriate promotion.

Another trend is the revitalizing of **strip centers,** or neighborhood shopping centers, as they are luring such national retailers as Ann Taylor and Gap. Strip centers, sometimes called "string streets" or "strip malls," are composed of a relatively small number of stores set beside each other, with the largest tenant perhaps a grocery store, variety store, or drugstore. Usually the remainder of the stores are convenience stores. Unlike larger malls, these strip centers are not enclosed. As regional mall construction slows and rents stay high, retailers are finding viable opportunities in new and remerchandised strip centers. Another change in some of these centers is the trend toward category killers and big box stores replacing small specialty stores. These big stores bring increased traffic to centers that had found it hard to compete with larger, neighboring, enclosed centers. Additionally, some anchor department stores have eliminated some categories and changed their merchandise selection as they rethink how this type of competition affects them.

Some new retail centers are being built around new residential and multipurpose structures (work/live/play) near mass transit, often with less parking than normally would be planned because residents walk to the stores. These mixed-use areas are sometimes called **"lifestyle centers"** or **"town centers."** Santana Row in San Jose, California, is an example of new development with upscale retail and apartments on the upper levels and again, a short walk to the stores and restaurants.

Another example of these successes is the new Midtown Atlantic Station in Atlanta, Georgia, which formerly housed the Atlantic Steel Mill. Having undergone a major transformation, it was actually described by some as "a modern-day Truman Show," a reference to the 1998 film *The Truman Show* set in the fictional perfect town of Seahaven where all of the needs of the main character were met inside town borders. The developers of Atlantic Station describe it as the national model for smart growth and sustainable development. Similar to Santana Row, it combines housing and employment with world-class restaurants, theaters, and retailers (www.atlanticstation.com).

INTERNATIONAL RETAILING

Successful U.S. retailers are going global—that is, opening stores internationally. As the world becomes smaller and as the U.S. market becomes saturated with retailers in an already over-stored environment, companies are looking to overseas markets as a way to increase their business. As some companies expand by merging or taking over other companies, others grow simply through internal growth, and international expansion is a natural growth step. Sears and JCPenney have been international for many years, with Sears having a very different and chic image in Mexico. Gap has stores in Great Britain, Canada, Japan, and, most recently, franchised stores in the Middle East and Southeast Asia. Barney's has stores in Japan, Ralph Lauren in Europe, and Wal-Mart in China and India. Levi Strauss has used European markets as testing grounds for such domestic action. Similarly, we see more and more Japanese and European retailers in the United States. For example, Uniqlo, often thought of the "Japanese Gap," recently opened its largest unit in SoHo in New York City, and TopShop, a popular fast fashion British retailer, has also just opened in SoHo.

Major retail expansion in Asia and the Middle East may bring competition—as European retailers have in the past—to U.S. retailers. An example is the retail boom in Dubai, United Arab Emirates, which is creating new business opportunities in the Middle East's shopping sector. Dubai is already known as the shopping center of the Middle East; in the future it may be known, as some have said, as the mall of the world, with retail space to rise to 20 million square feet (www.ameinfo.com). The Mall of the Emirates, opened in 2005 and best known for its indoor ski slope, welcomed a United Kingdom department store, Harvey Nichols, in 2007. Topping the luxury and scale of The Mall of the Emirates is The Dubai Mall (rendered in Figure 2.4), opening in 2009. *Case 12, To Commit or Not: The Indian Retail Affair* gives us insight into the rapid changes today in retailing in another part of the world—India.

Normally market research is done in an international location before opening a new store, just as it is done at home, and local preferences are taken into consideration. However, some retail formats successfully "export" to other countries intact with few if any changes from their U.S. formula because other countries prefer the American format. Williams-Sonoma and Toys "R" Us are examples (Williams-Sonoma's Tokyo store is slightly smaller in size because of high rent.) To succeed in international markets, a domestic company usually needs a proven, well-developed business; the commitment to adapt to the local environment; recruiting and training local employees; and the necessary capital for this type of expansion. Category killers are thought of as having real potential for international success. Mexico, Europe, and Asia are the areas holding the most opportunities for U.S. companies.

In some countries, such as China and India, international retailers can only own a percentage of a company in that country. Thus, an international and a domestic company would join together to form a new company. These arrangements are called **joint ventures**. See *Case 12, To Commit or Not: The Indian Retail Affair,* for a discussion of the current situation in India, where the government is encouraging joint ventures to modernize the country's retail industry.

MERGERS AND INTEGRATION

Mergers and diversification are common to sustain or enhance sales growth. Mergers are arranged combinations of business. They can take the form of horizontal or vertical integration. **Horizontal integration** can be thought of as one company buying or forming another company that is different than its customer or supplier. Horizontal mergers can include specialization and diversification mergers. Specialization mergers combine like businesses. The past 20 years have brought a plethora of mergers, with the result of larger conglomerates and, some say, less competition. It's hard to keep track of who owns what at any time. Diversification mergers take place with a combination of different types of companies. One example of this type of merger (which was not successful) is Mobil Oil buying Montgomery Ward many years ago. After attempts to make Montgomery Ward profitable, Mobil sold the company. Often there are disastrous results when a retailer is bought by a nonretail company, as they have no experience managing a retail-type of business.

Amongst all the merger mania in the mid-1990s and 2000s, retailers cleaned house and shed less profitable units. They also changed the names of purchased units, such as the Macy's name replacing Marshall Field's and Rich's, sometimes to the dismay of loyal customers. Store closures are a retailing fact of life as companies become more streamlined, keeping only profitable units. Additionally, this type of downsizing can occur before or after entering Chapter 11 bankruptcy, which allows protection from creditors and reorganization.

Vertical integration is another form of merger or diversification. Horizontal integration is generally more common in the apparel industry; however, there is a tendency for companies to become more vertical. Because profits are kept in-house, vertical integration helps increase margin. Vertical integration involves a company acquiring another company, or developing a function, that serves as either its supplier or its customer. When it serves as its supplier, it is called **backward integration**; when serving as its customer, it is called **forward integration** (see Figure 2.7). As an example of backward integration, The Limited acquired Mast Industries, which manufactures The Limited's apparel. Forward integration is when manufacturers have retail outlets for their products. Levi's opening its own retail stores is an example of this trend. There is also a tendency for smaller manufacturers to open their own retail outlets. ABS USA, a Los Angeles bridge sportswear firm, has ten stores in California, New York, and New Jersey. One of the main functions of the retail store is to test-market a collection. Comfort Cloud Shoes in *Case 7* is another example. Some manufacturers have only one retail store because they want to stay close to their customer. For example, Japanese Weekend, a small San Francisco maternity apparel company, started with one retail store in the downtown area and now has several stores in addition to its wholesale business. Some manufacturers open stores in the upper-end markets to provide a presence, thereby enhancing their image.

As designers have become more and more disillusioned with department store presentations and operations, they have begun opening their own retail stores too. Opening their own retail locations affords designers complete control of the presentation of their merchandise to the public. Armani has opened his Emporio-Armani shops across the country and a limited number of his Armani boutiques; others include Ralph Lauren, Calvin Klein, Todd Oldham, Donna Karan, Anna Sui,

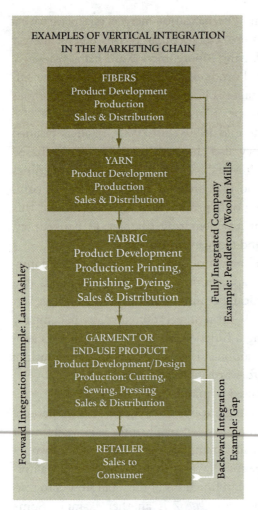

EXAMPLES OF VERTICAL INTEGRATION IN THE MARKETING CHAIN

FIBERS
Product Development
Production
Sales & Distribution

YARN
Product Development
Production
Sales & Distribution

FABRIC
Product Development
Production: Printing,
Finishing, Dyeing,
Sales & Distribution

**GARMENT OR
END-USE PRODUCT**
Product Development/Design
Production: Cutting,
Sewing, Pressing
Sales & Distribution

RETAILER
Sales to
Consumer

Forward Integration Example: Laura Ashley

Fully Integrated Company Example: Pendleton /Woolen Mills

Backward Integration Example: Gap

Figure 2.7 Three examples of vertical integration in the apparel/retail industry are shown in this diagram. Developing private-label merchandise to sell in Gap's retail stores is an example of backward integration. Laura Ashley, an illustration of forward integration, added retail stores as a vehicle to sell products that the company designs (including the design and production of their fabric). Pendleton Mills is fully integrated, as it is responsible for all levels of production and distribution from fiber to retail store.

Jean-Paul Gaultier, Gianni Versace, and many other American and European designers, as evidenced by boutiques on Rodeo Drive in Beverly Hills and Madison Avenue in New York City. In addition to designers opening their own boutiques, designers and manufacturers are also opening factory outlet stores in outlet malls across the country, as mentioned earlier. Like the upper-end boutiques, manufacturers/designers have an opportunity to offer a full range of their lines with merchandise presentation under their control.

PRIVATE-LABEL MERCHANDISING

A major phenomenon in the fashion business is the blending or blurring of retailing and manufacturing. In addition to manufacturers becoming retailers as they develop their own retail formats, retailers are also becoming manufacturers with their private-label development. Examples of this are such stores as Abercrombie & Fitch, H&M, and Gap, as they sell only their private labels. Private-label development is a form of vertical integration, because the retailer becomes the manufacturer and eliminates the buying level from the business. Gap eliminated Levi Strauss as a vendor when Gap went to a completely private-label operation. In the past, The Limited carried some vendors in its larger stores when experimenting with new looks, but as a rule it sells exclusively The Limited-labels, which are often interpretations or knockoffs of popular European styles. This private-label concept has become increasingly popular and an important part of department store inventories. Macy's Charter Club and Nordstrom's BP (Brass Plum) are examples of successful private labels.

SUMMARY

Retailers are classified by ownership, merchandise mix, and selection. They can be stored or non-stored, carry a range from general goods to very specific niche merchandise, and cater to upper-end or mass markets. Trends include an increase in online retailing, global retailers, large specialized category killers, and integrated companies. Also, small independent formats are closing due to strong competition from both chain stores and category killers.

KEY TERMS

anchor store
backward integration
big box store
boutique
category killer
chain
corporation
department store
destination store
direct marketing
discount store
e-commerce
factory outlet
factory outlet mall
forward integration
franchise
home parties
horizontal integration
independent store
joint ventures

kiosk
mail order
mass merchandiser
mom-and-pop store
non-stored retailers
off-price store
partnership
pop-up retail
sole proprietorship
specialty (or limited-assortment) store
stored retailers
strip center
television shopping
temporary retailer
town centers/lifestyle centers
variety store
vertical integration
vertical malls
warehouse store

BIBLIOGRAPHY

Atlantic Station, life happens here. Retrieved on September 9, 2007, from
http://www.atlanticstation.com.

Donnis, C. (2004). *e-tailing*. London: Routledge.

Dunne, P. M., & Lusch, R. F. (2007). *Retailing*. Norman, OK: South-Western College Publishing.

Levy, H., & Weitz, B. A. (2009). *Retail management*. New York: McGraw-Hill.

National Retail Federation. Retrieved on September 10, 2007, from www.nrf.com.

Poloian, L. G. (2003). *Retailing principles: A global outlook*. New York: Fairchild Books.

Seckler, V. (2006, April 26). The great shopping divide. *Women's Wear Daily*, p. 6.

Stern, L. (March 22, 2004). Wanna deal? Click here. *Newsweek*, p. 65.

Sternquist, B. (2007). *International retailing*. New York: Fairchild Books.

Thomas, C., & Segal, R. (2006). *Retailing in the 21st Century*. Hoboken, NJ: John Wiley & Sons, Inc.

U.S. Census Bureau. *North American Industry Classification System*. Retrieved on September 10, 2007, from http://www.census.gov/epcd/www/naics.html.

www.data360.org, accessed October 20, 2008.

Case 7

CORPORATE-OWNED STORES VERSUS FRANCHISING FOR COMFORT CLOUD SHOES

Denise T. Ogden, Penn State University,
Lehigh Valley
James R. Ogden, Kutztown University of
Pennsylvania

Comfort Cloud Shoes started in 1995 in the Midwest. The company is a manufacturer and specialty retailer of an innovative line of comfort shoes. The company started out as a sole proprietorship, then as the manufacturing portion of the business grew, Comfort Cloud incorporated and began selling to independent retailers. Its unique design of the shoe has aided in the expansion of the business, and there are 110 dealers throughout the Midwest that primarily sell the Comfort Cloud Shoe line. Because each of these stores is independently owned, they are considered "dealers" of the line. As such, dealers attach their own name and logo to their store. In addition to the dealerships, there are three corporate-owned stores. The corporate-owned stores outperform the dealers in terms of same-store sales. The shoes are manufactured in Mexico and shipped to a central distribution facility. Many of the family members are involved in running the corporation and are dedicated to future expansion.

The company recently held a board of directors meeting to determine how to best expand the operations. Russell Dak, one of the board members, is opposed to franchising. He believes that the company should pursue opening more corporate-owned stores instead. Maria Esquibel, another board member, wants to franchise. She believes this is the best way for the company to expand. With the franchise decision, the company would convert existing dealers to franchisees. Russell is worried about this because he is not convinced that the existing dealers will want to become franchisees. In addition, he fears losing control of operations once the company has to contend with franchisee owners.

Because the decision is one with lasting implications, the meeting lasts ten hours as each board member gives his or her thoughts on the pros and cons of franchising. At times there is heated debate; other times there are long pauses as each board member thinks of the alternatives. Russell argues that corporate-owned stores are better managed and will bring the company higher revenues and profits. Maria counters that it will be more difficult to open corporate-owned stores in different states and that this will place a greater burden on the management team. Maria states that franchising will help the business expand the fastest and, because the product is unique, the franchisees will become destination retailers.

The chief financial officer is called in to provide an estimate on the costs of both options. Although she did not have specific figures, she stated that initially both options are costly. The franchise option is costly due to the legal expenses that will be incurred be-cause the company will have to go through each state's franchise and legal process. The company will also need to hire a lawyer that specializes in franchising. The decision to expand through company-owned stores will require a higher investment in land and buildings than the franchise option. The meeting ends and the board members decide to meet back in a few days to make their decision.

That evening the board members individually review the advantages and disadvantages of corporate-owned stores versus franchising in preparation for the next meeting.

Major Question

If you were a member of the board of directors which option would you support? Why?

Study Questions

1. Do you think that Russell or Maria will support a decision other than the one he or she initially backed?

2. What are the benefits of a business person seeking to purchase a franchise (franchisee)?

3. Are there any drawbacks for a franchisee?

Case 8

eBAY[1]

Barton Weitz, University of Florida

The concept for eBay was born during a conversation between Pierre Omidyar and his wife, an avid Pez collector. (She currently has a collection of more than 400 dispensers.) She commented to Pierre how great it would be if she could collect Pez dispensers and interact with other collectors over the Internet. As an early Internet enthusiast, Pierre felt that many people like his wife needed a place to buy and sell unique items and meet other users with similar interests. He started eBay in 1995 to fulfill this need.

Luckily for Pierre Omidyar, he was living in Silicon Valley when he got the idea for eBay. If Omidyar's family had been living in France, his idea never would have gotten off the ground. It's not a lack of venture capital or Internet audience in France that would have stopped him; it was the law at that time. Under French regulations, only a few certified auctioneers are allowed to operate, so eBay could not have been opened for business in its founder's homeland back in 1995. Ten years later, eBay operated auctions in Argentina, Australia, Austria, Belgium, Brazil, Canada, China, France, Germany, Hong Kong, India, Ireland, Italy, Korea, Malaysia, Mexico, Netherlands, New

[1]Levy and Weitz, *Retailing Management*, 6th ed., The McGraw-Hill Companies. Reproduced with permission of The McGraw-Hill Companies.

Zealand, Philippines, Poland, Singapore, Spain, Sweden, Switzerland, Taiwan, and the United Kingdom.

Offering to Customers

Most retailers follow the business-to-consumer sales model. eBay pioneered online person-to-person trading, also known as the consumer-to-consumer sales model, by developing a Web-based community in which buyers and sellers are brought together. Initially, most of the items auctioned were collectibles such as antiques, coins, stamps, and memorabilia.

Many of the sellers on eBay are small *entrepreneurial* businesses that use the site as a sales channel. By 2003, most of the merchandise available on eBay had shifted from collectibles to practical items, such as power drills and computers. Now big businesses such as Disney and Sun Microsystems have discovered eBay. Retailers, manufacturers, and liquidators are using the site to unload returned merchandise, refurbished merchandise, and used products.

The eBay service permits sellers to list items for sale and enables buyers to bid on items of interest. All eBay users can browse through listed items in a fully automated, topically arranged, intuitive, and easy-to-use online service that is available 24 hours a day, seven days a week. However, even with automated bidding features, participating in an online auction requires more effort than buying fixed-price goods, and once the auction is over, buyers have to send a check or use Pay Pal and then receive the merchandise up to two weeks later. Buyers have the option to purchase items in an auction-style format or at a fixed price through a feature called Buy It Now.

More than 500 million items are listed for sale each year. From Civil War to *Star Wars* items, from kitschy collectibles to fine antiques, chances are that you'll find it among eBay's 45,000 categories of merchandise from 254,000 online sellers. "If you can't sell it on eBay, you might as well open up the window and throw it out in the backyard because it ain't worth a damn," says Bob Watts, an antique dealer in Fairfield, Virginia. The Web site has over 135 million registered users worldwide.

People spend more time on eBay than any other online site, making it the most popular shopping destination on the Internet. Users often refer to eBay as a community—a group of people with similar interests. For example, Dr. Michael Levitt by day is a distinguished medical researcher at the Minneapolis Veterans Medical Center, but by night, he is an eBay warrior. Levitt is a collector of antique California Perfume Company bottles. Every night he logs on to eBay to see if anything new is being offered. He has purchased hundreds of bottles through eBay simply because it's the most convenient way to connect with sellers.

The Web site requires that all new sellers have a credit card on file, insurance, authentication, and escrow accounts. Buyers and sellers can check the "reputation" of anyone using eBay. A Feedback Forum is provided, through which eBay users can leave comments about their buying and selling experiences. If you're a bidder, you can check your seller's Feedback Profile before you place a bid to learn about the seller's reputation with previous buyers. If you're a seller, you can do the same with your bidders.

Business Model

Unlike most e-commerce companies, eBay has been profitable from the very beginning. Table 2.1 contains net revenues, net income, employees, and net profit margin figures from 2000 to 2004. Most of the company's revenues come from fees and commissions (between 1.25 and 5.0 percent of the sale price) associated with on-

TABLE 2.1 Financial Overview for eBay

	2004	2003	2002	2001	2000
Net revenues ($ mil)	3,271	2,165	1,214	748	431
Net income ($ mil)	778	442	250	90	48
Employees	8,100	6,200	4,000	2,500	1,927
Net profit margin	23.8%	20.4%	20.6%	12.1%	11.2%

line and traditional offline auction services. Online revenues come from placement and success fees paid by sellers; eBay does not charge fees to buyers. Sellers pay a nominal placement fee, and by paying additional fees, they can have items featured in various ways. Sellers also pay a success fee based on the final purchase price. Online advertising on eBay has not made significant contributions to net revenues, and no significant revenue from advertising is expected in the near future. Additional revenues come from auction-related services, including bidder registration fees and appraisal and authentication.

Its online business model is significantly different from electronic retailers. Because individual sellers, rather than eBay, sell the items listed, the company has no procurement, carrying, or shipping costs and no inventory risk. The company's expenses are just personnel, advertising and promotion, and depreciation on the site's hardware and software.

Competition

Due to the popularity of auctions with consumers, a number of e-businesses have entered (and some exited) the market. Some competing Internet auctions offering a broad range of products are Yahoo!, uBid, and Overstock.com. In addition to these multicategory sites, there are vertical auction sites specializing in a single category of merchandise such as stamps or baseball cards.

Perhaps the most significant competitor was Amazon.com, which launched an auction site in 1999. Amazon has a well-known and highly regarded brand name and substantial traffic on its Web site. (Amazon is the most widely known e-business, with eBay ranking third in brand awareness.) In response to Amazon's entry, eBay took steps to make buying and selling easier. Amazon, however, did not chip away at industry pioneer, eBay's growth. eBay now offers a Personal Shopper program that searches out specified products and My eBay, which gives user information about a customer's current eBay activities, including bidding, selling, account balances, favorite categories, and recent feedback.

Major Question

As a seller on eBay what would you change about the business model?

Study Questions

1. What are the advantages and disadvantages from the buyer's and seller's perspectives of purchasing merchandise through Internet auctions like eBay?

2. Will a significant amount of retail sales be made through Internet auctions like eBay in the future? Why or why not?

3. What are eBay's competitive advantages? Will it be able to withstand the competition from other auction sites?

Exercises

1. Check the status of trademark infringement law suits against eBay.

2. Compare statistics on the growth of eBay over time.

Case 9

THE JUMBO e-RETAILERS CONTINUE TO INNOVATE[1]

*Source: Internet Retailer.com,
September 2006*

Amazon.com: Size and Skill

In a nutshell, Amazon.com just keeps getting bigger and better.

Having originally honed its science and art on books, music, and movies, Amazon.com has branched out so far that it defies categorization. A department store? Maybe, but one that has its own video show, "Amazon Fishbowl with Bill Maher," and gives floor space to a travel agent, Sidestep.com, and a financial services advisor, Fidelity Investments. What Minnesota's Mall of America did years ago to the United States is what Amazon.com is doing today: it's the Mall of the Known Universe. It is providing the operational underpinnings for a never-ending stream of partner stores, as well as making its own forays into groceries, movie downloads, jewelry and, to put it mildly, more.

Not only does the whole site function like clockwork, but the abundant features, which could be cluttered and distracting in lesser hands, work together to enhance the customer experience. In fact, the site does

[1]Copyright © 2006 by Internet Retailer. Reprinted with permission.

very well at letting the customers do the selling. There's Listmania, where customers post their "Best of . . ." lists, for example. And of course there's Amazon's longstanding product review feature, which has set the industry standard.

Whatever a customer buys, whenever he or she buys it, Amazon remembers and is right there with in-kind recommendations whenever a customer drops in. If the customer wanders off-target over time—if, say, a customer's juvenile reader has moved on to Harry Potter and no longer needs those "I Can Read" titles—the customer can visit "Improve Your Recommendations" to set things straight.

The company's tremendous cross-selling capabilities boost its sales. Seeing what else was purchased by fellow customers for a given item can lead a shopper far afield from his original quest to things he didn't even know he wanted.

In a newer feature, Amazon connects readers and authors through Plogs, or personal collections of blogs, where customers can read blog entries from, for example, authors whose books they've purchased. After all, who better to sell a Stephen King book than Stephen King?

Costco.com: Upscale, Online

Costco.com could be just an online version of the company's massive discount warehouse clubs, but it's actually more like an upscale department store.

There's a little overlap with the bricks-and-mortar locations, says Ginnie Roeglin, senior vice president of electronic commerce and publishing. "Some large, bulky items are in both places so that we can help get them home. Or if you buy a piece of furniture at the warehouse, there might be complementary pieces online. But we have our own buying team, and we offer merchandise that's more high-end." In other words, Costco warehouses might have a good mid-range digital camera, but for a professional model with interchangeable lenses, Costco.com is the place to go.

Costco has found that its online customers have money to spend and don't mind doing so, and they're more likely than the average warehouse customer to have researched a big-ticket purchase before they arrive. "We've done a number of tests on the site over the years and if we offer, say, a mid-level treadmill next to an upscale version that's much more expensive, it's the expensive one that sells," Roeglin says.

"Costco's online channel plays a very strategic role where they're looking to establish new categories or category extensions," says retail consultant Jim Okamura, senior partner at J.C. Williams Group. "Their online channel is rapidly growing, even if it's just a tiny fraction of the company's business. I really admire what Costco is doing, integrating the online channel into their core business and making sure it's consistent with the brand promise, yet using it strategically."

Costco revamped the site's overall look and feel, along with the navigation and all of the categories and subcategories, to make it easier to use, Roeglin says. "This year we'll take it down to the item level."

For FY 2006 Costco had e-commerce sales of $880 million compared with $542 million in FY 2005.

JCP.com: Winning Department

Big department store chains have struggled in recent years to maintain their position in retailing as growth among successful specialty stores has coincided with the decreasing popularity of department store-anchored shopping malls.

Further, department stores in general have been late to profitably leverage the Web—many of them launched a retail Web site as a completely separate and lowly valued channel. But JCPenney is one department store chain that placed a high value on its Web channel in the early days of Internet retailing, positioning it as part of a multichannel strategy back in 1995. It has continued over the years to develop and improve its multichannel strategy, reaching $1 billion in online sales last year and pushing its retail Web site to new heights as a rebranded JCP.com.

And there's plenty of growth ahead, says John Irvin, president of JCPDirect, JCPenney's e-commerce and catalog division, projecting $2 billion in Web sales within the next several years.

JCP.com has taken bold steps this year, investing in such technologies as state-of-the-art interactivity and imaging. It blended online video and TV advertising when it ran its Oscar awards TV commercials on the Web, with the extra attraction of letting viewers click into the videos to purchase the apparel worn by models. It also has improved more basic shopping functions. A new interactive shopping tool, for instance, lets shoppers mix and match 142,000 combinations of window treatments in visual room settings to preview how a particular choice might look at home.

"JCPenney has some great content within its site to help shoppers select the right product," says Colleen Coleman, an affiliate with retail consultants McMillan/Doolittle. JCP.com also makes it easy to shop apparel by letting shoppers navigate by size or brand, she says, adding, however, that the site should play up such features on its home page.

JCPenney also is positioning itself for growth by bringing JCP.com into its stores, where it's starting to let store shoppers see at POS terminals additional inventory available via the Web store. With that kind of multichannel integration, $2 billion may be closer than expected.

SmartBargains.com: Lookin' Smart

While all shoppers like a smart bargain, SmartBargains.com zeroes in on women 35 to 55. Whether it's a search engine that finds all the brown boots in a size 9W, a Smart Shoppers Club that gives members the first and sometimes only shot at the best merchandise, or a Buyer's Choice section that tags some merchandise as the best of the best, SmartBargains.com is not so much about economy shopping as it is about the unbelievable find.

SmartBargains.com focuses on women's clothing, shoes and accessories, but has a selection of menswear, home items, and toys—all the while recognizing that mom is probably the one doing the shopping. Within the confines of the virtual store, SmartBargains.com seeks to re-create the same sense of urgency that once led to bruised ribs at Filene's Basement, the company says. "SmartBargains has used real-time inventory capabilities to bring some merchandising tools to life online that have worked well in an offline world," says retail consultant Jim Okamura, senior partner at J.C. Williams Group, Chicago.

The "almost gone" notice on items that are running low appeals to those who want to snatch the very last one—no matter what it is. Particularly rigorous bargain hunters can sort their selections so that those with the "greatest percentage off" float to the top. A new jewelry section recognizes that even the rich like a good deal: the Vault Collection showcases deals like an 18-K diamond and gemstone bracelet for a mere $29,999.99 (64 percent off the $85,000 retail price).

There are enough major designer names—Kate Spade, Prada, Dolce & Gabbana—to give SmartBargains.com credibility among choosy shoppers and big enough discounts—usually 40 percent or more—to make the purchases more than worthwhile.

In 2005 SmartBargains.com introduced the Smart Shoppers Club, where for an annual fee of $9.95 members can get substantially discounted shipping, a special customer service phone line, and 48 hours of exclusive access to new items and new markdowns before they're available on the general site. While the company won't share membership numbers, vice president of marketing Mark McWeeny says the club is growing faster than expected and is an "important part of our business."

"We want to exceed customer expectations every time," he adds.

Study Questions*

1. Why were these retailers rated the best Internet retailers in 2006?

2. What do these retailers have in common besides being Internet retailers?

*Do not use the alternative solutions format for this case.

Case 10

HOME SHOPPING DILEMMA

Janice Ellinwood, Marymount University
Judy K. Miler, Florida State University

Michele Lansburg is a buyer for a major network home shopping television program called *Fashion Sampler*. Her program focuses on soft goods, and she is responsible for women's apparel. Several other programs focus on selling jewelry and such hard goods as sports equipment, small appliances, and tools.

Although her merchandise is termed "fashion," she knows, along with the other program employees, that her merchandise cannot be the highest fashion, as her target consumers are not primarily fashion leaders, but followers. The majority of the Fashion Sampler consumers are middle-income homemakers, with a lot of disposable time on their hands. Most have children at home, are married, spend leisure time outdoors, and attend their children's sporting and other extracurricular activities. They are also involved with their neighborhoods and in volunteer work, and are health-conscious. The profile of the Fashion Sampler customer is clearly atypical of what research indicates the majority of home shopping viewers are, as she does not like hot trends, nor is she a traditional stay-at-home mom. She seems to be a new, emerging type of television shopping customer that represents another market.

At this time, Michele must select merchandise to sell during the last 15-minute segment of a one-hour program (5:00 p.m. EDT/2:00 p.m. PDT) of a Thursday afternoon show, planned to air during the upcoming Spring season. The program is slated to run between the "Collectible Gifts" and "World's Best Dolls" programs. (See Table 2.2, Program Guide.) She has done some preliminary planning work and has narrowed the product choices down to three apparel merchandise groupings. Her task now is to determine which of the three apparel groups would be the best to sell.

One of the products under consideration is a sporty scarf hat in four colors: navy, bright green, turquoise, and fuchsia. These scarf hats can be arranged into three different styles on the head, and their poly/cotton fabric is an easy-care, year-round weight.

TABLE 2.2 Home Shopping Program Guide

EDT	PDT	Thursday	Hosts
12:00 A.M.	09:00 P.M.	The Jewelry Connection	Celia Harris
01:00 A.M.	10:00 P.M.	The Latest in Electronics	Ted Hanson
02:00 A.M.	11:00 P.M.	The Latest in Electronics	Ted Hanson
03:00 A.M.	12:00 A.M.	Baseball Hall of Fame	Will Smith
04:00 A.M.	01:00 A.M.	Car Shop	Will Smith
05:00 A.M.	02:00 A.M.	Car Shop	Will Smith
06:00 A.M.	03:00 A.M.	Clever Cookery	Jean Cohn
07:00 A.M.	04:00 A.M.	Work Out Today	Fred Haley
08:00 A.M.	05:00 A.M.	Work Out Today	Fred Haley
09:00 A.M.	06:00 A.M.	Northern Home	Suzanne Ames
10:00 A.M.	07:00 A.M.	Northern Home	Suzanne Ames
11:00 A.M.	08:00 A.M.	Beauty and Skin Care	Suzanne Ames
12:00 P.M.	09:00 A.M.	Time on Your Hands	Audrey Friend
01:00 P.M.	10:00 A.M.	Collectable Gifts	Audrey Friend
02:00 P.M.	11:00 A.M.	Collectable Gifts	Audrey Friend
03:00 P.M.	12:00 P.M.	Fashion Sampler	Trish Parsons
04:00 P.M.	01:00 P.M.	Fashion Sampler	Trish Parsons
05:00 P.M.	02:00 P.M.	Fashion Sampler	Trish Parsons
06:00 P.M.	03:00 P.M.	World's Best Dolls	Fran Stoessell
07:00 P.M.	04:00 P.M.	Travel Ease	Fran Stoessell
08:00 P.M.	05:00 P.M.	Sideline Sports	Jim McKay
09:00 P.M.	06:00 P.M.	Sideline Sports	Jim McKay
10:00 P.M.	07:00 P.M.	The Best of Gold	Celia Harris
11:00 P.M.	08:00 P.M.	The Jewelry Collection	Celia Harris

Additionally, one size adjusts to fit all heads, and they are manufactured by a major accessory resource, whose brand-name hats are in all the major department stores at a retail price of $15 each.

Another product considered for selection consists of separate tunic tops and slim skirts. The tops are solid colors and the skirts are matching pastel prints. They are the network's private label, sized small, medium, large, and have an average retail of $30 a unit.

The third group of merchandise to be considered is a signature line of golf apparel from a women's golf circuit pro. The coordinates of the licensed golf activewear manufacturer include polos, skirts, shorts, and cardigans. The golf apparel is cotton knit, in solid red, white, and navy along with argyle pieces that mix and match. Sizes of the golf wear are misses, 8 to 16, and the retail for each item in this line runs in the $20 to $35 range.

Michele's considerations in selecting what to sell differ somewhat from a conventional store buyer. She has to not only worry about profitability, return rates, and other traditional merchandising matters, but she also has to be accountable for the additional cost of airtime and/or attendant staff and production of the show as factors reflected into her bottom-line profitability. She knows that merchandise sold on television requires specific broadcasting and selling skills in the presentation to motivate customer purchasing. Additionally, information about the print, color, silhouette, price, and fabric should be effectively communicated, as these are factors that sell the goods. A lesson well learned by Michele, through trial and error, is that certain prints and colors do not show to advantage on television, especially stripes or close shades of a color. Program positioning is another consideration in determining what merchandise will sell best, because carryover watchers could very easily become customers. Michele must also consider the demographics of her customer audience. Then the merchandise must be picked, packed, and sent without error. She hopes to plan the right amount of inventory—not too little or too much—of the best merchandise.

Major Question

If you had Michele's responsibility, which of the three merchandise selections would you decide to promote and sell? Why?

Study Questions

1. As a buyer, what are some of the merchandising considerations upon which you would base your decisions to purchase any product?

2. What other information could be obtained to help make Michele's decision easier?

3. Why might it be harder to sell apparel on TV than at a store?

Exercises

1. Visit the Web site for HSN, QVC, or another home shopping channel. Check the program guide to determine at what time of day a particular type of merchandise is featured. Write an explanation for that decision using merchandising reasoning.

2. Select a program on a home shopping channel to watch. Write a report about the techniques used to motivate the viewer to purchase. Include whether or not you wanted to make a purchase and what motivated you.

3. Survey home shopping channels to identify a merchandise program linked to a celebrity. Watch the program and report to the class regarding the type, quality, nature, and price range of the merchandise. What techniques did the celebrity utilize to sell the merchandise? Do you think the effort was successful? Why?

Bibliography

Wilson, E. (2004, December 16). QVC on fashion's edge. *Women's Wear Daily*.

Case 11

CREATIVE KIDS WEAR'S SHORT RUN

Connie Ulasewicz, San Francisco State University

Creative Toys is a successful private company in California owned and founded by Suzanne Montgomery. Her philosophy is to provide for the whole child and to help the child develop self-esteem by producing enjoyable and educational products. These products are unconditionally guaranteed and can be returned by customers for any reason. Toys are sold only through home parties and catalogs, which are distributed by independent "customer representatives" similar to Avon and Amway. Company representatives buy samples to show and demonstrate to customers at the parties. Creative Toys carry a high price point, are of high quality, claiming to last "forever," and are available only through this distribution avenue. The Creative Toy customer is willing to pay high prices. Typically, she is a grandmother with high discretionary income or a mother who wants products for her children that are educational, good quality, and unique or special. She is not a Toys "R" Us customer but is a savvy shopper who recognizes high quality and good value.

Suzanne felt her customer would be a good prospect for high-quality children's apparel, a similar market to Hanna Andersson (an upper-end Swedish catalog carrying high-quality, functional children's apparel). The apparel could be sold in the same venues as the toys. Because the apparel business is in many ways different from the toy business, Suzanne hired Heather Hilstead and Jasmine Jones, consultants with extensive apparel production experience, to advise her on this new apparel end of the business. Suzanne wanted the following aspects incorporated into her apparel lines:

- A similar markup to what is achieved in her toy business (a 62 percent markup)
- The same type of educational element for the clothes as the toys have
- Special or unique qualities in the clothes to satisfy her savvy customer

Suzanne did not want her very visible Creative Toys logo to be incorporated into the apparel line because she was afraid that if the apparel line was unsuccessful, by association it could damage the good reputation of Creative Toys. She was not willing to take this risk, so a new name and logo, CKW for Creative Kids Wear, was developed for the apparel line.

Even though her customer is used to paying high prices for the toys, Suzanne wanted a lower price point in the apparel because her customer, who is a smart shopper, is aware of the competition in the apparel business (e.g., department stores, discount stores, off-price stores, factory stores, Web stores, and so forth). Therefore, prices on the apparel needed to be comparable to the local retail store competition. However, Suzanne is used to a high markup in her toy business, and she demanded a comparable markup in the apparel line. To beat the retail store competition, Suzanne wanted special features in the clothes such as a gusset in each shirt for easier maneuverability for active children and a special jacquard (patterned) knit collar rather than a plain, solid collar. A tab system, similar to the Sears' "Geranimal" concept, was incorporated into the garments so children could mix and match appropriate pieces. Also, instead of screen printing patterns directly onto plain T-shirts, Suzanne had screen prints specially made and appliquéd onto the T-shirts, a feature found in higher-quality apparel. Many items also had appliquéd logo patches.

The apparel collection consisted of two separate lines: one for boys and one for girls. The boy's line had pants, shorts, T-shirts, polo shirts, jackets, and a licensed cap and socks. The girl's line included jumpers, dresses, shorts, pants with a feminine ankle bow, T-shirts, and vests.

Similar to toy samples, sales reps purchased apparel samples. These were in the form of "kits." Suzanne had a full-time merchandiser who planned the lines and the kits. Reps did not buy samples of all garments in the catalog; the kits merely gave a representative look of the collection. For example, a kit might include one color of shorts, T-shirt, and jacket. The company provided all reps with fabric swatches of four solid colors and two prints along with sketches of other items produced by a CAD (computer-aided design) system. Reps were

not required to purchase the sample kits, but some did. Many felt the fabric samples, CAD sketches, and catalog pictures were sufficient to show customers, especially in the light of the added costs the reps would have to incur to purchase the kits.

Developing the catalog to include the apparel line was problematic because the photo shoot for apparel had to be scheduled far earlier than the toys. The apparel shoots had to wait until all the various pieces arrived from the different manufacturing sites. Toy styles didn't change often; therefore, many toy pictures were reused in new catalogs. On the other hand, the apparel line was more demanding because color pallets change each season, necessitating new shoots for each season.

To keep prices down and to achieve Suzanne's required markup, Heather and Jasmine sourced the jackets in Peru, T-shirts in Los Angeles, and the pants and jumpers in Mexico. As a result, pieces came into the warehouse at different times. After all the pieces arrived, workers assembled the items into packages to be sent to the customer representatives. The warehouse, which was set up for toys that all came in as a unit at one time, had to be rearranged to accommodate the apparel kit assembly, which was also a time-consuming process. Additionally, there was a scheduling problem for the warehouse. The toy business is essentially a holiday business, with November and December the busiest times in the warehouse. The Spring apparel line required a January delivery of the apparel sample kits to reps. This necessitated a December 15th delivery date to the warehouse so that kit assembly could be accomplished. This definitely interfered with the normal smooth operations of the toy distribution at the warehouse.

Manufacturers were very pleased to produce the apparel sample line because it was easy: one size (size 4), one color, and a large order. The problem was that the reps didn't buy the sample kits as anticipated, leaving the company with a huge inventory of a one-color/one-size product. However, after the reps showed the samples and pictures to customers, they loved the line. Orders came in, and the production had a great sell-through, with a 52 percent markup, appearing very successful. Especially successful were the higher-end products with special features. But the sample making was a losing proposition. After four seasons of production, Suzanne decided to discontinue the extensive apparel line and concentrate on the toys.

Major Question

What could Suzanne have done differently in the planning, merchandising, and production of Creative Kids Wear to ensure more success?

Study Questions

1. What should Suzanne do with the huge sample inventory?

2. What potential problems are there in combining toys and apparel in the same company? How are they the same and how are they different?

Exercises

1. Choose a children's clothing store, shop, and compare the merchandise in its store and catalog. Are the same styles carried in both? Compare the prices; are they the same? Compare return policies; are they the same? Write up your findings.

2. Research an example of another home-based business (e.g., Avon, Mary Kay). What is its business structure? Does it sell a variety of products? Source a sales rep from the company and ask how its line is sampled and what the cost structure is.

3. Find a branded line of children's toys (e.g., Lego, Barbie) that also sells clothing. Describe the styles by color, silhouette, size, and price. Describe how the clothing line works with or does not work with the toys.

Case 12

TO COMMIT OR NOT: THE INDIAN RETAIL AFFAIR

Jaya Halepete, Marymount University
Marina Alexander, East Carolina University

Intense competition in the American and European market has made U.S.-based retailers look at other venues for expansion. The two fastest-growing markets have been China and India. After having entered China, retailers are now looking at India as the next destination. The local retail market in India has been estimated to be U.S. $250 billion in

2005, and it is the eighth largest retail market in the world. The Indian retail industry is expected to grow at a rate of five to seven percent through 2011. Retail forms a large part of India's Gross Domestic Product (GDP). The Indian retail industry accounts for 10 to 11 percent of total GDP.

With global retailers analyzing India for their entry into the market, Indian retailers are preparing themselves against the increasing competition from foreign retailers. The existing local retailers are scaling up to cover all the important regions of India. Many companies are trying to invest in a substantial way in the Indian retail industry. Malls are not only opening up in every corner of the metropolitan areas but are also moving into the second tier cities. "Organized retailing" is the buzzword in the growing retail market.

The world's largest retailers, such as Wal-Mart, Costco, Ikea, Carrefour, and Tesco, have been trying to enter the growing Indian retail market. A recent policy put into place by the Indian government now allows for 51 percent foreign direct investment in a single-brand retail or cash-and-carry operation. With this new policy in place, Wal-Mart has recently moved a senior official from its headquarters in Bentonville, Arkansas, to head its market research and business development functions in India. Wal-Mart has joined hands with Bharati group to start a retail chain in a joint venture. Carrefour has also moved senior officials from Paris to explore opportunities and oversee work in India.

Reactions of Mom-and-Pop Retailers

With a possibility of Foreign Direct Investment (FDI) rules being further modified in favor of allowing more foreign investment, the traders (small mom-and-pop retailers) in India are unhappy with the government. Although the main reason the Indian government decided to open up its markets was to remain in the forefront of the global activity, the small retailers in India are upset. They believe that large malls and retail chains will eat into their share of business and eventually force them out of business. The competition from foreign retailers will add to the burden of innumerable trade laws, increasing prices of real estate, and low profit margins.

The two main reasons given by Indian government for allowing FDI are (1) improving technology in the food retail industry, and (2) modernizing the overall retail industry. The domestic small retailers believe that India had been on the path of improving technology as well as modernization even before the new FDI set up. Hence, they feel that the government should have allowed them to reach a comfortable level before forcing them to face competition from technologically advanced foreign retailers. According to Indian retailers, they were given no time to solidify their position before being burdened with competition.

Reactions of Organized Retailers

Most large organized retailers are in favor of increasing foreign direct investment, as they believe that Indian markets should open up

100 percent to foreign retailers. They believe that small traders will develop a niche market for themselves and consumers will benefit from availability of their better-quality products for lower prices. The quality of service in the retail sector will also improve along with better sourcing options available to Indian retailers. India is a large market with a large diverse customer base. There is a place for all kinds of retail formats to coexist.

Indian Consumers

Indian consumers' interest in foreign brands has remained static, but their confidence in domestic companies has been growing steadily in the past few years. Indians believe that not all foreign products are suited to their needs and that domestic brands understand their needs better and, hence, serve them better. The diversity among Indian consumers requires an intense amount of research to understand their needs. On another note, consumers who have been interested in buying foreign brands have usually traveled abroad to purchase these products.

But now, these consumers are expecting to get everything they need in stores in India. Hence, foreign brands may work toward targeting this consumer segment.

Summary

With the uncertainty around FDI, foreign retailers are being cautious about how much they want to invest in the country. India is attractive not only because of the size of the market but also because there is a retail boom in the country of which many want to be a part. Indian retailers are divided in their opinion about allowing foreign companies to enter the Indian market. Many consumers are indifferent as of now, but with their growing incomes, they are likely to be interested in buying global products at local prices. Foreign companies are now weighing pros and cons of investing in India. The Indian government is trying to open the retail sector to foreign investment.

Major Question

With so much uncertainty about the FDI policies in India, should global organized retailers take the risk of investing in the Indian retail industry?

Study Questions

1. What products or services would do well in India, one of the emerging economies of the world?

2. If foreign retailers decide to enter the Indian market, should they aim at its low-, middle- or upper-class consumers? Should they compete at the low, medium, or high price points?

Bibliography

Consumer lifestyles in India. (2006, June 26). *Euromonitor Country Report.* Retrieved on December 1, 2006, from Global Market Information Database.

CHAPTER DISCUSSION QUESTIONS

1. If you were starting a new business, what format would you choose? Why?

2. What are the advantages and disadvantages of conventional formats, for example, department and discount stores? Compare to new niche companies and such new formats as online services.

3. In the future, do you think all retailing and manufacturing will merge into large vertical companies?

4. Compare and contrast the various retailing formats illustrated in the cases. Are there any that you believe will not survive into the next decade? Which ones do you think will thrive? Why?

Merchandise/Store Positioning

CHAPTER OBJECTIVES

- Relate image, identity, and retail positioning to companies and products.
- Stress the importance of retail differentiation and successful merchandising.
- Discuss the relationship between competition, positioning, and target marketing in today's complex marketplace.
- Illustrate how changes in the population relate to redefining target markets and image.

*I*n today's fiercely competitive environment, companies must clearly articulate their identity, evidenced by a developed image in the marketplace. Businesses must differentiate their products from their competition to maintain success. Knowing who the target customers are and what level of fashion merchandise they want helps clarify the image a retailer or manufacturer wants to present. Additionally, market research is essential to profile a specific target market. Understanding how changes in the demographic and psychographic makeup of society affect business is vital in decisions to maintain or change one's image at both the product and retail level. The trend toward vertical integration, with retailing and manufacturing done by the same company brings a double need for clarity in image and positioning.

IMAGE AND IDENTITY

With the trend toward consolidation of retail stores because of bankruptcy and takeovers, and the redundancy of retail offerings that are found in many stores, a clear image, merchandise differentiation, and a distinct market position are all vital for success in today's over-stored, competitive retail environment. Image differentiation in the marketplace presents both challenges and opportunities to today's retailers. Not only is it important to convey a clear image to consumers, but retailers and manufacturers must also understand their ultimate customers: who they are, what their needs and desires are, what they think and feel, and what is affecting them and their purchasing habits.

Company Identity

A company must possess a clear **identity** before it can be conveyed to its customers. All personnel including owners, managers, and sales staff must be aware of and understand a consistent image and a well-articulated company mission, including the nature, purpose, and direction of the company. After this identity is made clear, it is easier to identify a target market and to choose appropriate communication channels to reach that market. Who the company is and what that company stands for influences the type of merchandise offered and subsequently the type of customer the company is trying to reach. A "fuzzy" or unstable image breeds trouble for retailers and manufacturers.

The **image** that a company possesses is the perception customers have of it. Because perceptions vary among consumers, not all customers perceive a particular company in the same way. Some find upscale, sophisticated stores quite intimidating and do not even enter the store because they perceive a situation in which they would be most uncomfortable. It may be the pristine appearance of the store, it may be the intimidating look of the sales personnel, or it may be the prices that create such an image or impression. On the other hand, stores that are crowded with merchandise with much promotional signage convey the image of a discount store or of lower-quality merchandise. This image might discourage a more upscale consumer, who is used to the ambience of a quiet, laid-back specialty store.

Fashion Image

A company's fashion image is based on its merchandise, promotion, and environment. Jernigan and Easterling (1990) differentiate fashion images with the terms advanced fashion, updated fashions, exclusive, trendy, traditional fashions, and classics. Some stores and manufacturers specialize in one of these fashion levels, while others (for example, department stores) offer more than one fashion level depending on the department focus. The **fashion cycle,** or **product life cycle,** which represents the adoption level of consumers of a particular style and the stages of a product's life cycle, is the traditional analysis of fashion stages. Retailers and manufacturers place themselves in a fashion position by targeting the consumer adopters as (a) innovators, (b) early conformists or early adopters, (c) mass market conformists, and (d) late fashion followers or laggards. (See Figure 3.1.)

Research has indicated that these categories are difficult, however, to utilize in terms of identifying and differentiating consumers at each level; therefore, for the sake of analysis, retailers and manufacturers might choose to use the more broad categories of **fashion leaders** and **fashion followers.** A company that is always showing the newest, latest styles is seen as **fashion forward,** which appeals to fashion leaders. This can be very risky because consumers do not always accept the new styles; also, fashion with such narrow appeal is generally produced in limited quantities, and is expensive and exclusive. If the store does not have an image for

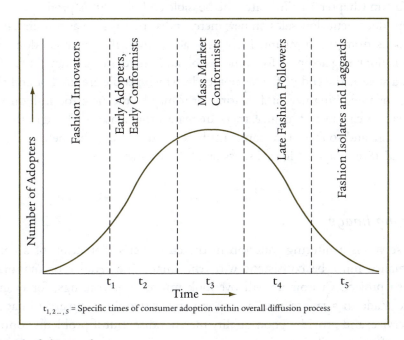

Figure 3.1 The fashion cycle.

fashion leadership, it can be perilous to bring in new fashion items as a large proportion of their offerings. Additionally, customers will not find the more traditional or classic styles they expect from the store and therefore can get mixed messages of the store's image. In *Case 13, Frustration in the Menswear Department,* this dilemma is illustrated by a cautious divisional merchandise manager who is hesitant to allocate a large portion of a menswear department to an untested style.

After consumers accept a new (or fashion forward) style, it is usually translated into a more affordable item with less expensive fabrication and detailing that is produced and sold by other companies at lower price points. This less expensive, more affordable item is generally referred to as a **knockoff.** Knockoffs are a way of life in the fashion industry and are indicative of general consumer acceptance and adoption of styles. See *Case 23, The Knockoff,* in Chapter 4, for an illustration of a buyer/vendor conflict that is caused by the retailer's copying the vendor's popular style.

Toward the end of the fashion cycle, acceptance of a style wanes and now only laggards are accepting and purchasing a style at discount or resale stores. The fashion has generally ended with an excess; that is, the knockoff manufacturers are left with unwanted stock that they must sell. Usually they give great deals to retailers at off-prices to move the merchandise out. Similarly, retailers usually put the style on sale to make way for newer, more profitable, more fashionable merchandise. *Case 67, Amber's Wave,* in Chapter 10, illustrates the possible end of a style's product life cycle as sales reps document slow sales on new merchandise that is seen as too similar to previous looks from the company. Fashion is acceptance. If consumers don't buy an item, it is not being accepted for some reason and, therefore, it is not "in fashion." It may be a style at the end of the fashion cycle, which people are tired of and they are looking for something new and exciting; or it may be too new, too fashion forward for the store's clientele. Of course, there are many other reasons related to the quality, color, brand, and so forth that can contribute to the reason why merchandise is not purchased. (See Chapter 4 for a discussion of these issues.)

Changing Image

Image serves as a filtering function in the customer's evaluation of a company. Performance must be consistent with the image the retailer or manufacturer wants to project. Customers will overlook minor shortcomings, for example, a mistake made in a transaction, in a company that holds a positive image, gives good service, and provides good-quality merchandise. But if problems continue to happen, the firm will lose that positive image. This happened on a large scale when many department stores reduced the number of sales associates available to help customers. Consequently, the overall image of department stores has changed from full-service to limited- or self-service; and with this image change has come a change in store patronage. If customers do not receive service but still pay high prices, why not go to lower-priced, self-service stores? Therefore, such stores as Wal-Mart and Target are doing very well and expanding, while many department stores are going out of business or merging.

Retailers and manufacturers often find that they wish to change their image and offerings or even their location because of events occurring around them. Increased competition may force a company to change in order to differentiate itself from that competition. A changing neighborhood may lead a store to relocate or change to merchandise that is more suitable to its clientele. Local clientele can be lost with store location changes, so there are definite risks with major changes. Often, however, there are more risks involved with no change.

New ownership often brings changes and new images, sometimes beneficial, other times not. Ownership by Gap brought complete, successful store makeovers for Banana Republic, which eliminated the safari decor and the original travel concept and added higher-priced, well-tailored merchandise. Abercrombie & Fitch has reinvented itself from its original outdoor, adventure image to contemporary in the 1990s as part of The Limited Corporation, and again in the first decade of the twenty-first century as it separated from The Limited. It is not an easy task to change an image, and not all attempts are successful. After an image is established, it is hard to change customer perceptions. It is possible to change from one image to another, but it can be very difficult and can take a great deal of time and promotion to acquaint the public with the change. Macy's did it in the 1970s when it abandoned its bargain basement and replaced it with the Cellar, an upscale kitchen and housewares concept. Spiegel, once known for value-oriented merchandise, now carries upper-end, well-known brands. Changed images imply changed target markets and companies risk the loss of the old market before gaining the new one.

Sometimes a company image can be damaged due to public opinion of company practices. Wal-Mart, the largest retailer in the world, has been in the news a great deal lately for a variety of reasons including criticism of discrimination, not paying fair wages, resisting unions, using contractors that hire undocumented workers, and selling counterfeit goods, among others. See *Case 14, Can Wal-Mart Improve Its Company Image?*, for the company's attempts to turn around this negative image.

Established, successful companies often think that all they need to do is more of the same to maintain success. That, unfortunately, does not always work in today's fast-paced, quick-changing society and marketplace. Formats that are on the

New Team at Altman's To Keep Its Traditions

B. Altman & Company, which has occupied its site on 34th Street and Fifth Avenue since 1906, has a new set of officers since its sale last year by the Altman Foundation. They held a breakfast conference this week to report that its traditions will continue and to show, through displays and models, the directions the New York store's two main areas, home furnishings and fashions, will take next fall.

"We're better known for our home furnishings than fashions, for reasons we do not yet completely understand," said Anthony C. Conti, the new chairman, who promised expansion into the fashion area.

Jack Schultz, the new president, described the store's style as "updated classic, somewhat traditional." He said special attention would be given to the working woman's needs through service and specialized merchandise from Europe, the Far East and the United States.

A new Ralph Lauren shop will open in the store's home furnishings area in September, said Anita Gallo, vice president for fashion direction. Other major themes running through home furnishings will be an emphasis on 18th- and 19th-century styles, including furniture, printed and woven damask fabrics, embroidered linen and cotton sheets and English silver serving pieces.

Gold accents will be stressed in dinner services and accessories, Miss Gallo said. Flowered pillows and platters will express a romantic theme. Pottery, glassware and rugs with primitive look represent another direction.

In fashion, suits will constitute an important category, geared especially to the working woman. Long jacket styles and knits were included in the fashion presentation. Store executives believe the one-piece dress will be significant and daytime separates will look more coordinated.

For men, classicism prevails, as in a one-button suit shown in a muted gray glen plaid with a white shirt and red tie. A navy double-breasted blazer was shown with gray flannel pants as Miss Gallo observed that more men are wearing sports coats to work. Polo coats were presented for both men and women.

No Bidder To Rescue B. Altman

6 of 7 Stores to Close
After One Last Sale

By ISADORE BARMASH

B. Altman & Company, the 124-year-old department store whose flagship establishment on Fifth Avenue was one of the first to cater to Manhattan's carriage trade, will be closed, a bankruptcy court decided yesterday.

After a month on the auction block and a decade of decline, the New York-based retailer failed to attract any acceptable bidders and will shut six of its seven stores after a clearance sale starting Friday, the start of the Christmas shopping season.

The closing of the stores, expected by Jan. 29, ends an era of dignified retailing in lush surroundings that began fading with the demise of New York City retailers like John Wanamaker, Best & Company and Arnold Constable. These stores boasted rich wood paneling, high ceilings with chandeliers and wide, carpeted aisles. Their merchandise was mostly higher-priced than the competition . . . .

The decision to close the Manhattan store and five branches on Long Island and in New Jersey and Pennsylvania was made yesterday in New York by Federal Bankruptcy Judge Tina Bronman in approving a request of the L. J. Hooker Corporation, the owner of Altman's . . . .

The closing of Altman's reflects the pressures that certain retailers have experienced in the last several years, particularly because of a decline in the women's apparel business.

In big city after big city, the quiet slow-paced retailing emporiums that catered to the affluent have either disappeared or adopted a snappier, more contemporary atmosphere . . . .

Today, only some large specialty stores, like the Saks Fifth Avenue chain, Brooks Brothers and Tiffany & Company have the traditional ambience, combined with a disdain for anything too modern or radical in fashion . . . .

Aside from the severe drain of merchandise created by Hooker's decision not to finance new merchandise so that goods could be delivered only when paid for in cash, Altman's suffered from a competitive weakness. It became saddled with an eroding image because of its failure to remodel sufficiently, a reluctance to enrich its merchandise with more diversity and an inability to project a clear image to the customer.

"You can hardly call it a strong carriage-trade store, or, an attraction to the affluent anymore, not anything like Saks," said a retailing executive in another city who asked not to be identified. "Altman's lost its way years ago and never found it again."

Figure 3.2–3.3 Two *New York Times* articles, originally published on June 12, 1986 (top), and November 18, 1989 (bottom), illustrate the hazards of failing to change with the times. After 124 years as a landmark institution on Fifth Avenue in Manhattan, the posh but old-fashioned B. Altman & Company department store was forced to close its doors.

rise include the super specialists or niche companies, and price-oriented companies. Those with high overhead and high prices are finding it a more difficult environment in which to be profitable. The demise of B. Altman in the 1980s and I. Magnin in the 1990s and the buyout of Marshall Field's and Rich's by Macy's in the 2000s are evidence of this. Businesses must change with the times to survive. In some instances, that means using technology to streamline operations to remain cost-effective. Other times it means changing a target market to coincide with societal, economic, and demographic changes. In *Case 15, Chico's Faces Fashion Slump,* Chico's makes several changes to turn around slowing sales. Has its target market changed?

PRODUCT DIFFERENTIATION/POSITIONING

Image must differentiate a company from others in the marketplace—that is, it must be different from competition. No two retailers or manufacturers are alike; each has its own unique personality or image, which emphasizes such factors as price, quality, physical environment, customer service, employee attitude, fashion level of merchandise, or unique or convenient location. These factors create a certain image that attracts a certain type of customer. The success of Nordstrom in competing with other department stores is attributed mainly to their reputation for excellent customer service—not only the perception of it, but the reality. Customers found the best customer service at Nordstrom and therefore were lured away from other department stores that were clearly losing the customer service battle. Indeed, customers of some stores have difficulty merely finding sales associates to help them. (For more on Nordstrom's customer service, see *Case 58, Customer Service and Relationship Management at Nordstrom* in Chapter 9.)

Retailers cannot be all things to all people. They must clearly target their customer and position themselves by differentiating their business from others. At a time when demand is greater than supply, many similar companies can be successful by merely offering certain types of merchandise. This has been the case at times throughout history, for example, after a war when previously scarce items finally became available. However, retailers and manufacturers are finding themselves in trouble if they compete for the same customer and cannot differentiate themselves from others in the marketplace. The closing of Gimbel's and Ohrbach's in 1986, Broadway Stores in 1996, and Mervyn's in 2008 was due in part to their inability to establish clear identities. Consumers could not differentiate these stores from others in the market. Each store must be clearly different or unique to the consumer.

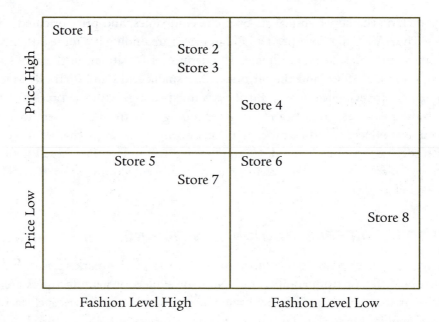

Figure 3.4 This diagram illustrates the positioning of stores based on fashion and price levels.

The term **positioning** refers to the image of a company relative to its competition in the marketplace. For example, where is Target positioned relative to Macy's, Nordstrom, or Wal-Mart? Is Target in direct competition with any of them, or above or below them in terms of fashion?

Using Figure 3.4, fill in familiar fashion stores in terms of fashion and price. Can you identify eight stores in these positions? Where would you put Wal-Mart, Target, Nordstrom, Sears, JCPenney, Macy's, Barney's, Dillards, Saks Fifth Avenue, Tiffany's, and other favorite stores?

Competition

Companies competing or vying for the same consumer business is called **competition** and is an important consideration when deciding whether to open a store in a new area. Is there too much competition in one area? Or is competition good for everyone? After an area is saturated, that market may have difficulty sustaining all the establishments, and many times stores will be forced out of business. On the other hand, a new store can bring more shoppers into an area and often can bring new customers to established stores. Of course, those businesses have to stay on their toes and not rest on past successes. Additionally, competition can be too much for some small stores. When Wal-Mart moves into areas that have been serviced by small, independent retailers, many of these will leave the area or will simply go out of business as the competition becomes too much for them to combat. Such large stores with huge buying power can achieve profits on small margins that small retailers cannot. An illustration of this issue is *Case 16, The Small Store Dilemma,* in which a small store's future is threatened by a large store and shopping center that is relocating into the area. A small store may be in trouble in such a situation if it cannot offer something better than the new competition, such as better selections (wide or deep), lower prices, or better customer service. This is what competition is about: the one that does the best job survives.

Niche Merchandise

Meeting the needs of a specific population **niche** (a narrowly defined customer segment) is one way of differentiating a product or store. Because niches have very specific needs, niche retailers offer deep assortments of one particular type of merchandise. A company could also serve a niche by defining its market in narrow geographic terms; that is, a retailer might serve only one small neighborhood, meeting many of its needs. Golf is an example of a niche that is becoming more popular with aging baby boomers and retirees, and has growing popularity with women—an untraditional golf market.

Large-size fashionable clothing is another niche becoming more popular lately. Lane Bryant has traditionally filled this niche. Today, Torrid is filling the needs of young women of sizes 12 to 26 who, in the words of the company, "want exciting and cutting-edge apparel and accessories" (www.torrid.com). On the other hand, companies like Bebe sell sizes 00 to 12 and do not have interest in selling anything larger. Some niches are so small that a Web site is more appropriate than a chain of stores. For example, www.2BigFeet.com specializes in large shoes for men up to size 20 and width 9E.

Case 17, A Hunka-Hunka of Burnin' Hot! A Case of Abercrombie & Fitch's Brand and Store Positioning describes A&F's controversial niche marketing plan over the years, from its magalogue to its shirtless male greeters. In addition, its atmospherics define its uniqueness. These include the A&F scent, distinctive music, and shuttered storefronts, all of which together create an air of exclusivity.

Figure 3.5 Stella McCartney's activewear for Adidas, focusing on golf, tennis, and running, illustrates niche merchandise.

Target Marketing

Market segmentation is a process of dividing a market into distinct subsets of consumers with different needs and characteristics. **Target marketing** is the selection of one segment to serve with a specific marketing mix. A **target market** is the group of customers that a company seeks to serve and is identified by several variables. This could be golfers, tween girls, baby boomers, or people interested in the environment. To reach a selected target, the product or service is positioned so it is perceived by the target customer to satisfy its needs better than other offerings. Refer back to Figure 3.4. Look at the position of one of the stores. What target market do you think they want to reach?

The bases for identifying a target can include **demographics** (e.g., age, income, gender), **psychographics** (e.g., values, lifestyle, activities, interests), geographic characteristics (e.g., region, city size, climate), sociocultural characteristics (e.g., subcultures, religion, social class, family structure), use (e.g., usage rate, brand loyalty), or benefit (e.g., value, economy, convenience). See *Case 18, Is Wal-Mart in Vogue?,* for an analysis of Wal-Mart's customer relative to its advertising in *Vogue* magazine. Keeping up with changes in its target market is important for a company to remain successful. Do you think Wal-Mart's target has changed?

The following are some trends that might affect retailers' offerings to their U.S. target markets:

- *Changing age groups.* There are 78 million **baby boomers** in the United States, the country's largest demographic group, and they are aging; the oldest are reaching retirement age. The elderly, **the gray market,** are living longer due to increased health care, and they want to live independently in their homes, not nursing homes. Both groups have an abundance of discretionary income to spend on themselves and their grandchildren. **Tweens,** the almost teenagers, are looking for feel-good products, and **Gen Y,** the college students, is wired and socially connected, thanks to the Internet.

- *Increase in ethnic subcultures within society.* African Americans, Hispanic Americans, and Asian Americans are the three fastest-growing ethnic groups in the United States. The increase of ethnic minorities can be seen in music crossovers such as Shakira, Christina Aguilera, and television and movie stars such as Jennifer Lopez, Eva Longoria, and America Ferrera. The U.S. Census Bureau estimates that by 2050, Hispanic Americans will grow to 24 percent of the U.S. population, with the nonminority population decreasing.

- *Use of the Internet and increase of technology for everyday consumers.* The lowered cost of broadband connection has brought the Internet to the masses. We all seem to be wired and connected today with our cell phones and Black-Berry devices. Also, more information is available to the everyday consumer regarding products and services, medical advice, and plenty of sharing through blogs and other Web sites such as Wikipedia, the everyman's encyclopedia. To combat the use of the Internet, retailers are turning to creating an exciting shopping experience for consumers, retailing as theater and experiential retail. Consider American Girl stores, where mothers can buy a doll for their little girls and even get the doll's hair styled while they wait. **Atmospherics,** the design of space to evoke certain effects, becomes more important. See *Case 17* for how A&F creates an atmosphere clearly targeted to their young market.

- *Increase in social consciousness.* This leads to an increase in social marketing, sometimes called **cause marketing.** When companies support a cause, consumers feel better about the company. Examples are Macy's support of

HIV/AIDS groups with their well-known Passport fashion show and many fashion companies that support breast cancer research.

- *Time poverty and life simplification.* Many people today feel pressed for time more than ever before. It may just be that we have more options for spending our time today and feel pressured to do it all. Even with many labor-saving household devices and spouses sharing housework, we feel the pressure of time in our family and professional lives. Products and services that can ease this feeling of time pressure are and will continue to be successful. Such things include prepared meals, digital cameras (the one-hour photo service being no longer fast or convenient enough for today's consumers), instant everything from puddings to dry-cleaning services, one-day delivery, or credit cards that are read instantly with just a wave. Can anyone stand dial-up after using high-speed Internet connections?

- *The rise of mass class and fast fashion.* With increased prosperity, more and more people desire luxury items. The marketplace has responded with "affordable luxuries," mass-produced products that still have a degree of exclusivity. H&M, Zara, Dell, Nike, and Uniqlo all offer fashion and service at low prices.

- *Diffusion of cultures.* With increased global travel, increased prosperity, and immigration we see fusion as a common theme in food, clothing, relationships, and other aspects of our lives. Western fashion affects people around the world, and U.S. consumers are seeing more global companies in the marketplace increasing our choices and introducing us to other cultures.

All trends have implications for retailers and manufacturers, including what type of merchandise to produce and offer for sale, where to locate production sites and stores, what services to offer, and what type of formats to provide for busy consumers. Such demographic, psychographic, and societal changes must be addressed by retailers if they want their businesses to thrive.

SUMMARY

Product differentiation is a vital part of competing in the marketplace. Many once strong retailers that have lost their uniqueness are no longer in business today. Niche merchandise, which serves a specific market, is one way that companies differentiate themselves from others. Image and identity must be clearly communicated to a retailer's consumers. Additionally, market research can identify consumer changes in makeup and needs.

KEY TERMS

atmospherics

baby boomers

cause marketing

competition

demographics

fashion cycle

fashion followers

fashion forward

fashion leaders

Gen Y

gray market

identity

image

knockoff

niche

positioning

product differentiation

product life cycle

psychographics

target market

target marketing

tweens

BIBLIOGRAPHY

Arnould, E. J., Price, L. L., & Zinkhan, G. M. (2004). *Consumers.* New York: McGraw-Hill.

Frings, G. (2008). *Fashion from concept to consumer.* Upper Saddle River, NJ: Prentice Hall.

Jennigan, M. H., & Easterling, C. R. (1990). *Fashion merchandising and marketing.* New York: Macmillan.

Levy, M., & Weitz, B. A. (2009). *Retailing management.* New York: McGraw-Hill.

Schiffman, L. G., & Kanuk, L. L. (2008). *Consumer behavior.* Upper Saddle River, NJ: Prentice Hall.

Solomon, M. R., & Rabolt, N. J. (2009). *Consumer behavior: In fashion.* Upper Saddle River, NJ: Prentice Hall.

U.S. Census Bureau, www.census.gov.

See trend Web sites such as:

> http://beauty.ivillage.com/trends/fashion/topics/0,,6xvzwplp,00.html
>
> http://www.fashiontrendsetter.com
>
> http://www.infomat.com/trends/index.html
>
> http://www.smallbiztrends.com
>
> http://t-r-e-n-d-s.blogspot.com
>
> http://www.trendwatching.com/trendreport

Case 13

FRUSTRATION IN THE MENSWEAR DEPARTMENT

Nancy J. Rabolt, San Francisco State University
Judy K. Miler, Florida State University

Jim Safford is the men's suit buyer for the Langley Department Store, Milwaukee, Wisconsin, and has been in this position for five years. He was employed directly after graduation from the University of Michigan, where he earned an MBA. After completion of the Langley Training Program, he was an assistant buyer, then an associate, and finally a buyer, all within two years. His first buying assignment was in the men's furnishings department, where he performed admirably for four years. His record was so good that management decided to give him the new assignment of buying men's suits, a department with declining sales. Despite this, Jim felt that this was a step toward a position on the upper-management team, an achievement that would take another year or two. In fact, it was common knowledge among personnel that he was a young man slated for higher management, so his thoughts were not just reveries.

Jim tackled his job with enthusiasm, care, and understanding. He gave the op-

portunity all it was worth—a lifetime career that was going to lead to big things. Unfortunately, Jim was the victim of circumstance, and soon some of the glitter began to fade. Despite all his efforts—which included advice from the buying office, peers in the field, and friendly manufacturers—business continued to lag. The trend toward sportswear hurt his business; losses of volume were suffered up to 10 percent per year; and after five years, the department's projected volume for the next year was 60 percent of what it was when Jim took over. Management was not deeply disturbed because they were aware of the fashion trend and had industry records that reflected similar regional and national results.

Despite management's support, Jim was grim and never ceased to search for the key to build the department and again assume the position of a man on the rise. Finally, during January of this year, the message came across loud and clear. The market, optimistic for the first time in years, reported a trend toward men's suits and a new silhouette, the revival of the double-breasted, European-cut suit—just what the doctor ordered as medicine to accelerate business. Jim visited the market and shopped it thoroughly. He spoke to all sources of information and learned of heavy manufacturer production concentrating on the new style, other stores' plans for strong promotions, and fashion magazine support. He was convinced—this was it. And he made up his mind that 80 percent of his suit budget should be put behind the trend.

Fortunately, his divisional merchandise manager, Dan Powers, was in the market and was able to meet him for dinner. As Jim enthusiastically presented his plan to Dan, he outlined the following:

- Men's suit orders must be given four to six months in advance of delivery.
- The lead time requires an early decision; it is not possible to purchase needed goods after the season starts. Failure to take an early stand means a serious loss during the best-selling period of the year.
- The new styling is not revolutionary; it is just right for the global marketplace of today.
- Competition is going all-out for the first good news in years.
- Coop ad money is available, and strong promotional efforts will not exceed last year's budget substantially.
- Customers are looking for styling that is wearable but fashionable. Moreover, the styling fits right into the Langley customers' taste level.

Powers listened carefully and then replied. "It all sounds great, but fashion is acceptance; anything less is an opinion. I suggest that we plan one early strong promotion, about 20 percent of your open-to-buy, which is an important investment." Jim was annoyed, "You were a fashion merchandiser of women's apparel; you just don't understand the men's business." One

word led to another, and an impasse developed. Both men were angry, and finally Powers said, "I've made my decision, and I will not countersign any order beyond 20 percent of the OTB." With those words, he got up and said, "That is final. Good night."

Jim was terribly upset. He understood the meaning of fashion and knew the difference between opinion and acceptance. But he also felt that even modest success would bolster the department's sagging volume. In fact, he worked up a chart proving that a markdown of 15 percent of net sales would still allow for a profitable season. He knew that the department needed stimulation, the store needed newness, and the sales personnel needed the lift of a new fashion look to promote. He considered going over Powers' head to the general merchandise manager, who was regarded as a logical thinker. His main arguments would be the following:

- He is a seasoned buyer who should be the selector of merchandise. After all, he is being paid to evaluate the market, study customers, and stock merchandise.
- Retailing demands that merchandisers take some risk. Staying with the same old, same old does not reflect fashion leadership or allow profits from selling early trends.
- The element of risk in this case is minute.

Before taking his next step and trying to convince Powers' boss with his arguments, Jim thought he would discuss the issues with friendly peers. He called several of his colleagues, explained the situation, and asked for advice on how to approach the problem.

Major Question

If you were one of Jim's colleagues, how would you advise him?

Study Questions

1. Why would promoting a new style or trend at the beginning of a season be a safe way for a retailer to test it?

2. Discuss the risks associated with the introduction of new styles and the maintenance of a store's fashion image.

3. What does Powers mean when he said "fashion is acceptance, anything else is an opinion"?

4. What type of stores show fashion leadership? How does the merchandise differ relative to non-fashion forward stores?

Case 14

CAN WAL-MART IMPROVE ITS COMPANY IMAGE?[1]

Hope Bober Corrigan, Loyola College in Maryland

Background from the Company

The company Sam Walton built has become the world's number one retailer. The organi-zation has grown in a variety of retail formats, including Wal-Mart Stores, Supercenters, Sam's Clubs, Neighborhood Markets, online, and internationally. Wal-Mart operated units in the following countries as of April 2005:

Country	Number of Stores	Country	Number of Stores
Argentina	11	South Korea	16
Brazil	151	Mexico	700
Canada	281	Puerto Rico	54
China	45	United Kingdom	286
Germany	89	United States	3,719

As Wal-Mart has grown, it has also become a large job creator. According to the company home page, "more than 1.2 million Associates work at *Wal-Mart* in the U.S. The majority of Wal-Mart's hourly store associates in the U.S. work full-time. That's well above the 20–40 percent typically found in the retail industry. We are a leading employer of Hispanic Americans, with more than 139,000 Hispanic associates. Wal-Mart is one of the leading employers of African Americans, with more than 208,000 African-American associates. More than 220,000 of our associates are 55 or older. We project we will create positions for more than 100,000 new jobs in 2005."

Wal-Mart Faces Criticism

Over the years, Wal-Mart has had its share of negative press about its labor and management practices. As a large company and

[1]Levy and Weitz, *Retailing Management*, 6th ed., The McGraw-Hill Companies. Reproduced with permission of The McGraw-Hill Companies.

employer, Wal-Mart has grown to expect attention and criticism. Some of the key areas of concern include discriminating against women, resisting unions, paying lower wages and offering fewer benefits, purchasing merchandise from China, employing contractors who hire illegal immigrants, and growing too rapidly. Constructive criticism has helped Wal-Mart improve its operations; however, the company takes issue when the criticism becomes an unwarranted attack that tarnishes its reputation.

Advertising Campaign to Improve Corporate Image

To reverse negative criticism and improve its public image, Wal-Mart launched an informative Web page, http://www.walmartfact.com\default.aspx, had key high-ranking executives appear for interviews on ABC, CNN, Fox, and CNBC; and took out full-page advertising in over 100 newspapers. Wal-Mart is proactively fighting back against critics and special interest groups to dispel myths about its employment and business practices.

To tell the Wal-Mart story and clear up misperceptions, the Web page contains company news and press releases, illustrates community impact and involvement programs, describes employee benefits and wages, and explains the status of current lawsuits facing the organization. This noncommercial Web page also summarizes Wal-Mart's diversity and equal employment opportunity policies, international operations, employee promotion strategies, charitable giving, and merchandise sourcing. An important objective of the Web site is to help associates, consumers, reporters, and investors learn about the company.

To reach the mass media and take control of its image, Wal-Mart's Chief Executive Officer, H. Lee Scott, appeared on many networks including ABC, CNN, Fox, and CNBC for interviews. As part of this promotional campaign to show Wal-Mart in a positive light, he also granted interviews with *USA Today* and the Associated Press.

Wal-Mart put a full-page ad in more than 100 newspapers including the *New York Times* and *The Wall Street Journal* on January 13, 2005. The ads contained a five-paragraph letter from CEO Scott in response to misinformation about Wal-Mart. To set the record straight, the national print ads stated that the average wage for full-time hourly workers at Wal-Mart is $9.68, which is almost twice the federal minimum wage of $5.15 per hour.

Major Question

Can this type of advertising campaign improve Wal-Mart's image in the eyes of associates, consumers, investors, and the press?

Study Question

What else could Wal-Mart do to improve its reputation?

Exercise

Go to Wal-Mart Stores home page and click on College Recruiting. Explore what this page has to offer. If a Wal-Mart recruiter came to your campus, would you consider Wal-Mart as an employer? Why or why not?

Case 15

CHICO'S FACES FASHION SLUMP

Denise T. Ogden, Penn State University, Lehigh Valley

Chico's FAS, Inc. is a retailer of women's private-label, sophisticated, casual-to-dressy apparel and accessories. The company owns Chico's, White House/Black Market, Soma by Chico's (intimate apparel), and Fitigues (activewear). Of the 909 stores, 541 are Chico's front-line stores and 32 are Chico's outlet stores. Chico's started in 1983 in Sanibel Island, Florida, as an independent retail chain, selling sweaters and Mexican folk art. Chico's went public in 1993 and evolved into one of the fastest-growing women's specialty apparel retailers in the United States.

Chico's targets women 35 years and older with an income of $75,000+ who are fashion-conscious. The size of the target market is estimated at 148 million women. The company prides itself on customer service. It designs most of its products in-house or through independent companies. Chico's fashions are relaxed, figure-flattering, and made with easy-care fabrics. The clothes at Chico's are sized 0 to 3. Size 0 is equivalent to sizes 4 to 6; 1 to sizes 8 to 10; 2, sizes 12 to 14; and 3, sizes 16 to 18. The sizing strategy gives customers a psychological boost. The in-house design process allows Chico's to realize average initial gross profit margins that are higher than industry average. In past years its operating income margin has consistently exceeded 20 percent, compared with 3.5 percent for the apparel retail industry.

In 2005/2006, the company reported that slow sales, payroll, and store upgrades will cut profits. Prior to this, the company had 113 consecutive months of same-store sales gains. President and Chief Executive Officer Scott Edmonds admitted that the company has had some missteps in its fashion merchandising. He stated that the main problems were Chico's own fashions, and catalog and marketing strategies, which were flat and stale. More often customers were leaving the stores without a purchase. Some of the items experiencing the greatest slowdown included their Southwest designed sweaters and jackets. In addition, the competition had lured customers away with innovative fashions. In an effort to reverse this trend, the company implemented several actions:

- Hiring Michael J. Leedy from American Eagle Outfitters as chief marketing officer to replace James Frain
- Redesigning the Chico's Web site
- Reexamining the stores to position them to better meet local customer tastes
- Lowering prices on selected items due to management admission that prices may have been raised too much

The problem with the merchandise is not an easy fix. To improve its fashion merchandising, Chico's hired Michele Dalahunt Cloutier, a former executive at Ann Taylor Stores, as general merchandise manager. Ms. Cloutier's responsibilities include overseeing and directing all merchandising activities for the Chico's brand. Ms. Cloutier reports to Patricia Murphy Kerstein, chief merchant for the Chico's brand.

Major Question

If you were Michele Cloutier, what changes would you implement?

Study Questions

1. Is Chico's hitting the saturation point in terms of number of stores? Why or why not?

2. What effect do competitors such as Coldwater Creek and J. Jill have on Chico's?

Bibliography

Cassidy, T. (2003). Chico's and J. Jill target same shoppers with different styles. *Boston Globe.* Retrieved on February 6, 2003, from Proquest Direct database.

Chico's. (2006, April 3). *Chico's FAS, Inc. fills senior marketing positions and announces additional management promotion.* Chico's Press Release.

Chico's. (2006, August 23). *Michele Delahunt Cloutier to join Chico's FAS, Inc. as EVP & general merchandise manager.* Chico's Press Release.

Chico's Annual Report 2005.

Chico's FAS Inc. Management Presentation. (n.d.). Retrieved on November 28, 2006 from http://www.chicos.com/store/investor_mgmt_presentation.asp

Covert, J. (2006, September 13). Chico's attempts to fashion rebound. *Wall Street Journal* (Eastern edition). Retrieved from Proquest Direct database.

Case 16

THE SMALL STORE DILEMMA

Nancy J. Rabolt, San Francisco State University
Judy K. Miler, Florida State University

Juan Romano is a small apparel speciality store owner in Dubuque, Iowa. He has had the store for 15 years, and while it has not been an easy road to success, he very much enjoys his work and lifestyle in this middle-American city. Prior to having his own business, Juan had worked for several major apparel retailers as a buyer and divisional merchandise manager. Life has been good to him, and he gives back to his community through philanthropic involvement and donations, granting him respect as a Spanish-American businessman in Dubuque.

The annual sales volume of the store is in the neighborhood of $500,000, which yields a comfortable living. Juan's store sales personnel consists of one full-time salesperson and two part-timers, a student at the local community college and a retired school teacher. The customers are in the middle to slightly above average income range. They are not fashion leaders in the sense that they want the latest market offerings, but they are fashion-conscious and highly selective. Juan's store sells a full range of men's and women's clothing, from sleepwear to outerwear, sportswear, and a small amount of seasonal, special-occasion merchandise. He has built up a loyal customer base of professional men and women who live and work in the area. Juan offers his customers the service they want, with the prices and styles they desire.

Juan enjoys the daily running of the store. It adds up to a most pleasant and profitable occupation—that is, until six months ago when Juan learned that one of the major chain stores in the state, with a national reputation, had filed plans to build and anchor a shopping center approximately one-quarter mile from his store. The shopping center will be ready for occupancy in eight months. This has Juan quite upset, as he knows that the ladies' sportswear and dress departments will be in direct competition with the merchandise classifications he carries, because he has shopped this major chain store himself, looking for inspiration of lines to purchase for his store.

Even though Juan already knows the character and practices of the department store that will be moving into Dubuque, he

starts an in-depth investigation. He travels to the nearest branch and studies it for a day. The store's departments offer a wider assortment of styles than Juan's store; maintain depth beyond his ability; have interesting and compelling regional advertising, including television spots; offer personal selling service, including personal shoppers; maintain liberal return policies; and accept any credit card under the sun.

Needless to say, Juan is more than a bit upset and disturbed by his findings. He knows that there is a possibility that he will not be able to stand the hard-hitting competition, let alone the pressure. One of his neighbors, the owner of a children's shop, remarked the other day, "I don't know what I'm going to do—look for another location? I don't know how to stand up to the competition."

Juan's full-time salesperson, Sara Cummings, keeps repeating, "I'm not afraid of them. They're big, but our customers are loyal. They've been our customers for years, and they like us and our merchandise." If Juan could only believe this, there would be no reason to fear the new store taking his customers away.

Juan, however, knows the threat is real and he must begin to prepare a proactive course of action. His store's location is in a strip shopping area with no strong pull from adjoining stores. They are all small retailers like himself. The strength has to come from within. Steps must be taken to ensure continued success. As a small store operation, Juan knows that he cannot obtain exclusivity of styling or preferential delivery, buy in promotional quantities, or use conventional promotional power like the big stores.

Juan visits his Dallas buying office, an operation that handles small specialty shops, but he feels that their advice is inadequate to meet the situation. As a matter of fact, he is somewhat annoyed by the president's major suggestion, which was to visit the market more often. This is very unrealistic. As a small store operator, how can he leave the store to visit New York, Dallas, or Atlanta more frequently? Not only is it too costly, as he does not have the volume to support more frequent purchasing, but he cannot see how it will position him better to meet the other challenges the new store is going to present.

Major Question

If you were Juan, what course of action would you take to combat the big, new competition moving into your store's area?

Study Questions

1. Today, many small, independent apparel stores are suffering from competition of large, national chains. What are some strategies that a small retailer could implement to help secure the maintenance of the store's market share when faced with new competition?

2. In what ways can a small store excel compared to a large department store?

3. If two stores carry the same merchandise, how can one store differentiate itself to ensure customer loyalty?

Case 17

A HUNKA-HUNKA OF BURNIN' HOT! A CASE OF ABERCROMBIE & FITCH'S BRAND AND STORE POSITIONING

Joseph H. Hancock, II, Drexel University

The History of Abercrombie & Fitch

In 1892, Abercrombie & Fitch (A&F) was known for traditional outdoor, camping, and adventure apparel for men and women. However, after being bought by The Limited Corporation in 1988, the company was reinvented reflecting a new contemporary image. In 1998 A&F separated from its parent company, The Limited, to become an independent retailer. By first quarter 2007, the company was operating 947 stores including: 355 Abercrombie & Fitch stores (target market age 18 to 22), 396 Hollister Co. stores (target market 14 to 18), 180 Abercrombie stores (kids—target market age 7 to 14), and 16 Ruehl No. 925 stores (target market 23 to 35). In their own words, A&F is the "Creator and Operator of Aspirational Lifestyle Brands." The company plans to continue its growth in Canadian and European markets and is searching for real estate in Tokyo (Abercrombie & Fitch, 2006).

The employees of the company pride themselves on having total control over stores, fashion design, sourcing, pricing, and marketing. A&F believes it offers the consumer excellent quality and key trends, and it prides itself with the ability to sell products at full retail. The company continues to focus on first-rate price levels with higher-priced and better-quality products reflecting Abercrombie's "Casual Luxury" theme.

The company's fashion assortment consists of basics for men and women that are composed of casual pants and shorts, T-shirts, polo shirts, fashion tops, woven shirts, sweaters, denim jackets, jeans, sweatshirts, zip fleece tops, leather belts, flip-flops, underwear, cologne, baseball caps, bracelets and other jewelry, as well as various other types of activewear. A&F brands its products by attaching traditional outdoor and rugged iconic patches on garments, allowing the retailer to gain strong product position and recognition. Symbols such as collegiate flags, sports mascots, and the letters A&F appear on almost all of the products. The company has even adopted the logo of a moose that it embroiders on all its polo and oxford shirts.

Niche marketing and in-store advertising displaying predominantly young half-naked muscle boys and trim girls has been a key vehicle for A&F to gain success in the retail market. During the late 1990s, A&F's marketing strategy gained momentum with promotions geared toward college coeds, gay men, and other Abercrombie enthusiasts.

The Abercrombie "magalog" (as it was identified by the *Wall Street Journal* on July 29, 1997; the official word *magalogue* is used in all other publications) was popular and went beyond a mail-order catalog, evolving into a lifestyle guide for thousands of consumers (Bird, 1997).

In his book *The Erotic History of Advertising,* Tom Reichart (2003) states, "Abercrombie is to fashion what *Maxim* is to magazines . . . both are extremely profitable, enjoying exponential sales increases, and both use skin to appeal to teens and young adults" (p. 235). A&F continues to employ the well-known fashion photographer Bruce Weber to create marketing campaigns that have gained extreme attention from the press. These photographic advertising magalogues are collected and continually sold on eBay.com for prices ranging from $35 to $100.

Although the magalogue was effective as a promotional device, many conservative activist groups protested this periodical's use of blatant erotic scenes in order to sell Abercrombie items such as cargo pants and muscle T's. An article by David Reines (2003) titled *All the Nudes That's Fit to Print* cites A&F's magalogue as sexually charged and reveals how the American Decency Association and other groups called for a national boycott of the retailer.

However, amongst teens and college coeds, owning A&F apparel is almost the norm. Some teens refuse to shop A&F because it is "too common." As Greg Lindsay (2003) suggests, the Quarterly made Abercrombie's name synonymous with a preppy and classic look found in its clothes and the all-American perfection of its models, but its edgy tone and imagery drove many critics over the edge. While the days of the risqué magalogue are gone, over the last few years, A&F has developed newer concepts to promote its products.

Abercrombie's Atmospherics, New Store Facades, and Shirtless Greeters

A&F is one retailer that continually re-creates its branding concept for product differentiation. It is constantly gaining market share by creating unique merchandise characteristics that are composed by reinventing traditional garments with fashion savvy design, washes, and fit. However, Abercrombie uses other methods to generate a unique store position. It appeals and entices consumers through the senses of sight, sound, and smell.

Anyone who has entered an Abercrombie store knows they all *smell* the same. Every one of the 355 Abercrombie divisional stores smells of the company's fragrance *Fierce* for men. For many merchandisers in the retailing profession, the joke is that to find an Abercrombie store a person just needs to follow his or her nose. Abercrombie is known for asking its associates to continually spray both the store and the garments in the store with the fragrance.

Another strategy Abercrombie utilizes to create an aura of excitement in its stores is techno, electronic, house, and dance music. By playing these genres of music, A&F gives the customer a clublike feeling when shopping its stores. The thump, thump, thump of the bass on a remix of *The Glamorous Life*, along with the smell of *Fierce* cologne, creates an atmosphere that arouses a customer's senses, possibly getting him or her to purchase more A&F brand products. While these strategies of differentiation are not unique to A&F, two of this retailer's other methods of market positioning are quite innovative.

In 2005 A&F opened a new store prototype in Manhattan at 720 Fifth Avenue. While previously known for its unique window displays, this new four-story space would change the company's window merchandising strategies forever. The Fifth Avenue store's façade and all windows were covered by wooden shutters (see Figure 3.6); eventually the company took the same position with all of its mall stores (see Figure 3.7), creating an aura of exclusivity.

While some customers may have liked the new shutter-covered facades, others may have felt that new look of the store was intimidating. However, this was not the biggest change in the company's niche marketing strategies. With the opening of the new A&F store on Fifth Avenue, the retailer also re-created the role of the store greeter. Unlike a typical greeter at Gap or Wal-Mart, A&F's new greeter was a sexy, shirtless, chiseled, ripped hunk who wore nothing but torn blue jeans (sometimes underwear) and flip-flops. (See Figure 3.8.)

The new greeters gained huge attention from both the press and industry professionals. Jade Chang's 2006 *Los Angeles Times* article, *The Ab in Abercrombie*, reveals that

Figure 3.6 The shutter-covered façade of the Abercrombie & Fitch store on Fifth Avenue in New York.

Figure 3.7 A typical Abercrombie & Fitch store located at King of Prussia Mall.

these greeters are successful marketing and store positioning techniques for A&F on both the West and East Coasts. An executive marketing manager of trend and scouting services for The Limited states, "When A&F opened in London last March, crowds of people lined up just to see all the shirtless muscle male models that Abercrombie had brought in for the store opening. Their shirtless greeters have gained an international reputation that has grown since they started the concept in 2005. Both male and female customers know when they go to A&F they are going to see half-naked men and *they love it!*" (Krista Lowther, personal communication, July 6, 2007).

"They love it" seems to reflect A&F's sales success. From 2005 to 2007, sales have continued to grow at A&F. The company reported gross profit increases of over 65 percent during both 2005 and 2006 (Abercrombie, 2007). Moreover, during these years the company expanded into Canada and England. Did the new aspirational market and brand positioning of shutter-covered facades and shirtless greeters impact sales? Or was the actual product so different that consumers wanted more?

Major Question

Should retailers use atmospherics such as music, cologne, and visual effects in order

Figure 3.8 A live model greeter at the A&F store on Fifth Avenue in New York.

to contextualize their products? Was Abercrombie & Fitch's decision to cover the store windows and hire shirtless greeters a good strategy? Why or why not?

Study Questions

1. Is Abercrombie & Fitch using strategies that are ethical? Why or why not?

2. Is the use of eroticism new to generating sales in retailing? Should retailers entice consumers sexually to sell products? Why or why not?

3. Was the covering of A&F windows a smart idea? Is the company going to hurt its sales or create an aura of exclusivity that will draw more customers into the store?

Bibliography

Abercrombie & Fitch Annual Report. (2005). Retrieved July 23, 2007, from http://library.corporate-ir.net/library/61/617/61701/items/198310/05AnnualReport.pdf

Abercrombie & Fitch Annual Report. (2006). Retrieved July 23, 2007, from http://library.corporate-ir.net/library/61/617/61701/items/246067/2006_Annual_Report.pdf

Bird, L. (1997, July 29). Beyond mail order: Catalogs now selling image, advice. *Wall Street Journal*, p. B-1.

Chang, J. (2006, September 10). The ab in Abercrombie: Hard bodies give the hard sell at this grove emporium. *Los Angeles Times*, Retrieved July 23, 2007, from http://www.latimes.com/features/printedition/magazine/la-tm-abercrombie37sep10,1,1129353.story?coll=la-headlines-magazine&ctrack=1&cset=true

Lindsay, G. (2003, December 11). Death of A&F's quarterly: Problem wasn't sex but brand's loss of cool, *Women's Wear Daily*, Retrieved July 23, 2007, from http://www.tiburonresearchgroup.com/pdfs/2003_1211_ANF_Mag.pdf

Reichart, T. (2003). *The erotic history of advertising*. New York: Prometheus Books.

Reines, D. (2003). All the nudes that's fit to print, http://www.nerve.com.

Case 18

IS WAL-MART IN VOGUE?[1]

Hope Bober Corrigan, Loyola College in Maryland

The September 2005 issue of *Vogue* magazine contained eight pages of advertisements from the world's largest retailer, Wal-Mart. The other 792 pages contained advertisements from Ralph Lauren, The Gap, Saks Fifth Avenue, Dior, Estée Lauder, Gucci, Lancôme, St. John, Louis Vuitton, Bill Blass, Yves Saint Laurent, L'Oreal, Guess, Michael Kors, David Yurman, Clinique, Marc Jacobs, Burberry, Calvin Klein, Manolo Blahnik, Donna Karan, Paul Mitchell, Vera Wang, and Jimmy Choo, to name just a portion of the brands in this fall issue.

The ads from Wal-Mart feature real customers including a martial artist, a musician, a mom, students, a cake decorator, a professor of art, and a fundraiser. Each woman is shown with a "Her Style" profile, locating her

[1]Levy and Weitz, *Retailing Management*, 6th ed., The McGraw-Hill Companies. Reproduced with permission of The McGraw-Hill Companies.

Wal-Mart and indicating what she is wearing in the photograph from Wal-Mart and from her own closet. These ads are a departure from the smiley-faced, low-price–focused messages seen from Wal-Mart in the past.

Do Wal-Mart ads belong in *Vogue* magazine? To help answer this question, describe the characteristics and attributes of the Wal-Mart shopper and the *Vogue* magazine reader. Use the following segmentation bases to complete this exercise:

Demographic. Gender, age, race, life stage, birth era, family size/stage, residence tenure (own/rent), marital status.

Geographic. Region, city size, climate, metropolitan area, density (urban, suburb, rural).

Psychographic. Personality, values, lifestyle, activities, interests, opinions.

Socioeconomic. Income, education, occupation.

Benefits Sought. To meet customers' desires.

Usage Rate. Purchase behavior (frequency), brand loyalty.

Study Questions*

1. Is there an overlap in these two consumer segments?

2. Can Wal-Mart change its image and appeal to an upscale shopper, or should it stick to loyal, cash-strapped customers?

3. Would you recommend that Wal-Mart purchase additional pages in *Vogue* magazine this year? Explain your rationale.

*Do not use the alternative solutions format for this case.

CHAPTER DISCUSSION QUESTIONS

1. What stores have closed lately? Analyze their images and positioning in the market. Were they clearly differentiated, offering superior merchandise and service to the public? Why do you think they went out of business?

2. Discuss successful retailers and manufacturers that offer niche merchandise and/or services. How do they differ from traditional department and specialty stores? What are the keys to successful niche merchandising?

3. Discuss the fashion level of The Limited, Gap, Saks Fifth Avenue, Nordstrom, Neiman Marcus, Bloomingdale's, Macy's, and other popular stores. How would you position them in terms of fashion leadership?

4. What demographic, psychographic, and sociocultural changes have you become aware of in the population where you live that would affect retail offerings?

5. How can small stores compete with larger stores that have more power?

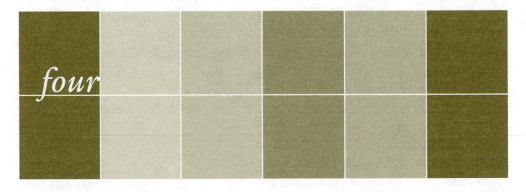

four

Merchandise Characteristics

CHAPTER OBJECTIVES

- Present and exemplify such major merchandise characteristics as style, fashion, price, and quality as related to image.
- Differentiate levels of fashion and explore the concepts of licensing, knock-offs, and counterfeiting.
- Relate the advantages and disadvantages of branded versus private-label merchandise.

*T*he characteristics of merchandise offerings of a manufacturer or retailer are defined by its mission, image, and target market. Customers expect to find certain price, quality, and fashion levels, in addition to their favorite brands at the stores they patronize. Brands are recognizable labels, whether they are store, manufacturer, or designer labels, which have specific expectations of performance defined as value by customers. These expectations are based on consistency of the defining characteristics. Successful companies understand their customers' preferences and strive to maintain their business by meeting those needs. Dominance in one or more characteristics helps a manufacturer or retailer stand out from its competition and gain the all-important competitive edge.

CHARACTERISTICS AND TYPES OF MERCHANDISE

Part of the image of a company is based on the type of merchandise it offers. Retailers and manufacturers must decide on the characteristics of their merchandise offerings. Among the many questions to be asked and decisions to be made are the following:

- Will the company offer soft or hard goods?
- At what price and quality level will the products be offered?
- Will the products be private label or branded?
- Will the products be basic or fashion goods? If they are to be fashion goods, at which fashion level will they be offered?

After these decisions are made (among many others), there are also marketing considerations and decisions to be evaluated. A company (retail or manufacturer) must decide how to market the merchandise (whether fashion or basic goods, soft or hard goods, private or branded). Merchandise can be marketed as **convenience goods** (for example, pantyhose), **shopping goods** (which are evaluated more by the consumer and include most clothing purchases), **specialty goods** (which are name brands), or **impulse goods** (which by their very nature are purchased with little or no planning). Obviously, the nature of the goods themselves (i.e., hard, soft, basic, fashion, and so forth) helps in making all these determinations, but merchandise characteristics can also identify and build (or hinder) the reputation of the business in the eyes of the consumer.

Soft Goods versus Hard Goods

Early American retailers sold general merchandise or dry goods. The term "dry goods" referred to bolts of fabric, while "wet goods" referred to rum, the two chief imports of Colonial days. Dry goods are now referred to as **soft goods,** which include apparel and textile products. **Hard goods** include home furnishings, appliances, electronics, and so forth. A company's merchandise mix can include either one or both types of merchandise. Since the mid-1980s, department stores have tended to decrease or even eliminate hard goods while increasing soft goods, which have higher turnover and profitability. Other retailers began selling strictly hard goods, and departments stores found it difficult to compete with their limited stocks. Because soft goods were consistently the majority of traditional department store sales, they frequently decided to drop many hard goods and to build up their apparel lines. JCPenney and Sears are two examples of the trend to-ward emphasizing soft goods over hard goods.

Price Levels

Price level is another characteristic of merchandise and store positioning. Certain stores are thought of as selling merchandise at certain prices. For example, dis-count stores sell lower-price point merchandise than regular-price stores, while tra-ditional department stores—which are regular-price oriented—sell merchandise at higher price levels. Prices of merchandise take into account more than just the mer-chandise; price also takes into account the services offered by the retailer and other non-price bases, for example, the store's environment, location, and level of cus-tomer service. Therefore, the same product may be found at two different retailers at two very different prices. Retailers with a monopoly position have the most free-dom to determine prices; that is, with no competition, they can ask any price de-spite merchandise cost. For example, shops at airports are notorious for this, with their excessively high prices due to the relative absence of competition. In a com-petitive situation, which is the case in most of today's retail environment, prices are affected by consumer demand and competitors' prices. Often apparel and other types of retailers meet their competitor's prices to make an individual sale and will also lower prices of branded goods when another store does. Consumer prices have been affected by government regulations through the Robinson-Patman Act, which has regulated the price retailers pay to suppliers. (See Chapter 11 for a discussion of this related issue.) However, a recent Supreme Court ruling may allow manufac-turers to set minimum prices for the sale of their brands at retail. In the past man-ufacturers could not set retail prices. The court ruling gives lower courts the leeway to determine, on a case-by-case basis, whether minimum pricing agreements are anticompetitive (Clark & Ellis, 2007). This could allow luxury brands protection from discounters but raise prices to consumers.

Some manufacturers and designers try to protect their reputations by selling only to full-price retailers and not to discounters. Similarly, some retailers try to protect their image by not selling any product that is also sold at a discounter. *Case 19, "With It" or Without* describes such a department store policy.

The price of goods is generally related to the quality and style level of the goods. Apparel is designated as designer, bridge, better, moderate, or budget, generally in respectively descending price and quality. Designer goods carry a de-signer name. These vary by price and exclusivity levels. **Designer collections** con-sist of the designer's high-end one-of-a-kind lines and ready-to-wear lines shown

Figure 4.1 Designer Carolina Herrera speaks to guests at a personal appearance and promotes her special occasion clothing.

to the press twice a year, while the **bridge** (or **secondary**) **lines** are somewhat more affordable and may be licensed to another manufacturer (thereby "bridging" the gap between designer and better). For example, Giorgio Armani has several prices levels, with his Armani Collezione commanding the highest price. One fur-lined woman's jacket was for sale on its Web site for $3,100. Emporio Armani could be considered a bridge line, found in Emporio Armani stores, for more affordable prices. Other lines include Giorgio Armani Prive, Armani Jeans, A/X Armani Exchange, Armani Casa, and Armani Junior. Some of these lines may be found in department stores. Similarly, the Donna Karan line is her collection, while DKNY at lower prices is her bridge line.

Bridge lines are often similar to the quality and price of **better goods**. Bridge goods, which carry a designer name and high price, may not necessarily be as high quality as better goods, however. This is because the status of the designer name, and not necessarily the quality, is the reason for the popularity; thus, the product can command a higher price. **Moderate goods** are lower in price and quality than better goods and are sold at many department stores, while **budget** or **opening**

price point goods are even lower priced and are offered at discount department stores and mass merchandisers. Opening price point goods are a manufacturer's first, or lowest, price level.

Style and Fashion Levels

Retailers often classify merchandise as basic or fashion. **Basics** (also known as **staples**) generally have a stable customer demand and generally don't go in and out of fashion. Some examples of basics are pencils, shoelaces, jeans, T-shirts, and hosiery. Although some basics are seasonal, this type of merchandise is often **nonseasonal,** as it sells all year long. At times, basics become so popular that they take on a "fashion" of their own. This happened in the 1980s with women's blazers and in the 1990s with Gap's "basic" look.

Fashion goods are thought of as something new, in demand, or popular—at any particular time. They are less stable, have a short life span, and therefore are more risky (financially) than basics. Generally, they are also **seasonal;** that is, they sell best during either the Spring or Fall season. As demand for fashion goods is not easily predictable, buying mistakes can be made and there can be more markdowns at the end of the season for fashion goods than for basics, which change less from season to season and can demand a more stable price. Fashion level is another characteristic of merchandise. **Mass fashion** appeals to the majority of consumers and is produced and distributed at moderate or opening prices at both mass retailers and department stores. Consumers who buy mass fashion are not fashion leaders but still want to be in fashion.

Fast fashion is a relatively new term used today in the retail industry referring to low-priced, fashionable items that don't last long in the stores. Mass fashion has generally been seen as knockoffs of well-known designer labels that "follow" rather than "lead." Recently we have seen such companies as Sweden-based H&M, London's TopShop, and Spain's Zara leading fashion with their own fashion shows held during fashion weeks and on their own. Also, the trend of mixing inexpensive fashion finds, vintage, and luxury brands is seen by some as true chic (Davidson, 2005). H&M has become known for featured designers such as Stella McCartney, Karl Lagerfeld, and Victor and Rolf with their "one-off" (one-of-a-kind) collections. Each collection has sold out instantly, with long lines waiting to get into the stores. Zara's successful business model involves changing stock every two to four weeks, rather than every season, and focusing on supply chain flexibility. Most apparel companies are producing where they find the cheapest labor (mostly China); however, fast fashion companies produce closer to home, since

Figure 4.2 Levi's jeans are classified as basic merchandise.

their short runs require more costly shipping. Zara can design and distribute a garment to market in just 15 days (Ferdows, Lewis, & Machuca, 2005). Short runs also add to the idea of exclusivity. See *Case 20, Buy It, Wear It, Chuck It: The Price of Fast Fashion,* for a different take on fast fashion.

High fashion is produced and priced for that small percentage of the population who want something new and different from mass fashion, with the added panache of exclusivity. High-fashion products are generally high priced because of these factors. The products of high-fashion designers sold at upper-end retail are often shown in a boutique style, where their merchandise is sold together in one space. Probably the best example of this type of merchandising is at Bergdorf Goodman in New York City, with an exclusive "boutiqued" floor plan. *Case 21, The Out of Fashion Inventory Problem* is an example of a change to this type of approach. There's a big leap between mass and high fashion, but some designers, such as Isaac Mizrahi, have straddled the line by creating both mass and high. Mizrahi's clothes are available both at Bergdorf Goodman and Target!

Figure 4.3 An example of high fashion, Giorgio Armani's Collezione is sold at boutiques and online.

Each retailer has to determine the proportion of fashion to basics in its merchandise mix that will meet its customer's needs. Gap is a retailer that sells mostly basics; sometimes, however, it offers fashion goods. Buying decisions related to stock and merchandise assortments often consider both basics and fashion groups together—not in isolation. (More on assortment planning may be found in Chapter 5.) Fashion items are often matched with basics in merchandise groupings that sell well together.

Merchandise Quality

The **quality** of merchandise is a major consideration in product selection and offerings by both retailers and manufacturers when determining merchandise positioning or the company's reputation, as well as the needs and wants of their market. Quality is often thought of as "degree of excellence." In apparel it is determined by many aspects, which are composed of many aesthetic and functional features. Aesthetics include appearance, fit, design, fabrication, construction, and

TABLE 4.1 Relationship of Styling and Price in Women's Wear

Market	Styling	Brand Example	Price Range
Designer collection	Unique, top-name designer fashion	Donna Karan	Designer (high-end)
Designer bridge	Designer fashion	DKNY	Bridge
Misses or petite	Adaptations of fashions	Liz Claiborne	Better to moderate
Contemporary	Trendy	BCBG, bebe	Better to moderate
Junior	Youthful, trendy	Forever 21	Moderate to budget (low-end)

details or decoration. Functional features include such attributes as durability and serviceability.

Consumers' perceptions of quality may be as important as the actual quality. It is difficult to judge some aspects (for example, durability) at the point of sale because some items must be "tested" before a true evaluation can take place; that is, many times apparel has to be worn and in some cases washed before it can be evaluated. Therefore, extrinsic characteristics are often used to judge quality. Extrinsic features include such factors as price, brand, reputation of the retailer or manufacturer, and country of origin.

Branded merchandise (discussed in the next section) is known for a certain expected quality. Private labels may be of comparable quality but are often not as well known. If expected or perceived quality is not achieved, reputations and customers can be lost.

Quality control is done at either the fabric manufacture, garment manufacture, or retail levels. Specifications of private-label merchandise are usually checked by the retailer against approved samples before being distributed to the stores. Some large retailers and manufacturers, such as JCPenney and Levi Strauss, perform extensive textile testing on products based on standards set by the American Association of Textile Chemists and Colorists (AATCC) and the American Society for Testing and Materials (ASTM). Normally, the manufacturer is responsible for checking the quality of materials before production—but not always. This is illustrated by *Case 22, The Fabric Problem,* in which fabric flaws were discovered after a garment was produced.

The relationship between quality and price, often thought of as **value**, is another important factor in merchandise selection. Off-price goods (discussed in Chapter 2) can offer many consumers good value because they are often brand-name goods that are being sold at lower prices. However, as these often are late-in-

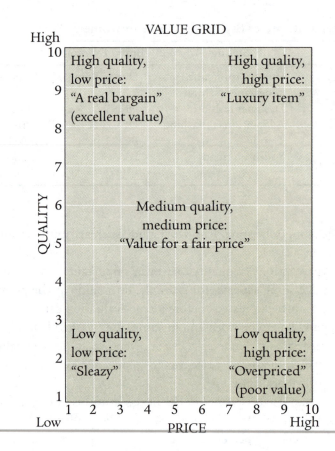

Figure 4.4 This figure, a "value grid," shows the relationship between quality and price.

the-season goods, they do not offer fashion timeliness and may not be of value to every consumer. Generally, however, a good value is defined as a high-quality product at a low price, which is seen as a "true bargain." On the other hand, an expensive but poor-quality product is seen as overpriced. Sometimes goods that carry a designer name can fall into this category. Figure 4.4 illustrates the relationship between value and price.

Cost per wear can also be used as a measure of value. An expensive item that is worn very often has a lower cost per wear and may be seen as a bargain or a good value, while an inexpensive item that is never worn has little value. This, of course, is evaluated after purchase, but consumers should try to keep this factor in mind when purchasing merchandise. Additionally, retailers selling "good value" should communicate all the quality features of the merchandise to their customers.

BRANDED AND LICENSED MERCHANDISE

A **brand** has been defined as "a known name associated with a specific product or group of products carrying with it an expectation of such perceived values as style and image, quality, price, fit, reliability, consistency, and confidence that you'll look good." A brand is produced and controlled by the manufacturer. Branded merchandise dominates most merchandise categories today, and in fashion apparel it is especially important in intimate apparel, hosiery, and footwear. A brand should set the product or company apart from its competition.

Consumers generally pay more for brands because they feel they are worth more than non-brands. Many consumers prefer branded merchandise because they make shopping easier; that is, the reputation of brands means they are a known entity, with an established fit and quality, and the manufacturer and retailer that sell these products stand behind them. As time and convenience are important factors in busy consumers' daily lives, brands become even more valuable. A popular brand has a loyal customer base, which is a very valuable commodity today that is worth protecting. See Figure 4.5 for information about consumer perceptions of brands.

Companies often register their brand names or logos as trademarks. Levi's has several trademarks, including the red tab stitched into the patch pocket seam, the arcuate stitching on the back pocket of its 501s, and the name Levi's. Some designs are copyrighted, but as most fashion is an interpretation and not original design, few companies register or enforce copyrights. Many, however, attempt to

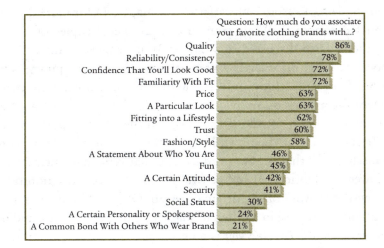

Question: How much do you associate your favorite clothing brands with...?

Quality	86%
Reliability/Consistency	78%
Confidence That You'll Look Good	72%
Familiarity With Fit	72%
Price	63%
A Particular Look	63%
Fitting into a Lifestyle	62%
Trust	60%
Fashion/Style	58%
A Statement About Who You Are	46%
Fun	45%
A Certain Attitude	42%
Security	41%
Social Status	30%
A Certain Personality or Spokesperson	24%
A Common Bond With Others Who Wear Brand	21%

Figure 4.5 This bar chart shows the relationship between brand merchandise and various consumer perceptions about the product.

Figure 4.6a and b Is this 2008 Forever 21 knockoff of YSL's 1965 Mondrian dress a counterfeit? Is it copyright infringement? Sometimes there is a fine line (resulting in lawsuits) between being inspired by another designer and illegally infringing on another's work. Mondrian began painting his most famous series in 1922. Yves Saint Laurent was inspired by Mondrian. Diane von Furstenberg was also inspired. Her version of the Mondrian dress sold at Bergdorf Goodman. Herve Leger and even Nike borrowed the Mondrian look. "Adventures in Copyrights: The Art of the Ripoff" on fashionista.com has an interesting look at many "inspired by others" designs.

protect their trademarks from counterfeits (see Chapter 11 for more discussion on this and related concepts). While counterfeits are illegal copies of trademarked goods, knockoffs (also discussed in Chapter 3) are copies or interpretations of popular styles at lower-price levels. Often referred to as "style piracy," knockoffs are a way of life in the fashion industry. Many manufacturers are referred to as *knockoff companies,* as they do no real designing on their own. Instead, they shop the market, find the most sought-after styles, and then "reinterpret" them or simply copy the style and put their own label on the merchandise. Some companies knock themselves off—that is, they produce a similar version of their own popular item in a lower-cost fabrication and generally lower-cost construction techniques, but they keep the "flavor" of the original design. Often referred to as a *secondary line,* these products are sold in a different market, at different stores, and to different consumers. *Case 23, The Knockoff* is an example of a buyer who finds a manufacturer to knock off a popular style of shirt, which then threatens her store's relationship with the vendor who produced the original design.

Figure 4.7 Manufacturers seek to become licensees due to the high recognition of the trademark. Licensees generally pay a percentage of the profits to the licensor.

Licensed goods, which carry the name of a famous person, character, or company, are an important part of the fashion industry. In this arrangement, a company (the **licensor**) allows a marketer or manufacturer (the **licensee**) to produce and sell a product with its registered trademark or logo (for example, Mickey Mouse nightshirts). Manufacturers seek to become licensees because of the high recognition of the trademarks. While designers make little or no profit on their

Figure 4.8 The Olsen twins, celebrity designers, promote their "Elizabeth James" apparel line.

couture collections, large profits frequently are made on licensed secondary lines, accessories, and fragrances. Advertising of the licensed product reinforces the sale of the principal product and vice versa. Corporate licensing increases brand awareness and allows for brand extension into other product categories. For example, in the mid-1990s Tommy Hilfiger, well known for men's wear, quickly broke into the women's industry by licensing his name out. Licensing involves many areas today including cartoon characters, sports figures, celebrities, designers, TV programs, music, and so forth. The success of licensed designer products depends on the continued quality of the product and often the continued success of the designer's collections. See *Case 39, Licensing Pitfalls,* in Chapter 6. Just because a designer's or celebrity's name appears on a product does not mean that she or he had anything to do with the design. Some designers, however, participate in the design and development of their licensed products, while others have little (if any) input. More and more fashion brands today carry the name of celebrities. It seems every popular singer has a fragrance named after him or her. Jennifer Lopez has a line of ready-to-wear, swimwear, accessories, footwear, among other categories (www.shopjlo.com); Sean "Diddy" Combs has sportswear, tailored, and children's lines (www.seanjohn.com); Beyoncé Knowles co-owns the House of Dereon with clothing and accessory lines. Madonna had a special line produced for H&M, Mary-Kate and Ashley Olsen have clothing and fragrance lines, Sarah Jessica Parker has a clothing line (inexpensive, which may seem quite out of character), and the list goes on. These lines are licensed to manufacturers with expertise in design and production.

TABLE 4.2 Top 20 Brands

1. Hanes	8. Old Navy	15. Nine West
2. Nike	9. Reebok	16. Tommy Hilfiger
3. Victorias Secret	10. Liz Claiborne	17. New Balance
4. Fruit of the Loom	11. Gap	18. Playtex
5. Levi Strauss	12. Ralph Lauren	19. DKNY
6. Timex	13. Calvin Klein	20. Jockey
7. LEggs	14. Adidas	

Source: Pogoda, D. M. (2008, July). Money talks, The WWD100, *Women's Wear Daily Special Report*.

With all the competition today with private and designer labels, manufacturers of existing brands are finding they must continue to strive for their brands to thrive. Popular one season, a brand can fade away the next. According to large denim makers in the United States, the following strategies are important to maintain brands: (1) advertise; (2) develop a unique relationship with the stores; (3) have up-to-date systems response; (4) bring value to the market; (5) license; (6) go international; (7) once it's built, protect it (Ozzard, 1995). Table 4.2 lists the top 20 brands in a *Women's Wear Daily* study of 2,000 consumers between the ages of 13 and 64 (Pogoda, 2008).

The list in Table 4.2 is interesting, as it shows a lack of distinction between national brands (Levi Strauss) and designer labels (Calvin Klein), and store brands (Gap). It appears that—at least in the minds of consumers—a brand is a brand is a brand, regardless of ownership or traditional definitions.

Lifestyle brands are an important part of the fashion industry. Companies produce complementary products that fit into every part of a consumer's life. With one company's products, consumers can dress, furnish their homes, even paint their walls, bathe with their products, wear their scents, drink their water, and even drive their stylish cars as they subscribe to a certain lifestyle. Ralph Lauren probably does this the best and was one of the first designers to market a lifestyle, from apparel to home. Visit Rhinelander Mansion, his flagship on Madison Avenue in New York City, to see how he does it; his smaller boutiques across the country also display his lifestyle products. Manufacturers and retailers such as Anthropologie, Urban Outfitters, Nautica, Nike, and Patagonia, to name a few, offer lifestyle products creating a life to which their consumer can relate or aspire.

PRIVATE-LABEL MERCHANDISING

The distinction between brands and private labels is becoming fuzzy, if not disappearing altogether. What is important is the consumer's perception of a brand, which now includes store and private labels, as discussed in the previous section. A *Women's Wear Daily* study indicated consumers refer to labels as "brand" or "not a brand." Sometimes there is little or no difference in these products, as manufacturers or contractors that produce brands also produce private labels for retailers at the same time; they just put different labels on the merchandise. Generally, consumers are not aware of this situation, and they judge the product exclusively by the label—thus illustrating the importance of image and reputation.

Store brands and **private labels** are produced and named by the retailer that sells them. Store brands literally carry the name of the store. Private labels may carry names other than the store's name, for example, Charter Club and INC, which are Macy's private labels. Some names refer to such real people as Target's Michael Graves and Isaac Mizrahi lines, while others are made to sound like designers, for example, JCPenney's Stafford.

Private and store brands have advantages for retailers. They are generally knockoffs and therefore more profitable than national brands, as there is no advertising to add to costs and no middlemen involved because the retailer manufactures them. As national brands saturate the market, stores begin to look alike; therefore, a private/store label is one way a retailer can differentiate itself from its competition. While national brands are sold to many stores, private labels are found only in one store—the store that created them—and they lend a sense of identity to the retailer. Despite the fact that branded merchandise dominates most categories, private labels' share of the market is increasing faster than traditional brands. Additionally, private/store labels may constitute all or part of a retailer's offerings. For example, both the Gap and The Limited's chains sell 100 percent private-label merchandise. Retailers change the proportion of private versus branded merchandise over time.

Department stores often have a percentage of private-label merchandise, with most of their goods being branded. Retailers need to find the right balance for themselves between branded and non-branded merchandise. There is a danger of putting too much stock into brands and/or private labels, as a buyer may not be able to capitalize on new trends or "hot" resources in the market. *Case 24, To Brand or Not to Brand,* which describes a men's department that may be over-branded, is an example of a store's relying too heavily on branded merchandise.

Retailers with private labels are becoming manufacturers as the merchandise is developed for the store by its product development department. Manufacturing, however, is not their expertise and sometimes private-label retailers can find themselves with new challenges. One is marketing a retailer's own brand. Such stores as Gap, Talbot's, Crate & Barrel, Nike Town, Abercrombie & Fitch, Anthropologie, The Limited, Ann Taylor, and Tiffany's have been very successful when using their own names as their brands. Department stores, however, do not always have the same success creating their own brands, with some exceptions. Customers purchasing from Tiffany's, for example, have a product with a name that has a certain reputation. This doesn't necessarily hold true for department stores unless that store has a clearly perceived image of quality. Two notable examples of department stores that have successfully marketed their own store brands are Bloomingdale's (Bloomingdale's Own) and Neiman Marcus.

SUMMARY

The characteristics of merchandise help to define its image and reputation. Consumers look for certain levels of fashion, quality, and price to meet their needs. Nationally branded merchandise is thought of as having high quality with a known reputation. Private or store labels offer more value to consumers and generally are profitable for retailers who are responsible for their manufacture. Some store labels have become as well known as nationally advertised brands and, consequently, the distinction to the consumer between national and private brands is less distinct. As retailers develop their own labels, the distinction between manufacturer and retailer also is becoming less defined.

KEY TERMS

basics	hard goods
better goods	high fashion
brand	impulse goods
bridge lines	licensed goods
budget goods	licensee
convenience goods	licensor
designer collections	lifestyle brand
fashion goods	mass fashion
fast fashion	moderate goods

nonseasonal goods

opening price point

private label

quality

quality control

seasonal goods

secondary line

shopping goods

soft goods

specialty goods

staples

store brand

value

BIBLIOGRAPHY

www.brandchannel.com (for current articles on lifestyle brands, books on brands, and debates)

Clark, E., & Ellis, K. (2007, June 29). Power to set prices: Supreme Court backs brands over retailers. *Women's Wear Daily,* pp. 1, 14.

The consumer says they are all brands. (1995, November). *Women's Wear Daily, Infotracs* Supplement, pp. 10–15.

Davidson, J. (2005, February 13). *Chic thrills.* http://www.living.scotsman.com.

Ferdows, K., Lewis, M. A., & Machuca, J. A. D. (2005, February 21). Zara's secret for fast fashion. *Harvard Business School Working Knowledge for Business Leaders.* http://hbswk.hbs.edu

Foroohar, R. (2005, October 17). Fabulous fashion. http://www.msnbc.msn.com

Frings, G. (2008). *Fashion from concept to consumer.* Upper Saddle River, NJ: Prentice Hall.

Interbrand. (2008). *Brands that have the power to change the retail world: Top performing European retail brands.* Available from www.brandchannel.com/papers

Jansen, M. (2008, summer). Brand fashioning: What brand managers can learn from fashion designers. Available at www.brandchannel.com/papers

Ozzard, J. (1995, October). How to build a brand. *Women's Wear Daily, Denim Network Supplement,* pp. 10–11.

Pogoda, D. M. (2008, July). Money talks. *The WWD100, Women's Wear Daily Special Report.*

Stamper, A., & Sharp, S. H. (1991). *Evaluating apparel quality* (2nd ed.). New York: Fairchild Books.

Stone, E. (2004). *The dynamics of fashion.* New York: Fairchild Books.

Wolf, M. G. (2006). *Fashion.* South Holland, IL: The Goodhear-Wilcox Co.

Case 19

"WITH IT" OR WITHOUT

Nancy J. Rabolt, San Francisco State University
Judy K. Miler, Florida State University

One of the hottest manufacturing houses in the New York market is "With It," which makes junior-size apparel that is very "in." Its styling is casual, young, and a symbol of being "with it" for high school and college students alike. The company motto being sung by fans is, "If you are not *With It,* you are out."

The company is owned by two relatively young men who had once been top ready-to-wear buyers for Macy's—John Sung and Bill Lipe. It is apparent that they know the business because they anticipate the latest trends and "hot" styles, and their use of marketing and positioning the business is very savvy. They have brought "With It" to a dominant name-brand recognition level in an extremely short period of time. Part of their business philosophy is to sell only to regular price stores, which they rigidly enforce. Discounters are not considered as accounts, not even as a way of dumping end-of-season merchandise. When "With It" was conceived, an underlying principle was that their merchandise would never be discounted. This strategy enables them to maintain a certain level of status in the

minds of their target consumer, which in turn keeps the retail price up and generates a high level of profit for the regular-priced retailer. Irregulars and closeouts (odds and ends and a mix of remaining broken lines), however, are disposed of at the plant level, but the labels are always cut or removed, and these garments are not sold to any regular-price customers.

The level of success has been ongoing. From the day John and Bill started the business five short years ago, some retailers, impressed with the acumen and record of the maker, opened "With It" shops within their stores, a strategy suggested by John and Bill. "With It" works closely with the retailers to set up these shops.

Main Street, California's largest department store chain, is one of the biggest users of "With It." They virtually ton out the goods, never seeming to have enough merchandise. The junior sportswear buyer, Carol Baker, has had a great working partnership with John and Bill for three years.

One store policy concerning resource criterion is that Main Street will never share a resource with a discount store within its trading area, so the exclusive sales policy followed by "With It" fits right in with Main Street philosophy. Two weeks ago, however, a comparison shopper for Main Street reported that The Mart, a 26-store discount chain, was carrying the "With It" jeans line. The labels, although cut, had not been removed and were easily identifiable as "With It" merchandise. A customer complaint involving a pair of jeans priced at $20 less at The Mart was the stimulus for the investigation.

Carol Baker, the buyer, called "With It" collect to find out why The Mart has the line. She got John on the phone. Excitedly she explained, "We do a great job. I can't understand how you can ship to a discounter and hurt us. It doesn't make sense, particularly because you're familiar with our store policy and you've told me it's your policy, too. It doesn't matter that you are a very profitable line for our stores, management looks at the long-term meaning to our customers. They'll refuse to allow me to carry your goods any longer."

John explained, "Don't get excited, Carol. We don't ship The Mart any part of our regular line. Any merchandise they have is irregular or last season's goods. The labels are removed or cut to show that they're not current or regulars. One more point, we have a big successful operation; but, like all manufacturers, we always own goods that must be sold, which are closeouts or are less-than-perfect. They are job lots, the kind most of our buyers can't use. This merchandise represents a lot of stock that must be liquidated and if we can sell it—we do. We don't want to hurt loyal customers and it represents too much money to sell for waste so we will sell to retailers who do not buy our regular line of merchandise."

"What you don't realize," John continued, "is that The Mart has given us an open order. Anytime we have $10,000 worth of goods, we ship what we want without notice. The price is cheap, but it gives us a pipeline to dispose of unwanted goods. Frankly, this arrangement is as important as any we have that sells at regular retail levels. I'm sure you understand that business is business. We want to keep our great working relationship with you and we want it to remain profitable for both of us, but this is one situation that we can't change. We will, however, make sure all labels are completely removed in the future, rather than just cut, if that will help."

"John," Carol replied, "what you say, I guess, makes sense. Our policy, though, is not to stock goods from manufacturers represented in discount stores, with or without labels, different styles, closeouts, or whatever. The problem is bigger than my department; it's one that I must take to a higher level. I'll be back in touch with you after my boss returns from Europe in a week. I don't want to go to the general merchandise manager, as he is apt to be tough and stick to the book. I just hope that he doesn't see the Comparison Office report and that no more complaints come in before my boss returns."

Carol is concerned and worried because she does not want to lose "With It"—one of her major vendors. The records show that 15 percent of her department volume is "With It" merchandise, and they are a key resource that she does not feel can be replaced. Even worse, the store has built up a trade for the label, and competition would love for her to give up the line so they could take her "With It" business. However, she understands that rules are rules and policy must be followed. But sometimes, rules are bent to fit circumstances. Hopefully, this situation fits into the latter. Anxiously, Carol starts to prepare a plan to present to her boss, who will return from Europe tomorrow.

Major Question

What strategy should Carol suggest to her boss that would best help her keep the "With It" line?

Study Questions

1. Does lower price always mean lower quality? Or lower fashion level?
2. How can one store retail the same product for $20 less than another and still be profitable?
3. If a retailer loses an important brand at a vital price level, how can a replacement be found?

Case 20

BUY IT, WEAR IT, CHUCK IT: THE PRICE OF FAST FASHION[1]

Martin Hickman, The Independent, *December 1, 2006*

Growing demand for cheap clothes is putting an increasing social and environmental strain on the world, a report has said. It questions the very sustainability of the "fast

[1]The text printed here represents an excerpted portion of a longer article.

fashion" that is growing in popularity among . . . shoppers.

Chains selling bargain outfits have boomed . . . in the past five years, with many fashion followers throwing away garments after one season. An academic analysis of the global textiles business indicates that such intense consumerism comes at a heavy cost to factory workers and the environment from intensive use of chemicals and greenhouse gases.

. . .

Shoppers are advised to lessen their environmental footprint by buying organic cotton and fewer but better garments, washing them at lower temperatures and drying them naturally.

Laundering is crucial because it can use more energy than the entire production process, with tumble driers identified as the most wasteful.

The throwaway culture is also a problem. Although the public recycles newspapers and bottles, only one eighth of clothes are recycled through charity shops . . . 70 percent goes straight to landfill or incineration.

Study Questions*

1. What is the relative environmental impact of fast fashion?
2. What could retailers do to lessen the negative impact of fast fashion?
3. What could consumers do to lessen the negative impact of fast fashion?

*Do not use the alternative solutions format for this case.

4. What, if anything, are you actually willing to do to lessen the negative impact of fast fashion?

5. From an ethical perspective, is it better for retailers to produce higher quality products that will have a longer life span and less negative impact on the environment or cheaper products more accessible to the masses?

Case 21

THE OUT OF FASHION INVENTORY PROBLEM[1]

Maryanne Smith Bohlinger, Prof. Emeritus, Community College of Philadelphia

Lloyd & Burns, located in a large New England city, has always catered to a well-to-do, conservative clientele. This large women's specialty store does an annual volume of approximately $35 million and prides itself on being a high-quality, personal-service type of retail establishment.

As a conservative business, however, L&B never really enjoyed the reputation of real fashion leadership. The management determined that a number of the store's competitors were using the "boutique approach" in merchandising to add a high-

[1]From *Merchandise Buying* (5th ed.). New York: Fairchild Books. Copyright © 2001.

fashion image to their stores. Management decided that Lloyd & Burns would try its hand at this new merchandising approach in an effort to gain higher fashion recognition.

Shortly thereafter, the "Royal Garb Boutique" was opened, with a buyer responsible for purchasing exclusive, high-fashion types of merchandise. The buyer was provided with an assistant, two full-time salespeople, part-time sales help, and stock personnel.

The "Royal Garb Boutique" was a success. Store volume increased as a result of the addition of the boutique, and L&B was gaining an image as a high-fashion store. After three years the buyer was rewarded with a promotion and took over the buying responsibilities of a much larger department: the women's better coat department.

When Gwen Franklin, an assistant buyer in fashion costume jewelry, heard that a buyer's position was available, and in the Royal Garb Boutique at that, she immediately applied for the position. After several interviews, she was informed that she was to be the new buyer for the boutique. However, Gwen was soon to discover that along with a successful department she was also about to inherit serious inventory problems.

For various reasons, Gwen's predecessor had allowed a large amount of old merchandise to accumulate in the stockroom. The merchandise consisted of expensive blouses, handbags, sweaters, and other accessory items. When Gwen checked the price tickets for the seasonal code, she was amazed to learn that some of the merchandise was more than two years old. She immediately realized that she must take a physical count of all merchandise on hand to determine the condition of the merchandise assortment. She soon discovered that over 25 percent of her dollar stock was tied up in old or slow-moving merchandise. For some reason, her predecessor had allowed old merchandise to accumulate in stock while new items were being sold.

The Christmas season was rapidly approaching. Gwen knew that almost half her sales volume would occur between November and January. However, she was overloaded with old and out-of-style goods, a limited open-to-buy, expensive markdowns, and limited storage and selling space. She was in trouble inventorywise, budgetwise, and seasonwise. The department's fashion image was in jeopardy.

Major Question

What plan of activities could Gwen follow to help her solve her inventory problems?

Study Questions

1. How could she avoid the recurrence of these problems in the future?

2. What other kinds of inventory problems can occur?

Case 22

THE FABRIC PROBLEM

Diane Cantua, U.S. Customs and Border Protection
Nancy J. Rabolt, San Francisco State University

Robert Rossi is a fabric sales representative carrying a line of wool fabrics of various types. He has set up an account with Jordan Luce, a new customer, who is new in the business. Jordan has always wanted to produce some of her own designs, and her husband—a wealthy doctor—is backing her venture. She will sell her designs in a small boutique that is owned by a friend. She was on her way toward this goal when she ordered six colors of wool jersey from Robert.

Because Jordan is a new customer, Robert very carefully explained the trade practices of the fabric business. On her request, he even took samples of fabric to her house for Jordan to choose. During this time, he showed her the Worth Street Rules, which itemize textile trade practices. The American Textile Manufacturers Institute (ATMI) revised these rules in 1986 (still in effect today). They include provisions for buyers' rights, sellers' rights, quality, and grading fabrics. Some of the provisions are outlined in Table 4.3. Robert did not give Jordan a contract outlining these conditions because they are normal business practice and are understood within the industry. Essentially, Robert indicated to Jordan that

TABLE 4.3 Summary of Revised Worth Street Rules

Buyers' Rights

If the buyer is going to reject or cancel a fabric order, the seller must be notified:
- Within ten days after the defect is known.
- Within three months after passing title.
- Prior to cutting.

Sellers' Rights

- If fabric has been invoiced but not shipped and the buyer is five days late in payment on previously shipped fabric (this could be 30, 60, or 90 days after delivery), the seller has the right not to deliver the fabric.
- Delivery by the mill within 15 days of a specified delivery date is acceptable.
- "If you cut it, you own it" rule has been somewhat modified. New rules allow a converter to dye or print a fabric and still make a claim for defects, but they deny an apparel manufacturer that right if the fabric is cut. It is assumed that a cutter or the contractor will be able to see defects in a fabric as it is laid up.

even though the fabric may be given a cursory glance as a quick inspection, the buyer or cutter should inspect the goods in sufficient light before cutting. It was explained that if there was a problem, for example, wrong color, color blotching, color streaking, yarn defects, or any other defect, Jordan should call immediately and a replacement bolt would be sent. After Robert reiterated this to Jordan, she carefully selected the fabrics that she wished to order. This order consisted of two bolts each of Plum Red, Chocolate Brown, Emerald Green, Sapphire Blue, Mustard Yellow, and True Black. Later that week, 12 bolts of wool fabric were shipped with COD terms.

Jordan took the fabric to her cutter and sewer, but neither of them inspected the goods. Long-sleeve dresses were constructed from the six colors of wool fabric. When the dresses were complete, Jordan took them to the store. She was very proud and happy. As the dresses were being displayed in the store, however, Jordan noticed color streaks in the four chocolate-brown dresses. She became very upset, removed the dresses from the floor, and called Robert immediately, demanding that she be reimbursed for the fabric and all labor costs involved in constructing the brown dresses. All the other dresses were fine, and they continued to be displayed in the boutique.

Robert reminded Jordan of their conversation and explained again that after the fabric was cut, the buyer owned it. It also was explained to her that reimbursement for labor charges was not industry practice and he was not prepared at all to do that. She was not satisfied with these answers. Two days later, Jordan's husband telephoned Robert and threatened to sue him and the fabric company. He is a powerful man in the community and is used to always getting his own way. He claimed that Robert did not give Jordan a contract that outlined the conditions of sale. Before hanging up the phone, he threatened, "If there are any legal loopholes my lawyers will find them!"

Major Question

What should Robert do?

Study Questions

1. What else could Robert have done to ensure that Jordan understood and abided by standard industry policy?

2. How is the fabric business different from the apparel business in regard to returns?

Case 23

THE KNOCKOFF

Nancy J. Rabolt, San Francisco, State University
Judy K. Miler, Florida State University

Gold & Silver, Inc., a women's fine jewelry and casual clothing store, is a unique type of retailer with an unusual but highly successful merchandise mix. Currently it has the best small independent retail financial record in the United States. Profits on sales and returns on capital investments outstrip any comparable retail organization in the country. This enviable record is the result of careful planning, risk taking, and imaginative controls by management and staff.

Merchandise policies and procedures are one type of control management abides by. One aspect requires management to keep detailed records on merchandise to the lowest tracking level possible, for example, color and size. Another of the merchandising policies that works is to establish in-depth stock of the most wanted items, promote on a consistent basis, and extend the selling period as long as possible.

Jeanette Jildor is the women's shirt buyer. She has been with Gold & Silver for almost six years and has done quite well with her department. As any good, aggressive buyer would, she is looking for her chance to shine through finding the "hot" new shirt of the year. Armed with well-thought-out and approved plans, Jeanette went to market in search of her "find." She visited several resources before she discovered her "star" shirt. There was no doubt in Jeanette's mind that this long-sleeve, solid shirt with the crested pocket was just the new look she'd been searching for to make her year! It was also gratifying that the manufacturer was already a highly respected supplier and a key resource to Gold & Silver.

What made it even more interesting, however, was the fact that the shirt was not being pushed by the sales rep. Jeanette saw the sales potential herself by relating the crested pocket on the shirt with the current popularity of crested blazers. She figured that this look was a natural winner.

Working with the manufacturer to her advantage, Jeanette was able to get assurances from the vendor on the quality of the fabric and workmanship, the colorfastness of the crest emblem, reorder capability, and delivery guarantees. As added insurance to these favorable factors, and as a safeguard to her strong position on the shirt, Jeanette also secured a promise from the resource that no similar merchandise would be shipped in quantities to support a promotion within her trading area for two months. This promise was not hard for the resource to make, because most buyers were just sampling the shirt or did not buy the style at all. The manufacturer was excited that someone found the shirt more exciting than even they had originally thought it to be. Consequently, both the vendor and Jeanette were very pleased with the sale and the commitment Jeanette was going to take with the shirt.

She advertised—and was on target—the style took off. Week after week there was an ad that invited Internet and telephone orders; the latter was supported by a 24-hour phone ordering service. She "milked" the item through every means possible. The sales during the season were just short of phenomenal: 3,000 a week, with no abatement. It just kept rolling along, to the delight of Jeanette, her merchandise manager, upper management, and the manufacturer.

The resource was most cooperative in supplying even more merchandise than Jeanette had originally anticipated and planned. They put aside production orders for other styles to help Jeanette fill her promotional needs. Sales were soaring, with

seemingly no end in sight. After three months of record-breaking sales, however, Jeanette decided that the "party" would probably end in a couple of weeks. She couldn't imagine the life of the shirt being much longer, as she had never experienced such success in her life as a buyer.

Deciding to act on her hunch, Jeanette visited the manufacturer, talked to the decision makers, and advised, "You've made my season, which will be over soon. However, have you considered the volume potential if we reduce the retail price from $40 to $19.99, a level that will open up a new customer group, develop individual multiple sales, and, above all, extend the selling season? I think that we need to plan on promoting the shirt to conclude the season and end with a bang."

The resource balked. "You've had your party; now it's our turn. We're going to make it a basic shirt and get the distribution we missed on the first selling round. You showed us the way. Now we want to capitalize on an item that can have a successful run for several years."

"Be realistic," Jeanette responded. "Sure, your name is nationally known, but don't you know that the style is going to be knocked off at lower prices? If you don't take action, others will."

The manufacturer again disagreed, replying, "Apparently you're not aware that one of the largest men's brand houses features a shirt that has been at one price for 20 years, despite knockoffs."

The conversation ended in a stalemate, with no conclusions or agreements drawn.

Knowing that she wanted to do what she had planned, a day or two later Jeanette took the shirt to another resource that she used regularly. Jeanette explained her success with the shirt and how she now wanted to position it promotionally in her store to conclude the season. The manufacturer was interested and listened intently. The sales manager called the production manager in to get her input. After close inspection, the production manager said, "We can make this style at a cost of $9.75, or less, depending on what you want to change about the shirt." Jeanette did not want to change anything about the styling, because the crested pocket really was what made the shirt.

Jeanette took a position. She placed a verbal order on the spot for promotional depth at $9.75 in a narrow range of colors suitable for the current time of year. She also indicated that she would send a confirming written order countersigned by her merchandise manager tomorrow. Jeanette said her goodbyes and happily left the resource feeling good about her new find.

Three weeks later she advertised the shirt at $19.99. The stock consisted of the original shirt marked down to $19.99 and the knockoff received five days previously. Again, she was right in her prediction for success. The momentum continued at peak levels for several weeks. Her real problems centered around forecasting just how long this could continue and what quantity should be committed for reorders.

The national brand house from which Jeanette originally purchased the crested shirt watched events at Gold & Silver. They re-sented the store's course of action and made their feelings known in the market and to other retailers. A letter was received by Jeanette's divisional merchandise manager, which stated, "We have decided to cancel any future business arrangements with you and are taking steps to sell to additional stores in your area, to those retailers from whom we previously declined to sell, as negotiated with you." Jeanette's merchandise manager is upset and disturbed by the letter, because a major sportswear promotion was in the works for the next season, and this resource was to be a major player in that promotion. He wants them back—and soon.

Major Question

If you were Jeanette, what would you do in regard to the resource's choice to terminate business with Gold & Silver? How would you go about luring them back to your store?

Study Questions

1. How often do you think brands are copied or knocked off? Is that illegal?

2. What is the difference between a counterfeit and a knockoff?

3. At what level of fashion is a popular style knocked off? Who buys the original and who buys the knockoff?

4. Do you think Jeanette was right in knocking off a style from one of her major branded manufacturers, then selling it, along with the manufacturer's style at a reduced retail price?

Visit high-end and lower-end stores. Note similar styles that appear to be knockoffs, and record price and other differences. Do any appear to be counterfeits?

Case 24

TO BRAND OR NOT TO BRAND

Nancy J. Rabolt, San Francisco State University
Judy K. Miler, Florida State University

Jones Department Store is one of the few remaining privately owned department stores left in the still thriving downtown area of Philadelphia. The store has been passed down from generation to generation of Jones family entrepreneurs for over 125 years and still remains in the same location on which it was originally built. While tradition has been discarded by many long-term retailers, Jones Department Store has kept their merchant family traditions alive and it has served them well, as generations of Philadelphians have continuously made Jones their preferred place to shop, particularly since the leading department store in Philadelphia was bought out and renamed by a large conglomerate. Locals still make it a day to come downtown to shop and lunch at Jones.

Bruce Gregory is the recently hired buyer of men's furnishings on the main floor of Jones Department Store. Store sales volume is over $50 million a year. The men's furnishings department, as is the case in many major stores, is a well-developed, well-trafficked section that alone brings in approximately $1 million a year. A major sales contributor, furnishings is an important department.

Bruce has been studying the operation with extreme care—not only because he is new but also because he has been advised by his divisional merchandise manager that he is going to be called upon soon to make several important merchandising decisions. The owners hired Bruce partially because they knew that some improvements need to be made in furnishings and he comes with experience in that area. Bruce had been a men's furnishings buyer in a major New York City store prior to coming on board with Jones, and he is up-to-date on market trends and developments.

One of the aspects that surprised Bruce is the dominance of brand names in his inventory. Practically all of the merchandise stocked is from nationally known manufacturers. When this fact came to his attention, he spoke to several of the salespeople about it. Their remarks indicated that the store's policy favored heavy concentration on labels and that most of the brands had been carried for many years. He also learned that the customers seemed to prefer major brand names, as indicated by a continuous department sales growth. However, he also learned that, on many occasions, Jones Department Store had been beaten out by other stores because new styling that was available from small, private-label resources was not available from the larger, branded resources that concentrate on traditional, classic looks. He recognized that over-branding can be prohibitive—shutting the door to new creativity. He studied the classifications and could readily see that at least six items that deserved to be included in stock were absent: pocket squares, cuff links, sunglasses, formalwear accessories, leather nail grooming kits, and Jones signature merchandise for those loyal Jones customers.

He knew that he had to take a stand in regard to introducing private-label merchandise. He realized that the department produces well but is not realizing its full sales potential. Another disturbing element is that the store has shut itself off from the benefits of newness in the market. As a buyer, he concluded that if things remained as is, he would have a narrow selection of merchandise offerings from relatively few resources. His market associations would be of no real value, and, from a selfish point of view, he would lose all his meaningful contacts that he worked hard over the years to develop. "Besides," he wondered, "how long will it be before customers recognize that Jones is standing still in a new, exciting market and then shop elsewhere?"

Now that he has analyzed the department's situation, Bruce is quite concerned and feels some changes should be made in regard to merchandise assortment and private labeling. The aphorism "a new broom sweeps clean" is very much on his mind. He knows that he must take special care when confronting his boss because logically his superior would conjecture:

- You are new and do not understand the operation, and our policy favors carrying name-brand merchandise.
- Which resources would you discard?
- Our customers depend upon specific brands; to a large degree they mean customer patronage.

Bruce is well aware that he cannot make a presentation in regard to his recommendations without data that prove his thesis, "It is possible to be over-branded."

Major Question

What steps would you recommend to Bruce? How would you present your findings to management?

Study Questions

1. What are the advantages and disadvantages of using national branded sources?

2. What control in merchandise selection does a buyer have when buying from national brands? Who makes the decision to carry a national brand?

3. How does the type of merchandise vary the importance of branded versus unbranded or private label merchandise?

Exercise

Compare the level of fashion, quality, price, and degree of advertising of several successful national brands with the hottest new looks of today.

CHAPTER DISCUSSION QUESTIONS

1. How do price and fashion level relate to the quality and value of a product?

2. How do retailers determine their merchandise mix based on these characteristics?

3. Which is "safer"—fashion or basics? Which is more profitable? How does a retailer determine the mix of fashion and basic goods? Use case examples to support your argument.

4. What are the advantages and disadvantages of carrying national and private brands?

5. List your favorite brands and then identify them as national, store, or private label. Why are these your favorite brands? What makes them distinct from other merchandise on the market?

6. When is it appropriate to knock off a popular style? What is the relationship between national brands, private labels, and knockoffs?

Merchandise Planning, Buying, Control, and Profitability

CHAPTER OBJECTIVES

- Highlight the importance of merchandise planning and forecasting.
- Distinguish between dollar, unit, and assortment planning and consider their importance in merchandise management.
- Stress the critical role of standards and controls in successful retail management.
- Relate planning, pricing, productivity, and profit to buying.
- Describe the major technological systems that aid retail and apparel merchandising.

*C*areful planning and control, using the most accurate information available, guides a re-tailer to profit. Any plan, however, should always be regarded as a flexible and adaptable guide that is not written in stone and that allows for all the revisions that constantly occur in the retail business. The merchandising division is responsible for the buying and/or production of the goods that a retailer sells. This division is also responsible for the planning, pricing, and ultimate profitability of the retailer through the sales generated. Dollar and unit planning and controls are the major means of merchandise management that lead to the profit goal. Today, through technology, more detailed and accurate planning and control can be accomplished, which is faster than ever before because of the information that is available literally at our fingertips. The better the planning and controls, the more the retailer and manufacturer will achieve the goals that have been set. Monitoring, and, in many cases, adjusting plans (up or down) is necessary because retailing is dynamic. Even the most experienced buyers or planners cannot always accurately predict, for example, how many customers purchase, how much they will purchase, or just what will be purchased.

MERCHANDISING AND PROFIT

Technology can be applied to all levels of retailing and manufacturing to manage merchandise and ultimately lead to profit. Sophisticated software utilized by most businesses today plan, purchase, and monitor sales and stock; this results in increased efficiency and improved quality of decision-making. The retailer has joined in partnership with the manufacturer, who in turn has joined with suppliers, in an effort to make service the number one priority.

Merchandising is one of two necessary retailing functions, without which the business could not exist. **Merchandising** is the buying and selling of goods and/or services for the purpose of making a profit. The first and foremost aspect of merchandising is satisfying the customer's wants and needs. Doing so, however, requires preparation and planning. Additionally, the type of retail organization plays an integral part in achieving the set goals. Controls also play a major role in helping to ensure the profitability the retailer is looking to achieve, by helping to monitor the business and keep it on track. Prior to establishing controls, however, the merchandise that the customer needs and wants must be bought.

Buying

One of the major functions of the merchandising division of a retail organization is **buying.** It is the purchasing of goods and/or services for the retailer to sell to the ultimate consumer. This function can be separated out as a division, as is most often the case in large organizations, or it may be combined with the operations function, as it often is in smaller companies. The individual given formal authority to undertake the purchasing for a retailer is the **buyer.**

Most experts agree that buying is both an art and a science. As an art, aesthetic and visual principles are considered. As a science, the mathematics of budgeting are primary in forecasting (or predicting) the needs and wants of the retailer's customers, by knowing just who your customer is. Some of the skills can be taught, others are an inherent part of the buyer and who that person is as an individual—including the knowledge and experience an individual brings to a buying position.

Buying, of course, is also undertaken at the manufacturing level. In that context, however, it is usually referred to as **purchasing** and refers to obtaining the materials to make the end product. The individual given buying authority at the manufacturing level is either given the title buyer, **product manager, purchasing agent, merchandiser,** or **sourcing agent.** Many of the techniques and preparation for purchasing (including the information that is gathered and analyzed) are often the same or very similar from either a retailing or manufacturing perspective. Many large retailers and manufacturers have designers and buyers who work together on the creation and manufacturing of merchandise. A technical design associate works closely with a buyer to create just the right looks for the retailer in *Case 25, The Confrontation*; however, disagreement between the two causes some difficulties to occur. Also, because of the complexity of the apparel and retail environments today, often the retailer and manufacturer are one and the same, and buying is undertaken at both levels. In some cases, buying from vendors, as well as manufacturing, is done by the same individual. Additionally, the buyer is sometimes the designer and/or product manager for private-label merchandise. A good example of a retailer that is also a manufacturer is The Limited. To muddy the waters a little more, The Limited calls their buyers "merchants."

There are plenty of benefits to a buying career, such as travel and opportunities to meet and work with a variety of people; however, the buyer's job has changed somewhat from years gone by. The world has become smaller, as we live in a global marketplace today where there are more resources from which to select merchandise, and change occurs more rapidly, so the very nature of buying has altered. A buyer must act and react faster, and there is more information to use in operating and managing a retail or manufacturing business than ever before. Consequently, in some cases, the challenges are even greater than in the past, making the job even more exciting.

Buying merchandise for retailers—whether stored or non-stored, small-independent operations or large chains—has become a complex effort that requires major preparation and planning, time, and effort. Gone are the days of buying by the seat of one's pants, so to speak. Most large retailers and manufacturers today use sophisticated software and point-of-sale systems to track sale and manage their merchandise.

Point-of-sale (POS) systems are the major technological control that retailers use today to track inventory and sales by the use of computer software programs. Additionally, information systems and communications technologies have improved retail productivity and profits. These include **universal product coding (UPC** magnetic bar coding) and EDI (discussed next), which are utilized at point of sale. In retailing, there has been an increase in computerized POS systems and a decrease in manual cash registers. Although it is a major capital expense, stores invest in sophisticated POS terminals that provide up-to-the-minute information on sales at all locations of a company. Sales data are captured instantly at the terminal and, in a quick response relationship with vendors, are then relayed to the vendor for automatic reordering.

The UPC system is widely used by apparel manufacturers and retailers today. It creates a unique code to identify a product according to manufacturer, brand, style, size, and/or color. A magnetic base is read (scanned) at the POS terminal, which captures sales and inventory data and tracks the movement of merchandise within a retail organization. This gives the retailer such instant information as what is selling best and what is not selling, which leads to better and faster decisions in regard to reorders and markdowns. Controls must be input by the retailer and/or supplier, however, to effectively use the data. An automatic replenishment system can save many manual inventory and reorder hours, but there must be an excellent relationship between vendor and retailer for this system to work effectively and efficiently. The vendor must clearly understand the needs of the retailer and the nature of the business. (See Chapter 7 for more on retail/vendor relationships.)

Manufacturers and retailers work closely today partnering for profit. Electronic systems enable them to work intelligently and quickly to meet the needs and changes that occur in merchandising. **Electronic data interchange (EDI)** is a communications system that electronically transfers information from one point to another via computers. Everything from sales and inventory to the processing of purchase orders between manufacturer and retailer is kept up-to-date electronically. **Optical character recognition (OCR)** that utilizes scanning of paperwork is often used in place of manual data processing to speed up document processing and increase accuracy.

MERCHANDISE PLANNING AND FORECASTING

Planning is a critical element of retailing and merchandising. Successful merchants must plan their businesses in today's sophisticated retail environment.

People and products, or, in other words, the target customer and the merchandise, along with the desired profit must be anticipated and planned, for these three are inherently related. Running a business by the seat of your pants can rarely result in profit. Planning is a means of control that helps provide the buyer with information to make the best decisions in purchasing, which hopefully results in a profit. Big businesses today have expanded their merchandising staffs to include **planners** and **allocators,** who work with the buyers and their assistants to ensure that the right merchandise gets to the right place at the right time. An allocator works with the planners and buyers in *Case 26, Planning and Allocation of a Basic Business.* She is able to improve overall business, though she must determine how to raise sales for a slow-selling line carried by the buyer in the department.

Profit results when operating expenses are less than the gross margin. **Gross margin** is the difference between the net sales and the cost of goods sold and usually is an indicator of profit. A retailing business can be planned manually, but more and more frequently today it is done by computer. Using computer technology to plan and track a business is a time-savings method that is within the reach of almost all businesses and that allows for better and faster planning than in the past. There are inexpensive turnkey programs for even the smallest independent retailer of today. Computer technology enables easy tracking of **stock keeping units (SKUs),** allowing the retailer to continuously keep up with sales and inventory levels along with other merchandise specifics. An SKU is the smallest unit level of merchandise and includes style, color, size, and any other information that needs to be tracked.

Planning involves determining what, for whom, and how much to buy. Also considered are where to buy, what method of buying to undertake (centralized versus decentralized), as well as what type of buying in which to partake (regular, off-price, promotional, and so forth). There are so many options available today that generally this is not an easy task.

The buying preparation (or forecasting) and **dollar and merchandise planning,** directly involves the five "rights" of merchandising that Mazur (1927, p. 66) brought to our attention many years ago. These are purchasing the *right merchandise,* at the *right time,* at the *right place,* in the *right quantities,* and at the *right price.*

Forecasting is predicting the styles and trends to purchase for the customer. It is a part of the buyer's job that is dependent on a lot of work and effort, due to the dynamic nature of the retail environment. Forecasting the right merchandise, as well as the expected or right amounts to be sold, is a crucial part of the merchant's job. The better a buyer or retailer is able to forecast, the better the likeli-

Figure 5.1 Textile reps showing their fabric lines to apparel designers and manufacturers. Because fabric and color decisions are made at least a year in advance, textile companies must be able to successfully forecast future merchandise trends.

hood that the projected sales and resultant profit will be obtained. Forecasting involves decision making that uses as much input as possible to predict what the customer wants next.

Scanning the **environmental factors,** from both an internal and external perspective, impacts the buyer's decision making. Internal environmental factors include information from store records to the store's particular culture and goals and vendor history. External environmental factors include aspects of technology, the economy, society, and culture, along with political and legal issues that affect the business and the customer being considered. Data that are gathered from within and/or outside the company supply the retailer with a wide range of information to interpret, to analyze, and on which to act. The more information the buyer is able to synthesize, the better he or she will be at projecting the needs and wants of the consumer.

Figure 5.2 shows a page from a trend book provided by Doneger. Organizations such as this resident buying office compile information and forecast the major trends in colors and styling for an upcoming season in apparel, accessories,

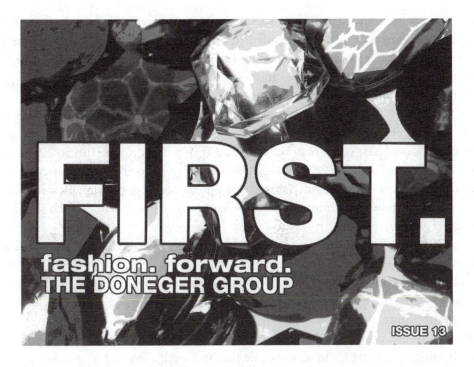

Figure 5.2 This page from a Doneger trend book is an example of forecasting style trends.

cosmetics, and home furnishings. Such information is available for purchase from numerous sources or may be provided to member stores by the buying offices of corporations, such as Macy's, or private buying offices, such as Doneger. *Case 27, Forecasting Fashion in Menswear* examines the complexity of forecasting the right merchandise trends from a menswear buyer's perspective.

The history of the retail organization, including the past performance records, can also be of significant help in planning. Measured results, such as sales and profit or loss of past years, may aid the planner in predicting the future with more precise accuracy. In *Case 28, The Inexperienced Buyer,* a novice buyer must make a multifaceted sales planning decision based on last year's poor sales, a current and strong open-to-buy position, and a single key market trend about which she does not feel confident.

Retail planning can be long-range or short-range, as well as top-down or bottom up. **Long-range planning** entails looking toward the future for a business and projects goals of five or more years. If a retailer considers how to diversify a business over the next ten years, then long-range planning is a necessity. **Short-range planning** involves looking at the most immediate concerns and setting goals of the business to achieve them. Examples of short-range planning include such subjects as what to do about a sale that is a week away or how to meet a sales plan for the week, month, or season. How much of the planning is done and by whom is dependent on the size and type of retailer, as well as how the retailer operates and is organized.

Top-down planning involves goal setting at the highest level of the organizational structure and management, then filtering the goals down to the other levels. For example, a corporation and its president plan the company's total sales goal, then it is broken down by division, and to the category or department level and the buyer. Next, the buyer breaks the sales down from a department (or category) to the classification, subclassification, and perhaps even to the brand, price, style, size, and color. Generally, merchandise is planned to (at least) five levels:

1. A **division** is the largest breakdown of merchandise for a retailer. It contains categories, departments, classifications, and subclassifications. Examples of divisions are: soft goods, hard goods, women's, and children's.
2. A **category** is a major grouping of merchandise that includes all types of departments, classes, and subclasses that a particular type of customer would shop, for example, women's or men's apparel.

3. A **department** is a segment of a retailing establishment that groups classifications of merchandise together that are complementary to one another, such as a junior's department or a men's department.

4. A **classification (class)** is a group of items (or the same general type of merchandise that are housed within a department), for example, sportswear or eveningwear.

5. A **subclassification (subclass)** is the term used to describe a group of merchandise within a classification that is closely related in styling, such as bottoms or tops under the classification of sportswear, or it could even be a vendor.

The level to which detailed planning is done is dependent on the type and importance of merchandise to the buyer and retailer. **Bottom-up planning** involves goal setting at the lowest levels of management—and even sometimes non-management—then filtering plans up the organizational structure to the highest management level. It is planning from the lowest level to the highest level. An example of bottom-up planning is when sales volume is being predicted by the department manager, who then tells the store manager, who finally relays this to the company's operations manager.

DOLLAR AND UNIT PLANS

A major portion of the buyer's role involves planning what merchandise to purchase. Buyers rely on **dollar plans** and **unit plans,** or what may also be referred to as the **merchandise budget,** to guide them in making the best purchases. These plans forecast the merchandising activities for a department or store for a specific period of time. The buyer usually has direct involvement in creating the merchandise budget. Dollar planning is regarded as the money budget preparation of retail dollars to meet sales plans. This plan is quantitative and results in the planned purchases. **Unit planning** refers to the physical units and most often to the assortment planning and qualitative aspects. This type of plan involves decisions about what types of merchandise (or mix) should be bought and stocked by a retailer down to the number of pieces in inventory. Dollar and unit plans usually include calculations in dollars and percentage figures that relate to net sales.

Unit and dollar merchandise planning covers two 6-month time frames within a calendar year—Spring/Summer (February–July) and Fall/Winter (August–January)—and are referred to as **six-month plans.** An example of a six-month plan is shown in Figure 5.3. This plan presents the projected sales, beginning- and end-of-the-month stocks, reductions, retail and cost planned purchases, along with other critical elements for planning. These elements include: initial and maintained markup, gross margin, operating expenses, expected net profit, and turnover. Last year's actual sales, a plan for this year, and actual sales figures are all recorded on the plan. For an example of how a six-month plan is developed, see *Case 29, McFadden's Department Store: Preparation of a Merchandise Budget Plan.*

Planning, whether the dollars and/or units, includes five progressive steps:

1. Planning the retail sales
2. Planning the inventory or stock (beginning of the month and end of the month)
3. Planning the reductions (markdowns, employee discounts, and shortages)
4. Planning the markup (retail minus cost)
5. Planning the purchases (needs to meet projected sales)

These five steps are explored in the next sections.

Sales Planning

The first step in developing the merchandise budget is **sales planning,** which is the estimation of the sales that a retailer will make over a period of time. If sales history is available, planners can use these figures as a base, and the sales from year to year and from season to season are planned, based on increases or decreases to a set figure. If no past sales figures are available and original sales plans are being created from scratch, then more work and research in sales planning will be necessary. Environmental information, trends, and industry data need to be collected and analyzed to help estimate first-time sales. The accuracy of the sales plan is important, because all other merchandise plans are based on this, and consequently, if it is unrealistic, then the other plans will most likely be as well. A **sell-through** plan often is also developed, which sets a certain percentage of the amount of merchandise sold as a goal to achieve.

Inventory and Assortment Planning

Inventory (stock) planning is accomplished after sales planning, and entails the determination of the stock levels necessary to meet the sales plan. (The terms inventory and stock are used interchangeably.) **Beginning-of-the-month (BOM)**

SIX-MONTH MERCHANDISING PLAN

DEPARTMENT NAME _____ DEPARTMENT NO. _____ PERIOD COVERED _____

	LAST YEAR	PLAN			LAST YEAR	PLAN
Initial Markup	_____	_____		Gross Margin	_____	_____
Reductions	_____	_____		Operating Expense	_____	_____
Maintained Markup	_____	_____		Operating Profit	_____	_____
Cash Discount	_____	_____		Season Turnover	_____	_____
Buyer	_____	_____		Date Prepared	_____	_____

Spring	Fall	Sales +			E.O.M. +			Reductions -			B.O.M. =			Retail Purchases			Cost Purchases		
		Last Year	Plan	Actual	Last Year	Plan	Actual	Last Year	Plan	Actual	Last Year	Plan	Actual	Last Year	Plan	Actual	Last Year	Plan	Actual
Feb.	Aug.																		
Mar.	Sept.																		
Apr.	Oct.																		
May	Nov.																		
June	Dec.																		
July	Jan.																		
Total																			

Figure 5.3 An example of a six-month merchandise plan form.

and **end-of-the-month (EOM)** inventory/**stock** levels are calculated for each month of plans, as a means to ensure that enough merchandise will be stocked to cover the planned sales. The planner must remember that the planned BOM for a month is also the planned EOM for the preceding month. There are four methods of inventory planning that can be used to arrive at the "right" beginning of the month stock levels:

1. **Basic stock method,** which relies on having a minimum level of stock no matter what, as a reserve stock level and also enough stock to meet projected sales each month. Basic stock is equal to the average stock for the season minus the average monthly sales.

2. **Percentage variation method** determines stock for a high turnover rate (six or more per year). It allows for stock fluctuation and is based on the premise that the variation of monthly stock from average stock should be half as much as the percentage variation in monthly sales from average sales.

3. **Stock-to-sales ratio (SSR) method** arrives at a planned stock level that is based on what should be on hand at any given time, rather than on an average stock basis. It may be arrived at by multiplying the planned sales for the month by the BOM stock-to-sales ratio.

4. **Week's supply method** is used when calculating a needed stock level by week. With this method, planned stock is equal to the average stock in a week's supply multiplied by the planned weekly sales.

Different factors help a merchant determine which method of stock planning is best to use. Turnover is one factor that is always considered. **Turnover (TO)** or **stock turn (ST)** describes how many times stock is sold and replaced within a period of time. Stock turn rate helps ensure that the amount of merchandise available is adequate to meet the sales. A retailer or buyer must be careful, however, not to have too much more inventory than is needed. There is often a fine line between too much and not enough, or just the "right" amount of inventory. An overstocked position causes problems in *Case 6, Sell or Buy: What's Right?,* in Chapter 1, because there is plenty of merchandise but not the "right" merchandise on hand.

Inventory problems that need immediate attention are presented in *Case 21, The Out of Fashion Inventory Problem,* in Chapter 4, in which there is an accumulation of old stock that the buyer's predecessor never moved out and action is needed to bring in fresh, new stock. What kind of action to take can sometimes present problems, and when goals conflict there may be negative repercussions.

An **assortment** of stock (or what particular types of merchandise will be purchased) is determined. Merchandise **assortment planning** regards not only what

UNIT AND ASSORTMENT PLAN EXAMPLE

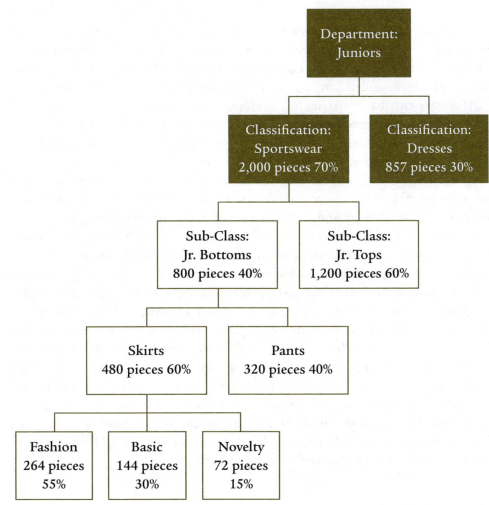

Figure 5.4 This unit and assortment plan breaks merchandise down into management control levels, showing both the number of units and the corresponding percentage of stock.

retailers will carry, but the number of units and stock levels, price ranges, styles, sizes, colors, fabrics, and even the level of fashion. In essence, it plans the mixture of merchandise. An example of a simple unit and assortment plan by department, classification, and subclassification that breaks the merchandise down into specific types of styles, level of fashion by percentage, and number of units is presented in Figure 5.4.

An assortment is sometimes referred to as a **merchandise mix.** A golf pro-shop wants to make some improvements in its merchandise mix but is unsure how to do so in *Case 30, Sub-Par Inventory.* Unfortunately, a lack of planning and control in the past provides current problems in stock that may have been otherwise avoidable, so an analysis of the assortment is necessary. Merchandise assortment planning is also considered in *Case 31, A Competitive Dilemma: Advance or Retreat?*

There are two basic systems of developing assortment plans: creating basic stock plans or model stock plans. The type of merchandise being planned for—either basic or fashion—helps the retailer or buyer determine the type of plan to use. **Basic stock planning** involves staple merchandise, while **model stock planning** sets a determination of merchandise levels according to factors important to the buyer, for example, fabric, price, style, and so forth. A model stock plan is for fashion and/or seasonal merchandise within a particular merchandise category.

An effective, salable assortment of balanced stock should be strived for by the buyer. In doing so, two dimensions of stock are considered—the breadth and depth. The **breadth** of merchandise refers to the number of different product lines, styles, or brands that are carried in a retailing establishment. The **depth** refers to the number of units within a product line, style, or brand. Figure 5.5 shows several types of breadth and depth plans—with sizes or colors used for the depth dimension and styles or brands used for the breadth dimension in an assortment plan. Descriptions of assortments are often presented in terms of breadth and depth. For example, merchandise within an assortment may be described as **broad** (lots of styles), **narrow** (few styles) **deep** (many colors and sizes), or **shallow** (few sizes and colors). An assortment can also be described in combinations, as in narrow and deep (few styles, many colors and sizes), broad and shallow (many styles, few sizes and colors), and so forth.

Planning Reductions

A means of lowering or marking down the retail price of merchandise, **reductions** are planned because only rarely can all the merchandise purchased be sold at the originally set retail price. Reductions are a provision used by retailers to reduce the retail price of merchandise and encourage the sale of stock so that it can be replaced with fresh, new goods. Markdowns, markup cancellations, and discounts are all types of reductions that a retailer should plan to incur. **Markdowns** are either **promotional** or **permanent;** these adjust the initial retail price downward temporarily or set a new retail, respectively. **Markup cancellations** adjust the amount of markup that was put on an item originally, thereby lowering the price.

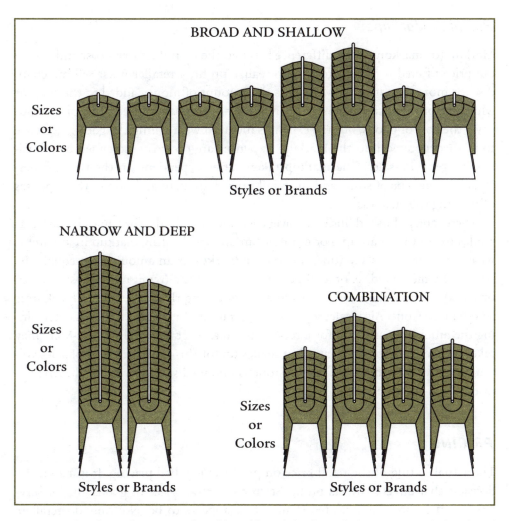

Figure 5.5 This figure shows examples of breadth and depth stock dimensions, including broad and shallow, narrow and deep, and combination.

Different reasons for reductions help the retailer decide what type of mark-down to take. Special events, sales, clearance, old or damaged stock, the competi-tion, or buyer's errors in purchasing or pricing are the more common reasons for markdowns. **Discounts** can also lower the retail price as a concession to employees (i.e., employee discounts) or other special customers.

Planning Markups

Markup (or **markon**) is the difference between the manufacturer's cost and the retail price offered to the customer. To realize profit, a retailer must sell merchandise for more than it costs. Markup is the amount of money added to the cost (or wholesale price) of the merchandise. Not only does markup need to be planned to cover the cost of goods, but the expenses incurred with selling the goods also have to be incorporated into the markup. **Expenses** are the costs expended by a business to generate sales. The markup taken varies dependent on the type of merchandise, the type of store, and the retail price desired, in addition to the expenses of running the business.

There are published industry averages and standards that may be used as guides for setting markup. For example, an average, healthy markup in apparel is what is referred to as keystone. A **keystone markup** is an amount that equals the cost of the merchandise, or a 50 percent retail markup (retail minus cost, divided by retail). That is, the retail is arrived at by doubling the cost. A **short markup** is less than keystone. Also, sales volume (i.e., total sales) may play a role in determining the amount of markup for a retailer to take. A retailer such as Wal-Mart may take less than keystone markups but makes up for this in the amount of sales volume acquired. Often more than keystone is obtained with private-label merchandise at high-end boutiques.

PRICING

The actual setting of the retail price on products is called **pricing.** It is a strategic decision that directly affects profit. Setting the retail price of goods and/or services is much more complicated than it first appears to be. Not only do retailers have to consider all the expenses incurred in the price, but they must also consider the type of merchandise, the competition, and the target customer when determining the best retail price to set on a product. The consumer today is cognizant of the relationship between value and price; however, value today means much more to the customer than just price. It is more situational and varies depending on who the customer is, what merchandise the customer is shopping for, and where the customer is shopping. "Getting your money's worth" is a real and often major factor in consumer purchase decision-making. Today there is not the stigma associated with inexpensive fashion that there once was, and consumers at all economic levels shop for moderate clothing at mass merchants or specialty stores. Many retailers compete with others for the customer's patronage through price alone. Therefore, setting the right retail price is a very important—and is often the deciding factor—in whether or not a sale is made. This can be a difficult decision to make.

The **retail price** for merchandise is calculated using a number of important factors. The cost (i.e., wholesale price) of a garment plus all expenses that need to be figured into the markup are itemized and added into the total retail selling price. The proportional expenses that are included in the markup of a retail price varies from retailer to retailer; however, all these expenses must be included in the markup. If not, part of the cost of merchandise is not being accounted for, and consequently, sales will not cover all the expenses incurred. Expenses include not only the cost of the merchandise, but allowances for markdowns, shortages and theft, salaries and benefits, and business overhead. Also, expected **profit** should be planned and worked into the markup, so there will be a residual profit after all the expenses are accounted for. No matter what the amount is, the retail price is the sum of the cost and markup.

Deciding on the correct and profitable retail price for a proven seller can be a problem for both a buyer and a retail owner, who must consider a cost increase, markup, and gross margin. A cost increase also warrants a retail increase in *Case 43, Tying One On,* in Chapter 7. This case exemplifies the fact that setting retail prices may be dependent on outside factors.

Pricing strategy is the determination of the type of pricing policy a buyer or retailer will use along with the practices the buyer or retailer will employ. It involves understanding not only who the target customer is and what his or her needs and/or wants are, but also a number of other such factors as the image and identity that a retailer wants to project, as discussed in Chapter 3. Additionally, there is usually a direct relationship between the retail price, quality, and style level of merchandise in most customers' minds as illustrated in Chapter 4.

Merchandise pricing policies are the methods that retailers use to set retail prices on their merchandise in addition to the thought processes behind their pricing. A policy is selected by a retailer to help set the price on merchandise and to also convey a message (or image) to the customer about the retail operation and the merchandise being carried. Psychology often plays a role in determining the type of pricing to use. As mentioned, both who the customer is and what type of merchandise a retailer wants to sell to that customer play an important role in what price should be the "right" price to place on the merchandise to sell it. Pricing policies and strategies must incorporate the psychology to best match the correct price with the merchandise being sold so that the customer will feel that the price is fair for the merchandise being bought. Pricing determinations are made on such issues as:

- Will **price ranges** and/or **price points** be used? That is, will the retail price be determined by keeping the dollar amount between one retail price and another or will a single, predetermined price be used? For example, at a dollar store everything would sell for one dollar. Another example is a retailer who marks everything at whole and mid-dollar points, for example, $5 and $7.50.
- Will the merchandise be **promotionally priced** (i.e., have a sale price) or **regularly priced** (i.e., not on sale)? A discounter might sell all merchandise at the .49 or .99 price point ending to indicate a sale price, while a department store might price and sell all regular merchandise at whole number prices, such as $60 or $100.
- Will the merchandise be **odd priced** (i.e., ending with an odd number or a round number) or **even priced** (i.e., ending with numbers that can be divided evenly)? Odd price point endings, such as .95 or .99 often reflect sale merchandise, while .00 or evenly divisible numbers usually indicate non-sale prices.
- Should the merchandise be priced as a **loss leader** (i.e., priced at or below cost) to attract customers, as many discounters do?

Pricing and pricing practices are regulated by the Federal Trade Commission (FTC), which helps to protect the retailer and consumer alike from deceptive, unfair, and/or illegal pricing tactics. Several examples of the FTC's involvement in regulating pricing can be found in Chapter 11.

PLANNED PURCHASES AND OPEN-TO-BUY

Planning the dollars and units for the open-to-buy and the planned purchases (needs) must take into consideration the five merchandising rights. These include the determination of the best (right) merchandise desired, the correct (right) quantities, the setting of the best (right) retail prices, the most accurate (right) timing and delivery, and the proper (right) placement of the merchandise.

A **planned purchase** is the difference between what is needed and what is on hand. The amount of planned purchases that is projected is based on the planned sales, BOM and EOM inventory levels desired, and the amount of reductions that are being planned. Failing to plan can cause many merchandising and retailing problems, as it does in *Case 64, Katie's Kloset in Cedar Spring Grove: Sales, Smoke, and Small-Town Business,* in Chapter 10.

The **open-to-buy (OTB)** is an adjustment to the planned purchases that takes into account what is already **on order** (i.e., what is due in). It is calculated on a frequent basis, usually weekly or monthly, and aids the buyer in making necessary adjustments throughout the season to help control inventories and profitability. After purchases are originally placed, the OTB is then periodically determined by subtracting the on-order from the planned purchases.

Adjusting plans is a means to change what can realistically be done and more accurately ensure that goals will be met. *Case 32, Is the Purchase Worth the Risk?* involves a buyer who is in an overstocked and overbought position, but is offered an attractive promotional package of merchandise from a vendor. She desperately wants to make the purchase, and then adjusts her plans to allow her to make the buy. Her merchandise manager, however, does not want to approve the purchase based on the adjusted plans, even though the buyer feels the merchandise is just what she needs to stimulate business.

Setting the best, most realistic, reasonable plan is not always easy. A plan needs to be realistic enough to be achievable, yet aggressive enough to be a challenge, which will increase sales and improve profit. In *Case 33, The Planning Impasse,* a buyer disagrees with the merchandise manager, who wants to increase the department planned sales.

Incorrect and/or poor merchandise planning and purchasing can result in poor sales performance from stock-outs, high markdowns, lost sales, and ultimately a poor bottom line, or profit. In *Case 4, The Impossible Goals,* in Chapter 1, the buyer is challenged by the merchandise manager to improve profit. She met her sales, but not her profit goal. Successful buyers regularly review and revise their plans throughout the season to act upon changes that may affect their business. To make the best buy, the prepared buyer should purchase goods armed with plans that are often loaded into the buyer's laptop carried with him or her to market. When planning is not done or is improperly done, disaster can strike.

CONTROLS

Measuring and evaluating performance productivity and resulting profitability of a business is reliant on planning and controls. **Controls** are the methods employed to help a retailer track the business to see how it is doing and how effective the merchandising strategies are. Effective control systems have established **standards**, a means of measuring performance through accepted guidelines that help to monitor performance. Consequently, the resulting analyses allow for change to the business that is based on the information provided with the control. When retailers discuss controls, they usually refer to the financially based aspects of their business and those accounting and merchandising measures that help ensure profitability. Controls can also be records that track data or compare and contrast information.

The importance of maintaining merchandising standards as a control in an effort to run a profitable business is brought to light in *Case 4, The Impossible Goals*. Planning and controlling such specific aspects of a buyer's business as markup, turnover, markdown, and sales as related to improving sales and profitability are also examined. Controls also aid a business in reacting to events that occur, in order for adjustments to be made as needs arise. Usually controls are built into management objectives during the business planning stages. For example, the dollar and unit control of a retailer is often built into the merchandise planning budget.

Merchandise planning is a necessary control for retailers. However, there are tools other than budgets that may be utilized to control a retailing business and help to make it profitable. Inventories (both periodic and perpetual) are types of retail controls taken to keep track of stock. **Periodic inventory** is a method of stock control in which the retailer physically counts merchandise at designated time periods. Many apparel retailers take periodic inventories twice a year, in July and January. These dates coincide with the end of the six-month planning periods and also correspond to the lowest inventory levels of the year. In contrast, **perpetual inventories** are stock control methods that provide a continuous record of the movement of incoming and outgoing merchandise which is easily done today through POS systems.

Records help management follow and guide businesses to success. Retailers generate various reports to help monitor their businesses, which may include many types of planning reports and records. Reports on units, dollars, assortment, pricing, fast or slow sellers, sell-through analysis, vendors, and other information desired are frequently used methods of retail control.

Another aid for control used by numerous large retail chains is a **vendor matrix** or **key resource list**. These matrices or lists are based on the premise that fewer resources or suppliers are better than many, in order for the resources to be as beneficial to the retailer as possible. The matrix or key resource list incorporates the company-approved key vendors from which a buyer is recommended and/or required to purchase. An example of a vendor matrix may be seen in Table 5.1. Pertinent performance information on vendors is contained on the matrix. Such information is reported as dollar purchases, sell-through, the amount of markdowns, markup, and gross margin. Often the vendors are listed according to the most profitable resource, unlike this matrix in which the vendors are alphabetized but still ranked according to profitability. Sometimes purchasing rules are given to buyers, for example, the 80/20 rule. This guideline instructs the buyer to purchase 80 percent

TABLE 5.1 Key Vendor Matrix

Vendors	Ranking	*Pur	*Sales	% Sell-Through	% MM+	% Mk downs	S* Mk downs	% GM++
All That Jazz	5	40	32.0	80	46	4.0	1.60	36
Allyn Paige	13	23	9.2	40	30	15.0	3.45	28
Blondie & Me	10	8	2.0	25	44	9.0	.72	38
Brioche	7	12	6.6	55	50	6.3	9.45	32
Byer Too	16	17	8.5	50	32	14.0	2.38	30
City Triangles	3	9	6.3	70	46	8.0	.72	34
CLE Paris	8	15	6.3	42	41	7.0	1.05	42
Dawn Joy	19	7	2.1	30	40	22.6	1.58	31
Hearts Divine	12	13	5.5	46	49	16.0	2.08	34
Jalate	18	42	28.6	68	29	55.0	23.10	19
Jump	20	8	7.2	90	60	36.0	2.88	29
Just Choon	2	24	18.0	75	52	4.0	.96	38
La Belle	11	29	9.3	32	36	20.0	5.80	22
Marian & Maral	6	10	3.2	32	48	3.5	.35	37
Rampage	14	8	5.4	67	42	22.0	1.76	20
Tickets	4	30	22.2	74	52	7.2	21.60	32
Triangle Blues	15	4	6.0	15	34	19.0	.76	26
XOXO	9	22	32.0	15	37	14.0	3.08	31
XTRMZ	17	6	3.6	60	41	9.0	.54	29
You Babes	1	30	25.5	85	49	6.0	1.80	35

* Dollars in thousands (purchases and sales)
+ Maintained Markon
++ Gross Margin

of their department needs from the top 20 percent of their vendors, which helps to ensure proven profitability and vendor consistency in assortment.

PRODUCTIVITY AND PROFIT

The retailer's bottom line, and the objective of most retail businesses, is to realize a profit. The evaluation of a company's profitability is reported on a **profit and loss statement (P&L)** or **income statement.** This is also a control that helps to monitor the budget. It summarizes the financial workings of a business during a certain period of time and documents whether or not there is a profit or loss. Profit results when revenues generated exceed the costs incurred in producing those revenues. On the profit and loss statement, **net sales** are first compared to **cost of goods** sold to arrive at **gross margin.** Next, the expenses are subtracted for resulting profit or loss. Such reports as the profit and loss statement can help direct a retailer as to whether or not changes are necessary to a business. In *Case 31, A Competitive Dilemma: Advance or Retreat?*, facts and figures are presented on which to base the determination of whether or not a store owner should keep the business as it is or change it. Records that provide information on the maximization of sales potential, productivity, and profitability of the store in general, as well as the separate departments are considered.

The profitability of a business may also be used as a gauge to determine the direction in which a retailer should plan growth, as well as how to specifically plan that growth.

SUMMARY

Forecasting the needs and wants of retail customers through research and careful planning helps to predict sales more accurately, as well as ensuring a retailer's and manufacturer's success through profit. The need for effective internal controls in monitoring the dollars, units, and assortments should never be underestimated by a retailer. Today, the managing of merchandise from planning, purchasing, pricing, and inventory is often done through a computer and the systems created to do such, allowing faster and more detailed reports to monitor a business. The closer a retailer monitors and manages a company, as well as adapting to changes that occur in both the external and internal environments, the more profitable and rewarding a business will be.

KEY TERMS

allocators

assortment

assortment planning

basic stock method

basic stock planning

beginning of the month (BOM)

bottom-up planning

breadth

broad assortment

buying

category

classification (class)

controls

cost of goods

deep assortment

department

depth

discounts

division

dollar plans

electronic data interchange (EDI)

end of month (EOM)

environmental factors

even priced

expenses

forecasting

gross margin
income statement
inventory (stock) level
inventory (stock) planning
key resource list
keystone markup
long-range planning
loss leader
markdown
markup/markon
markup cancellations
merchandise budget
merchandise mix
merchandise planning
merchandiser
merchandising
model stock planning
narrow assortment
net sales
odd priced
on order
open-to-buy (OTB)
optical character recognition (OCR)
percentage variation method
periodic inventory
permanent markdowns
perpetual inventory
planned purchases
planners
point of sale (POS)
price points
price ranges

pricing
pricing strategy
product manager
profit
profit and loss statement (P&L)
promotional markdowns
promotional pricing
purchasing
purchasing agent
records
reductions
regular pricing
retail price
sales planning
sell-through
shallow assortment
short markup
short-range planning
six-month plans
sourcing agent
standards
stock keeping unit (SKU)
stock-to-sales ratio (SSR) method
stock turn (ST)
subclassification (subclass)
top-down planning
turnover (TO)
unit plans
universal product code (UPC)
vendor matrix
week's supply method

BIBLIOGRAPHY

Bohlinger, M. S. (2001). *Merchandise buying*. New York: Fairchild Books.
Brannon, E. L. (2005). *Fashion forecasting: Research, analysis, and presentation*. New York: Fairchild Books.
Clodfelter, R. (2003). *Making buying decisions: Using the computer as a tool*. New York: Fairchild Books.

Clodfelter, R. (2003). *Retail buying: From basics to fashion.* New York: Fairchild Books.

Cushman, L. M. (2005). *Using computerized spreadsheets: Mathematics for retail buying.* New York: Fairchild Books.

Diamond, J., & Pintel, G. (2005). *Retail buying.* Upper Saddle River, NJ: Prentice Hall.

Donnellan, J. (2007). *Merchandise buying and management.* New York: Fairchild Books.

Easterling, C., Flottman, E., & Jernigan, M. (2003). *Merchandising mathematics for retailing.* Upper Saddle River, NJ: Prentice Hall.

Guthrie, K. M., & Pierce, C. W. (2003). *Perry's department store: A buying simulation.* New York: Fairchild Books.

Kang-Park, J., & Kotsiopulos, A. (2007). *Merchandising mathematics.* New York: Fairchild Books.

Kunz, G. (2005). *Merchandising: Theory, principles, and practice.* New York: Fairchild Books.

Mazur, P. (1927). *Principles of organization applied to modern retailing.* New York: Harper and Bros.

Rosenau, J. A., & Wilson, D. L. (2006). *Apparel merchandising: The line starts here.* New York: Fairchild Books.

Sherman, G. J., & Perlman, S. (2007). *The real world guide to fashion selling and management.* New York: Fairchild Books.

Tepper, B. K. (2007). *Mathematics for retail buying.* New York: Fairchild Books.

Case 25

THE CONFRONTATION

Jenny Greene, Harold's Stores

Jaime has been working with the same small retailer for four years. She really likes the people she works with, and especially her boss, Cathy. However, lately there's been a lot of employee turnover with the company's corporate office, and many new people for Jaime to work with. As a technical design associate, it is Jaime's job to conduct weekly meetings with the buyers, assistant buyers, sourcing team, and trend and design team to communicate all fit changes on ladies top styles with them. This is necessary because the fittings for all ladies tops happen with Cathy in the New York office, and they must be sent down to the corporate office afterward to be approved by the aforementioned teams.

In these meetings, Jaime works with the senior tops buyer, Megan. Megan is new to the company. Her performance is being watched closely by the executive-level vice presidents because ladies tops have not been selling well. Megan knows she must take all of her top styles very seriously or it will be her job on the line if the tops' selling performance does not improve. In the weekly review meetings, Jaime starts noticing that Megan is overly scrutinizing the fit changes made to all the tops styles, even though they have been very carefully made and approved by Cathy in New York. Jaime becomes slightly irritated at Megan's constant need to not only pick apart every fit change they review but also to add a few more of her own to each style. It is causing the review meetings to run overtime, and it is obvious that the meetings are becoming tense. Jaime is finally asked by Cathy if she thinks Megan is overstepping her authority in these meetings. Jaime is unsure of what to tell Cathy, because while Cathy is her boss and she feels a duty to tell her the truth, she also doesn't want to jeopardize her professional relationship with Megan as they will have to work closely together for the duration of their employment. And Jaime knows it would be obvious to Megan that she's the one who reported her, if anyone discusses the issue with Megan.

Major Question

How would you handle the situation if you were Jaime?

Study Questions

1. Is there an alternative way to handle the situation in which all parties win?

2. What is the best thing to do when you're faced with someone difficult at your job? Answer this question two ways: one if the person is a peer, another if he or she is a superior.

PLANNING AND ALLOCATION OF A BASIC BUSINESS

Abigail Johnson, Assistant Buyer for Watches and Color, Friedman's Jewelers

Alex worked at the corporate office of a moderate-sized jewelry store chain of about 400 stores. She had been working there for about a year and had learned the basic processes of merchandising pretty quickly. Alex started out as an intern, then was hired as a merchandising detail assistant. Her basic functions in that position were sample coordination, maintenance of the mock store (where samples were displayed as if in a real store), vendor coordination of meetings, and scheduling her buyer's trips. Within seven months of her employment, Alex was promoted to allocator of watches. With her goal of someday being a buyer, Alex was excited to finally arrive at the next stage of her career progression. Her position as a detail assistant helped her learn more of the buying functions, and allocator was the next step toward becoming an assistant buyer. After assistant buyer, she would go into Planning, where hopefully she would move to either associate buyer or buyer of a division. This is the career path Alex's company wants for their associates so that they are more "fiscally responsible" buyers in the future.

As an allocator, Alex is the front person for replenishing the watch business to stores. Watches are a very basic business, with new items coming in only twice a year and basic replenishment monthly based on sales and vendor availability. Alex must work closely with her planner to make sure that her stores are stocked up to their presentation quantities, which are two per SKU so that when one watch sells there will be a backup until the one that sold can be replenished. With this, she must track her sales by SKU and replenish weekly. She does this with ladder plans by SKU, which help her forecast, based on the number of stores, what the item will sell each week. The basis of this forecast is done by what class the SKU is in within the division and how that class has sold in the past as a percentage to the year. So depending upon what class the SKU is in, Alex will be able to use a percentage for that item as to what the performance might be during the year. This is all a guess. As sales come in, Alex will adjust her ladder plans according to how the item trends up or down. Therefore, her work with the planner involves matching her bottoms up number (SKU to total plan) to her planner's top down number (company plan to division plan to class plans). Sometimes this is not such an easy task, and the buyer has to help figure out which items are more important to be stocked on if the dollars are higher than her open-to-buy allows for purchases. If Alex's buyer feels the need to cut back on an item, it may be because sales are slowing or she

knows that this item will soon be on clearance or put on sell-down. (Sell-down means that the company will no longer be cutting orders and replenishing an item and will just let it remain in the stores to sell down at the full price).

Alex was enjoying her position as allocator, as it was fun for her to figure out what would be selling better in certain regions of her stores and to figure out the constant "puzzle" of her numbers for replenishment versus her planner's. She also enjoyed talking with the stores one-on-one. During her time as an allocator, Alex was able to improve the business by working with her buyer and determining certain store groups for brands that were hard to determine where they were selling.

One example of this was the chain's ESQ line. ESQ is a division of Movado, and it has a very distinct styling compared to the Japanese brands within the company. This was an attractive new addition to the watch assortment, and with nine-month sales history Alex was noticing that the line was not doing as well as it should (even after being rolled out to an additional 100 doors from the original 75). Stores with ESQ were in stock, but overall sales were low despite this. To help the performance of this brand, Alex compared it to Wittnauer, the other Swiss brand within the company. Alex must now figure out what steps she should take to correct the ESQ business as there is an opening for assistant buyer coming up and she knows that solving this problem will help her attain her goal of securing that position.

What should Alex do to correct the problem with ESQ's sales performance?

1. How do you think the planning meetings with the buyer work? Explain.

2. What do you think are potential reasons that ESQ is not working in this specialty store?

Exercise

Research ESQ. Is there any indication of how this company is doing on a global scale?

Case 27

FORECASTING FASHION IN MENSWEAR

Janice Ellinwood, Marymount University

On this particular morning, Naomi Hicks was especially anxious to get to work. After several years of assisting in the buying of women's sportswear and dresses at a regional chain of stores called Edmonds, Naomi was beginning a new job as buyer of men's related separates.

Edmonds is situated in the suburbs of a major, eastern city in the United States. With a central buying structure, it enjoys a reputation for quality apparel, generally a mix of brand-name and private-label merchandise. The chain even has its own import program. Its main competition comes from larger, departmentalized stores like Bloomingdale's, Macy's, and JCPenney.

Edmonds provides personalized service, building customer loyalty that may combat competition. The stores occasionally run sales timed with those of competitors. It is not considered a fashion-forward store; however, it aims for uniqueness in product mix as a defense against the competition.

Paul Clay, the menswear merchandise manager, greeted Naomi. He defines Edmonds' male customers as "age 30 to 60 years old, educated, white-collar, family-men who spend 20 percent of the week in leisure activities." Naomi oversees these classifications: polos, rugbies, crew-neck shirts, workshirts, sport pants, and shorts.

Paul presented two immediate concerns to Naomi. It is time to prepare for the buying of Spring season merchandise, but simultaneously, product information must be assembled and presented to upper management for the store's import of its own merchandise during the following Fall. Naomi learned that Edmonds' theme for its Fall merchandise was "Crew." She is not sure what "crew" means and feels immediately overwhelmed, having to formulate merchandising ideas for two different seasons. Paul suggested that she compile a list of sources of relevant fashion forecasting information because this is her first buying experience. She draws on her experience as an assistant, and using information she remembers from school research sources, she compiles a list of information:

1. Color reporting service—for example, Color Association of the United States.
2. Resident buying office, especially the one serving Edmonds, which is Certified Fashion Guild.
3. Consumer menswear publications, for instance, *Gentleman's Quarterly.*
4. Online fashion reporting sources, such as men.style.com.
5. Historic costume books.
6. European menswear collections, like those designed by Gianni Versace, Romeo Gigli, Nino Cerruti, or Jean Paul Gaultier.
7. Trade publications for the menswear market, for instance, *DNR.*
8. Edmonds' best sellers from last season.
9. Local store competitors.
10. Local art museum.
11. Museums that feature historic costume, such as the Metropolitan Museum of Art.
12. New York's most prestigious stores: Barney's, Bloomingdale's, Bergdorf Goodman, and so on.
13. Apparel on local college campuses.

Paul reviewed Naomi's list but knows that she cannot possibly research all the information contained on the list because time will not allow it. He wants plans by the end of the week and it is Tuesday. He also thought the list lacked order and feels that narrowing the list down and/or rank-ordering the information could help Naomi prioritize her research. He asked Naomi to look at the list a second time and rerank the sources for her research and pare the list down. Naomi is a bit disappointed, as she spent quite a bit of time compiling her list, but she knows that if her plans have to be in by Friday, she had better get to work. She does know that the more information she has, the better her decisions will be, so she is somewhat frustrated because she really wants her first buying plans to be great.

Major Question

How should Naomi rank these sources in order of importance, and what information would you eliminate if you were Naomi? Analyze each source for relevance to Naomi's situation.

Study Questions

1. Should any of Naomi's choices be omitted from the list?

2. Did Naomi forget any other sources of fashion information?

Exercises

1. Locate trade publications for the menswear market, such as *DNR*. What apparel do you find that is appropriate for Naomi's target market (30- to 60-year-old, educated, white-collar family men who spend 20 percent of the week in leisure

activities)? Bring the visuals and present your thoughts to the class.

2. Find photographs of athletes competing in the collegiate sport "crew." List the characteristics of their attire that suggest styling possibilities for Edmonds' stock of men's related separates, considering the target market.

3. Research online fashion reporting sources to identify trends in menswear for the current season. In your overview of trends, note any that might relate to the target market.

Case 28

THE INEXPERIENCED BUYER

Judy K. Miler, Florida State University
Nancy J. Rabolt, San Francisco State University

Loretta Fall is the women's sportswear buyer for Culver Fashions in Culver City, California. It is July, and she is about to submit a six-month merchandise plan (August thru January) for her department. Loretta has reviewed last year's sales figures and events and has remembered that weather in August and September was horrible, with lots of rain and winds keeping a lot of shoppers off the roads. She has also remembered that the heat was constant, and this caused consumer lassitude. The computer printout indicates her figures for the two-month period were off about 18 percent from the previous year. She also recalls worrying herself sick to make figures.

This year, Loretta visited the market in June for Fall merchandise and was not impressed with the trends. Although she has been a buyer for only a year, she believes one color trend—heather gray—may spell trouble because it is a rather dull color and not one that most of her target customers will want to buy and wear. Lately, consumers have been refusing to buy if they do not become excited about the new merchandise. Accordingly, Loretta has bought small amounts of merchandise well below her budgeted figures. She is in a strong open-to-buy position, with money in her budget for other types of trendy purchases.

Loretta assumes that business will not be adversely affected to the extent of last year. She figures that she can't have such a disastrous Fall season two years in a row. If the market shows real strength with some trends, she could plan a strong increase of sales for the two opening months of the plan with some hustling. If she plans for a decrease, it may be considered as a defensive measure by a new buyer. Should Loretta plan for a strong increase and sales remain flat, she could be strongly criticized and look like an inefficient new buyer. Because she is a fairly new buyer, she is between a rock and a hard place.

The other ready-to-wear buyers are more confident, and they don't have the same misgivings about this season. They suffered some losses last year, but they have affirmative feelings about the opportunities for increases this year. Business this year, they maintain, will be better than last year's disaster.

Loretta considers going to her merchandise manager, George Ramos, to discuss the dilemma with him. Loretta knows George is a fair person, but she knows that he has some misgivings about her as a buyer because he feels she lacks experience. Actually, he hired her after considerable soul-searching and at the time shared his misgivings with her. Therefore, Loretta discards the idea of going to George.

Finally, she decides to talk with Matt Washington, another buyer who went through the Culver Fashions' buying training program a few years earlier than she did. They shared many of the same experiences during their programs, and Matt has always given her good, solid advice. Also, he is familiar with the current market conditions.

Major Question

If you were Matt, how would you advise Loretta?

Study Questions

1. Discuss the advantages of maintaining an open-to-buy during the selling season. What are the disadvantages?

2. How else can an inexperienced buyer research fashion trends when planning? Is the Internet a good source?

McFADDEN'S DEPARTMENT STORE: PREPARATION OF A MERCHANDISE BUDGET PLAN[1]

Michael Levy, Babson College
Harold Koenig, Oregon State University

McFadden's Department Store has been a profitable family-owned business since its beginning in 1910. Last year's sales volume was $180 million. More recently, however, many of its departments have been losing ground to national stores moving into the area. To complicate this problem, the National Retail Federation (NRF) predicts a recession. The NRF estimates a 6.5 percent drop in sales in the coming year for the Pacific Coast, where McFadden's operates.

Department 121 has one of the more profitable departments in the store, maintaining a gross margin of 55 percent. Its basic merchandise is young men's clothing. Last year, sales reached $2,780,750 for the July–December season. The highest sales period is the back-to-school period in August, when autumn fashions are supported by strong promotional advertising. Reductions (including markdowns, discounts to employees, and shrinkages) typically run 20 percent of sales. The

[1]Levy and Weitz, *Retailing Management*, 6th ed., The McGraw-Hill Companies. Reproduced with permission of The McGraw-Hill Companies.

TABLE 5.2 Percentages of Reductions

July	August	September	October	November	December
10	20	15	10	10	35

TABLE 5.3 Percentage of Annual Sales for Department 121

	July	August	September	October	November	December
2002	3.5	10.1	9.2	6.4	4.8	9.1
2003	3.5	10.3	9.5	6.8	5.3	8.8
2004	3.5	10.5	9.6	6.2	5.5	8.2
2005	3.0	10.3	9.8	6.6	5.5	8.0

TABLE 5.4 Average Stock-to-Sales Ratio

July	August	September	October	November	December
3.0	1.9	2.1	2.4	2.5	2.2

percentages of reductions are spread throughout the season as shown in Table 5.2.

By month, the percentage of annual sales for Department 121 within this six-month period had been distributed as shown in Table 5.3.

A pre-Christmas sale has been planned in an attempt to counterbalance the slackened sales period following the first of the year. The buyer has decided to bring in some new merchandise for the sale to go along with the remaining fall fashion merchandise. The buyer expects that this will increase December's percentage of annual sales to 30 percent above what it would be without the sale. Top management has emphasized that the department should achieve a gross margin return on investment (GMROI) of 250 percent. Forecasted ending stock level in December is $758,000.

Additional information is available on the historical stock-to-sales ratio for this type of department. This information is taken from a similar department in another store that happens to have a lower average stock-to-sales ratio, as shown in Table 5.4.

*Exercise**

Your task is to prepare a merchandise budget plan. You may do the plan by hand, using the form in Figure 5.6 or by using an Excel spreadsheet. Plug in the numbers from the case. On a separate sheet of paper, explain how you determined the sales forecast, percentage of sales per month, and the monthly stock-to-sales ratios.

*Do not use the alternative solutions format for this case.

McFadden's Merchandise Budget

Planning Data

SALES FORECAST $

$$\text{Planned GMROI} = \frac{\text{Gross Margin}}{\text{Net Sales}} \times \frac{\text{Net Sales}}{\text{Inventory Costs}}$$

$$\boxed{} = \frac{\$}{\$} \times \frac{\$}{\$}$$

$$\frac{\text{Sales}}{\text{Inventory Costs}} \times (100\% - \text{GM}\%) = \frac{\text{Inventory}}{\text{Turnover}}$$

$$\boxed{} \times \boxed{} \% = \boxed{} \%$$

$$12 \div \text{Inventory Turnover} = \text{B.O.M. Stock/Sales}$$

$$\boxed{} \div \boxed{} = \boxed{}$$

Markdowns % $\boxed{}$
Discounts + % $\boxed{}$
Shortages + % $\boxed{}$
Total Reductions % $\boxed{}$

Forecasted Ending Inventory $\boxed{}$

The Plan

		Jan	Feb	Mar	Apr	May	Jun	Jul	Aug	Sept	Oct	Nov	Dec	Total (Average)	Remarks
% Distribution of Sales by Month	1													100.0%	History/Projection
Monthly Sales	2														Step (1) × Net Sales
% Distributionh of Reductions/Mo	3													100.0%	History/Projection
Monthly Reductions	4														Step (3) × Net Sales
B.O.M. Stock/Sales Ratios	5														Adjusted by Mo. Sales Fluctuations
B.O.M. Stock ($000)	6												Forcasted End Inventory		Step (2) × Step (5)
E.O.M. Stock ($000)	7														EOM Jan = BOM Feb
Monthly Additions to Stock ($000)	8														Steps 2 + 4 + 7–6 Sales + Reductions + EOM–BOM

Figure 5.6 Form for a merchandise budget plan.

Case 30

SUB-PAR INVENTORY

*Antigone Kotsiopulos and Molly Eckman,
Colorado State University*

Golf clubs and golf courses are organized in different ways, but there is typically a person called a "pro" who manages the golf side of the business. This person may also be responsible for the restaurant business, the golf course greens, and other areas of the operation such as retail space, typically referred to as the "pro shop." Many golf pros and club managers are unfamiliar with retailing when they accept the position of "pro." Jerry Kyros was typical because he came from a golf background but knew little about retailing. Jerry was on the college golf team and was recruited by fraternity friends to come to a very small community in the Midwest to run their golf course seven months of the year. The golf course had several potential revenue sources including the driving (practice) range, golf lessons, the restaurant, and the long-term potential of a retail shop. Jerry worked on developing each revenue source and eventually had enough capital to expand his retail sales beyond the basics of golf balls, gloves, towels, and caps to include men's and women's apparel. Within the club house he created a separate room for retail sales and ultimately developed signage, purchased professional fixtures, and even designed a club logo for monogramming.

Frequent tournaments were held at the club, and typically prizes were gift certificates to be used in the pro shop. Therefore, Jerry felt he had a built-in percentage of golfers who would automatically be looking for golf and related merchandise. If he capitalized on the opportunity, he thought he could generate more revenue through multiple sales. A real bonus was that the club was not charging him for rent or utilities, because they wanted some type of retail operation on-site and they were already paying his salary. Therefore, any profit he generated was his to retain.

Jerry knew a great deal about golf equipment and men's clothing, but the most difficult market for him to buy for was women's golf apparel. As the rest of his retail business grew, Jerry became more and more frustrated with his inability to derive more profit from this area. The main problem seemed to be markdowns because he would sell some items but not others and good sellers seldom outnumbered the bad. When he went to golf shows to buy merchandise, he would talk with the vendors and other store buyers, but most of them were involved with very large, year-around operations. His club was rural, smaller, and seasonal. At last he decided to consult with a merchandiser to see what could be done to enhance his overall business potential.

Tammy Baker, the consultant, suggested she visit Jerry's location to get a better idea of his operation. She also asked Jerry to gather any sales data and inventory information from the previous season, which would allow her to examine trends and possible areas for development. Jerry told her he had never kept sales records, other than his daily sales figures. When Tammy visited the pro shop, she was able to see part of the problem by merely examining the merchandise that remained at the end of the season, by asking questions about what items Jerry originally had in inventory, and by reviewing purchase orders.

Tammy took notes throughout her examination of the pro-shop. The total profile of beginning inventory was as follows:

- *50 percent equipment—golf bags, clubs, head covers, towels, balls, tees*
  - Most of this merchandise can be easily reordered and carried over to next year if necessary.
  - Special orders compose the majority of sales in this category.
  - Typically generates his most profitable markups (little need to markdown).
  - Biggest competitors are catalog/on line companies.
- *20 percent men's apparel*
  - Pretty basic in styles and colors (not trendy).
  - Seems to sell well and selection of size ranges is very good.
  - Logo merchandise looks good and could probably be developed further.
  - Now has logo on shirts and caps only.

- *10 percent shoes for both men and women*
  - Has some samples and does most of his business by special order.
  - Good markup items.
  - Shoes are classic and can be carried over to next season.
- *20 percent women's apparel*
  - Area of greatest concern.
  - Currently carries no logo merchandise.

Further examination of women's sizes:

- *Size 3/4*
  - Most of what remains are fashion colors, stripes, and prints.
  - Short styles that remain are full, baggy and long.
  - Much had to be marked down to move it.
  - A dozen pieces remain at the end of the season.
- *Size 5/6*
  - Most colors remaining are fashion colors.
  - Styles remaining are varied; plaid shorts remain as the matching tops have sold.
  - Sold better than 3/4 but still have about a dozen remaining.
- *Size 7/8*
  - Total sales in this size looked better, but more was bought than in the two smaller sizes—about two dozen pieces left.
- *Size 9/10*
  - Sold well compared with other sizes and has a few pieces left—

Concepts and Cases in Retail and Merchandise Management

could probably have sold more if there was more inventory.

- **Size 11/12**
  - Again, fashion colors remain.
  - Styling of tops and bottoms are full cuts.
  - The shorts that remained tended to be shorter than regulation length on a tall figure.
  - Remaining tops tend to be sleeveless.
- **Size 13/14**
  - Has three dozen pieces remaining after big markdowns.
  - Same styling as 11/12 leftovers.
  - Jerry buys most of his merchandise at golf shows (which means golf brands and higher prices) and a considerable amount of this merchandise in prepacks from vendors. Many are packs of 18 units with sizes and colors predetermined. Jerry has an older clientele; apparently not many young women in this geographic area are golfers and those who do golf tend not to buy much at the pro shop (they're obviously purchasing golf apparel elsewhere). He sells no women's accessories.

Major Question

If you were this consultant, what changes would you recommend to Jerry related to his merchandise assortment?

Study Questions

1. What specific changes would you make in the sizing of the women's apparel?

2. Are there any buying strategies, including possible items for negotiation, that you would recommend to Jerry?

3. Would you expand the club logo business? If so, in what classifications?

Exercises

1. Visit a golf course or country club pro shop in your area and document the merchandise mix, prices, and unique aspects of the business.

2. Interview golfers and ask why they buy in a pro shop versus other retail options. Where do they buy most of their golf related merchandise and why? If they are not currently buying most of their merchandise from the pro shop, what would motivate them to do so?

3. Look online to see what golf apparel and merchandise is available to consumers. How might this alter the recommendations you make related to this case?

4. Develop guidelines that could be used by pro shop buyers to select garments appropriate for various sizes and ages. If you are not a golfer, what else might you want to do to find out more about the needs of various segments of the market?

Case 31

A COMPETITIVE DILEMMA: ADVANCE OR RETREAT?

Antigone Kotsiopulos and Molly Eckman,
Colorado State University

Ken Lincoln owns a clothing store in a Midwest rural community. Ranching and farming families within a 60-mile radius shop at his store, as do many of the 6,000 members of the community. Lincoln's Family Apparel is the only store of its kind in the community catering to the entire family. However, there are three women's specialty stores, two shoe stores, a western wear retailer, and a trendy apparel store catering to the youth market. Two general-merchandise stores carry limited clothing items as well. Summer brings thousands of tourists through the community as they head to the largest lake in the region, which is just ten miles north of town.

While Ken's business is good, he feels it could be better. He has a valuable Main Street location with ample parking and an effective, hard-working sales staff. Being his own best critic, Ken always looks at what is not up to par. He knows that in an effort to serve a wide range of family needs, he is carrying a little bit of everything using broad assortments of styles, colors, and sizes. He carries national brands but also looks for special purchases at market that

would be suitable for his price-conscious consumers. To be the full-service clothing retailer in the area, Ken carries men's, women's, and children's apparel and everything from undergarments to outerwear. This leads to a steady stream of markdown merchandise that attracts perpetual bargain hunters and reduced profits.

Ken's latest concern comes from a local chamber of commerce representative who verified that a large chain operation was looking at possible building sites in the community. Ken is familiar with the chain and knows it carries a broad assortment of brand-name clothing at reduced prices, as well as a variety of household items. Ken decided to seriously examine his own business being as unbiased as possible. He looked at all the facts and figures related to his business to objectively determine whether he would keep his business as is, narrow his merchandise assortment, or possibly relocate to another community.

Ken's figures from the previous business year are shown in Tables 5.5 and 5.6.

Major Question*

What general assessment and recommendations would you make of the situation after examining the data? (Calculate: stock-to-sales ratio, turnover, gross margin dollars and percent, shortage and markdown percentages.)

*Do not use the alternative solutions format for this case.

TABLE 5.5 Brand Name Merchandise

	Annual Sales ($)	Average Stock ($)	Annual Stock ($)	Cost of Goods sold ($)	Shortage ($)	Markdowns ($)
WOMEN'S APPAREL						
Accessories	8,887	2,279	29,627	3,560	249	1,564
Blouses/sweaters	40,221	22,345	290,484	19,306	1,006	9,774
Dresses	10,553	7,035	91,455	4,643	201	2,712
Slacks	8,705	6,696	87,048	3,656	157	2,403
Jeans	7,442	1,815	23,595	4,837	193	1,660
Skirts	4,378	3,127	40,651	1,839	70	1,173
Outerwear	3,615	1,247	16,211	1,746	69	1,038
Lingerie	4,083	1,167	15,171	2,050	102	890
MEN'S APPAREL						
Accessories	11,667	3,646	47,398	5,483	233	2,998
Shirts/sweaters	55,356	26,360	342,680	27,124	996	13,562
Slacks	65,422	18,172	236,236	34,019	1,374	16,355
Jeans	72,198	34,380	446,940	46,929	1,733	13,284
Outerwear/sport coats	12,321	4,928	64,064	6,161	234	2,698
Underwear	24,835	10,798	140,374	11,921	621	3,055
CHILDREN'S APPAREL						
Accessories	6,278	2,511	32,643	3,202	82	1,726
Shirts/blouses	25,384	11,035	143,455	12,184	584	7,615
Dresses	6,218	10,363	134,719	3,109	81	1,660
Slack/shorts	48,084	60,105	781,365	23,561	817	13,127
Outerwear	18,832	7,847	102,011	9,793	226	5,631
Underwear	20,745	5,186	67,418	9,750	187	4,875

Study Questions

1. Which department did best with branded merchandise, men's, women's, or children's?

2. Which department did best with generic label merchandise?

3. Which department and category of merchandise performed best overall?

4. How can a specialty store like Ken's compete with a large chain store if it comes to town?

Exercises

1. Visit a small retail operation and attempt to ascertain what product categories the retailer might be using and the percentage of stock in each category. (A) Interview the owner/manager to obtain actual categories

TABLE 5.6 Generic Label Merchandise

	Annual Sales ($)	Average Stock ($)	Annual Stock ($)	Cost of Goods sold ($)	Shortage ($)	Markdowns ($)
WOMEN'S APPAREL						
Accessories	9,261	2,437	31,681	2,964	204	1,510
Blouses/sweaters	53,687	26,843	348,959	21,474	966	11,864
Dresses	9,095	8,268	107,484	3,638	191	2,201
Slacks	5,924	3,949	51,337	2,488	53	1,499
Jeans	3,083	907	11,791	1,541	65	808
Skirts	3,506	2,062	26,806	1,473	46	873
Outerwear	4,273	1,378	17,914	1,923	64	1,141
Lingerie	3,008	912	11,856	1,053	57	596
MEN'S APPAREL						
Accessories	8,782	2,927	38,051	30,737	149	1,748
Shirts	56,629	22,651	294,463	23,784	849	11,552
Slacks	50,326	14,379	186,927	20,130	654	11,222
Jeans	63,887	16,381	212,953	31,944	1,342	10,924
Outerwear/sport coats	9,285	5,158	67,054	3,993	158	1,894
Underwear	21,054	10,527	136,851	7,799	463	2,737
CHILDREN'S APPAREL						
Accessories	8,935	4,964	64,532	3,574	80	2,234
Shirts	30,347	11,240	146,120	11,835	637	8,254
Dresses	7,483	9,354	121,602	3,517	60	1,856
Slack/shorts	55,194	55,194	717,522	24,837	773	15,509
Outerwear	20,452	5,843	75,959	8,181	143	5,461
Underwear	22,539	13,258	172,354	9,241	270	4,846

and percentage of stock in each. Compare and contrast your perceptions with the actual (if available). (B) With the owner/manager, discuss how much he or she uses classifications when buying and determining merchandise assortments. (C) Also, discuss the company's use of generic and branded merchandise. Which does he or she feel is more profitable and why?

2. Examine a community such as the one in which you live, where you grew up, or where you attend school. Is there market saturation with a particular type of store? Is there a void in a particular product type or category? Identify potential niches that offer further retail opportunities. Provide the background information and cues that lead you to your determination.

Case 32

IS THE PURCHASE WORTH THE RISK?

Judy K. Miler, Florida State University
Nancy J. Rabolt, San Francisco State University

Beverly Manners is the coat and suit buyer for ABC Bargain Stores in Kankakee, Illinois. It is a hard-hitting retail organization that features merchandise at low discount prices. The store's slogan is *ABC—Always Better and Cheaper.*

Beverly was a department store buyer for six years prior to her position with ABC and is fully experienced in working retail figures: she can plan, adjust, and achieve. She is a professional in every sense of the word.

Recently, she has been in a bind because of the unavailability of promotional merchandise suitable for the store's needs. The market has been depressed because of poor business; manufacturers have cut back on production so there are just not enough goods to go around and no quick reorders because of all the offshore manufacturers. The result has been that few manufacturers have disposable stock and the bargains have dried up because of supply and demand. Beverly has been looking everywhere for goods, and it does not look promising.

A few days ago, however, a manufacturer, who also happens to be an old friend, called her to advise her of the availability of promotional merchandise—stylish winter coats—which could rejuvenate her business considerably. She was very excited and went to tell her merchandise manager, Artie Lang, about the fantastic deal she was being offered. He knew she needed merchandise to promote—even though she was overstocked—so he advised her to fly to New York to check out those goods and the possibility of others. While in New York, she planned to see 15 to 20 other manufacturers for possible future promotions. "Perhaps," she thought, "if I planned ahead, the results will be better for my future needs."

She arrived in New York and immediately visited Link Brother's, her friend's firm. Inspection of the coats, an overrun made for a large mail-order firm, proved that they were indeed a great deal: 40 percent below original wholesale cost, fashionable, in great colors, and a complete size spread.

She thought it was a bonanza—just what the doctor ordered. There was one problem, however: Link Brothers will only sell the goods on the condition that the entire joblot of 2,500 garments is purchased. "That's a lot of merchandise," she mused, "but because we are in the middle of the season, they will probably sell with a short markup. The store needs the business, and this group can stimulate heavy traffic, so other areas will probably benefit as well." That evening she called Artie, relayed her good news, and outlined the details. Artie was impressed with Beverly's intensity and desire to perk up the business, but he had strong doubts about such a large quantity purchase.

"In the first place," he said, "2,500 coats are an awful lot of garments, which represents a big investment of $100,000. Second, business is poor, and your actual BOM stock is 15 percent over your plan. Finally, if the sale is a disaster—and there certainly is no such thing as a sure winner—you'll be in deeper trouble stockwise. Can't you talk Link into a partial purchase with an option to buy the remainder? When sales are realized we can run a fast promotional sale and establish a rate of sale, then unload all of them if we're successful. He's your friend; press him."

"I've tried that," she replied. "I've tried every possible tactic. He's anxious to sell, and he knows he can get rid of the goods in one shipment to any number of stores. He called me first out of friendship, thinking I probably wouldn't want to pass this purchase up."

"Beverly, I see your point, but good business practice dictates that you shouldn't take such a huge risk. You are overbought and don't have a dime of open-to-buy, let alone $100,000 with one vendor."

Furiously, Beverly snapped back, "I just can't believe you won't let me buy the merchandise; you sure aren't a risk-taker."

"Sorry," he responded, "you'll just have to keep looking for a smaller deal."

After hanging up the phone, Beverly was quite depressed and angry. She has the chance to buy the perfect promotional merchandise, which could make her season, but she can't get Artie's approval. She knows her store's stock position but feels it could be greatly reduced with a successful promotional ad. "That darned merchandise plan. Does one have to live and die by it?" she asked herself. "Plans are made to be revised," she thought, "they are not supposed to be set in stone!"

Beverly, being a fighter, does not give up easily. She prevailed on her friend to give her a 24-hour option on the promotional merchandise, which he did, and she promised to call him after returning home. She is now on the plane heading home and is planning a strong case to overcome Artie's objections.

Major Question

If you were Beverly, what approach would you plan to obtain some open-to-buy from your boss for the purchase?

Study Questions

1. Should Beverly, or any buyer, create OTB for additional purchases when she is overbought? How would you suggest this be done?

2. What controls and/or policies do you think ABC should institute to avoid further gross departmental overstock positions?

Case 33

THE PLANNING IMPASSE

Judy K. Miler, Florida State University
Nancy J. Rabolt, San Francisco State University

About four months ago, the Midwest Department Store in Sheboygan, Wisconsin, hired a new divisional merchandise manager, Richard Blum, who had a great history at Marshall Field's in Chicago before they were bought by Macy's and renamed. He was assigned to the women's apparel departments.

The store had brought in merchandise consultants prior to hiring Richard to determine ways to increase the ready-to-wear volume that was not up to comparable stores. The recommendations included the goal to increase turnover, which ranged from four to a little less than five times per year. This was below the standard of other stores in the region devoted to moderately priced merchandise. One of the strategies suggested was to set up an advertising program featuring specially priced merchandise.

Shortly after he arrived, Richard held a meeting with the six buyers on his staff and outlined his plans. He said, "We are shooting for a minimum turnover of six times with a stock-to-sales ratio of two to one. With additional advertising, thorough shopping of the market, and good vendor relations, we should be able to make many good buys and pass them on to our customers."

On July 14, Marjorie Porter, the accessories buyer, was with Richard at the weekly buyer review meeting and presented her merchandise plan (as seen in Table 5.7). Richard scanned the plan and commented: This plan is okay, but the sales are increased only 10 percent despite twice as many ads, improved displays, and strong store programs. I'd judge that a 10 percent increase would be a pretty poor estimate in view of the cost and efforts to stimulate real volume."

Marjorie was taken aback. She did not understand his concern and felt that a 10 percent increase was aggressive enough. She thought Richard was overplaying the recommendations of the consulting firm. She defended her plan to him, explaining, "A plan is a flexible tool. If conditions warrant additional increases in sales and open-to-buy, the plan can be changed later. I can't see any reason for being unrealistic and for projecting unobtainable figures."

"Listen," Richard responded, "modest increases indicate to management a lack of confidence and motivation, and I don't want to project that. I also feel that you won't be under sufficient pressure to top the planned figures. My philosophy is that pressure helps realize goals."

Marjorie retorted, "If I submit high figures, I leave myself vulnerable to downward revision and high markdowns, and to me that makes me look worse than exceeding sales. So, I'm not going to look bad, and I don't want to play an unfair game—period."

Richard was surprised that Marjorie was standing her ground. He had never before been challenged by a buyer not to do what he was asking. He did not expect this response. Since his arrival, this was his first

TABLE 5.7 Marjorie's Six-Month Plan

	Aug.	Sept.	Oct.	Nov.	Dec.	Jan.	Total
SALES							
LY (actual)	90,000	100,000	70,000	90,000	120,000	60,000	530,000
Plan	99,000	110,000	80,000	99,000	132,000	66,000	586,000
RETAIL STOCK							
LY (actual)	225,000	250,000	175,000	225,000	300,000	150,000	1,325,000
Plan	198,000	220,000	160,000	198,000	264,000	132,000	1,172,000

LY=Last year

real encounter with Marjorie, and he had not established a track record at the store, so he felt vulnerable. He was trying to win over the buyers and impress management with his business knowledge and management skills. He simply could not afford an impasse at this early stage; the results could do him no good and might even make him look ineffective as a manager.

Major Question

What do you think Richard should do in regard to Marjorie's refusal to increase her plan even more?

Study Questions

1. Who do you think should make the final decision in setting the sales plan? Why?

2. Do you agree or disagree with Richard's response to Marjorie that "modest increases indicate to management a lack of confidence and motivation"?

Exercise

Using the numbers provided, create a revised plan that would increase Marjorie's plan so that Richard would find it more acceptable.

CHAPTER DISCUSSION QUESTIONS

1. Discuss planning as a merchandise control, distinguishing between the three major types of merchandise planning. What part do standards play in retail control?

2. What are the five sequential steps in merchandise planning? Explain exactly what is involved with these planning steps.

3. What direct role does merchandising play in retail profit? Be specific in your explanation.

4. Compare unit and dollar planning. Why are both equally important?

5. What are the advantages of modifying merchandise plans? What are the disadvantages? Justify your opinions with examples from cases in this chapter.

6. Identify and discuss the internal and external sources of information that may be used in determining what merchandise retailers should purchase from vendors.

7. Discuss the major technological applications that are used in merchandise planning, buying, and control. What are the benefits?

Sourcing

CHAPTER OBJECTIVES

- Examine the challenges and opportunities of domestic and international sourcing.
- Differentiate between centralized and decentralized buying.
- Distinquish between methods of buying origination and types of orders.
- Explain the use and importance of buying offices and markets.
- Emphasize the importance of careful merchandise source selection.
- Examine the interaction of technology at the manufacturing level.

*T*here are many sources and suppliers to meet the needs of manufacturers and retailers alike. Understanding who the target customer is helps to guide a retailer to the best resource for goods to supply the customer. Today, manufacturers have become their own retailers, and retailers have become their own manufacturers, but procuring the materials to create the merchandise is still often an arduous task with all the choices available. Also today, technology plays a major role at the manufacturing or sourcing level. Both domestic and international sourcing offer challenges and opportunities that must be considered when determining where to buy. Other helpful criteria for determining the best selection of goods for the best price, along with the best supplier, include (1) the appropriateness of merchandise;

(2) the policies of the supplier (i.e., delivery, specs, distribution, advertising, pricing, terms, and so forth); and (3) timing. There are advantages and disadvantages to all sourcing methods. The pros and cons must be weighed against the company objectives to determine just how to supply the desired merchandise and what to supply. Often the sourcing decision may be quite difficult because of the many choices and factors involved in the decision making. But in many instances, cost advantage is the deciding factor, when all other factors are equal.

RESOURCES AND SOURCING

After retailers have planned their needs (i.e., planned purchases), they must then begin the search for the procurement of merchandise. In today's world there is an extensive selection of merchandise available to the retailer globally no matter what the classification or category. The number of available sources is so vast and their locations are so varied that it is impossible to list all of them—let alone shop all the resources. The Internet has enabled anyone in the world to purchase from anyone else in the world. Today, manufacturing concerns have proven that incorporating technology and linking to their customer results in faster and better service.

Sourcing is the term used to describe the process of determining how and where goods will be procured. The selection of types of merchandise from manufacturers and contractors involves decision making on the part of the retailer as to which resource would be the best from which to purchase. Retailers may select from a variety of types of resources, of which there are several major kinds. These include: manufacturers, wholesalers, middlemen, and cooperatives. **Manufacturers** offer goods for sale that they have produced. Manufacturers are also referred to as **vendors, suppliers,** or **resources,** and these terms often are used interchangeably. **Wholesalers** are resellers of merchandise. Normally, wholesalers buy merchandise in large quantities to break down and then sell the goods in smaller quantities. **Middlemen** is a term used to describe agents who process goods in one way or another from the manufacturer to the retail distributor. For example, a manufacturer produces a garment and does not do the finishing or packaging but sends the garment to another company (the middleman) for these steps. After finishing and packaging the garment, the product is then shipped directly to the retailer. A wholesaler can also be a middleman, as is a drop shipper or broker. **Drop shippers** take title to merchandise, but do not take actual possession of the goods. A drop shipper just arranges shipment of the goods to the retailer. **Brokers** are middlemen who help negotiate business between the buyer (retailer) and seller (manufacturer). **Jobbers** sell closeouts and job lots. Others may be able to supply a retailer's needs depending on the timing and status of merchandise that they hold, as a major vendor like Levi Strauss would. Levi's sells regular merchandise preseason, reorders, and promotional goods in season, and even closeouts and off-price goods at the end of a season.

Today, many retailers are vertically integrated and produce their own merchandise by manufacturing goods in-house under their own private label. Label names are created to identify and gain recognition by consumers for that label. It is interesting to note that many of these retailer brands (or store brands) become known in the minds of consumers as major brands, often competing with major manufacturer's brand names. Examples are JCPenney's Arizona Jean Company and Aeropostale, which began as a private label for Macy's but then became a branded label and specialty store chain (www.aeropostale.com). When a retailer also manufactures merchandise or vice versa, the company is referred to as vertically integrated, because they are performing more than one function in the marketing channel. (See Chapter 2 for examples of vertically integrated companies.)

How and where private-label merchandise is produced varies from company to company. For example, retailers who rely totally on private-label merchandise, do so primarily by manufacturing offshore. They have specialists, however, in their offshore locations to oversee the smooth operation of business.

Most apparel production today is done offshore and contracting the production of merchandise is a common method of obtaining apparel by both the manufacturers and/or the manufacturer/retailers. A **contractor** is an independent producer who performs aspects of manufacturing, such as sewing, cutting, and finishing. Whether or not to choose a contractor that is domestic or international, exclusive or not, however, must be determined by the manufacturer or retailer who is searching for goods. An **exclusive contractor** is a supplier that only works for a particular company. Exclusive contracting can help or hurt the company a contractor is providing for, or even the contractor itself. For example, dealing exclusively with a producer, a company can be assured of continued consistency and resulting quality. If, however, the contractor is the only producer being used and that contractor runs into trouble, then the company relying on the contractor must also deal with the consequences of that trouble, which very often can hurt its business. Similarly, if something happens to a business that a contractor is dependent on, then the contractor may suffer consequences as well.

The use of key resources by the retailer is one method of containing and narrowing the resource structure. A benefit of this method is that it enables vendors and retailers to be better business partners than would be possible if retailers had no vendor consistency and different resources were used from season to season.

Figure 6.1 A computer-aided design (CAD) system. This scene shows the pattern layout (or marker making) on the monitor and plotter. Also shown is a skilled worker digitizing the pattern pieces into the computer for grading (sizing) and marker making.

The vendor matrix presented in Chapter 5 is one method retailers use to concentrate on purchasing from key resources.

TECHNOLOGY AND SOURCING

Technology can play an important and often critical role in the production and delivery of goods. Quick response (QR) and just-in-time (JIT) are terms that describe technologically based strategies that help cut the time from the production of the goods to the sale of the product. Technological linkages between the producer and the retailer speed communication and help to reduce the lead time for receiving merchandise. As mentioned in Chapter 5, the manufacturer and retailer are often linked through EDI systems that are designed to serve them both well. **Lead time** refers to the amount of time that lapses between the placement of an order and the arrival of the merchandise at the retail establishment. Today, it is critical to obtain merchandise when it is needed, and technology is a major contributor in doing so.

Computer-aided design (CAD) and computer-aided manufacturing (CAM) have enabled manufacturers to significantly speed up the production process from initial design to grading and marker making. Controlled by computer, lasers for specialized cutting and robotics are being utilized to reduce the use of manual labor.

Agile manufacturing, incorporating modular production rather than the traditional piece goods line method, allows for special orders at the last minute without disruption. Similarly, **mass customization** allows for individualized sizing to be incorporated into regular mass production.

Levi Strauss takes this a bit further, offering a collection of men's and women's jeans, under the Levi's registered (Capital E) TM line, which is made by hand but standard sized, allowing each garment to be an exclusive, unique item. Some better apparel manufacturers, such as Brooks Brothers, also offer their customers one-of-a-kind, made-to-measure merchandise. Technology has made it feasible for computers to quickly choose one of over thousands of possible combinations of variables to arrive at a "custom fit."

Quick response (QR) shortens the pipeline of getting a product from its conception to the retail consumer by capitalizing on EDI. Quick response was developed as a strategy to fight imports because domestic manufacturers have the advantage of proximity to the marketplace over the offshore manufacturer and therefore have the capability to deliver faster. It also serves as a competitive advantage for domestic manufacturers competing with each other. However, today the technology is used by offshore vendors as well. QR is effective if manufacturers and retailers are true partners, in which retail sales data are shared with the manufacturer who then can arrange for **automatic replenishment** of stock. For example, LeviLink is a program offered to retailers selling Levi's to maintain a model stock program, referred to as VMI, for vendor managed inventory, where stock is replaced when sold. This gets the goods to the customers when they want them—fast.

Just-in-time (JIT) is a concept used in manufacturing to lessen costly inventories. Communications and partnerships with suppliers enable fabric and other supplies to be delivered to the manufacturing site "just-in-time" for production. *Case 34, Safeguard Limitations* illustrates a problem that can happen with this technology when an importer utilizes this concept a little too closely and finds the quota category closed.

DOMESTIC AND INTERNATIONAL SOURCING

Merchandise can be procured domestically or internationally. **Domestic sourcing** is the purchasing of merchandise within the borders of the United States. **International sourcing** is the process of buying goods **offshore,** from countries other than the United States. Buying merchandise offshore and bringing it into another country to sell refers to importing or purchasing **imports.** Both types of sourcing have pros and cons, and the retailer must weigh them before deciding how and where to source goods. Price, quality, and availability are some of the many factors that must be regarded when evaluating whom to use as a resource. Today more and more retailers and manufacturers are going to offshore production because of costs (see *Case 34*). The next two sections examine domestic and international sourcing.

Domestic Sourcing

Domestic sourcing can be either advantageous or problematic to the retailer. For example, a faster lead time is usually available with domestic goods, as is more assurance of getting exactly what was ordered. Unfortunately, the cost of goods in apparel is often higher (due to higher labor costs) for domestic merchandise than imports. Even when only domestic suppliers are used, there are factors to compare vendors for selection, such as quality, delivery, and cost. Also, close proximity to the source does not always protect against problems. For example, miscommunication and the resultant errors can occur whether two parties are in the same city or on different continents. Similar merchandise is obtainable from two domestic sources, and a department store buyer must determine which of the two suppliers would be the most profitable to use in *Case 35, Treadwell's: The Buyer's Decision*.

International Sourcing

International sourcing is used to obtain a healthy markup for the retailer and is almost universally done today for apparel. Figure 6.2 shows the countries and areas of the world that provide these imports. Although there are risks and challenges that have to be met, the major advantage to sourcing overseas is a cost advantage and markup, which often result in increased profit. Imports, at one time viewed as inferior and of lesser quality than domestic merchandise, generally are no longer viewed as such, although quality still can be a major problem. The lead time needed for delivery is often longer for imports than domestic merchandise. Other matters, such as government regulation or the politics of a country, can also add to the complexity of determining who and where the best resource is. In *Case 36, Where Will Yongmei Go?*, a Chinese manufacturer has to work within government policies and a drop in government financial support to manufacturers, which results in increased costs and a multitude of problems for the manufacturer that may keep him from staying in business. Trade sanctions and quota safeguards may limit availability of goods, and shipping costs and/or tariff rates may add more cost to goods than make it reasonable. Also, today the ethics of producing in certain countries

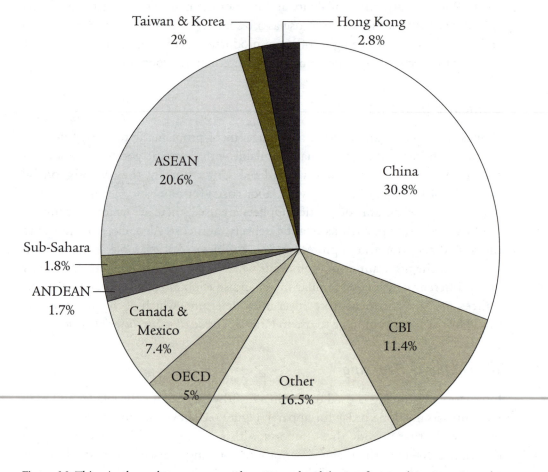

U.S. Apparel Imports by Country

Figure 6.2 This pie chart shows a country-by-country breakdown of apparel imports into the United States. CBI includes 25 countries in the Caribbean; OECD includes most developed countries (these data exclude OECD members Japan, Mexico, and South Korea); Sub-Sahara includes 48 Sub-Saharan African countries; ASEAN includes 10 Southeast Asian countries; ANDEAN includes four countries in the Andean Trade Preference Act (source: http://otexa.ita.doc.gov/msrintro.htm).

are paramount in many consumers' and manufacturers' decision making. (See Chapter 11 for this discussion.)

Quotas and Tariffs

The limit to the number of units of specified merchandise permitted to be brought into a country for consumption during a specific period of time is called a **quota.** Quotas can be a hindrance for both manufacturers and retailers. For example, if a quota for specific merchandise is filled, no further entries of that type of merchandise into the country is allowed for that year. Therefore, even if retailers and customers have a desire for more of these particular goods, they will be unobtainable and those sales that could have been realized will be lost. Similarly, if a manufacturer wants to sell goods in a particular country and the quota category for those goods is closed, these goods cannot be imported. Companies can check quota levels for various categories online at www.otexa.ita.doc.gov.

The concept of **free trade** (no barriers to trade) is subscribed to by most business and government officials. In 1994, as a result of the extended Uruguay Rounds of talks under **GATT (General Agreement on Tariffs and Trade),** the **World Trade Organization (WTO)** was formed. The WTO facilitates trade agreements and serves as a permanent forum for members to address trade relations. **The Multifiber Agreement (MFA),** which outlined quotas by category and by country under GATT, was replaced with the Agreement on Textiles and Clothing (ATC) under WTO. With the phaseout of MFA through 2005, quotas were eliminated for WTO countries, leaving tariffs (discussed below) as the main form of protection of domestic goods against most apparel imports. However, there is a provision for temporary **safeguards** (additional quotas imposed after 2005) if certain categories are disrupted. Sometimes safeguards are initiated by WTO members. *Case 34* discusses the purpose of these restraints and presents a situation where a manufacturer has finished product and a closed safeguard quota category.

A visa may be required when importing from certain countries. A **visa** is a document from the exporting country guaranteeing country of origin and is a way for the exporting country to monitor the amount of its exports to the United States.

Tariffs also complicate importing merchandise for the manufacturer and retailer. A **tariff** (also known as **duty**) is a special tax, paid to the government, placed on imported merchandise that adds to the cost of goods. Two common types are as follows:

- **Specific,** which is a rate of duty that is based on a set amount per each unit imported, such as $1 per dress.
- **Ad valorem,** which is a rate of duty that is based on a percentage of dutiable value, such as 6 percent of the value of the shipment.

The **U.S. Harmonized Tariff Schedule (USHTS)** itemizes all products imported from other countries that are subject to tariff. (This itemization can be found online at www.usitc.gov.) There are many special trade agreements made between the U.S. government and other countries that provide free or low tariff provisions. One such agreement, the North American Free Trade Agreement (NAFTA), which went into effect in 1994, eliminated tariffs and other trade barriers among the United States, Canada, and Mexico. This was followed by the Central America Free Trade Agreement (CAFTA), an effort to unify all of North, Central, and South America in free trade. Others include the African Growth and Opportunity Act (AGOA), the Bahrain Free Trade Agreement, the Israel Free Trade Agreement, and many others. It is important for buyers to be aware of these agreements and for companies to work with Customs brokers who know the specific regulations. The U.S. **Customs and Border Protection** department (CBP) oversees imports to the United States involving quota safeguards, tariffs, and counterfeits. Its major roles are to collect revenue and to ensure that the trade laws and sanctions that the U.S. government legislates are upheld. These efforts help to ensure that the economic and political goals of the government are met.

Understanding import law is complex and time-consuming. Manufacturers and retailers who are involved in importing need to clearly understand the policies and procedures so that they can work within the law and work closely with an import broker whose job is to know the complexity of the law and to advise the importer. The paperwork accompanying imported merchandise (and sometimes the actual merchandise) is inspected by CBP to ensure that the importer has complied with the law and has honestly declared those goods that are being imported into the country. If the law is not upheld, or if there has been any dishonesty or errors, serious repercussions may result. These may include delay of deliveries, confiscation of merchandise, and the imposing of fines and/or penalties. **Embargos** also limit the items imported into a country: These legal bans on trade with certain countries may prevent a company from obtaining exactly what they need or want.

THE CHALLENGES OF SELECTING SOURCES

Even with the duties, shipping costs, and complications of imports, they are still often highly competitive with domestic goods or hold a true advantage. Today, most customers look for cost advantages above other advantages, so in many cases, they purchase the less-expensive imports over domestic goods.

Choosing between domestic or offshore resources can often be difficult because of all the factors that must be considered. Sometimes the political situation in a country may cause difficulties and uncertainty of getting the merchandise desired. Even more difficult for some retailers and manufacturers is deciding between countries to

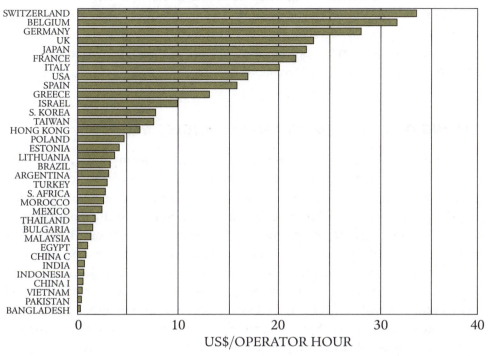

LABOR COST TEXTILE INDUSTRY 2007

US$/OPERATOR HOUR

Figure 6.3 This chart shows labor cost comparisons of many countries around the world.
Source: www.wernerinfotex.com

use as a source due to the potential problems that may arise. In *Case 37, The Saudi Arabian Sample Situation,* apparel samples to be shown to a major retailer are manufactured in a country against which the receiving country has an embargo, creating problems in entry to the country as well as for sale of the items.

Often the cost of goods and humanitarian concerns must be considered in resource selection. In many situations, rising costs and the need for more profit is the major deciding factor of where to source. The issue of sweatshop labor—and even child and slave labor—in certain countries has raised public concern about the true cost of goods at the expense of exploitation of labor. Many are objecting to the low retail price of much imported apparel, due to the appalling conditions and the pittance workers are paid. (More ethical matters related to retail and manufacturing may be found in Chapter 11.) Figure 6.3 shows sharp contrasts of labor costs in the textile industries around the world. The cost of textiles is an important component of a garment's total cost.

The choice of where and from whom to source could be an elective decision, or it could be imposed upon the business by another party. For example, if a vendor can no longer provide a retailer's needs as a result of changing the way in which the business is done, the retailer must look for a replacement resource—based solely on the need for specific merchandise.

BUYING ORIGINATION AND MERCHANDISE NEEDS

Accessibility and availability of merchandise in different forms (such as quantities and assortments) are also factors for the merchant to consider in sourcing. The type of merchandise desired and/or reason for the retailer's purchase often narrows down the selection of resources, what type of source to use, and where the buying should originate. A specific determination of needs can assist in the method of buying (centralized versus decentralized), the origination of buying (buying office, market, or direct), place to buy (manufacturers, middleman, or broker), and type of ordering to be done (regular versus off-price). For example, a retailer needs merchandise for a special sale promotion in November. Luckily, this particular retailer can sell Spring merchandise in November because of the geographical location of the store. Just the fact that sale Spring merchandise is desired—for November selling—can help the retailer determine who the best vendor would be. Such factors as type of merchandise and the styles wanted could also help further narrow down and target the search.

Types of Orders

Different types of merchandise orders can be placed to cover the specific needs of a retailer, and often the origination of the merchandise is determined by placement of different types of orders. A retailer can purchase merchandise by way of several types of orders:

- **Regular orders** are placed for goods purchased in season as part of a regular line of a manufacturer's merchandise.
- **Exclusive orders** are those placed for merchandise that can only be sold to one particular store or buyer. Exclusive merchandise is usually a special arrangement between vendor and retailer.

- **Off-price orders** are placed for merchandise that is purchased at a price below the regular line price. Usually, this is regular merchandise being sold later in the season or is surplus merchandise.
- **Job lots** are groups of merchandise that are odds and ends of remaining styles, which a manufacturer wants to sell. Often they are broken sizes, colors, and/or styles and are sold at a considerable discount as a group.
- **Prepacks** are assortments of merchandise that are chosen according to a manufacturer's or retailer's direction. These predetermined choices direct that a certain amount of sizes and/or colors of a style or styles are shipped to the retailer.
- **Closeouts** are an assortment of merchandise that is left over from a seasonal line. Usually closeouts include all remaining items and are sold at a discount.
- **Reorders** are purchases placed on merchandise that have been purchased at least once before by the retailer. Normally merchandise is reordered if it has sold out and has further demand (and there is the possibility of receiving it in a timely manner). However, in *Case 47, Good Results No New Business,* in Chapter 7, to the frustration of a sales manager, a buyer does not communicate the reasons for not purchasing more goods despite the great selling success of a new product. Reorders are more common with basic merchandise than with fashion items.
- **Promotional orders** are placed for goods at a better-than-regular manufacturer's cost. These are often special purchases from vendors that can be promoted by the retailer at a savings to the customer.
- **Open orders** allow a manufacturer the discretion of shipping merchandise when deemed necessary, rather than locking into a set delivery date. Open orders may also specify a dollar amount that must be purchased, but not always the specific styles, sizes, or colors.
- **Advance orders** commit the retailer to a long-term delivery because of the nature of the merchandise or the needs of the retailer. Often, imported goods and seasonal merchandise require advance orders.
- **Back orders** are full or partial orders that are still outstanding (i.e., not shipped) by the manufacturer but will be completed when the merchandise (or the balance of the merchandise) is available.
- **Blanket orders** are those that do not have specific information spelled out but that commit the retailer to a certain number of units or dollars that will be detailed at a later date.

CENTRALIZED AND DECENTRALIZED BUYING

How a retailer originates the buying and placing of orders (purchasing of goods) is also a decision that has to be made. This is usually dependent on where the merchandising division of the company is located. The two methods of buying are centralized and decentralized. **Centralized buying** entails focusing all the purchasing activities in one place, where it is initiated and overseen by one individual or group. Many large retailing chains use centralized buying exclusively. **Decentralized buying** centers the purchasing activities at the local or retail-outlet level. This method of buying is used less frequently by large retailers; some companies like JCPenney use both methods because they feel that better purchases are made when the buyer considers the specific needs and wants of the local or regional customer. Deciding whether or not to strictly utilize centralized buying is the quandary for a chain store president in *Case 38, Should All the Eggs Go in One Basket?*

Buying Offices

Buying offices provide yet another way to supply a retailer with merchandise. Traditionally, a **resident buying office (RBO)** has been an organization located in a given fashion market that serves as a retailer's market representative for the procurement of merchandise. Years ago, buying offices purchased merchandise for their member retailers and served no other purpose. This is not necessarily true today. Many serve all the varied needs of a retailer. The two major types of resident buying offices are store-owned and independent. **Store-owned buying offices** are those that are owned and operated by a retail firm or group of retail stores. The **independent buying office** is owned and operated separately from its client retailers. Its functions can also include forecasting, finance, personnel, advertising, and promotion, as well as providing consultation services and the manufacture of private-label merchandise. Just as there were major shakedowns of stored and mail-order retailers in the 1980s and 1990s, so were there parallel consolidations and buyouts of buying offices. An example is when IRS (Independent Retail Service) merged with Doneger in the 1980s. Recently, Tobé trend forecasters, one of the largest and oldest in the business, and Here & There, another forecasting company, merged with the Doneger Group in order to strengthen all the organizations, continuing the move toward consolidation into bigger, stronger companies.

A variety of buying offices are now available that serve almost any type of retailer and their needs. From women's to children's, regular to off-price, bridge to opening price-point lines, men's clothing to women's sportswear—there is a

Figure 6.4 Member buyers working with Doneger, the largest U.S. resident buying office. In addition to buying, RBOs can assist retailers in forecasting, finance, advertising and promotion, as well as many other services.

buying office to fill all their needs. Buying offices can help small and large retailers alike, because of the numerous services offered. Sometimes retailers turn all their buying over to a buying office for economic reasons, as is considered in *Case 38*.

Markets

From a retail and merchandising perspective, markets have several definitions that can cause confusion. A store manager or a market researcher may refer to a "market" as the target customer group (i.e., the target market). To the buyer and manufacturer, however, the **market** is the actual physical place where the retail buyer and seller come together to purchase or sell goods and services. This marketplace may be at a merchandise mart or trade show, or even a specific city site as in New York City. A market may also refer to a time when buyers and manufacturers come together, such as the Spring market.

Merchandise marts are trade centers built to house manufacturers' representatives and provide a center for retailers and manufacturers to come together to do

Figure 6.5 The WWD MAGIC marketplace covers over 250,000 square feet in Las Vegas.

business. Major marts are located in such metropolitan areas as Dallas, Atlanta, and Chicago. Secondary marts are located in such smaller cities as Charlotte, Pittsburgh, and Seattle. Costs associated with a major mart's showrooms are of concern to a licensee (manufacturer) in *Case 39, Licensing Pitfalls.*

Trade shows are a means for buyer and seller to meet and do business. Existing facilities are used temporarily to house a trade show and its exhibits, often at convention centers, fairgrounds, or hotels. Figures 6.5 and 6.6 are interior shots from two major apparel trade shows. In addition to trade shows, retailers can also source merchandise directly with vendors, working with them in their headquarters and/or production facilities.

Today's global marketplace is serviced by **international markets,** located all over the world. Paris, London, Milan, and Tokyo are just a few of the larger international markets. **Domestic markets** refer to those in the continental United States, ssuch as New York City, which also happens to be a major international market. Localized **regional markets,** which may provide a mart, serve the U.S. retailer as a g eographical convenience. Atlanta, Dallas, and Los Angeles are examples of regional markets.

Market calendars publicize the dates (called **market weeks**) and locations of trade shows and markets that are available. Markets coincide with the seasonal delivery of

Figure 6.6 A view of the floor at the CPD Dusseldorf Trade Show.

goods by the manufacturer and are set up according to type of merchandise. For example, there are menswear and womenswear markets. The traditional apparel planning seasons of Spring, Summer, Fall, and Winter have been broken down further for more frequent availability and purchasing of goods, because today's fashion customer is looking for newer looks more often. However, there are at least five standard seasonal markets for apparel: Spring, Summer, Transition/Early Fall, Fall, and Holiday/Resort. See Figure 6.7 for a market calendar and trade show listing.

The decision to use a specific market depends on the type of retailer and who the target customer is. Some fashion apparel manufacturers break their line releases into further seasonal market time periods that coincide with such specific holidays or events as Back-to-School and President's Day Sales. Liz Claiborne, for example, and fast-fashion retailers such as H&M and Uniqlo release merchandise on a monthly basis, because they feel that their customer wants new merchandise more frequently than the traditional seasons.

The National Retail Federation (NRF), a major organization of retailers in the United States, publishes an annual retail calendar in *Stores* magazine at the end of each year to aid the retailer in shopping the markets and meeting other specific needs. The calendar lists all monthly events that are related to retail—from regional and international market dates and sites to trade shows such as MAGIC

DNR Events Calendar

January

ASI
01/03/2008 - 01/05/2008
Orlando Convention Center
Orlando, FL
http://www.asishow.com/Orlando
877.274.7469

CHILDREN'S CLUB OF NY
01/06/2008 - 01/08/2008
Javits Convention Center
NEW YORK, NY
http://www.enkshows.com
2127598055

MIAMI MEN'S & BOYS
01/06/2008 - 01/08/2008
Sheraton Mart Plaza Hotel &
Convention Center
Miami, FL
http://www.sunshinestateexhibitors.com
5619676040

THE NILES SHOW
01/08/2008 - 01/10/2008
The White Eagle
Niles, IL
http://www.nilesshow.com
630.584.9513

PITTI UOMO
01/09/2008 - 01/12/2008
Fortezza da Basso
Florence, Italy
http://www.pittimmagine.com
0030553693224

SURF EXPO
01/10/2008 - 01/13/2008
Orange County Convention Center
Orlando, FL
http://www.surfexpo.com
6787817978

**DENVER INT'L WESTERN/
ENGLISH APPAREL & EQUIPMENT
SHOW**
01/11/2008 - 01/15/2008
451 E.58 th Avenue
Denver, CO
http://www.denver-wesa.com
3032951040

Direction
01/15/2008 - 01/17/2008
Penn Plaza Pavilion 401 Seventh
Avenue
New York, NY
http://www.directionshow.com
9737615598

PRINTSOURCE NEW YORK
01/15/2008 - 01/17/2008
Hotel Pennsylvania 401 Seventh
Avenue
New York, NY
http://www.printsourcenewyork.com
2123521005

SEATTLE TREND SHOW (PNAA)
01/15/2008 - 01/18/2008
Qwest Field Event Center 800
Occidental Avenue South
Seattle, WA
http://www.seattletrendsshow.com/showdates
2067679200

BREAD & BUTTER
01/16/2008 - 01/18/2008
Fira Barcelona Avenida Rena M
Christina s/n
Barcelona, Spain
http://www.breadand butter.com
0114930400440

IMPRINTED SPORTSWEAR SHOW ISS
01/18/2008 - 01/20/2008
The Long Beach Convention Center
300 East Ocean Boulevard
Long Beach, CA
http://www.issshows.com
8009338735

TRANOI HOMME
01/18/2008 - 01/21/2008
Palais de la Bourse
Paris, France
http://www.tranoi.com
0113153018496

BLUE NEW YORK
01/20/2008 - 01/22/2008
Pier 92
New York, NY
http://www.EKNshows.com
2127598055

COLLECTIVE
01/20/2008 - 01/22/2008
Pier 94
New York, NY
http://www.EKNshows.com
2127598055

NORTHSTAR FASHION
01/20/2008 - 01/22/2008
Minneapolis Merchandise Center 1300
Nucolette Mall
Minneapolis, MN
http://www.northstarfashion.com
6123335219

CAPSULE
01/21/2008 - 01/23/2008
Angel Orensanz Foundation Center
172 Norfolk Street
New York, NY
http://www.capsuleshow.com
2122068310

PROJECT NEW YORK
01/21/2008 - 01/23/2008
7 World Trade Center
New York, NY
http://www.projectshows.com
2129516787

TEXWORLD
01/22/2008 - 01/24/2008
Javits Convention Center 655 West
34th Street
New York, NY
http://www.texworldusa.com
77709848016

OUTDOOR RETAILER
01/23/2008 - 01/26/2008
Salt Palace Convention Center 100 S.
West Temple, Salt Lake City, UT
http://www.outdoorretailer.com
9493768155

WHO'S NEXT
01/24/2008 - 01/27/2008
23 Rue Du Maille
Paris, France
http://www.whosnext.com/Whosnext
33140137474

**DALLAS MEN'S & BOYS MARKET
CENTER**
01/24/2008 - 01/27/2008
2050 North Stemmons Freeway
Dallas, TX
http://www.dallasmarketcenter.com
2146556100

ASR (ACTION SPORTS RETAILER)
01/24/2008 - 01/26/2008
San Diego Convention Center
San Diego, CA
http://www.ASRbiiz.com
9493768144

AGENDA
01/24/2008 - 01/26/2008
San Diego Concourse 202 C Street
San Diego, CA
http://www.agendachows.com
323.653.0066

AMERICA'S MART ALPHA
01/26/2008 - 01/29/2008
250 Spring Street NW
Atlanta, GA
http://www.americasmart.com
4042203000

MERCEDES BENZ FASHION WEEK
01/27/2008 - 01/31/2008
Postbanhof Berlin Mitte
Berlin, Germany
http://www.mercedes-benzfashionweek
berlin.com

PITTI FILATI
01/30/2008 - 02/01/2008
Forteza da Basso
Florence, Italy
http://www.pittimmagine.com
00390553693224

February

MERCEDES BENZ FASHION WEEK
02/01/2008 - 02/08/2008
Bryany Park Tents Sixth Avenue at
41st Street
New York, NY
http://www.mbfashionweek.com/newyork
6468712400

**DALLAS MEN'S & BOYS MARKET
CENTER**
02/02/2008 - 02/02/2008
2050 North Stemmons Freeway
Dallas, TX
http://www.dallasmarketcenter.com
2146556100

TRAFIK SOUTH BEACH MAIMI
02/03/2008 - 02/05/2008
Maimi Beach Convention Center 1901
Convention Center Drive

Figure 6.7 DNR international menswear trade show calendar for January through March.

Maimi Beach, FL
http://www.trafiktradeshows.com
8878723451

FASHION NORTH
02/03/2008 - 02/05/2008
International Centre 6900 Airport Road
ON, Canada
http://www.fashionnorth.com
9066076131

ASI
02/06/2008 - 02/08/2008
Dallas Convention Center 650 South
Griffin Street
Dallas, TX
http://www.asishow.com/dallas
8772747469

BOSTON MENSWEAR COLLECTIVE
02/06/2008 - 02/08/2008
Best Western Comelot Inn 1330 Silas
Deane Highway
Weathersfield, CT
http://www.bostoncollective.com
5086657158

OFF-PRICE SPECALIST
02/10/2008 - 02/14/2008
Sands Expo Convention Center 201
Sands Avenue
Las Vegas, NV
http://www.offpriceshow.com/index
2627821600

MARKET LAS VEGAS
02/11/2008 - 02/13/2008
Venetian Resort Hotel & Casino 3355
Las Vegas Boulevard South
Las Vegas, NV
http://www.mrketshow.com
2127107414

ASAP GLOBAL SOURCING
02/11/2008 - 02/14/2008
Venetian Marco Polo Ballroom 3355
Las Vegas Boulevard South
Las Vegas, NV
http://www.asapshow.com/futureshow
.html
7037979049

POOL
02/12/2008 - 02/14/2008
Las Vegas Convention Center C5
Entrance of Central Hall 3150 Paradise
Road
Las Vegas, NV
http://www.pooltradeshow.com
3236665587

MAGIC
02/12/2008 - 02/15/2008
Las Vegas Convention Center 3150
Paradise Road
Las Vegas, NV
http://show.magiconline.com
8185935000

MODA IN
02/12/2008 - 02/15/2008
Portello Fairgrounds Fieramilanocity
Milano, Italy
http://www.modain.it/ehtm/home
390266103820

PROJECT LAS VEGAS
02/13/2008 - 02/15/2008
The Sands Expo Convention Center
201 Sands Avenue
Las Vegas, NV
http://www.projectshow.com
2129516773

BOSTON MENSWEAR COLLECTIVE
02/13/2008 - 02/15/2008
Shriners Auditorium 99 Fordham
Road
Wilmington, MA
http://www.bostoncollective.com
5086557158

TEXWORLD
02/18/2008 - 02/21/2008
Paris Le Bourget
Paris, France
http://interstoff.messefrankfurt.com/t
exworld/en/fakten_133.thml
331552687158

March

NORTHSTAR FASHION
03/02/2008 - 03/04/2008
Minneapolis Merchandise Center 1300
Nicolette Mall
Minneapolis, MN
http://www.northstarfashion.com
6123335219

THE NILES SHOW
03/04/2008 - 03/06/2008
The White Eagle 6839 N. Milwaukee Av.
Niles, IL
http://www.nilesshows.com
6305849513

IMPRINTED SPORTSWEAR SHOW ISS
03/07/2008 - 03/09/2008
Atlantic City Convention Center One
Miss America Way
Atlantic City, NJ
http://www.issshows.com/issshows
8009338735

CHILDREN'S CLUB
03/09/2008 - 03/11/2008
Javits Convention Center 655 West
34th Street
New York, NY
http://www.enkshows.com
2127598055

MERCEDES BENZ FASHION WEEK
03/09/2008 - 03/13/2008
Smachbox Studios
Los Angeles, CA
http://www.mbfashionweek.com/losangeles
6468712400

**Texgate International Textiles and
Accessories**
03/13/2008 - 03/15/2008
CNR Expo Hall 1
Istanbul
http://www.itf.texgate.com
90.212.663.0881 x3251

FILO
03/19/2008 - 03/20/2008
Centro Congressi Stelline
Milan, Italy
www.Ui.biella.it
39.015.403.978

Jitac European Textile Fair
03/26/2008 - 03/27/2008
Tokyo International Forum / 5-1
Marunouchi 3-chome
Chiyoda-ku, Tokyo, Japan
http://www.jitac.jp/
203.698.7460

Made in France by Fatex
03/26/2008 - 03/27/2008
Carrousel du Louvre
Paris, France
http://www.salonmadeinfrance.com
33.014.730.5494

INTERTEXTILE
03/27/2008 - 03/29/2008
China International Exhibition Centre
Beijing, China
http://www.messefrankfurt.com.hk/fair_
hompage.aspx?fair_id=2&exhibition_id=2
861065171388

YARN EXPO
03/27/2008 - 03/29/2008
China International Exhibition Centre
Beijing, China
http://www.messefrankfurt.com.hk/fair_
hompage.aspx?fair_id=3&exhibition_id=3
861065171388

**DALLAS MEN'S & BOYS MARKET
CENTER**
03/27/2008 - 03/30/2008
2050 North Stemmons Freeway
Dallas, TX
http://www.dallasmarketcenter.com
2146556100

Tallahassee Urban Fashion Week
03/27/2008 - 03/30/2008
Tallahassee, FL
billyba@netscape.com

**China Intl Clothing & Accessories
Fair**
03/28/2008 - 03/31/2008
China Intíl Exhibition Center
Beijing, China
86.106.505.0546

New England Apparel Club
03/30/2008 - 04/01/2008
Oncenter
800 S. State Street, Syracuse, NY
http://www.Neacshow.com
781.326.9223

(Men's Apparel Group in California, now shown in Las Vegas) and conferences on technology, promotion, control, visuals, and fabrics. Calendars also appear in *WWD* and *DNR*, both in print and online.

SUMMARY

Determining when and what to buy involves more than might first be realized. The search for the right goods for a retailer's customer, however, can be an easy or difficult undertaking because of the tremendous availability of resources. Selecting where and from whom to source should entail thorough, deliberate decision making that weighs the advantages and disadvantages of each method and supplier considered. Technology has made this process easier and more reliable, from production, distribution, and even the selling of the product. Primary in determining the best merchandise to procure is knowing your company's customers and their wants and needs.

KEY TERMS

ad valorem tariff
agile manufacturing
automatic replenishment
advance orders
back orders
blanket orders
brokers
centralized buying
closeout
computer-aided design (CAD)
computer-aided manufacturing (CAM)
contractor
Customs and Border Protection (CBP)
decentralized buying
domestic market
domestic source/sourcing
drop shipper
duty
embargo

exclusive contractor
exclusive order
free trade
General Agreement on Tariffs and
 Trade (GATT)
imports
independent buying office
international market
international source/sourcing
jobber
job lot
just-in-time (JIT)
lead time
manufacturer
market
market calendar
market week
mass customization
merchandise mart

middlemen
Multifiber Arrangement (MFA)
off-price order
offshore
open orders
prepack
promotional order
quick response (QR)
quota
regional market
regular order
reorder
resident buying office (RBO)
resource

safeguard action
sourcing
specific tariff
store-owned buying office
supplier
tariff
trade shows
U.S. Harmonized Tariff Schedule (USHTS)
vendor
visa
wholesaler
World Trade Organization (WTO)

BIBLIOGRAPHY

Diamond, J., & Diamond, R. (2008). *The world of fashion.* New York: Fairchild Books.

Diamond, J., & Pintel, G. (2008). *Retail buying.* Upper Saddle River, NJ: Prentice Hall.

Dickerson, K. (1999). *Textiles and apparel in the global economy.* Upper Saddle River, NJ: Prentice Hall.

Kunz, G. I., & Garner, M. B. H. (2007). *Going global: The textile and apparel industry.* New York: Fairchild Books.

Poloian, L. G. (2003). *Retailing principles: A global outlook.* New York: Fairchild Books.

Reamy, D., & Steele, C. W. (2006). *Perry's department store: An importing simulation.* New York: Fairchild Books.

Sternquist, B. (2007). *International retailing.* New York: Fairchild Books.

www. usitc.gov

www.wto.gov

Case 34

SAFEGUARD LIMITATIONS

*Nancy Anabel Mason, Senior Port
Process Specialist, Customs and Border
Protection
Rebecca A. Lucas, Operations Specialist,
Customs and Border Protection
Tonda K. Fuller, Import Specialist,
Customs and Border Protection*

Preface

In 1995, the World Trade Organization (WTO) converted the MFA (Multifiber Agreement) into an Agreement on Textiles and Clothing (ATC), which gradually phased out all quotas on textiles and clothing, resulting in an elimination of quotas on January 1, 2005, between WTO member countries.

Although the goal of the ATC was to eliminate quantitative import restrictions among WTO member countries, there is a provision that allows a WTO member country to restrict imports of a product temporarily, which is referred to as *safeguard action.* Safeguard measures are defined as "emergency" actions with respect to increased imports of particular products, where such imports have caused or threaten to cause serious injury to the importing member's

domestic industry" (www.wto.org).

Textile safeguard restraints were a condition of China's accession to the WTO. The Accession Agreement allows WTO members who believe imports of Chinese origin textiles and apparel products are, due to market disruption, threatening to impede the orderly development of trade in these products, to request consultations with the People's Republic of China with a view toward easing or avoiding such market disruption.

On January 1, 2005, quotas were to be removed as scheduled in the ATC. However, the United States exercised its right to activate safeguard actions on certain imports from China. The wavering status of quota on textile imports from China created an unpredictable trading environment for both countries.

In the attempt to create a stable trading environment for the apparel and textiles industries in both countries, the "Memorandum of Understanding (MOU) between the Governments of the United States of America and the People's Republic of China concerning Trade in Textile and Apparel Products" was signed on November 8, 2005. The governments of the United States and China established restraint levels for certain textile products produced or manufactured in China and exported to the United States during three one-year periods beginning on January 1, 2006, and extending through December 31, 2008.

M-Wang Enterprises is a manufacturer and importer of women's wearing apparel and textile items for the home. Jerry Lee, the owner of M-Wang, has struggled to remain competitive in the clothing and textile industry operating within the global economy. Maintaining a competitive stance has been challenging and has required many business changes and swift decisions by management.

The goals of M-Wang include maintaining flexibility in selecting the countries in which to establish relationships with manufacturing facilities and nurturing relationships with major retailers. Jerry is continually working to establish new accounts while striving to deliver goods as contracted, which requires clearing merchandise through Customs and Border Protection (CBP; formerly the United States Customs Service), without delays. To meet these goals, M-Wang employs an individual responsible for studying manufacturing trends. This person must be aware of statutory changes made in Washington, D.C., trade agreements, and import restraint limits (formerly quotas) establishment, and be able to identify the most cost-effective manufacturing locations. See Table 6.1 for information on selected countries regarding import restraints, visa requirements, and duty rates.

Originally, Jerry operated factories in Thailand, the Philippines, Hong Kong, and China. Today, his staff works aggressively to establish operations in countries with low wages and countries that are not subject to U.S. import restraints/limitations. Such countries as Canada, Costa Rica, El Salvador, Israel, Korean Republic, Macedonia, Malaysia, Mauritius, Mexico, Peru, Sri Lanka, Turkey, and Vietnam are all potential new manufacturing locations. Vietnam was previously subject to Column Two rates of duty, which are prohibitively high; however trade agreements have changed and now Vietnam is under Column One duty rates (normal trade relations and lower rates) and is now a competitive manufacturing location without import restraints/limitations. (To contrast this, imports from North Korea have a Column Two duty rate of 72% as shown on Table 6.1.) To control costs associated with clearing merchandise through CBP, M-Wang has developed a small in-house import department managed by an individual who has a customhouse broker's license.

A significant challenge and potentially a disastrous obstacle to marketing popular apparel and textiles is importing items subject to safeguards (restrictions/limitations), formerly referred to as quota. Although the number of wearing apparel and textile items subject to safeguards has been reduced dramatically since 2005, there are still restrictions/limitations for a number of countries, including China. For numerous Harmonized Tariff categories there is always a risk of reaching the quantity limit and closure prior to the goods entering the commerce of the United States.

In an attempt to retain profit margins and meet the competitive pricing of the retailing environment, Jerry Lee has established a form of just-in-time inventory. The merchandise is delivered immediately to the retail establishment or retail warehousing facility upon

TABLE 6.1 Comparison of Quota, Visa Requirement, and Duty Rates for the Cotton Underwear HTS 6108.91.0005, Category 352, for Selected Countries, as of 2008.

| Country of Origin | Quota* | Visa | Column 1 | | Column 2 |
			Duty Rate	Special Rate of Duty**	Duty Rate
Canada	N	N	8.5%	–	–
Canada—eligible for NAFTA**	N	N	–	FREE	–
Costa Rica	N	N	8.5%	–	–
Costa Rica—eligible for CAFTA**	N	N	–	FREE	–
Israel	N	N	8.5%	–	–
Israel—eligible for ILFTA**	N	N	–	FREE	–
Korean Republic	N	N	8.5%	–	–
China	Y	Y	8.5%	–	–
Malaysia	N	N	8.5%	–	–
Mauritius	N	N	8.5%	–	–
Mauritius—eligible for AGOA**	N	N	–	FREE	–
Mauritius—eligible for trade preference level (TPL)***	Y	N	–	FREE	–
Mexico	N	N	8.5%	–	–
Mexico—eligible for NAFTA**	N	N	–	FREE	–
Sri Lanka	N	N	8.5%	–	–
Turkey	N	N	8.5%	–	–
Vietnam	N	N	–	–	–
North Korea	N	N	–	–	72%
Australia—eligible for AUSFTA**	N	N	–	7.6%	–

*This includes both quota limitations imposed as part of a Trade Preference Level Agreement as well as Safeguard Limitations that are allowed under the WTO Agreements.

**These are Free Trade Agreements. If the goods qualify under the agreement they can be entered at a lower rate of duty listed in the HTS under the "special rates of duty" column. If they don't qualify, they pay 8.5% duty. For example some goods imported from Canada, but not all, qualify for special rate under NAFTA.

***Some Free Trade Agreements also have provisions for a Trade Preference Level, which gives the lower Free Trade rate of duty to goods that do not qualify as originating under the Free Trade Agreement, but do meet a secondary set of requirements, i.e., tariff rate quota (tariff increases from 0% to 8.5% after a quota level is met).

clearance through CBP. This practice requires precise planning, transportation coordination, knowledge of CBP requirements and monitoring of Harmonized Tariff Schedule category status. Applying a just-in-time methodology to importing goods attempts to limit liability and overhead, reducing time for the disposition of merchandise, and reducing or eliminating prolonged warehousing costs.

One of Jerry's clients ordered 100 dozen pieces of cotton underwear, category 352, and 100 dozen pieces of cotton terry towels with an embroidered holiday theme. Underwear of 100 percent cotton from China is classified as HTS 6108.91.0005 and dutiable at 8.5 percent rate of duty. Cotton terry towels from China, made from 100 percent woven cotton, are classified as HTS 6302.60.0020 dutiable at 9.1 percent. (See Table 6.2 for the resulting duties on these orders.)

The contract specifies a delivery date of no later than November 25. Based upon past experience, Jerry is aware that safeguards in certain HTS categories start to reach restraint limits and are at risk of closing in November or December, the last two months of the calendar year restraint limit cycle. His items have the special embroidered holiday theme phrases "Happy Holidays," "Happy New Year," and "Peace on Earth." A major retailer

is planning to advertise and merchandise these items together, positioning them as special gift ideas for the holidays.

Production of the underwear and terry towels is complete. Labeling, packaging, and invoicing documents have been prepared. Visas have been obtained from China, and transportation has been scheduled. The merchandise enters the Port of San Francisco. The import manager, David DeMarcio, prepares the required merchandise clearance documents and submits them to CBP for release of the goods. Upon input into the CBP national computer system, Automated Commercial System (ACS), Alva Bostick, a CBP Entry Specialist, discovers the categories have closed.

When merchandise arrives after the closure of a safeguarded HTS category, the consequences can be disruptive and expensive. The importer must choose one of the following options:

- Destroy the merchandise under CBP supervision.
- Enter the merchandise into a Foreign Trade Zone (FTZ) and store the merchandise.
- Export the merchandise.
- Warehouse the merchandise.

TABLE 6.2 Rates of Duty

Item	Quantity	Value	Duty Rate	Duty
Cotton underwear 6108.91.0005 (category 352)	100 dozen	$1,966.00	8.5%	$167.11
Cotton terry towels 6302.60.0020 (category 363)	100 kilograms	$223.00	9.1%	$20.29

If one of the above is not chosen, the articles will go General Order (GO). This happens when articles are taken into CBP custody and placed in a public or general order bonded warehouse by a CBP officer at the risk and expense of the consignee. The shipment will be designated General Order 30 calendar days after the arrival of the importing vessel. The duration of a general order period is six months from the date of importation (Customs Federal Regulations 19 127.1). After the general order period is exceeded, Customs may exercise the right to auction or destroy the merchandise.

Jerry has been notified by CBP that both categories 352 and 363 from China have closed.

Major Question

Given the above options, what should Jerry Lee do since the quota category on merchandise Jerry is importing is closed?

Study Questions

1. In the future, how can M-Wang guard against this problem?

2. What are ways of ensuring your merchandise will arrive before the closing of a safeguarded (restricted/limited) category?

3. What other risks are there in importing merchandise into the United States?

Exercises

1. Research the countries in Table 6.1 for production capabilities. In addition, review the restraint, visa, and duty rate status of each country on the table. Where would you recommend producing M-Wang's orders? What are the advantages and disadvantages of producing in each country?

2. Go to www.usitc.gov to investigate current tarrifs, and www.otexa.ita.doc.gov to check on the status of filled quotas from China in different categories.

Bibliography

Black, H. C., Nolan, J. R., & Nolan-Haley, J. M. (1990). *Black's law dictionary* (6th ed.). St. Paul, MN: West Academic Publishing Company.

Code of Federal Regulations 19. (1992). Parts 1 to 199, Revised as of April 1, 1992. Washington, DC: Office of the Federal Register National Archives and Records Administration.

Taylor, S., Mishulskis, J. V., & Penn, M. (Eds.) (1995). *Introduction to Customs Brokerage.* Allegan, MI: Boskage Commerce Publications.

USITS Publication 2831. (1995). *Harmonized Tariff Schedule of the United States.* Washington, DC: U.S. Government Printing Office.

World Trade Organization Web site: http://www.wto.org/english/thewto_e/whatis_e/tif_e/agrm8_e.htm

Case 35

TREADWELL'S: THE BUYER'S DECISION

Judith Everett, Northern Arizona University

Treadwell's Department Store is a traditional department store that was founded in 1898 by Oliver Treadwell in the American Southwest. Treadwell's has symbolized the spirit of the Southwest for nearly a century, maintaining exclusive merchandise related to the region as well as providing moderate to better apparel, accessories, and home furnishings for the entire family. The regional department store retailer has 18 branch stores located at the major cities in Colorado, New Mexico, Utah, and Arizona. Treadwell's has its buying offices and distribution center in Phoenix, Arizona, and sends merchandise to all of its branches from the central distribution center. James Treadwell Stephenson, the great-grandson of the founder, is the current chief executive officer. He is very concerned about maintaining the image of the company as well as the profitability of the firm.

Recently, Tiffany Brentwood has been promoted to the position of buyer of women's sleepwear and loungewear after successfully managing the intimate apparel and children's departments at the Santa Fe branch for four years. She also had held the position of assistant buyer for children's sleepwear and accessories for almost one year. Her long-term professional goals include becoming a divisional merchandise manager and store manager.

After her interview with CEO Stephenson, Tiffany realized the importance of the company philosophy to enhance images of the Southwest yet maintain profitability. She has sought unique merchandise that will reinforce the Southwestern image for Treadwell's. She found a resource for a group of pajamas, nightshirts, and tunics with matching leggings. This merchandise features Southwestern motifs and would fit perfectly with the goals of the firm to offer such merchandise. She believes that this style is not a passing fad in this part of the country and it should be a staple item in her department.

The merchandise featured tasteful interpretations of traditional Native American blanket designs. The garments were made from 100 percent cotton knit and produced in fashionable colors. Tiffany was confident that this merchandise would be popular with Treadwell's target customer.

Upon further investigation, Tiffany discovered that similar styles and colors of merchandise were available from two different resources: Southwest Specialties, a vendor in Los Angeles, and JC Enterprises, a local Phoenix vendor.

Southwest Specialties requires a minimum order of $5,000 at cost, offers terms of 3/10, net 30, and does not provide transportation costs. Transportation costs may be estimated at approximately $4.50 per dozen garments. There is a rumor, however, that there may be a trucking strike and Southwest transports by independent truck lines. South-

TABLE 6.3 Tiffany's Initial Order

Quantity	Style	Southwest Specialties Cost	JC Enterprise Cost
12 dozen	Pajamas	$174/dozen	$180/dozen
6 dozen	Nightshirts	$150/dozen	$155/dozen
20 dozen	Tunics	$117/dozen	$120/dozen
15 dozen	Leggings	$117/dozen	$120/dozen

west Specialties is willing to participate in a cooperative advertising program. This Los Angeles firm assures Tiffany that merchandise will be in stock and available for reorder.

The local vendor does not have a minimum purchase and will deliver the merchandise for free. JC Enterprises also offers terms of 3/10, net 30. (Refer to Chapter 7 for terms of sale.) This firm is not willing to share in the costs of a cooperative advertisement, since it is a small company. JC Enterprises cannot guarantee immediate delivery. This firm needs a 48-hour delivery notice.

Tiffany decides to bring the merchandise into the stores. She calculates her initial order, which is shown in Table 6.3. Tiffany prepares a financial analysis of the purchase, also taking into consideration the discounts and shipping costs that would be applied to her orders to determine which vendor might be the best to purchase from. She studies her analysis, and then she takes it, along with the pros and cons about each vendor, to her divisional merchandise manager. Because Tiffany is new as a buyer, she does not feel confident about making the decision on her own and wants some feedback from her divisional manager.

Major Question

From which vendor should Tiffany recommend purchasing? Why?

Study Questions

1. What is the difference in the total cost of the merchandise from the two different vendors?

2. What factors in addition to price, discounts, and shipping should be considered in making this decision?

Case 36

WHERE WILL YONGMEI GO?

Dong Shen, California State University, Sacramento

Yongmei is a government-owned cotton manufacturer located in Beijing, China. Established in 1950, Yongmei originally produced different types of cotton yarns. Under the government's planning economy, all of its products were sold domestically to fill the domestic demand. Then in the 1960s, when the domestic needs were met, some of its products were exported to other countries, all of which were third-world countries due to China's political goals of helping other third-world countries. Under the planning economy, as a government-owned manufacturer, Yongmei experienced another two decades of development and success in the 1970s and 1980s. Because the Chinese government was in charge of everything from sourcing and sales to marketing and distribution, Yongmei only needed to focus on production. What it needed to produce, to whom it would sell its products, and how to sell its products were all decisions made by the government. At the peak of its history in the 1980s, Yongmei achieved three highs—high production, high efficiency, and high profit.

In 1992, dramatic changes took place in China after Deng Xiaoping, the leading Chinese government official, visited Southern China. Deng encouraged Chinese people to get rich instead of being ashamed of being rich. Along with that, a major innovation occurred in the Chinese exporting policy system. Before 1992, there was only one company allowed by the government to export and import textile and clothing products. This was China Textile Import & Export Co., a government-owned company. All the textile and clothing imports and exports were dealt with by this one company. After Deng's Southern visit, the Chinese government started to give some permissions to individual manufacturers, especially those

large-scale government-owned manufacturers, to import and export limited amounts of products. Meanwhile, the transition from their planned economy to a market economy was further deepened in that the government was no longer in charge of buying and selling products including textile and clothing products for those government-owned manufacturers.

With this new freedom and flexibility given by the government, Yongmei started to experience major changes. For the first time in its history, Yongmei could decide what it wanted to produce, from whom to buy raw materials, to whom it wanted to sell its products, and how to sell its products. Meanwhile, it still enjoyed some protections and benefits from the government, such as help on technology updates and introduction to new market demands. The government still offered those benefits to the manufacturers because in the 1990s the majority of the manufacturers in China, including the textile sector, were still government-owned. Even though the government was not responsible for everything, the success of these manufacturers greatly affected the national economy.

In the middle of 1990s, Yongmei started to go downhill, and by 1995, at one point it showed no profit at all. Two main factors triggered this trend. First, the price of domestic cotton, the raw material, was much higher than the price in the international market, whereas the price of their final products, cotton yarns, was low. Two questions become apparent: (1) If the price of cotton in the international market was much lower, why didn't Yongmei buy raw materials from the international market? (2) If their products were made of domestic cotton, why couldn't they increase their final price? The answers to these two questions related to the government economic policy of the time. Even though the transition from the planned economy to the market economy had been going on for several years in China and the government started to give more freedom and power to individual manufacturers, it didn't mean that the government was not still in charge. As a matter of fact, even though individual manufacturers could import and export products, they were not allowed to import and export everything they wanted freely. For example, in order to protect domestic cotton production, the government had strict limits on the amount and types of cotton that manufacturers could import from other countries. Meanwhile, the price was not driven purely by market demand. Instead, the government was still controlling the general price range in the market.

The second factor that triggered the downhill situation also related to the transition from a planned economy to a market economy. When the government started to provide more freedom to individual manufacturers, it also stopped providing financial support to them. Under the planned economy, the government provided a budget to the manufacturers to purchase new equipment and machinery to update their technology. However, under the market economy, it was the manufacturer's responsibility. Therefore, while Yongmei was facing the situation of decreasing profit due to the high cost of

raw materials and low final price for its products, it also had to find money to update its equipment and machinery, which further deepened its financial crisis.

In 1996 and 1997, while Yongmei's situation continued to get worse, other types of textile and apparel manufacturers started to emerge showing a promising future. Because of the new economic policy, more and more nongovernment-owned manufacturers were established in China. These tended to be smaller in scale compared to the large long-standing government-owned manufacturers. They were more flexible, efficient, and competitive than the government-owned manufacturers. Based on this phenomenon, the government believed that the reason why Yongmei and other government-owned manufacturers had more and more problems was because they had too many employees and not enough efficiency. Therefore, a new policy was established by the government to require the government-owned manufacturers to increase efficiency and decrease employment by laying-off employees and downsizing its facilities. Following this policy, Yongmei started the difficult structural reformation. During 1998 to 2000, Yongmei downsized its production facility from 300,000 spindles to 170,000 spindles, and decreased its employees from 17,000 to 2,000. Laying off employees didn't mean that Yongmei had no responsibilities toward them; as a matter of fact, according to the government policy, Yongmei still had responsibility for the laid-off workers that included providing stipends and benefits continuously, providing training, and helping them find other employment. Meanwhile, for every single retired employee, according to the government policy, manufacturers like Yongmei have full responsibilities that include providing health coverage, housing, and stipend throughout the rest of their lives.

After several years of struggle, Yongmei continues to fight for survival. Today the company is faced with the following problems: (1) how to continue to allocate and provide for the employees who were laid off; (2) how to financially support the retired employees; (3) how to slow down the pace of the structural reformation in order to avoid too many changes and uncertainties in a short period of time; and (4) how to face the competition that comes from other forms of manufacturers, such as private-owned, joint-venture, and foreign-investor.

Currently, the textile and apparel market in China is mainly dominated by private sector, joint ventures, and foreign-investors; they occupy most of the market share, while the government-owned manufacturers are shrinking. The future doesn't look bright for Yongmei and other government-owned manufacturers in China. Many experts believe that due to the difficult structural transition under the market economy, the word "sunset" is a good way to describe the government-owned textile and apparel manufacturers in China. The leaders of Yongmei have also realized that. They believe that their main mission is to finish the structural change smoothly without causing any social uncertainty. Their main goal is not to make money and profit, to expand the business, and to compete with other forms of manu-

facturers. Instead, finding ways to support the retired workers and workers who got laid off is their main goal. When all the laid-off workers find new jobs and all the retired workers have enough financial support, their mission will be accomplished.

Major Question

If you were part of the leading team of Yongmei, what would you do to address the problems it faces today?

Study Question

If you were an owner of an American retailing company, would you do business with Yongmei? Why? Why not?

Case 37

THE SAUDI ARABIAN SAMPLE SITUATION

Lorynn Divita, Baylor University

Nicole St. Lawrence is a merchandising assistant at Racer Jeans, a division of Chapman Jeanswear, one of the world's largest jean manufacturers, headquartered in St. Louis, Missouri. Nicole's job is to work with all of Racer's licensees. Racer Jeans only manufactures jeans, but it recognizes the importance of marketing itself as a lifestyle brand with a wide array of products, such as knit and woven shirts, socks, accessories, and leather products, each branded under the Racer name. Rather than become the manufacturer of these products, Racer has chosen to stick with what it does best—making jeans—and license the use of its name to manufacturers of these other products. Of the 15 licensees with which Racer has agreements, its main licensees include Hill Hosiery sock manufacturers in North Carolina, Ranchero Leather Products belt and leather goods manufacturers in Arizona, Habbott Brothers knit shirt manufacturers in New York, and its largest licensee, Sammy Shirts, a woven shirt manufacturer also in New York City.

Racer allows each company to develop a line that it markets under the Racer name, in exchange for payment of five percent of all sales from the line to Racer. Racer provides each licensee with co-marketing dollars and support materials, such as computer files containing the artwork for the most recent product labels and hangtags that licensees then adapt to their own merchandise.

It can be difficult for Nicole St. Lawrence to stay on top of what all 15 licensees are doing at all times, particularly because of how geographically dispersed they all are. Sometimes problems occur and relationships between Racer and one of its licensees get strained. For example, one time when Nicole requested product samples from each licensee to feature in a display, she realized that Sharp, the Racer's jacket licensee, was using outdated hangtag art and the colors on the logo on the hangtag were not the approved "Racer Red" that was specified. When she called the company to tell it that it had to reprint new hangtags, it had to discard more than 3,000 hangtags and was not pleased. But Nicole understood it was her job to preserve the integrity and continuity of the Racer brand, even if it made some of the licensees mad.

Nicole was busy getting product ready for a big meeting with Smithson, its largest retailer in Canada, with company headquarters in Toronto. Smithson requested a replica of a floor set in its offices for the meeting, complete with actual store fixtures filled with Racer product to see how the merchandise will look on the store floor. Providing jeans for the floor set has been no problem, but Nicole has had to coordinate merchandise from all 15 of the licensees. Finally, with just three days to spare, Sammy shirts delivers its products to Nicole, giving her just enough time to ship the product with the rest of the licensees' merchandise to Toronto. Just before contacting Racer's shipping department to show them the order, she realizes something that could disrupt the entire shipment: Sammy sent them an entire shipment of sample shirts manufactured in Saudi Arabia, and Canada has an embargo on clothing from Saudi Arabia and won't permit it to enter the country. The production shirts, however, will not be produced in Saudi Arabia. After many telephone calls to government offices, Nicole finds out that the shirts can enter the country as long as they are mutilated so that it is obvious they are only samples and can never be sold. The recommended way to do this is to cut a swatch of fabric out of the back of the shirt, so that they look fine on the rack but obviously can't be worn by anyone. This brings a whole new set of problems for Nicole. Sammy has sent a few thousand dollars worth of shirts at retail for the show with the expectation that they will be returned to them for future sales. They do not want their shirts mutilated because they will not be able to recoup any of their money. Smithson is equally adamant that if Racer expects to get any shirt orders, they need to see how the sample merchandise looks in a store environment. Sammy has put a great deal of pressure on Nicole to just lie about the country of origin on the shipping label, saying that "There's no way anyone's going to check it." Nicole isn't sure how to handle the situation, but she knows she needs to make a decision quickly.

Major Question

What should Nicole do about the sample shirts? Lie or demand that the shirts must be mutilated?

Study Questions

1. How often do countries embargo goods from other countries? Why would a government do that? Goods from which countries are embargoed by the United States?

2. What are advantages and disadvantages of licensing products?

Case 38

SHOULD ALL THE EGGS GO IN ONE BASKET?

Judy K. Miler, Florida State University
Nancy J. Rabolt, San Francisco State University

Lawrence Collins is the president of Blake's, a privately owned chain store operation, consisting of nine moderately priced stores located in West Virginia. He founded the stores over 35 years ago and feels fortunate that they are still doing well. The company has been built on loyal customers and loyal employees. Collins considers his company his second family (as a matter of fact, he named the chain for his deceased wife, Blake). Most employees remain until they retire, as everyone seems to get along very well and morale is excellent. Blake's company office is in Charleston and operates with four buyers, two divisionals and two merchandise managers, who visit the New York market four or five times a year. The exception is Rose Rockwell who handles women's better and bridge sportswear—she is in New York every two months because her departments are the most fashion oriented. The total volume of the dress and sportswear departments is $600,000 a year (about 40 percent of the total company volume), of which dresses contributes $250,000.

Even though Rose's formal training is limited, having come up from the ranks as a salesperson, she has paid her dues over 15 years and Rose is considered a dedicated, fairly knowledgeable merchandiser. Rose works with the company's New York corporate buying office sometimes but essentially makes all the merchandising decisions herself, including what goods to buy.

Collins, although satisfied with Rose's performance, believes that the chain is not obtaining its full share of volume potential in her areas, as compared to industry figures that show women's sportswear usually bringing in about 50 percent of the total sales volume of comparable retailers. He has never entertained the thought of replacing Rose because he is essentially a small-town man who believes in loyalty and appreciates that trait in all his employees—especially buyers. In fact, Rose is unmarried and considers her job the biggest, most important part of her life and she always puts the company first.

Collins was in New York last week and was reviewing his operation with the management staff of the corporate buying office, Associated Small Stores, Inc. In addition to Collins, Leonard Carroll, the buying office president, and Marvin Black, the buying office merchandise manager of women's better and bridge apparel, were present. During the meeting, Carroll—a dynamic businessman whom Collins has worked with for a number of years—suggested that the Blake's chain switch to the buying office's unit control service as so many of their other retail groups had. This move would probably free up management for other concerns. Carroll concluded his compelling suggestion by

stating, "The central operation is a way for a smaller group like your stores to save expenses. We can do all your buying so your buyers are not needed, and the fee is only 2 percent of net sales. You can make your buyers department managers, who then can concentrate on the stores' site business. We can almost guarantee a better business in sportswear by controlling the merchandise plans, buying, and designing ads. Above all, your stores will be stocked with all the latest, freshest merchandise in demand, because we are in the market and our buyers work the market every morning finding new resources and the latest trends."

Carroll's arguments were so powerful and logical that Collins's sense of loyalty to his employees, particularly Rose, began to waiver. He was on the verge of saying, "Okay, we'll try centralizing buying for a year," but his business acumen dictated a cautious approach. He decided to mull it over before coming to a conclusion.

He then sought out his corporate controller and trusted, long-time friend, John Slattery, a level-headed pragmatist. Collins explained his predicament to him. After listening to what had transpired, Slattery said, "The economics of the situation are probably just as presented by Associated Small Stores; we might be better off in the long run using their buying service. However, you realize that there are two negative points. One, you're going to 'destroy' Rose Rockwell, who will never accept the job of department manager, like your other buyers probably will; and, two, what does a New York office really know about the local conditions in West Virginia? Having Rose where the customers are provides the advantage of her being on top of the local customers' needs and wants. She even has the opportunity to meet and talk to her customers, giving them personal attention."

Collins replied, "John, you're saying just what I've been thinking, and I'm feeling like I'm up a creek without a paddle. I'll have to give this matter some more careful consideration in weighing the pros and cons."

Major Question

If you were Lawrence Collins and these facts were presented to you, would you decide to switch to corporate centralized buying? Why or why not?

Study Questions

1. What are the advantages and disadvantages of merchandising centralization? Decentralization?

2. Should the size of a retailing operation be a factor in determining whether centralized or decentralized buying and control be used? Why or why not?

Exercise

Do research to find examples of retailers who do centralized and decentralized buying.

Case 39

LICENSING PITFALLS

Suzanne G. Marshall, California State University, Long Beach

Licensing has become an increasingly important method for a well-known name (designer, cartoon character, athlete) to increase visibility and build the name into a "brand." Licensors "sell" the right to use their names by charging a royalty on the sales of products featuring their names. Licensees increase their earnings by the profit made from producing and selling these products. If the product is successful, both the licensee and the licensor win; at least, that's the way it looks at first glance. Typically, the licensor does win as the majority of the risk is born by the licensee. If the licensee does his job—makes a quality product, promotes, sells, and supports it adequately—the licensor earns royalties. But what about the licensee? How does the scenario play out for him or her?

The licensee in this case is Lunada Bay, which currently produces women's swimwear for a variety of companies. It formerly produced licensed swimwear for Mossimo and Ocean Pacific (OP).

Let's examine some of the pitfalls of licensing arrangements from the licensee's perspective. Lunada Bay employees spoke of several areas that cause concern for the licensee that are grouped under four main categories: (1) lack of control/power, (2) lack of visibility, (3) increased expense, and (4) multiple "masters."

1. Lack of Control/Power

In short, in a licensing agreement, the licensee's success is tied to the decisions made by the licensor.

- *Distribution decision changes.* In the mid-1990s, OP executives decided to change their product distribution from specialty stores to low price-point department stores. Lunada Bay was opposed to this change of strategy. Lunada Bay's president, Susan Crank, felt that this new policy would alienate OP's customer base and weaken the cache factor of its product. She reasoned that if customers can find a product anywhere, they see it as less valuable. In discussing this issue with OP, Lunada Bay sales reps pressured her not to lose the OP account because a large percentage of their income came from the commissions from the sales of OP-labeled swimwear.
- *Licensor changes his business and drops licensee.* When Giannulli Mossimo sold his business to Target in 1995, Lunada Bay lost his license. This is common for a licensee.
- *Licensor decides to lower product quality.* (This issue is a corollary to the one above. Typically, changes in distribution to lower-price stores necessitate reducing the wholesale cost, and

therefore quality, of the product): In order to sell to lower price-point stores, the product would need to be priced at a lower wholesale price. OP informed Lunada Bay that the suits must cost $7 or less. Lunada Bay had built its reputation on a high-quality product and said it could not produce a suit for this point.
- *Promotional differences.* At the time, Mossimo's preferred method for promoting his name was to feature head shots with no product. Lunada Bay prefers product shots, as do the department stores that purchase its product. In addition, for one of its catalogs, Macy's wanted to put Mossimo swimwear on the cover. This privilege came with a hefty charge—a move that Mossimo resisted. When Macy's pressured Lunada Bay to comply with its request, Lunada Bay had to support its licensor, whether or not they were in agreement.
- *IPO.* In the mid-1990s, Mossimo made the decision to go public. He called to inform Lunada Bay's president. She had misgivings about both the decision and the timing. She felt that part of the appeal of Mossimo's products were the result of his cache factor built from having a product that stores were always chasing, rather than one that was so widely distributed that the original customer base felt alienated. Crank knew once Mossimo went public, stock managers would increase the

pressure to expand the number of Mossimo retail stores and to sell to more department stores. She knew that for her company, it would have to increase production to meet the increased product demand. As she was unsure of the longevity of this increased demand, increasing production was risky. (Later, Mossimo inked a deal to produce for Target under his label.)

2. Lack of Visibility

- *Not promoting own brand.* As a licensee, you are always promoting another's product—not your own brand. Thus, if you are replaced by the licensor, your business is lost because you are unknown in the marketplace. The licensee finds it difficult to ensure its own longevity.
- *Licensee's designers feel invisible.* When Mossimo swimwear won the Dallas Fashion Award, the Lunada Bay designer, Becky Fortune, who designed the swimwear, went to the award show but sat at the table while Mossimo accepted the award. "It's hard on Becky to have only Mossimo accept the award. She gets to go but Mossimo gets the credit. She's invisible. No one knows she did the designs." Another Lunada Bay designer explained that he increased business for their licensor by four percent but still feels unappreciated and invisible. He said, "We're creating an illu-

sion. They told me when I interviewed for the job, I'd be invisible. We promote Mossimo. He has input into the product—but to the world, he does it all. We are nothing. We perpetuate his ideas to the world for him."

3. Increased Expense

- *Royalties.* The licensee pays the licensor a percentage of the selling price of each garment sold. Royalties range from a low of 2 to 15 percent to as much as 20 percent for avant-garde products. The added expense for the licensee necessitates an increase in the wholesale price. Often the licensor requires the same royalty on the sales of marked-down products as well, which is frustrating to the licensee.
- *Advertising/promotion.* The licensee is required to pay a fee for advertising and promotion of the products to the licensor. Often the licensee disagrees with the promotional strategy. For example, Lunada Bay disagreed with some of the media placements of OP and some of the sporting events it supported. Lunada Bay felt that this was not the best use of its money.
- *Staff duplication.* Occasionally the licensees' employees do not meet the expectations of the licensor and thus additional staff must be hired to work with a specific licensor, resulting in a duplication of effort and expense.

4. Multiple "Masters"

- *Two showrooms.* At the California Mart (http://www.calforniamart.com), all swimwear companies Lunada Bay licenses show the products during market weeks. Lunada Bay must staff each showroom before the market opens, as well as continually run from one floor to another answering questions, working with models, selling, negotiating, and working with sales reps—a tiring experience for all.
- *Differing images.* In licensing for several brands, the licensee must keep the images distinct for each licensor. This occasionally presents a problem for the design staff. Distinct products must be developed for distinct target groups. They must promote them in unique ways and sell them to a buyer from different retail store types and target customer groups.

- *Various leadership styles.* A licensee must please each of its licensors. Some licensors have a "hands-off" policy and allow the licensee to do business as it sees best. Others want total authority—a voice in every decision. A licensee must juggle the demands of both.

Major Question

How would you advise the manufacturer to address pitfalls mentioned in the case?

Study Questions

1. What general advice would you give a manufacturer who is considering adding a licensed product to its offerings?

2. Can you think of any way to give visibility to the real designers of a licensed product?

3. What are the advantages of producing only licensed products?

CHAPTER DISCUSSION QUESTIONS

1. Explain the opportunities and challenges of international sourcing. Compare and contrast it with domestic sourcing. Use case examples from this chapter to reinforce your discussion.

2. How can types of orders fulfill specific merchandise needs of retailers? Incorporate examples from the chapter cases differentiating the types with needs.

3. Compare and contrast centralized and decentralized buying. Note examples from cases that support your arguments.

4. Discuss the importance of careful research and decision making in the selection of resources and merchandise. Explain how the customer helps retailers select their products.

5. How has exclusive private labeling altered sourcing practices of many retail chains today, for example, Gap and The Limited, from traditional sourcing? Explain the advantages and advantages of private labels to retailers, whether they are exclusive users (e.g., Ann Taylor) or partial users (e.g., JCPenney).

6. Discuss the reasons that retail buyers search globally for the best-value merchandise.

7. Discuss how quick response and other computer applications link the manufacturer and the retail processes.

Sourcing

seven

Retailer/Vendor Relationships

CHAPTER OBJECTIVES

- Stress the importance of good retail/vendor partnerships.
- Present the reasons for negotiations between buyer and seller.
- Identify and explore major problems and resolutions between vendors and retailers.

Retailing success may be due in part to the kinds and types of relationships that a retailer has with suppliers. The building or formulation of retailer/vendor relationships is of critical concern because the type of relationship and partnership between a retailer and vendor often can make or break a business. Building an open, honest working relationship through mutual understanding, resolution of problems, communication, and partnerships helps both realize their goals. Today, retailers look to their vendors for help in meeting or exceeding sales goals by partnering with them to build business. The smart vendors know, of course, that if they help the retailer do well, they too will have success. In today's marketplace, new ways in which the retailer and vendor can work more efficiently are constantly being created to gain the competitive edge in meeting the consumer's satisfaction with the goods and services they desire. Speed is of primary concern in all phases of marketing *distribution channels and technology is the major force driving it—from negotiations through to order processing and delivery. Interactive links between customer, retailer, and manufacturer result in speedy delivery of the desired goods and services to the customer, which also helps ensure an effective, positive working relationship between retailer and vendor.*

VENDOR PARTNERSHIPS

Effective working relationships between a retailer and resource are often the result of a partnership. A **partnership** is a working relationship that is formed to achieve a mutually beneficial goal. Today, even vendor and retail planning is often part of a partner relationship, because managing merchandise is no longer just the retailer's job. The supplier and retailer can no longer afford to work independently but must partner for success. Most manufacturers invest in and use leading technology that benefits not only their business, but their retail accounts. Many vendors today take the leading role in training and/or supplying retail sales help, as well as instore merchandising support. This is done in an effort to ensure that the vendor's merchandise is presented in the manner in which it was intended. A vendor may also supply support fixturing and signage for their goods to help present their merchandise.

As mentioned in other chapters, many retailers are also manufacturers today. Manufacturers/retailers must depend on their suppliers, just as retailers do with their vendors, so a good working relationship is necessary to benefit both.

Hard work, time, and energy is needed to build solid, open, and mutually beneficial relationships between retail companies and their vendor representatives. Sometimes, however, problems create the need for reworking an established relationship. The next section examines some of the circumstances involved that can create conflicts between retailers and vendors.

Causes of Partnership Conflicts

There are a number of difficulties that can arise between manufacturers and retailers that must be resolved to continue working together effectively. Following are some of the most common specific causes of conflicts between retailers and venders:

- Cancellation of merchandise by the retailer
- Substitution of merchandise by the vendor
- Merchandise returns and adjustments
- Delivery and transportation
- Exclusivity

- Special orders, reorders, and minimum orders
- Discounts and allowances
- Unreasonable conduct and dishonesty

The following is a brief examination of each of these critical problem areas.

Problems can occur when merchandise orders are canceled (i.e., not accepted) by the retailer or when substituted merchandise is shipped by the resource. This is particularly true if the action (i.e., cancellation or substitution) is taken without informing the other party. See *Case 68, To Go or to Stay: Ethics in the Workplace,* in Chapter 11, in which a retailer wants to cancel orders due to declining sales in an economic downturn.

Sometimes unauthorized **returns to vendor (RTV)** on the part of a retailer create difficulties between a resource and the retailer. These returns may be due to not liking the merchandise or inherent problems (e.g., poor quality) in the product; following proper procedures, however, might prevent bad feelings. (Reasons for RTVs are shown in Figure 7.1.) See *Case 40, Elegance, an Upscale Specialty Retailer, Uses Data Mining to Solve Vendor Fit Problems.* A retailer's data mining system indicates that one of its major vendors has a fit problem that has caused reduced sales and increased alterations costs. **Data mining** entails electronically tracking product, sales, and customer information to use in a business. **Adjustments** to the cost of goods may also be requested and sought by the retailer because of problems with the merchandise or because the items were returned. This can also create ill will if retailers do not go through the proper procedures to remedy the situation or if vendors do not fulfill their end of the bargain.

Delivery of the goods from the manufacturer to retailer may be another source of difficulty and conflicts if communication is unclear or incorrect delivery information is given (e.g., wrong delivery dates or method of transportation, late shipments, and so forth). With so many imported goods coming into our country, delays can present major problems. See *Case 41, Credit Problems and Order Nightmares.* A buyer has to choose between using a vendor with past credit problems that created subsequent delivery problems and another that replaced that vendor while it dealt with its problems; this is a problem for the buyer. Also see *Case 42, Retailer/ Manufacturer Conflict.* Retail chargebacks, readying merchandise for the floor (i.e., tagging, adding labels), providing merchandisers for the retail store, and other profit-cutting demands create pressure for a manufacturer to keep its prices competitive and seek compromise with its retailers. Specific and clear instructions should be stated up front, in order to lessen the chance or type of error and the resultant problems in delivery and/or transportation.

RTV REASON CODES			
Reason: Three letter code identifying the reason the merchandise is being returned to the vendor **AND who pays the freight charges outbound**			
Reason	Description	Frt. Out/HC Responsibility	Frt.-IN*Respons.
DAM	Damaged Merchandise	VENDOR	VENDOR
WRG	Wrong Merchandise	VENDOR	VENDOR
NOR	Not Ordered	VENDOR	VENDOR
CAN	Order Cancelled	VENDOR	VENDOR
LAT	Received Late	VENDOR	VENDOR
AGV	Agreement—vendor pay	VENDOR	N/A
AGS	Agreement—store pay	STORE	N/A
SMV	Sample—vendor pay	VENDOR	N/A
SMS	Sample—store pay	STORE	N/A
JBV	Job Out—vendor pay	VENDOR	N/A
JBS	Job Out—store pay	STORE	N/A
*Freight In will be charged back to the vendor ONLY if the store payed the original inbound freight.			

Figure 7.1 A department store's RTV reasons codes. Many times, unauthorized returns to vendors cause difficulties between retailers and vendors. A list such as this can help both the vendor and the retailer follow the proper procedures, thus avoiding problems in the retailer/vendor relationship.

As discussed in Chapter 6, exclusivity of merchandise or territory may be requested and promised to a retailer but not delivered by the vendor, which in turn angers and upsets the retailer. Exclusivity is under consideration in two cases in which negotiations need to be conducted. In *Case 43, Tying One On,* a retailer must determine the best action to take after being pressured by a resource to either accept a cost increase—and subsequently raise the retail price—or lose merchandise exclusivity. In *Case 44, Exasperations with Exclusivity,* a vendor has to decided whether or not to sell to a retailer's competitor, which will result in the retail account losing exclusivity of the vendor and the possibility that the vendor may also lose the retail account.

Special orders (those that are placed with a vendor generally for a specific customer), **reorders** (an order that has been placed previously), and **minimum orders**

(a specific amount of merchandise that must be placed) are other situations that can cause relationship conflicts. For example, if a vendor cannot fill special orders or reorders when it has been previously stated that it can, unhappy retailers and their unsatisfied customers result.

In *Case 45, Celebrity Fragrances: The Art of Negotiation,* required minimums cause concern for a buyer who wants to try new products. She is unsure how well the product will sell and therefore is hesitant to purchase the merchandise. Compounding the problem is that the buyer recently had a slow-selling item from the same vendor who wouldn't take the product back and, even worse, began selling to discount stores. Perhaps some negotiated compromise could help resolve the predicament.

Discounts and allowances are price concessions given by the vendor to the retailer in return for certain actions that the retailer takes. Orders may be affected and not be what was originally arranged. When an invoice arrives at the retailer and there is a discrepancy or variation to an agreed-upon discount or allowance, it can create conflict and distrust between a vendor and a retail account.

Unreasonable conduct and dishonesty on the part of either party can also be a major problem or can build tension between the people involved in a transaction. Retailer/vendor partnerships must rely on trust and honesty in order to be a successful alliance. See *Case 46, Customer or Competitor?,* where a major retailer seemingly knocks off a new innovative product line from one of its key vendors, presenting a problem to the manufacturer as it doesn't want to risk losing the retailer's business by confronting them. See Chapter 11 for more on this topic.

All of the matters discussed (i.e., cancellation and substitution of merchandise, merchandise returns and adjustments, delivery and transportation problems, exclusivity, special orders, reorders, minimum orders, discounts, and allowances) could be initially negotiated to arrive at what both the buyer and the vendor want, or they could be issues that can create conflicts and then will need to be resolved through further negotiations.

Negotiations

A partnership is often dependent on **negotiations** because the parties involved may not be seeking the exact same outcome and are looking out for their own best interests. Negotiations can result in a settlement and mutual agreement between two or more parties on any matter. This settlement is based on communication and the satisfaction of a goal of one or more of the parties. From a retailer's or manufacturer's perspective, negotiations are often undertaken to solve problems, resolve conflicts, reduce costs, and/or improve profit. The means to do this, however, are numerous. Often a compromise is realized when negotiations occur and the "best" (i.e., the most workable, most equitable) settlement is worked out.

A retailer negotiates with many people for various reasons. Negotiations might be undertaken with a vendor for a certain delivery or cost. A retailing manager might negotiate with sales employees of the company to increase sales. Knowing when and what to negotiate—as well as how—ensures successful negotiations. Negotiating for what is desired may begin a good working relationship, help a failing alliance, or even salvage an association that is not beneficial to one or both parties. Being an effective negotiator is often a learned skill that takes years of practice and listening. See Table 7.1 for nine techniques of successful vendor negotiations.

TABLE 7.1 Nine Techniques of Successful Vendor Negotiations

1. *Act Collaboratively, Not Competitively.* Negotiation is not "me against you." Recognize that the other party has to come away with a benefit, too. Show them how giving you what you want will help them get what they want.
2. *Prepare.* Do your homework about the other party; gather as much information about them as possible. Even rehearse and outline your remarks.
3. *Know What You Want.* Being able to state specific proposals or plans gives you strength. Don't wait to "see what they offer us." Know in advance what you must have, and what you can afford to give up. Each time you make a concession, get something in return.
4. *Don't Let Your Ego Get in the Way.* When you think of the negotiating process as winning or losing, you have too much ego involved. Don't get sidetracked by personalities or emotions. Stick to the issues.
5. *Learn to Make Time Your Ally.* Time is at the heart of every negotiation. Learn to make it work for you. Try to learn the other party's deadline without giving away yours. Most concessions occur at somebody's deadline.
6. *If You Can't Agree on Point One, Go to Point Two.* Agree even in small increments. Don't get hung up on one issue. It is easier to come back to an issue after you have reached some agreement, and the other person has invested time and energy in working with you.
7. *Be a Creative Risk Taker.* If you are known to not take risks, you are predictable and can be easily manipulated. Create your own solutions; there is usually more than one way to get the results you want.
8. *Closing the Negotiation: Wrap It Up.* Don't stay around and chat after you have reached an agreement. If you have what you want, close the negotiation. Don't linger too long, or it may unravel.
9. *Develop Long-term Relationships.* Focusing on long-term goals will keep both parties from being sidetracked by short-term frustrations. Knowing you are both in for the long haul means you can solve any problem that arises.

Prepared by Elizabeth Tahir, former retailing executive, now president of Liz Tahir Consulting, a retail marketing and management consulting and training firm in New Orleans, Louisiana.

Following are some matters that are frequently negotiated between the retailer and resource in an effort to help improve the retailer's bottom line:

- Obtaining specific merchandise (for promotions or other specific needs)
- Markdown money (to help with profitability)
- Transportation and delivery charges (to reduce costs)
- Cooperative advertising (for media costs or instore promotions)
- **Terms of sale** (conditions in a purchase agreement between retailer and vendor that include discounts, delivery, and transportation costs)
- **Dating** (a predetermined amount of time during which discounts can be taken and the invoice is to be paid; for example, 8/10 EOM means the retailers can take an 8 percent discount if the invoice is paid by the 10th day of the month)

Additionally, other sales, marketing, and merchandising needs are negotiated when necessary. Sometimes personal and professional behavior causes problems between vendors and retailers. At other times, ethics come into play. (See Chapter 11.) Negotiations can occur between the retailer and resource, but often specifically between a manufacturer's representative and the retailer's representative, as in *Case 44, Exasperations with Exclusivity.*

SALES REPRESENTATIVES

A **sales representative** is an individual who represents a manufacturer's product. Often sales representatives are the major link between the retailer and the manufacturer or manufacturer and supplier. Sales representatives can provide invaluable information to the retailer, in the same way that retailers can help relay information about their customers to the manufacturer through the sales rep. Figure 7.2 depicts a sales rep showing an apparel line to retail buyers.

The type of vendor and the sales representative determines the type of partnership that exists between the retailer and resource. An **independent rep** may be under contract to a specific company as its sales agent but may also represent other firms. Pepper's, for example, represents many major dress manufacturers, as shown in Figure 7.3. **Company reps** or **corporate reps** on the other hand are those persons who work exclusively for a supplier and are company employees. There are fewer and fewer independent reps today, partially because of the merging of retailing operations into mega-corporations. These giant corporations (e.g., Macy's and Wal-Mart) are now becoming major accounts to many suppliers.

Figure 7.2 A sales rep showing a line of clothing to retail buyers. Often, a manufacturer's representative will negotiate the terms of sale with buyers.

Major accounts often work corporately with the principals of the suppliers rather than through a sales representative because they are such an important part of the resource's business. For example, Wal-Mart made a major change away from dealing with reps to only working with the principals of their suppliers, which, of course, angered many reps. Even the number of corporate reps has diminished within some resources because of this trend.

After the buyer (or other authorized retail representative) determines what to buy, and from whom, and has negotiated the conditions and terms of the sale, the order is placed. A **purchase order (PO)** is the legal contract that binds the buyer and seller. All pertinent information that must be relayed between the two parties for the purchasing of merchandise should be contained on this document, as shown in the example in Figure 7.4. Often purchase orders are placed and processed electronically, which speeds up the delivery and reduces errors. A purchase order ensures that what the retailer wants is being requested, and it also verifies any special requests that have been negotiated.

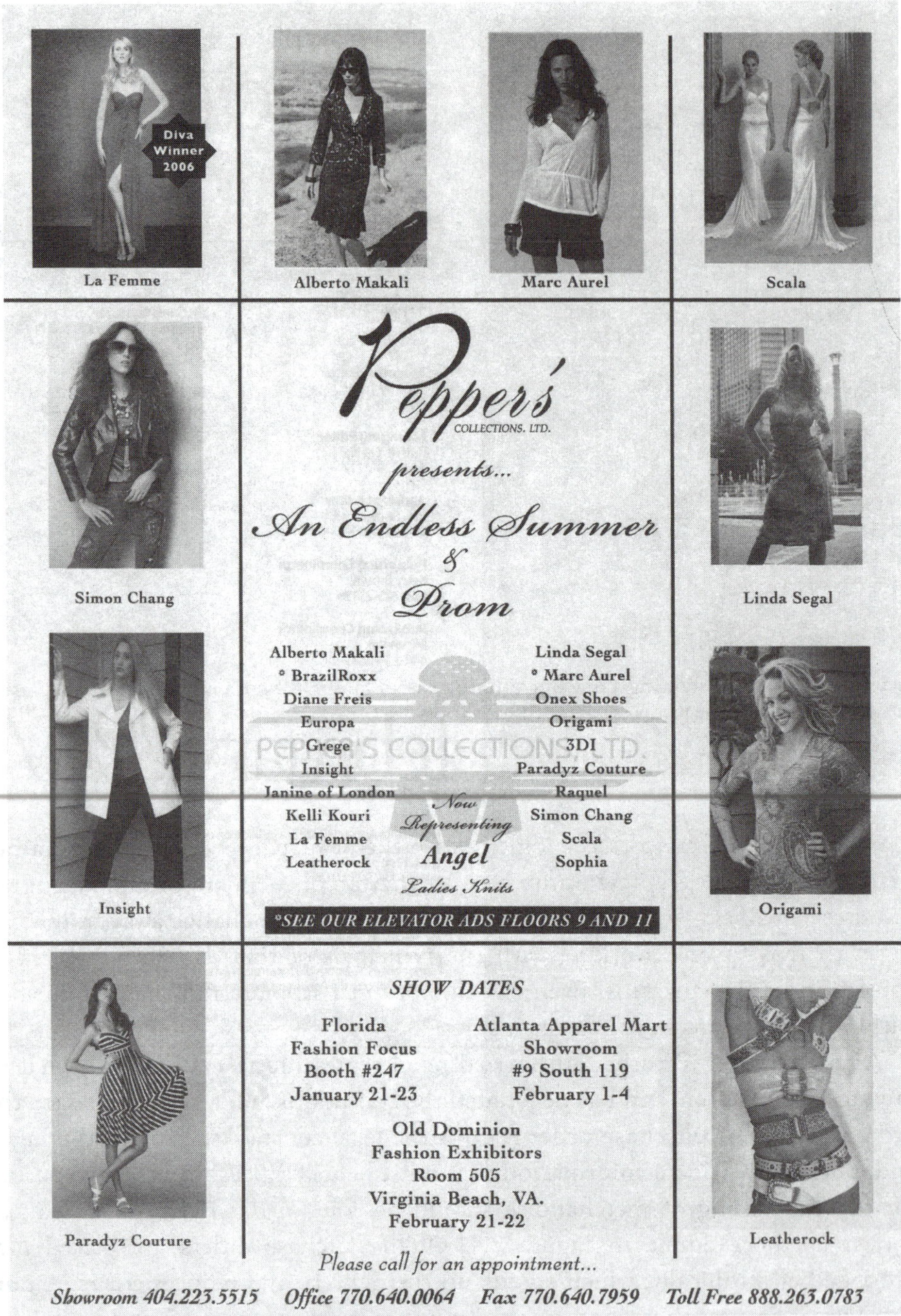

Figure 7.3 Pepper's is an independent sales rep that carries numerous non-conflicting apparel lines.

PURCHASE ORDER FORM VIEW

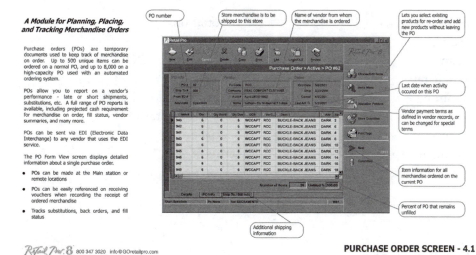

A Module for Planning, Placing, and Tracking Merchandise Orders

Purchase orders (POs) are temporary documents used to keep track of merchandise on order. Up to 500 unique items can be ordered on a normal PO, and up to 8,000 on a high-capacity PO used with an automated ordering system.

POs allow you to report on a vendor's performance - late or short shipments, substitutions, etc. A full range of PO reports is available, including projected cash requirement for merchandise on order, fill status, vendor summaries, and many more.

POs can be sent via EDI (Electronic Data Interchange) to any vendor that uses the EDI service.

The PO Form View screen displays detailed information about a single purchase order.

- POs can be made at the Main station or remote locations
- POs can be easily referenced on receiving vouchers when recording the receipt of ordered merchandise
- Tracks substitutions, back orders, and fill status

Callouts:
PO number
Store merchandise is to be shipped to this store
Name of vendor from whom the merchandise is ordered
Lets you select existing products for re-order and add new products without leaving the PO
Last date when activity occured on this PO
Vendor payment terms as defined in vendor records, or can be changed for special terms
Item information for all merchandise ordered on the current PO
Percent of PO that remains unfilled
Additional shipping information

Retail Pro 8 800 347 3020 info@GOretailpro.com

PURCHASE ORDER SCREEN - 4.1

Figure 7.4 This is an example of an electronic purchase order from a training manual. It spells out the shipping instructions, merchandise information, terms of sale, and any other information negotiated between the vendor and retailer, serving as the contract to help avoid retailer/vendor problems and misunderstandings.

As discussed in Chapter 6, the type of merchandise and/or vendor helps determine the type of order that is placed. The method of ordering is an issue that needs to be addressed by both the buyer and seller, and is dependent on their relationship and partnership.

SUMMARY

Building positive relationships between retailers and vendors takes time, energy, openness, and honesty; however, the benefits result in more business success for both. The possible difficulties a retailer and resource may encounter are numerous today due to many factors, but particularly the complexity of business and the interactive nature of the marketing channel. Resolving the problems mutually may depend on partnerships between the parties involved. In some instances negotiations may be necessary to settle a matter of concern and aid in ensuring that the benefits desired are achieved.

KEY TERMS

adjustments

allowances

company rep

corporate rep

data mining

dating

discounts

independent rep

minimum orders

negotiations

partnership

purchase order (PO)

reorders

returns to vendors (RTV)

sales representative

special orders

terms of sale

BIBLIOGRAPHY

Berman, B., & Evans, J. R. (2007). *Retailing management: A strategic approach.* Englewood Cliffs, NJ: Prentice Hall.

Dunne, P. M., & Lusch, R. F. (2007). *Retailing.* Norman, OK: South-Western College Publications.

Donnellan, J. (2007). *Merchandise buying and management.* New York: Fairchild Books.

Clodfelter, R. (2003). *Retail buying: From basics to fashion.* New York: Fairchild Books.

Diamond, J., & Pintel, G. (2005). *Retail buying.* Englewood Cliffs, NJ: Prentice Hall.

Levy, M., & Weitz, B. (2009). *Retailing management.* New York: McGraw-Hill/Irwin.

Case 40

ELEGANCE, AN UPSCALE SPECIALTY RETAILER, USES DATA MINING TO SOLVE VENDOR FIT PROBLEMS

Ellen McKinney and Steven McKinney

Retailer

Elegance, an upscale specialty retailer with sales over $4 billion, has 30-plus stores nationwide. Store values include providing distinctive merchandise and superior service to customers. The company focuses on the luxury retail market, selling brands including Armani, St. John, Zegna, Ellen Tracy, and Kate Spade. Women's apparel accounts for 35 percent of sales. Elegance is also known for strong vendor relationships, often working closely with vendors to develop products that will be desirable to its clients.

Vendor

A luxury knit apparel vendor, Luxe, in California, has been designing, manufacturing, and marketing women's clothing and accessories for 45 years. The company has wholesale as well as retail sales business segments. Luxe employs 4,000 people and operates dozens of offices and manufacturing facilities worldwide. Wholesale business segments include Knitwear, Sport, Shoes, Jewelry, Accessories, and Home Accessories. The vendor manufactures its products primarily to order. Products are sold by upscale specialty retail stores, such as Elegance, with whom the vendor has long-term relationships, as well as through company-owned retail boutiques. Luxe's top clients include Saks Fifth Avenue, Neiman Marcus, Nordstrom, and Bloomingdale's. The vendor works with retailers to get product to the selling floor quickly. Often product is shipped directly from the factory to stores, bypassing retailers' distribution centers.

Case

This case concerns a problem that occurred with the fit of the vendor's knitwear products. Knitwear is organized into four groups: Collection, Evening, Basics, and Couture. The vendor twists and dyes its own brand of wool and rayon yarns. The garments are made of a special type of knit that is known for being wrinkle-free. Luxe's collections are manufactured at the company-owned manufacturing facilities. Alterations to the garments are labor-intensive, requiring the un-knitting and re-knitting of the garment to shape. The vendor's alterations policy is to provide their services to retailers who currently carry their garments. Repairs/alterations are done through the retailer where the garment was purchased. Some retailers have their own skilled alteration staff that can accommodate requests, and some send garments directly to the vendor.

Elegance, like most retailers in the segment, provides alterations service for all garments sold. Clients are not charged for basic alterations to full-price garments. Certain more extensive alterations, along with alterations to discounted merchandise, are charged a fee. Total company alterations costs (including salaries, equipment, supplies, and transportation) always exceed income collected from fees. The company constantly seeks to minimize losses from alterations.

Elegance has a long-standing relationship with Luxe, which is one of the top ten vendors for the retailer. The knit suits are popular with its core customers. This customer is an older woman with high income and high net worth. The vendor made a change in their basic suit pattern to make the arms narrower. Clients were upset because they had to buy a larger size than they did before or have more alterations than before. Elegance realized that it was having an increasing number of alterations on garments from Luxe and sought to find where the majority of problems were occurring. Through its innovative use of a data mining system, which they use to track sales, cost, and customer information, they were able to mine its alterations by vendor and type of alteration, and by doing so Elegance was able to isolate the cause of this problem. These fit problems were causing reduced sales and increased alterations costs.

Major Question

What should Elegance do about the alterations problem with Luxe?

Study Questions

1. Are alterations and other services important for buyers to understand and use in their relationships with vendors?

2. Much of the information retailers collect about customers is proprietary and used to give them a competitive advantage. What information do retailers typically share with vendors? What information could a retailer share to improve the relationship? What potential implications might Elegance face by sharing alterations data?

3. How might the size of either the vendor or retailer in relation to the other affect the relationship and the sharing of "problem" information?

Exercises

1. Research data mining systems that are used by retailers to track sales and cost data. Name systems that are available. List all types of data that can be tracked. From where are these data collected? Are there multiple sources? How could this data be used by retailers to improve sales and reduce costs? How could this data be used to improve vendor relationships? What is the cost of implementing such systems?

2. Find an article in a trade publication discussing the implementation of data mining by a retailer. What system was used? Why was this system selected? What were

the benefits and costs of implementing the system? How does this real-world scenario compare with the pros and cons in the various alternatives in this textbook case? Does the article discuss benefits to retailer/vendor relationships? If so, what are they?

Case 41

CREDIT PROBLEMS AND ORDER NIGHTMARES

Courtney Cothren, Stephens College

Kelsey began her career at an upscale specialty store in Dallas, Texas. After working for two years as an assistant buyer, she moved to Carson's, a small men's and women's specialty retailer. Kelsey became adept at working with branded products in Dallas, and during her time as an assistant at Carson's, she quickly learned the ins and outs of the private-label fashion business. As Carson's is a private-label retailer, Kelsey had to learn about technical design, tech packs, sourcing, and many other aspects that she hadn't dealt with before. One of the most difficult things that Kelsey had to learn was the timing of a private-label business. Since all merchandise must be designed and manufactured by the retailer, the orders had to be placed much earlier than with the branded products she had helped buy before.

Kelsey worked as an assistant buyer at Carson's for about a year and a half in the women's tops division. She quickly realized that she could be much more creative in this business than she was in her last job. She did so well that she was promoted to the position of men's sportswear buyer. This position came with a whole new set of challenges. The first one was learning the men's business. Kelsey had previously only worked with women's accessories and apparel. However, she loved her Divisional Merchandise Manager (DMM) and everyone on the men's team helped her get acclimated very quickly.

One of her first tasks was to learn the current vendor matrix and place fall orders. Fall is the largest season for Carson's both in terms of volume and orders. Carson's believes that its customers are always looking for newness. It wants them to see new merchandise each time they enter the store. Because of this, Carson's delivers 12 assortments per year to stores—or one assortment every month. This seems to work well for the ladies business, but men shop a little less often than women, so some of the men's deliveries are very small (approximately four SKUs per department). In addition, Kelsey's total SKU count for fall is decreased from last year's numbers. (See Table 7.2.) She is buying five departments of merchandise for both July and August delivery. Records show that last year Carson's delivered a total of 112 SKUs between the two deliveries. Kelsey already took this year's purchase plans and her average unit retails to come up with this year's planned SKU count. It is smaller than last year, at 97 SKUs, because of poor sell-throughs and an overstock situation after Christmas.

TABLE 7.2 Estimated SKU Count

Fall 1 (July)

Dept	Plan	Avg Units	Avg Retail	# SKUS	LY SKU
220	$ –	0	$ –	0	0
250	$ –	0	$ –	0	2
270	$ 135.0	400	$ 69.50	5	12
280	$ 900.0	500	$ 69.50	26	20
290	$ 200.0	300	$ 79.50	8	14
	$ 1,235.0			39	48

Fall 2 (August)

Dept	Plan	Avg Units	Avg Retail	# SKUS	LY SKU
220	$ 200.0	250	$ 135.00	6	5
250	$ 350.0	700	$ 79.50	6	9
270	$ 243.4	350	$ 69.50	10	9
280	$ 600.0	400	$ 69.50	22	21
290	$ 382.9	300	$ 89.50	14	20
	$ 1,776.3			58	64

Kelsey has worked with the company's head designer, and they have decided on the styles for the 97 SKUs. Her presentation is only two days away, and her last step is figuring out which vendors will produce the products. A recap she completed shows the percent each vendor was to the total orders for the past two years. (See Table 7.3.) This reveals that two years ago almost all of the company's production was done by one vendor, Westplex. Kelsey has learned that Westplex received no business from Carson's the following year because it came under new management and had some credit problems. Apparently, Carson's had tried to do business with Westplex, but all orders were canceled due to its credit problems and Carson's gave its business to other vendors on the matrix. Because of the vendor changes, the deliveries were late, and because the products had to be produced so quickly, they weren't up to company quality standards.

Kelsey now has some very tough decisions to make. She met with Westplex on her first trip to New York, and they assured her that their credit problem is taken care of and they are once again ready to become Carson's number one private-label manufacturer. They apologized profusely and offered to show her detailed financial statements and references from other retailers that have been using them for the past eight months. Kelsey

TABLE 7.3 Vendor Percent to Total

	LY U Placed	% TTL	LLY U Placed	% TTL	% Change	LY $ Placed	% TTL	LLY $ Placed	% TTL	% Change	LY SKU	LLY SKU
Westplex	0	0%	26360	89%	−100%	$ –	0%	$ 1,790.53	89%	−100%	0	47
Texport	11700	26%	0	0%		$ 813.23	27%	$ –	0%		18	0
TFS	2950	7%	0	0%		$ 208.53	7%	$ –	0%		6	0
RIC	11700	26%	0	0%		$ 779.60	25%	$ –	0%		18	0
H. Oles	0	0%	1948	7%	−100%	$ –	0%	$ 135.39	7%	−100%	0	4
V. Furman	3500	8%	0	0%		$ 227.50	7%	$ –	0%		4	0
Turkey	8730	19%	0	0%		$ 559.90	18%	$ –	0%		14	0
Chinatex	600	1%	0	0%		$ 41.70	1%	$ –	0%		1	0
Kravitz	2050	5%	0	0%		$ 153.80	5%	$ –	0%		4	0
Oxport	600	1%	0	0%		$ 41.70	1%	$ –	0%		1	0
Martin	1700	4%	0	0%		$ 118.20	4%	$ –	0%		4	0
Forth St.	1650	4%	1372	5%	20%	$ 114.80	4%	$ 95.35	5%	20%	3	3
	45180		29680		52%	$ 3,058.95		$ 2,021.27		51%	73	54

LY = Last year
LLY = Two years ago
%TTL = Percent of total
U Placed = Total units placed last year or two years ago
$ Placed = Total dollars placed last year or two years ago

knows that the Carson's/Westplex relationship was very strong and that Westplex manufactured many of Carson's most successful items over the years. Kelsey also feels some loyalty to the vendors that picked up Westplex's slack when the orders had to be canceled. These vendors went out of their way to cut their production time in half to make Carson's cancel dates. They produced the goods in record time, and it was a miracle Carson's even had product on the floor that fall season. Sure, the quality wasn't up to par, but Carson's also didn't have time to see fit or preproduction samples on any garments, as they were under such time constraints. Kelsey feels that with her increased supervision, these manufacturers could turn out quality products. She has two days to figure out who she is giving her business to in terms of units, dollars, and SKUs.

Major Question

To which vendor(s) should Kelsey send her business for this fall?

Study Questions

1. Do you think the decision to lower the SKU count from 112 to 97 this year was the right thing to do? Why?

2. What other options could Carson have adopted to improve the business over last year without decreasing purchases?

Exercises

1. Make a table showing each vendor's percent to this year's total business in terms of dollars, units, and SKUs.

2. Do you think that 12 deliveries a year is smart for a men's business? Make a Time/Action calendar with your recommendation for the number of deliveries Carson's men's division should purchase. Be sure to include timing of when the orders should ship from vendors and when they should be merchandised on the sales floor.

3. Using your answer to the major question, make a worksheet showing your proposed SKU count for the June and August deliveries.

Case 42

RETAILER/ MANUFACTURER CONFLICT

Suzanne G. Marshall, California State University, Long Beach

The ability of manufactures and retailers to negotiate the terms under which they conduct business has eroded over the past two decades due to the power of the retailer increasing and the power of the supplier decreasing. Vera Campbell, president of Design Zone, a manufacturer of misses and junior knitwear with sales of $20 million annually, and Susan Crank, CEO of Lunada Bay, a women's swimwear and activewear licensee for Mossimo and others, with sales of $60 million annually, speak of the power shift in the apparel industry and its negative impact on small manufacturers.

Prior to the 1980s, apparel manufacturers held a high degree of channel power because the demand for their products exceeded supply. This is described as a "push" system—whatever goods are produced are pushed through the system to buyers who had limited choice options. In the 1980s, department stores began to merge into large ownership groups such as Federated Department Stores (today known as the Macy's Group). As a result, buying became more centralized. Buyers bought in large quantities to supply inventory for large groups of stores all over the country rather than for a small chain in one city.

Simultaneously, the number of apparel manufacturing companies grew at a rapid pace, which increased competition. As a result of the mergers of retailers into fewer but more powerful conglomerates, and the increased competition among a large number of apparel manufacturers, channel power shifted to those retailers with the "big pencils."

Realizing its high elevation on the power channel, the retailer began to shift some of its traditional responsibilities to the manufacturer. Manufacturers, especially smaller ones, felt that they had little power to negotiate, knowing if they refused to comply with large retailers' demands, there were plenty of other manufacturers who would supply them. Crank and Campbell cite several examples of demands by retailers that cut into manufacturer's already narrow profit margins:

- *Chargebacks.* Each of the major retail ownership groups writes a routing guide that sets forth rules of shipping to which the manufacturer must strictly comply. The rules cover areas such as where to attach the address label, whether the invoice goes inside or on the outside of the box, and whether shipments should be consolidated or broken down and sent to individual stores. Each notebook of rules is complex in its details, and each retailer has its own notebook of rules. "I'd have to hire MBAs to work in my warehouse to understand this," complained Crank, knowing if she did not strictly comply, she would be levied a heavy "chargeback" fee (a deduction from the invoice amount) from the retailer for having to correct the problem.

- *Merchandise preparation.* Manufacturers are now responsible for tagging merchandise, a process that involves not only price tagging, but also care labels and promotion-related tagging (which indicates the maker of certain fibers such as Invista's Lycra). Crank was pressed to purchase both a hanging rack system and a bagging system for her warehouse, costing thousands of dollars, so that she could ship her swimwear on hangers and in bags, making them "floor ready."

- *Merchandisers and specialists.* Manufacturers (Quiksilver, St. John, Liz Claiborne) now hire merchandisers whose main job is to visit the manufacturer's retail accounts and ensure their product is being given visibility and is visually appealing. Merchandisers also work with the receiving department to ensure that the goods are placed on the floor in a timely manner. Similarly, many manufacturers hire all specialists and place them in their key retail stores to sell only that manufacturer's merchandise.

- *Profit-cutting demands.* There are several common retail practices that cut into the potential profit of their suppliers:
  - Advancing the season—Campbell explained that retailers are breaking price (taking a markdown) on goods earlier and earlier each year, which eliminates the potential of a sell-through at the original price. Retailers explain that if they have a sale on January 15, they must "anniversary" that sale the next year to make their figures.
  - Markdown guarantees—The retailer expects the manufacturer to share the loss of profit from any markdowns, regardless of how early the markdown was taken in the season.
  - Automatic deduction for damages—Several retailers automatically deduct a percentage from the manufacturer's invoice to cover potential damages. Crank explains that she has only .3 percent damages and resents having to pay for the poor quality of her competitors.

In summary, both Campbell and Crank feel increased pressure from their retail customers. On one hand, they want to sell to the power retailers because of the larger orders, but on the other hand, they feel these retailers "own you."

Major Question

What do you think Campbell and Crank should do in regard to retailers' demands?

Study Questions

1. Develop a compromise strategy that might work for both sides. What are the strengths and weaknesses of your strategy?

2. What do you think is the future for small manufacturers? How can they remain competitive?

Case 43

TYING ONE ON

Judy K. Miler, Florida State University
Nancy J. Rabolt, San Francisco State University

Kendall's Department Store is located in Memphis, Tennessee, and caters to an upper-middle-income clientele. In all the departments, and particularly in the ones dealing with fashion merchandise, the buyers are under constant orders from the general merchandise manager, and especially from their divisional merchandise managers, to be on the lookout for highly original, exclusive merchandise. Alexander Henley, the general merchandise manager, has made it a practice to have all such merchandise privately labeled either as *Made Exclusively for Kendall's* or *Designed Exclusively for Kendall's.*

One of Henley's favorite departments is the men's furnishings department. Even though Kenneth Mackay is the divisional merchandise manager for men's and boys' wear, Henley himself keeps a close eye on many of the merchandise segments in the men's furnishings department because of his own personal shopping preferences. Henley is forever sending Francine Woods—the men's furnishings buyer—memos, clippings, and ads, all intended to prod Francine into investigating and buying new lines or styles. It is an awkward situation for both Kenneth and Francine, but one that they tolerate with good humor.

One of Henley's chief contributions to the men's furnishings department is his encouragement and approval of buying from relatively unknown designers—especially men's ties. These designers are usually young and ambitious, and they generally do well with Kendall's. Probably the best-selling designer of ties in this *Designed Exclusively for Kendalls* merchandise is Theo Moore. Henley is one of the most avid collectors of Moore's highly original tie designs.

When Moore began to sell exclusively to Kendall's, the store was charged $40 per tie, which was retailed for $80. As Moore's ties became more popular, his price was raised by $5 each, and Kendall's passed on this increase to their customers, who did not seem to mind paying higher prices for these one-of-a-kind tie creations. By the end of Moore's second year with Kendall's (after yet another cost-price increase), customers were paying $90 per tie.

Now, halfway into his third year as an exclusive Kendall's designer-resource, Moore is getting restive, and a bit demanding, and is now commanding $50 (cost-price) for the ties, which are still selling quite well at $100 each. Moore recently has had offers to sell his ties to Kendall's competitors under his own name (as opposed to the *Designed Exclusively for Kendall's* label). This would help him gain name recognition and obtain a wider, healthier distribution for increased volume.

After Moore had received the third offer to sell his ties to another store, Theo arranged for a meeting with Francine. At this meeting, Theo laid his cards on the table and told Francine that the alternative to going to another store (i.e., staying with Kendall's exclusively) would be another substantial increase in the cost-price to make up for the lost potential volume. He then told Francine that he would be asking $55 per tie. This would translate into $110 per tie for Kendall's customers.

Francine considers Theo's merchandise valuable both to the store and to her department but wonders if another price increase will cause Moore's customers to shy away from buying more ties. Either losing Moore or sharing him with another retailer—the other alternative—is not an appealing idea to Francine.

Major Question

If you were Francine Woods, how would you resolve this with Theo Moore?

Study Questions

1. Discuss some instances of negotiations that you think should result in compromise between a retailer and vendor. What instances do you think would not result in compromise?

2. Do you think maintaining retail price levels is important to maintaining customers? Why or why not?

Case 44

EXASPERATIONS WITH EXCLUSIVITY

Judy K. Miler, Florida State University
Nancy J. Rabolt, San Francisco State University

The Seasonless Store is located in Kennebunk, Maine, and prides itself on the better merchandise that it carries for an affluent clientele. The store's name indicates merchandise of a nonseasonal nature, but The Seasonless is a specialty store with the emphasis on fashion merchandise that can be worn all year long. Like many specialty stores, there is at least one outstanding merchandising area for which it is widely known—in this case, the dress department. Oscar Shepherd is the well-respected divisional merchandise manager of the misses and women's departments and has been with The Seasonless for over 25 years. Sybil Duncan is the women's dress buyer and is also highly regarded.

One of the women's dress department's key resources is the Dixie Dress Company. Dixie has showrooms in New York City, Atlanta, Dallas, and Los Angeles and a magnificent new state-of-the-art manufacturing facility in Flatrock, North Carolina, one of the few remaining large domestic manufacturers. Sybil brought the Dixie Dress line with her when she came to The Seasonless from her last position in Chicago. She has close ties to Dixie Dress and its sales manager, Garret Evans, because they are both from the same town in Georgia. Sybil felt that Dixie Dress shipped a very well-made garment that was styled particularly well for the larger, more matronly woman. Evans had agreed at the beginning of the relationship with The Seasonless that Sybil's department would be the exclusive distributors for Dixie Dress in her trading area. In return for this exclusivity, The Seasonless invested a large portion of its advertising space and money over the three years that Dixie Dresses had been featured. Sales, also, had come along splendidly after Kennebunk and the surrounding area's customers began to appreciate the fine fabrics, well-fitting designs, and excellent finishing details of Dixie dresses. Sybil's annual volume with Dixie had increased to well over 1,500 dresses with an average cost of $120, which translated to over $300,000 at retail for The Seasonless. As a result, Dixie Dress now accounted for a sizable portion of the women's dress department's volume.

This ideal arrangement came to a grinding halt one day when Ike Plunkett, the sales representative for Dixie Dresses, called and asked to meet with Oscar and Sybil. Actually, Garrett Evans should have called for this meeting, but his personal ties to Sybil embarrassed this southern gentleman. Hence, Plunkett drew the "dirty work" assignment.

In essence, Plunkett brought this message from the Dixie Dress management:

- Dixie Dress needs more sales volume. The firm is in an expansion cy-

cle, and it was looking for more outlets for its merchandise and more cash flow.
- Dixie Dress is approaching stores they had refused to sell to before because of their previous policy of granting exclusivity to the best store in a trading area.

In The Seasonless's trading area, Woodward's Department Store has long sought to buy some of Dixie's lower-priced lines but had never succeeded. Woodward's is a full-fledged moderate department store with highly promotional merchandising policies. At times, its ads give the impression that it is a discount organization. While The Seasonless's emphasis is on quality and service, Woodward's image, as reflected by its ads and other communications, shouts "PRICE!"

Oscar was livid. "You mean to tell me, after all this time, effort, and money, you want us to share your merchandise with that 'cheap' store?"

Uncomfortably, Ike Plunkett pointed out, "Mr. Shepherd, we have definite assurances that with their overall sales volume, we can more than double our sales in this area."

"Do you know what this will do to The Seasonless's customers?" Sybil asked. "The status associated with the dresses will most certainly be lowered."

Plunkett assured her that this would not happen because each store would have exclusive rights to certain styles that would be confined to that store. Additionally, there would be less chance of conflict because Woodward's price zones would confine its buyers to those numbers that The Seasonless never bought anyway.

"Have you ever seen Woodward's ads?" Oscar queried. "They scream PRICE, PRICE, PRICE! They frequently cut prices at the slightest pretext. With a nationally known name like Dixie Dress, they will damage your reputation as an upscale manufacturer."

Both Oscar and Sybil continued to argue, plead, and cajole, but it soon became apparent that Ike Plunkett was only the "messenger" who was there to deliver the message from Garrett Evans.

Major Question

What should The Seasonless Store do in regard to the decision by Dixie Dress to sell merchandise to one of its competitors?

Study Questions

1. Discuss the reasons why a retailer would want exclusivity from a vendor. Are there any reasons to not want such an exclusive arrangement with a manufacturer?

2. What might be negotiated by a retailer for obtaining exclusivity of a brand?

Exercise

Visit local retailers and find examples of exclusive brands.

Case 45

CELEBRITY FRAGRANCES: THE ART OF NEGOTIATION

Dee K. Knight, University of North Texas

The Jackson Company was founded in 1901 by the Jackson family in west Texas. Through the generations, the family continued to successfully operate the stores and grow through acquisitions and new store development. The company now operates more than 56 stores under 12 different names in 11 states, mostly in the Southwestern and Midwestern regions of the United States. As the company acquired stores in small towns to mid-sized cities, the names of the stores were retained to help ensure customer loyalty.

Today the future of the company seems brighter than ever before, as they plan for the future. The philosophy of Jackson's, which has remained unchanged throughout the generations, is that of providing quality, branded merchandise for the family and home at competitive prices with personalized service quality that exceeds customers' expectations.

The company carries prestigious cosmetic lines such as Estée Lauder and Lancôme, to name a few. Recently the cosmetic buyers met with their sales representative of a cosmetic line (not one of the prestigious lines) to discuss the launch of two new celebrity fragrances. The first was developed to appeal to a young, hip customer. The second fragrance line was classically elegant and targeted a more mature consumer. Promotion of this fragrance would be primarily through major advertisements in magazines.

The buyers and sales representatives discussed the marketing program for the product launches and also the company's opening order. Typically a cosmetic company has a large budget to launch a fragrance and allocates from $20 to $30 million in television, radio, and other media to launch a single fragrance. In addition, there could be a promotional CD to run in the stores and entertainment spots, or personal appearances; in other words, they would create a lot of buzz about the line.

Jackson's buyers were cautious and followed the philosophy that they did not want to be in an overstocked position and risk having a lot of markdowns. Rather, they preferred to be in a position to reorder the merchandise if it began to sell well. Just recently, the buyers had a fragrance from this same company that had not sold well, and it had refused to allow the Jackson company to return the product. This is a bit unusual, as most cosmetic companies allow retailers to return slow-moving product and replace it with merchandise that will sell more quickly. They do this in order to avoid markdowns. However, the cosmetic company was suffering some problems of its own at the time and decided to disallow the return. Some of the

items in Jackson's stock were over a year old, but still they were denied the return of the slow-selling merchandise.

There also were other issues. The vendor sold to two nationally known discount stores some of the same fragrances they had sold to Jackson's, and the product was being sold at a lower margin. This practice had the effect of decreased sales at Jackson's. The sales representative also no longer offered cooperative advertising to help promote the fragrances locally. This change of policy was a decrease in support from just one year ago.

Another consideration was the fact that the number-one-selling fragrance at Jackson's was a product purchased from this same company. In the end, both the buyers and the sales representative had the same goals in mind. They came to an agreement and wrote a purchase order for the two new celebrity fragrances, even though Jackson's still did not have permission to return the dated product. The next day, the buyers discussed the order with upper management and released the order as written the previous day with the sales representative.

Much to the surprise of the buyers, the sales representative informed them that the company could not accept the order because it was below the minimum level that had been established for the two new celebrity fragrances. Even the regional manager of the cosmetic company had not been aware of these minimums for an opening order. The cosmetic company was expecting even companies such as Jackson's with small stores to carry the same minimum number of units that was expected of larger stores such as Macy's. Jackson's senior buyer had been buying from this sales representative for more than 20 years and was surprised at this turn of events.

Major Question

If you were the Jackson's buyer, what would you do?

Study Questions

1. Should Jackson's continue to do business with a company that is selling to discount stores?

2. How important to consumers are celebrity fragrances?

3. Did the cosmetic company conduct business in an ethical manner?

Exercise

Role play. Select one group of students to represent Jackson's buyers, and designate another group as the fragrance sales representative. Each group must determine its ultimate goal(s) before negotiating with the other party. The goal of the buyers may be stated in terms of their open-to-buy, the return of the slow-selling merchandise in the celebrity lines, or exclusivity on the new celebrity fragrances. The sales representative may have predetermined unit or dollar goals for an order with no returns to vendor and no co-op advertising. After the groups have reached consensus, choose one student to represent each group during negotiations.

When Jackson's buyer and sales representative have concluded their negotiations, other members of the class may offer other options or suggestions, or ask questions.

Case 46

CUSTOMER OR COMPETITOR?

Lorynn Divita, Baylor University

Annmarie Powell is a merchandising assistant at Knight Underwear, a company with a rich history of more than 100 years and a diverse portfolio of men's, women's, and children's T-shirts, underwear and socks, and other products. Knight enjoys excellent brand recognition among consumers and is the industry leader of many of the product categories in which it sells merchandise.

Knight Underwear's sales volume has increased dramatically in the last 20 years. One of the reasons Knight has grown so much in recent years is its relationship with PrimeKo, a large global retailer. PrimeKo also carries Knight's main competitor, Harrison Underwear, as well as its own private-label brand, so competition for shelf space is high. PrimeKo's strategy of selling a large volume of merchandise at razor-thin profit margins has kept Knight's profits down as well. In response to these pressures, Knight's strategy has been to emphasize branding through national print and television advertising campaigns and to focus on product innovation as a way of keeping consumer demand high.

One recent product innovation that the merchandising department has been excited about is its new Shimmer line for its My Own Knight underwear line. The product incorporates a new synthetic fabric in the front panel that is very fashion forward for Knight, a company known for its cotton jersey knit products. The fabric is sheer yet shows a print very well and has a slight sheen on the surface. Knight has decided to do the fabric in a "Wild Hearts" print in two colorways, pink and blue. One package with two pairs of underwear will retail for $5.49.

Underwear merchandising at mass retailers is traditionally done on high, temporary walls with several columns of "peg hooks" that each holds about a dozen packages of underwear. Each column holds about eight to ten peg hooks. Because Knight is such a significant vendor for PrimeKo, it has been allocated several columns on the women's underwear wall to feature its merchandise. Most of the columns are taken up with Knight's different lines, including Knight Sport, Knight Beautiful (a plus-size line), and its basic line, Knight for Her. These lines all have a traditional spring/fall product line, and the merchandise changes just two times per year. The final column is called a "flex column" and is where the most fashionable merchandise is featured. This column has four different lines per year, and the merchandise changes every three months. Because of the rapid change, the merchandise featured on this column has a more seasonal feel than with the other lines, and the pressure is always on to come up with something that will strike a chord with consumers and encourage them to buy the product because of its uniqueness.

The biggest season for underwear purchases is Christmas, because many people purchase underwear as a stocking stuffer or other small extra gift. Because of this, the merchandising team at Knight has decided that the Shimmer line will be a huge hit on the flex column. However, before they plan their production calendar, they must know how many pairs PrimeKo will commit to ordering. In January, the Knight merchandising team heads out to PrimeKo's headquarters in Kennett, Missouri. The merchandising team pitches the line to PrimeKo's Women's Underwear Buyer, Kendall Stewart, and she seems very interested in the product. Before she can place her order, however, she needs to meet with some other vendors. Kendall tells Annmarie and the merchandising team to leave their product samples with her and she'll think it over and get back to them. They comply and return back to their own headquarters in Columbia, South Carolina, feeling good about how the meeting turned out.

Six weeks later, Annmarie and her boss are in PrimeKo doing some competitive shopping to see what other brands are doing. They are going through the racks, when all of a sudden, Annmarie is stunned. She finds herself holding a bra and panty set from Wishes (PrimeKo's own private-label line) that is an undeniable knockoff of the Shimmer line. The material is of lesser quality than

Knight's product, but the fabrication, the print, and the color stories are almost exactly the same. This means that PrimeKo's customers will have seen the style for almost eight months before Knight's product hits the stores in October. Also, the bra and panty set retails for just $6.89, and since a bra is more difficult to construct than a pair of panties, this makes Knight's own product offering for two pairs of panties for $5.49 seem like less of a deal.

Annmarie buys the pink and blue bra and panty sets and brings them back to Knight's offices for an emergency meeting. Everyone on staff is just as surprised and disappointed as Annmarie was. The question before them now is how to best react to the situation.

Major Question

If you were Annmarie, what would you do when Kendall calls to place her order for the line?

Study Questions

1. Would you work with this retailer? Do you think they are being honest?

2. Is there another explanation for PrimeKo producing something that looks like a knockoff of Knight's product?

Case 47

GOOD RESULTS = NO NEW BUSINESS

Billy Christensen, JCPenney

Bobby was the sales manager for a new, high-end dress shirt market. His product had a unique construction technique, one that no one else could offer for anything less than an exorbitant price. Bobby and his company were having considerable success in specialty stores with these shirts and took them to Nelson's, one of the nation's largest and most respected stores.

Nelson's had made its name in selling high-quality products, matched with a service standard that was second to none. Getting your product in Nelson's and it doing well there almost ensured your business would grow at an extremely fast pace.

Bobby secured an appointment with the buyer in the southern states region and gave an impressive and effective presentation. Nelson's decided to test the dress shirts in two of its stores, one with established success and the other an up-and-coming store in a growing area. They selected the assortment to be tested and the product hit the stores on September 1.

In the presentation to Nelson's, Bobby had offered himself and his designer, David Faison, to do appearances in each store. The shirts had David's name on them, and giving the public the opportunity to meet the designer was something that would help build the brand in the stores with the associates and help to build brand awareness in the public. Bobby and David appeared in each store motivating the sales staff, meeting and greeting customers, and working with management to ensure the success of the shirts.

After the first four weeks, the shirts had achieved a sell-through a full two percentage points higher than the department average. After six weeks, that result climbed to 2.5 percent. After eight weeks, the shirts had averaged sell-throughs 2.4 percent points above the department average.

Bobby called the buyer to discuss what the next the step would be. Clearly the shirts had outperformed the department average, beating many of the established labels. Sure the sales volume was less than those established names, but being a test, there wasn't the inventory behind it to complete for sales volume. The results showed that the shirts were not only a winner for Nelson's but should be expanded to a complete rollout in the tested stores, and the shirts should go into new stores as well.

The buyer saw things differently. She saw the success and acknowledged it, but said that the shirts would not be bought again at this time. Taken aback, Bobby asked why. The buyer's response was elusive, just saying that while the success was there, they wouldn't be going forward at this time.

Frustrated, Bobby began to probe the buyer, asking what results would need to have been achieved to get a rollout into more stores. The buyer gave an evasive answer that made it clear that the issue(s) had nothing to do with the success of the product. Bobby knew that there had been some tension between David and Nelson's in the past, but had been assured that those things were in the past and not prohibitive to business.

The conversation went on for 20 more minutes, with Bobby asking more and more questions but getting nowhere. Bobby thought about contacting the buyer's boss and discussing the results. But he decided that would be a bad idea. So Bobby left things with the buyer according to the buyer's wishes.

Major Question

Bobby is not happy with his buyer's decision. If you were Bobby what would you do next?

Study Questions

1. What else could Bobby have done to get more business?

2. Did David's involvement hurt the business with Nelson's? If so, do you think there is any way to remedy this in the future?

3. If you were the buyer, how would you have handled the conversation with Bobby?

4. Do you think it was a wise decision for Nelson's to not continue carrying the product? Why or why not?

CHAPTER DISCUSSION QUESTIONS

1. Discuss the major causes of problems between vendors and retailers and how negotiation may help to resolve these difficulties. Specify those matters that are most frequently negotiated.

2. Why are "good" retail/vendor partnerships and relations particularly important in the apparel industry today? Justify your answers with examples from the cases in this chapter.

3. How are the types of merchandise and/or vendors related to the determination of the types of orders placed by retailers? Use examples of order types in your discussion.

4. What can exclusivity do for a retailer? Discuss the pros and cons of negotiation with this type of arrangement.

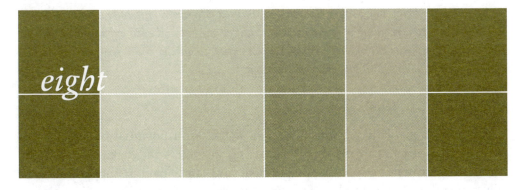

Sales Promotion, Advertising, and Visual Merchandising

CHAPTER OBJECTIVES

- Present the methods of communication between retailers and customers and discuss their effectiveness.
- Define promotional mix and relate it to media selection.
- Relay the types and importance of advertising, visual merchandising, promotional planning, and budgeting.

*A*ppropriate communication with customers is one of the keys to successful business. To communicate effectively with their target audience, companies must plan and coordinate promotional mixes to reach customers and project clear images. A promotional budget typically is divided among various elements, including sales promotions (which provide for short-term objectives), special events (which are planned by the company to attract large amounts of customers), institutional advertising (which achieves long-term objectives of goodwill, service, and prestige), displays (which capture the customer's interest at point-of-sale and promote on-the-spot purchases), and visual merchandising (which serves to present salable merchandise in different settings and also promotes consumer purchases). These elements

231

(along with publicity and public relations), when used effectively, efficiently, and in a timely fashion, can help a retailing operation reach its target market and even expand it. By reaching and increasing its customers, a company can expect to achieve more recognition, greater numbers of customers, and, therefore, more profit.

COMMUNICATIONS

Communications with a company's target market and potential new customers take many forms and are primary to attracting customers and making sales. Communications can be personal or nonpersonal, and can be paid or unpaid. Table 8.1 illustrates the relationship between these four factors. Generally, unpaid communications hold more credibility with consumers than those that are paid. Also, testimonials and blind tests by everyday consumers are believable, whereas commissioned sales associates often are thought of as saying anything to make a sale. **Publicity** is information reported in the media by a source outside the company such as a newspaper with no vested interest. This is the primary method of generating unpaid communications. A firm's **public relations** department is responsible for creating public impressions about the company. They are responsible for press releases and press conferences to release facts about a company.

Store location communicates a great deal about a store without any additional effort from the retailer. Certain shopping areas have an image or reputation, such as Rodeo Drive in Beverly Hills, Union Square in San Francisco, Madison Avenue in New York City, the Champs-Élysées in Paris, or Oxford Street in London. Often locations come with association dues, which support and promote area activities. One successful boutique owner in Union Square in San Francisco indicated she has no promotional or advertising budget, as she sees her location as all the advertising she needs.

TABLE 8.1 Methods of Communications with Customers

	Impersonal	Personal
Paid	Advertising	Personal selling
	Store atmosphere	e-mail
	Visual merchandising	
	Sales promotion	
	Web sites	
Unpaid	Publicity	Word of mouth

Source: Levy and Weitz, 2009.

PROMOTION AND SPECIAL EVENTS

Sales promotion is thought of, in the broadest sense, as all the efforts that attract consumers, build customer loyalty, and overall contribute to generating sales. The purpose of sales promotion is to inform, persuade, or remind customers about the business and its product. A company's **promotional mix** can include personal selling (see Chapter 9 for more on personal selling), advertising, displays, publicity, and/or special events. **Promotional campaigns,** overall focused efforts, often attempt to communicate a message to consumers in various ways. These can include television, radio, and print advertising, store and/or mall signage, and articles written in local newspapers about an event. The more coverage, the more apt the message is to get to the customer. Having the same message on television, radio, and print, for example, can be effective because they all reinforce each other. See Table 8.2 for a comparison of the advantages and disadvantages of various advertising media.

Special events can be classified as paid/personal communication and can include demonstrations, trunk shows, fashion shows, celebrity appearances, or other events (such as the Macy's Thanksgiving Day Parade, pictured in Figure 8.1), which are used to gain the interest of consumers. Manufacturers' personnel often are involved with such special events. Demonstrations require a knowledgeable person to show the correct usage of a product, for example, cosmetics, cooking implements, or household tools. **Trunk shows,** which are presentations of apparel lines by designers or vendors to store personnel or to customers, have become very popular. (Figure 8.2 is an example.) For some designers, trunk shows have provided the bulk of their sales in some stores. **Fashion seminars** (a presentation and discussion of new fashions) and **fashion shows** can attract large audiences into both stores and malls and can be very effective forms of promotion of new, seasonal merchandise.

Retail stores often have annual or monthly sales and promotions, which their customers come to expect. Table 8.3 lists the dates of some common promotions, although individual stores usually have a special time for such annual promotions as Anniversary Sales or Founder's Day Sales. Nordstrom, for example, only has their Anniversary Sale and Half-Yearly Sale, while Macy's and other department stores have sales once a month or even more often—depending on the competition. These sales have all sorts of names, for example, January White Sales, Big Sales, One-Day or Three-Day Sales, Customer Appreciation or Sales Associates Appreciation Day, and some discount stores run Dollar Day and Buy-One-Get-One-Free Sales. Some sales are planned in conjunction with other promotional events such as for Mother's Day or Christmas. *Case 48, The Founder's Day Special*

Figure 8.1 Macy's famous Thanksgiving Day Parade is an example of a special event.

TABLE 8.2 Advantages and Disadvantages of Different Advertising Media

Medium	Advantages	Disadvantages
Television	• Most powerful, versatile medium • Some flexibility; can be changed on short notice	• Expensive to produce and air • Local TV may not be available in some areas • Cannot target specific audiences except with cable or satellite
Radio	• Can target particular demographics • Spoken message more persuasive than print • Can be changed on short notice	• Less impact than television • Message is short-lived • Cannot show or demonstrate product
Magazines	• High-quality photographs show product to best advantage • Can target specific markets and regions	• Expensive • Ads must be placed far in advance • Large wasted circulation
Newspapers	• Often used as shopping guide • Ads can be purchased or changed quickly • Products can be shown	• Cannot target specific audience • Color reproduction poor • Short life of individual issues
Direct mail	• Can address very specific target market • Low total cost • Complete control over timing of message	• High cost per person contacted • Requires appropriate mailing list • Often seen as "junk mail"
Outdoor/ billboards	• Frequent exposure • Low cost per impression delivered • Can target specific region	• Much wasted exposure • Very little text possible • Unwilling audience; some resentment
Internet	• Combines visuals, audio, and text • Low cost after initial investment; unlimited "hits" • Can be revised at any time	• Customer must initiate contact • Reaches only people with Internet service

Figure 8.2 Francisco Costa personally shows his designs and interacts with customers at an in-store trunk show.

TABLE 8.3 Typical Sales Promotions by Month

Month	Promotions
January	White Sales, Winter Clearance, After-Holiday, Super Bowl Specials
February	President's Day (Weekend) Sale, Valentine's Day
March	Easter/Spring, St. Patrick's Day
April	Easter/Spring, Pre-Summer
May	Mother's Day, Memorial Day, Bridal, Graduation
June	Father's Day, Vacation
July	Summer Clearance, Fourth of July, Dog Days
August	Summer Clearance, Dog Days, Back-to-School
September	Labor Day, Autumn
October	Octoberfest, Halloween, Columbus Day
November	Thanksgiving, Resort, Election Day, Pre-Holiday
December	Holiday, After-Holiday

illustrates a problem between a buyer and a merchandise manager with the selection and pricing of merchandise for a retailer's annual sale.

ADVERTISING

Any form of paid/impersonal communication from a company is called **advertising.** Manufacturers may advertise to retailers, which is called **trade advertising,** for example, in *WWD* or *DNR.* Manufacturers offer advertising directly to consumers, which is called **national advertising,** as illustrated by Levi's ads on television or fragrance ads in magazines. Retailers advertise to consumers—called **retail advertising**—and, generally, the advertising is done through local media, with specific information of place, dates, and prices.

Advertising has two main objectives: (1) to sell a product, which is called product or promotional advertising, and (2) to sell an image, which is called institutional advertising. **Product ads** promote immediate consumer action—that is, the ad urges the consumer to come into the store and buy that specific product. **Institutional ads** are concerned with building a company's reputation or image rather than selling a product. They may illustrate the good deeds a company is doing in the community, the services it offers, or the prestige it maintains or desires. Some examples are oil company ads, which promote the idea that the oil company is helping to protect the environment; store ads, which show the store support of local school programs, offer special services for the elderly or handicapped, or support causes, such as Macy's Passport fashion show with proceeds going to HIV-AIDS prevention groups; or department stores, which offer top designer merchandise (if fashion leadership is the image to be projected). Nordstrom, Target, and Wal-Mart all run institutional ads for these purposes. Calvin Klein, Guess, and Benetton are well known for their image advertising, which is also a form of institutional advertising. This type of image advertising has brought Benetton especially a great deal of notoriety. In the 1970s and early 1980s Benetton concentrated on product ads, while in the late 1980s and 1990s it changed to pure image advertising, which usually depicted a social situation with no product at all, just the Benetton name. Their purpose was consciousness-raising in regard to social issues, while promoting the Benetton name. Some critics feel their ads were exploitative and inappropriate, but they were successful in reaching consumers and establishing more name recognition for the company. *Case 49, Sandini's Corporate Image* presents a case of similar, controversial image advertising.

Cooperative (co-op) advertising normally involves retailers and suppliers sharing the costs of advertising. Generally, retailers are reimbursed for part of the cost of the ad by vendors upon receipt of tear sheets (copies of the ad). Figure 8.3 is an example. Another type of co-op advertising is when a group of merchants cooperate and run one ad that benefits all of the retailers. Co-op advertising is often utilized when considering the advertising/promotion budget. However, the addition of advertising dollars to a budget through co-op advertising should not be the foremost consideration when choosing the right merchandise for a retailer's customers. *Case 50, The Co-op Advertising Fiasco* illustrates a situation in which co-op ad money was used to supplement an advertising budget in an unorthodox way, which ultimately backfired on the buyer.

Media Selection

Companies must choose the medium (i.e., television, newspaper, tabloid inserts, magazine, radio, direct mail, and so forth) to use for advertising. Media selection is key to a successful advertising/promotion plan because it is vital that advertising messages reach their intended market. The next five sections briefly examine the common forms of media used by retailers and manufacturers for advertising and promotion.

Print Media

Newspapers, magazines, flyers, and direct mail are all included in **print media. Newspapers** are the most widely used media for retailers because they are the most flexible and have a wide circulation. Because most newspapers are daily, advertisements can be very timely. These ads are called **run of press/newspaper (ROP)** ads and often are used for weekly store specials. **Tabloid inserts**—often called **preprints**—are printed separately from the regular newspaper and are usually inserted into Saturday or Sunday papers. These can be done in color and are cheaper than the ROP. **Magazines** are generally geared to a national audience and are relatively expensive, but provide good-quality print and color that are usually missing from ROP. Many national magazines, however, produce regional editions in which an ad can be targeted to local retailers. Because they are often published monthly, these ads are generally more image-related than geared toward immediate customer reaction.

Direct Mail and Marketing

A broad concept, **direct marketing** is utilized today by retailers and manufacturers. This term refers to the various ways a company can communicate directly with potential customers. This can include the use of toll free numbers, telemarketing (those dinnertime calls and cell phone messages trying to sell you something), catalogs, television shopping programs, and other forms of electronic interactive retailing.

Co-op Advertising Offer

This offer is the official Co-op Advertising Plan for the OshKosh Mens Wear Division, effective November 1, 1993. It replaces the plan printed in 1992. This offer is the only means by which our retailers may obtain the advertising assistance available from OshKosh B'Gosh, Inc.

Who is eligible for the OshKosh Men's Wear Co-op Offer?

Co-op funds are available to every men's wear retailer who buys first-quality men's wear directly from OshKosh. This co-op offer is available to all competing retailers on a proportionately equal basis.

Our co-op offer applies to advertising or sales promotions executed January 1 through December 31. Unused funds from one year cannot be carried over into the following year.

How are funds accrued?

Co-op funds will accrue in an amount equal to 3% of the net billing price of first-quality OshKosh men's wear products excluding off-price items, close-out merchandise and products purchased from OshKosh B'Gosh, Inc. licensees.

Your OshKosh net purchase from the previous calendar year will be compared with those made during the current calendar year. Your co-op fund is calculated on the amount that is greater. Accrual information is continually upgraded as the year goes on. To assist you in budgeting, the previous year's net purchases are used as a baseline until they are exceeded by the current year's net purchases.

Credit will not exceed, in any calendar year, your accrued advertising allowance applicable to that year.

How will you be reimbursed?

Spelled out on pages 5 through 8 are the basic content and documentation requirements an advertisement or sales promotion must meet in order to qualify for reimbursement. When these requirements are satisfied, you will be reimbursed with a credit memo. We will reimburse 50% of the net media and/or merchandising/sales promotion costs (less discounts and rebates)—providing the reimbursement does not exceed the limit of funds accrued.

If there are insufficient funds to pay a claim in full, it will be paid to the limit of the funds available. The balance will be a "pending" file so it can be paid when sufficient funds become available. If the claim has not been fully paid by the end of the calendar year, it will be paid to the limit of the funds available at that time, then closed.

Obtaining reimbursement is as easy as 1-2-3!

1. To receive reimbursement, submit your co-op claim within 75 days of the end of the month in which your advertising or sales promotion occurs. For example, if you run an ad on January 15, you will have until 75 days from January 31. Therefore, you must submit your claim by April 15. Extensions are available under special circumstances, with the approval of the OshKosh Co-op Department. Please do not send a co-op claim to your OshKosh Sales person or OshKosh corporate headquarters. This could result in a lost or misdirected claim, and delayed payment.

2. Along with your claim, include the required documentation as specified in the Print Advertising, Broadcast Advertising or Sales Promotion, Merchandising & Other Advertising sections of the OshKosh Co-op Offer.

Figure 8.3 OshKosh's cooperative retail advertising program.

Developing Your OshKosh® Advertising Plan

Your Media Mix

Each medium has strengths and weaknesses. It will take a combination of media to reach your target market most efficiently. You'll need to study each medium to determine the media mix right for you. The following media charts summarize the strengths and weaknesses of each medium in five crucial areas and explain how each medium is sold. You can use the charts as a quick reference to aid in your advertising decisions.

Media Tips

- Running an ad smaller than full-page, but big enough that no one else can advertise on the page, is a good way to get exclusivity.
- Always request a proof of your print ad prior to publication to make sure it's correct.
- Include easy-to-follow directions to your store in your broadcast and print advertising.
- Outdoor advertising requires long lead times, from 45 to 70 days. So plan well ahead. Billboards require prior approval of location, layout, timing and estimates of costs should you desire OshKosh® co-op reimbursement.
- A direct mail envelop that hints at the offer is better than a "blank" envelope.

Your Results

Advertising objectives set earlier allow you to evaluate your results. Increased sales is the most obvious measurement of your advertising. It's not always the most accurate, however, especially if you only count the sales immediately after you ran the ad or spot. You should also consider increased floor traffic and how that might affect your sales in the long run.

Set up a permanent scrapbook or file for the ads you run. Measure their pulling power by counting floor traffic a few days before and a few days after the advertising has run. (Remember to take note of weather conditions or competitors' advertising that appeared when yours did. They could have a bearing on how well your advertising pulled.) You'll soon learn which approaches and appeals bring prospects into your store.

Once you have established a regular advertising program, you'll be able to measure the pulling power and sales success of one ad or commercial against another. Soon you'll know exactly which ingredients work and which don't.

Advertising Efficiently

Planning not only makes advertising more effective, it can also make it more efficient. Most media will give discounts when you buy a regular planned schedule.

"Regular" doesn't have to mean every day or every week. Smart advertisers often "flight" their ads—they run a good solid schedule for two weeks, take a week or two off, then start up again. It's a good way to stretch an advertising budget while maintaining visibility. Try not to stop advertising altogether. Removing your name from the marketplace also removes it from consumers' minds.

If you have a small budget, it's better to do a few things well and create a big impact over a few shorter periods. Don't spread yourself too thin. Never put just a little bit everywhere. Concentrate your efforts in the right places. And remember, cost is a big factor, but don't ever buy the wrong medium for your target audience just because you got a "deal."

Putting It All Together

With this Ad Planner as your guide, you can coordinate your advertising across all media. Projecting the same image and tone throughout your OshKosh advertising will result in a multi-media campaign that has a consistent look and message. This consistency will help the consumer immediately recognize you as an OshKosh retailer.

Figure 8.4 OshKosh's advertising plan tips to retailers.

Direct mail (a type of print media) is used by both retailers and manufacturers, to send flyers, catalogs, or other literature to target customers. Catalogs increased tremendously in the last 25 years as busy families found less time to go downtown or to the mall. With such improved customer service as Spiegel's easy method of returning merchandise and the use of 24-hour toll free numbers for ordering, some of the disadvantages of catalog shopping are being eliminated. Neiman Marcus, for example, has become so well known for its Christmas catalog that it is sold to the public at newsstands and is a major form of advertising for the store.

Broadcast Media

Television and radio encompasses **broadcast media**. Generally television is used the most by retailers, while radio is used the least. This is understandable in that a product often sells better if the target consumer can see it. However, for special-events advertising (e.g., fashion shows, celebrity appearances, and so forth), radio advertising can be quite effective. Television reaches a mass audience and is expensive, but it can create dramatic results not easily achieved in other types of media. Generally, only such large retailers as Target, Wal-Mart, and JCPenney utilize national television advertising. However, the use of local television and cable shows is increasing, lending itself for more use by local and regional companies and is succeeding in reaching more specifically targeted audiences.

Outdoor Advertising

Billboards, the roving billboard (on wheels!), posters at train and bus stations, and on the buses, trains, and subways themselves are all included in **outdoor advertising**. In larger cities, kiosks are used to advertise retailers, manufacturers, banks, musical or theatrical performances, and other city events. San Francisco utilizes 90 JCDecaux kiosks, which are expected to provide $3 million of advertising revenues per year. These revenues are intended to help pay for the upkeep of matching sidewalk toilets, similar to those in Paris. Also, in cities, sides of buildings are sometimes utilized for advertising; for example, Adidas, Samsung, Barney's, Levi's, and DKNY all have ads painted on the sides of New York City buildings. These ads are variously institutional, product, retailer, and manufacturer/designer ads. Similarly, in rural areas or along the sides of highways, the roofs or sides of barns are often utilized in similar ways to either advertise products or to direct drivers to attractions. With improved digital printing technology, new methods of printing on vinyl are replacing painted billboards and the art of painting on sides of buildings. These images can be replaced quickly and less expensively than traditional billboards. However, with rampant advertising and too much "visual pollution" some American states, such as Vermont, and international cities, such as São Paulo, Brazil's largest city, have banned billboards. Companies in these areas have to be more creative in getting their message to consumers. Can you imagine Times Square after a ban on outdoor advertising? Companies have used other such nonconventional places to advertise as ballparks and stadiums. For example, marketers put their Web sites or company names on backdrops that are caught on camera during sporting events and then often seen again during sports highlight shows or in the sports sections of newspapers.

Internet Advertising

Have you been annoyed by pop-up ads when browsing the Internet? Pop-ups are a popular method of **online advertising** that can be infuriating to some Web users who aren't interested in the ad flashing at them. Pop-unders are a variation that opens a window under the active window; this window can be seen when the active window is closed. Internet advertising hit a record revenue of a phenomenal $5.8 billion for the first quarter of 2008, the second highest quarter ever recorded (Interactive Advertising Bureau, www.iab.net, 2008). These numbers indicate that companies are increasingly utilizing this medium. There are many companies that will create ads for companies to be placed on thousands of Web sites. Site-targeted ads are one popular method of ad placement. Some are set up where companies only pay for the clicks that they receive. Ads such as banner ads, mini Web sites, and buttons are easy to set up, and there are lots of them today. With over 138 million domain names, there are plenty of places for companies to place their ads (www.interntadsals.com, 2007).

Many apparel retailers and manufacturers also use blogs, or hives, as branded social networking and virtual shopping sites. This allows consumers to connect with their favorite brands, designers, and friends via message boards, forums, and reviews on events and merchandise, while also receiving promotional material from companies. MySpace, YouTube, ThisNext, and Stylehive are just some of these popular Internet sites that bolster the customer's confidence to buy. See Figure 8.5 for an example of a "hive." Some companies are experimenting with text messaging directly to cell phones to contact the customer. Some may see this as electronic junk mail.

Video Displays

Video walls (i.e., many television screens displaying the same visual and/or large screen projections) are being used more and more by large retailers. They make a dramatic display—bombarding the customer with messages—and are effective in

Figure 8.5 Manufacturer Ron Herman uses a "hive," or social network, where users can blog about their favorite products online.

Figure 8.6 Utowa, a Japanese company with a New York City location, unites fashion, cosmetics, and flowers to create an exhilarating sensory experience. The store uses plasma TVs as a visual merchandising technique to engage customers and persuade them to make purchases.

gaining consumer attention. Smaller stores utilize videos from designers to showcase their latest collections. (See Figure 8.6.)

Effectiveness of Promotions and Advertisements

Advertising effectiveness is measured by achievement of the objective. For example, product advertising is supposed to sell a product; therefore, the success of such an ad is measured in relation to the amount of sales generated by the ad. Experimentation with alternative promotional events at different times, using different media, or targeting different groups can be used to evaluate methods. When a company has a complex promotional mix, it is difficult to separate the parts to evaluate the effectiveness of each part because they often work together in creating results. Institutional ads are also hard to evaluate because the results are not produced immediately. Additionally, evaluation can be difficult because such outside factors as the economy or other competing events can affect the results.

Figure 8.7 Controversial ads such as this print ad by Dolce & Gabbana are sometimes banned from markets, but can be effective in creating a fashion image.

Some ads are sensational and even objectionable to consumers, but are these the ones people remember? Calvin Klein pathed the way for cutting-edge fashion advertising starting in the 1980s with Brooke Shields stating, "Nothing comes between me and my Calvin's." Since then he has continued to remain controversial with ads featuring Marky Mark, Kate Moss, and Christy Turlington. Some of his more controversial ads have included his Obsession ads, one with a naked Kate Moss lying on a couch, and his CK One ads depicting groups of young people who are paired off in ways that suggest alternative sexual lifestyles. Calvin Klein continues to use sexually charged images of men and women in his ads with supermodel Natalia Vodianova and Swedish soccer midfielder Freddie Ljungberg in an international campaign. And in 2006 Kate Moss returned to Calvin Klein after many years, teamed up with Jamie Dornan this time. Kate will always be associated with Calvin Klein in the public's mind (Karimzadeh, 2006).

Other companies such as Diesel, Guess, Dior, and Dolce & Gabbana have used sexually suggestive ads (see Figure 8.7). At times, these advertisements have been deemed too explicit to be run in some print publications or to appear at all in some countries. Victoria's Secret, to cite another example of a company that has used sexually suggestive ad campaigns, keeps the heat on with its steamy fashion shows that are broadcast on television and available online.

Controversy with Benetton, Sandini (see *Case 49, Sandini's Corporate Image*), or Calvin Klein ads may be remembered, but research has not definitively shown a direct relationship with sales. And that is the bottom line for businesses.

VISUAL MERCHANDISING

Visual merchandising is a general term that is used to describe everything that is seen when a customer enters a store. It is the presentation of a store and its merchandise in ways that will attract the attention of potential customers and motivate them to make purchases (Diamond & Diamond, 2007). This includes the exterior appearance of the store, window displays, signage, and all interior displays of merchandise on fixtures and lighting that are used to create an overall effect. Much visual merchandising is concentrated on internal displays with the objective of increasing sales, rather than elaborate and costly image window displays. The exception is large flagship stores such as Macy's, Saks Fifth Avenue, Neiman Marcus, Barney's, and Bloomingdale's. Traditional window displays often have been replaced with wide-open entryways where shoppers view the main selling store. The store itself is the display. However, new outside malls bring the opportunity for more small-store window displays.

Visual merchandising has become not only a conduit for sale, but entertainment, creating an experience and engaging the customer. Some methods are interactive, such as kiosks to find or price merchandise. Onscreen fashion shows, seen in many designer boutiques, give the customer product information in an exciting way. Others are more experiential. Young customers of American Girl can have their doll's hair done at the "salon" and can learn about their doll's "history" on www. americangirl.com. For example, "Samantha Parkington is a generous and loyal orphan growing up in Victorian times." Doll owners can play games related to Samantha, read book excerpts, send e-cards, and use wallpaper featuring her images.

Some manufacturers send their specialists to the retail store. Liz Claiborne was the first apparel company to provide stores with a merchandising specialist for that department, setting up displays and selling the merchandise. These specialists work for the manufacturer and/or the retailer. Many brand specialists periodically visit their retail clients to restock inventory, display the merchandise, and provide product knowledge to the sales associates. Effective visual merchandising can sell the merchandise without any other type of promotion. It can draw customers into an establishment and create the desire for purchase, encourage impulse buying, and provide self-service in addition to entertaining and engaging the customer. With the trend of less personal sales assistance in many stores—especially department stores—effective visual merchandising is especially important. Many stores use an instore approach for the majority of their promotion rather than utilizing media advertising. Often corporate offices develop strict standards to create merchandise presentation consistency in all stores. See Figure 8.8 for an example of visual display standards and Figure 8.9 for an example of a presentation plan.

VISUAL MERCHANDISING BASIC STANDARD

DIVISION: Moderate Sportswear
DEPARTMENT 127, 121
CLASSIFICATION: "Innovation"/Career Related Separates
FIXTURE STANDARD: Face out, Flat bar (for side hanging merchandise), Presentation shelf. T-stands, Small capacity four-way racks, Fourth arm displayer with abstract mannequin (prototype), "Innovations" sign wardrober (prototype)/or mannequins.

MERCHANDISE PRESENTATION STANDARD:
- Merchandise as a collection by fashion trend.
- Divide floor by fashion trends, according to quarterly zone-o-gram
- Utilize flat bar for side hanging under presentation shelves, or post out.
- Walls without valances should be broken up by using buttons, or broken up by use of presentation shelf.
- Consistent rack height adjustment, front arm one notch higher than rear and side arms.
- Norton McNaughton, Chaus and Chaus Sport should be merchandised within the innovations area.

VISUAL PRESENTATION STANDARD:
- Presentation shelf with wall enhancement and costumer layered as an outfit, minimal accessories or hanging wall forms.
- Rack top costumers/or 3/4 forms.
- "Innovations" sign unit with abstract mannequins/or wardrober.
- Layer face outs and front arm of floor fixture as would be worn.
- Place acrylic forms in sets of three on focal wall.

SIGNING STANDARD:
- "Innovations" floor fixture sign (prototype).
- 11"×14" key item signing.
- 7"× 5 1/2" price point signing, where applicable.

Figure 8.8 An example of corporate visual merchandising standards. This particular example comes from a major department store chain; the information contained in this report is relayed to all the branches of the chain and each store is expected to comply with these standards.

Figure 8.9 A computer-aided design (CAD) presentation plan for an apparel retailer.

Anthropologie is somewhat unconventional in that it doesn't do major advertising campaigns and doesn't have standard appearances for each of its stores, but rather puts its effort into interior and exterior store displays, with two full-time display employees for each store. See *Case 51, Anthropologie: Display and Store Image,* for a discussion of this approach to entice customers to spend time and money in its stores. Also see Figure 8.10 for an example of Anthropologie's displays.

Window displays are an important part of visual merchandising. Window displays can be open or closed. Traditional store window displays are enclosures with solid backings that isolate the merchandise to be presented. These are called **closed** or **closed-back window displays.** Often stores use **open window displays** enabling the viewer to see directly into the store through the display. Effectiveness is often more challenging to achieve in an open window display, however, because the interior of the store competes with the display. Open window displays are

Figure 8.10 This Anthropologie interior represents a lifestyle presentation of merchandise, where everything from books to switch-plates, jewelry and clothing entice the customer.

Figure 8.11 Saks Fifth Avenue's extravagant Christmas windows draw many shoppers to the store during the holiday season.

Figure 8.12 A junior fashion wall display plan, which shows how to present several types of pants and tops. Note how the items are grouped, which can suggest various combinations to the customer.

more common in malls where there are no outside windows, while department stores in downtown areas most often use closed window displays. These closed window displays perform a selling function even when the store is closed, in addition to pure entertainment for "window shoppers." Saks and Bergdorf Goodman have extremely effective closed window displays, and Barney's New York has become well known for its creative, entertaining, unconventional windows in which nothing is sacred and often common objects are used in offbeat ways. Some stores (e.g., Barney's, Lord & Taylor, Saks Fifth Avenue) have become known for their elaborate Christmas displays, which bring large numbers of shoppers just to view them. This is a time when many retailers try to "outdo" one another in window presentations under the presumption that the more people that view the Christmas windows, the more customers that will come in the store and purchase. See Figure 8.11 for an example of a Saks holiday window display.

Case 14, A Hunka-Hunka of Burnin' Hot! A Case of Abercrombie & Fitch's Brand and Store Positioning, in Chapter 3, explains Abercrombie & Fitch's new philosophy of no window displays. Its shuttered windows create mystery and entice customers to come in the store to see what's new because nothing can be seen from the street. A&F's Ruehl No. 925 stores are similar as its storefronts look like a house; again, customers need to enter the store to see what it has to offer.

Effective **interior product displays** help customers locate merchandise and can illustrate how the merchandise is used or worn. Additionally, product displays can show how the merchandise can be accessorized, which encourages the consumer to purchase that merchandise and the accessories. Most displays have a sales (product) objective; some displays, however, project an image of prestige without a sales objective (this is a type of institutional display, which serves much the same purpose as an institutional ad). For example, a very expensive designer gown with limited stock (or no stock at all) may be displayed for prestige and not a sales purpose. The various types of interior displays include the following:

Figure 8.13 This open-selling display in the Tom Ford store allows for easy customer self-service.

- **Countertop** or **point-of-purchase displays** in which the merchandise can be touched and self-selected by the customer.
- **Showcase displays,** which are often used for small or expensive items. These are usually enclosed and locked.
- **Wall** or **ledge displays,** which utilize dead or unused space to show merchandise.
- **Aisle displays,** in which merchandise might be layered and accessorized and then hung at the end of the display case (often these are the items that sell first!).

Displays can be either open or closed. **Open-selling displays** are those that enable customer self-service, but they have a higher potential for shoplifting (see Figure 8.13). **Closed-island displays** provide less customer access, which results in

Figure 8.14 In contrast to open-selling is this closed-island display of Tom Ford accessories. Because of the expensive nature of these goods, as well as their relatively small size, this type of closed display not only protects against shoplifting but projects an image of quality and exclusivity.

fewer thefts, but also possibly fewer sales. Closed displays also require a salesperson to be present (to open and close the display), which under certain circumstances could result in higher operating costs (i.e., employee salaries). See Figure 8.14 for an example of a closed display.

Often customers need suggestions on how to put apparel items together because they cannot visualize this for themselves. The employee display, or modeling of the merchandise, is one of the most effective selling tools. In stores in which such "employee racks" are used, those items sell out the fastest. Also, visuals from vendors can show how merchandise is intended to be worn or used.

There are many elements for creating productive, effective displays. Props, signage, and lighting are important components for creating displays. Other principles to remember when planning a display include the following:

1. Select the most in-demand merchandise.
2. Plan for installation time.
3. Consider the timeliness of the goods and display.
4. Keep the display clean.
5. Keep the display appropriate to the store's image.
6. Use elements and principles of design properly.
7. Change the display often.

Remote displays are used away from a store's location. These freestanding units can target tourists because they are often placed in hotels, while a department store that is located at one end of a mall might also use a remote display at the other end to alert customers of its presence.

PROMOTION AND ADVERTISING BUDGETS

Retailers and manufacturers develop **promotional plans** by carefully considering their budgets. They must consider what percent of their budget will be spent on the type of promotion and then choose the appropriate type of media to utilize. Often a percentage of sales is used to determine the amount to be spent on promotion. This could be a percentage of either past or anticipated sales. For example, with last year sales of $200,000 and 5 percent of sales allocated for promotion, the promotion budget is $10,000. That amount would be divided among television, magazine, and newspaper ads, special events, publicity, displays, and other general promotion items according to plan. In addition to allocating monies to departments, some companies divide budgets on a seasonal or monthly basis. Another method some small stores use is the "all-you-can-afford" method, which allows for promotions only if there is available cash. Sometimes the "meet-the-competition" method is also used when needed—that is, when a direct competitor has a sale or promotion, a retailer might meet that competition with its own promotion.

Some unpaid communications cost nothing; however, companies do incur costs to stimulate them, especially for some forms of publicity. Developing events worthy of media coverage can be costly, even if they are very effective. Macy's annual Spring Flower Show, Fourth of July Fireworks display, and Thanksgiving Day Parade receive a great deal of media coverage but are extremely expensive to produce. Word-of-mouth may be the best promotion (if it is positive) and it is free; however, negative word-of-mouth information can be very detrimental to retailers and manufacturers. That is why most companies care about the impression customers are left with after transactions.

Retailers should allot promotional dollars first to their **primary trading area,** which is the area in which it can serve its customers in terms of convenience better than its competitors, and then to its **secondary trading areas,** which yield customers despite a competitor's location advantage. Generally, there is a maximum distance that customers will travel to shop at a certain retailer or mall. A primary trading area is usually three to five miles from the site, while a secondary trading area is seven or more miles away. This, of course, varies from state to state and city to city. A retailer's promotional efforts should be geared toward those consumers who are most likely to shop at the retailing establishment.

Case 52, Promoting a Sale gives you the chance to develop a promotions budget for an electronics chain.

SUMMARY

Sales promotion, advertising, and visual merchandising are vital components of a retail business as they convey specific and general information to potential and current customers. Companies plan and budget a promotional mix to communicate their message, which can consist of paid, nonpaid, and personal and impersonal types of communication. Whatever the method, promotion, advertising, and visual merchandising are essential elements to a successful, growth-oriented business.

KEY TERMS

advertising

aisle display

broadcast media

closed/closed-back window display

closed-island display

cooperative advertising

countertop display

direct mail

direct marketing

fashion seminar

fashion show

institutional advertising

interior product display

ledge display

magazines

national advertising

newspapers

online advertising

open-selling display

open window display

outdoor advertising

point-of-purchase display

preprints

primary trading area

print media

product advertising

promotional campaign

promotional mix

promotional plan

publicity

public relations
remote display
retail advertising
run of press/newspaper (ROP)
sales promotion
secondary trading area
showcase display
special events

tabloid inserts
trade advertising
trunk show
video wall
visual merchandising
wall display
window display

BIBLIOGRAPHY

Corcoran, C. T. (2007, May 16). Shopping online now more social. *Women's Wear Daily*, p. 8.

Diamond J., & Diamond, D. (2007). *Contemporary visual merchandising & environmental design*. New York: Fairchild Books.

Internet advertising revenues up 18.2% yoy, $5.8 billion for Q1 '08, second highest quarter ever (2008, June 17). Interactive Advertising Bureau, www.iab.net.

Karimzadeh, M. (2006, June 26). Kate Moss comes home to Calvin Klein jeans. *Women's Wear Daily*, p. 5.

Kaufman, S. (2006, December). The whole cake or is it crumbs? *Visual Merchandising & Store Design*, p. 22.

Levy, M., & Weitz, B. A. (2009). *Retailing management*. New York: McGraw-Hill/Irwin.

Monget, K. (2005, December 5). Victoria's Secret keeps the heat on. *Women's Wear Daily*, p. 21.

Monget, K. (2006, January 9). Calvin Klein underwear ads turn up the heat for spring. *Women's Wear Daily*, p. 20.

Pegler, M. M. (2006). *Visual merchandising*. New York: Fairchild Books.

São Paulo: A city without ads. Retrieved September 8, 2008, from http://www.adbusters.org/magazine/73/Sao_Paulo_A_City_Without_Ads.html.

Web consumer info: Latest VeriSign domain name industry brief underscores growth of Internet internationally. (2007). www.interntadsals.com

Case 48

THE FOUNDER'S DAY SPECIAL

Nancy J. Rabolt, San Francisco State University
Judy K. Miler, Florida State University

Every October, the Young Company, a specialty store in Orlando, Florida, runs a Founder's Day Sale, which is a storewide clearance sale. The event lasts for one week and features stock goods ranging from 25 to 40 percent off regular prices. The yearly event, which has been held for the past 20 years, has become a store tradition and has always been highly successful. From the store's point of view, it is an excellent sale because (1) it helps to clear merchandise from the store and brings the inventory levels down to accommodate for new holiday merchandise, and (2) it yields customer satisfaction because of the great bargains that can be found.

The Young Company advertises this sale through an ad and a flyer. The flyer is sent directly to credit card customers and is also available in the local paper on the Sunday before the sale begins. The ad is run every day in the local paper during the week before the sale. The flyer and ad consist of a list of every sale item in the store. Every buyer submits a list of items to be included in the ad and flyer. The list describes the merchandise, the regular retail prices, and the new reduced prices. This strategy creates a large amount of traffic through the store and the sale has become the largest revenue producer of all the Young Company's promotions.

Ethel Frommer, the coat buyer, who has been with the company for five years, submitted her list to her divisional merchandise manager, who reviewed it for sufficient quantities, original values, and new price levels. They were satisfactory and approved. Two days before the ad was to appear, Sidney Smith, the general merchandise manager, visited the department with a proof copy of the first series of ads.

He said, "Ethel, I'd like to review the merchandise and check it against the copy." "Fine," replied Ethel, and she followed him to the stock room.

Sidney and Ethel entered the stockroom off the selling floor and checked each group to get a feeling for the bargain aspect of the merchandise. As he was nearing the end of his research, he spotted one group of coats originally priced at $150 marked down to $75.

"Ethel, didn't you run these coats at $75 last month?"

"Yes, I did," she replied.

"And wasn't it a bust—about four coats out of seventy-five?" he retorted.

"You have a great memory; that's the case."

"Well, you aren't going to run them again. We don't repeat failures," he stated in no uncertain terms.

"Please, Sidney, market conditions have changed; cold weather and sparse market supply make these coats worth $150. In fact, if I had to fill in colors and sizes, I'd have to pay the regular $80. At $75, the customers are getting the bargain of the season," Ethel pleaded.

"Sorry," Sidney responded, "go up to the advertising department and change the price to $60. First, of course, be sure to take the markdown and enter the reduction in the system."

Ethel was extremely angry. She felt the decision was arbitrary and without respect for her judgment.

Major Question

What should Ethel do regarding Sidney's request to reduce the promotional coats to $60 and run them in the ad?

Study Questions

1. What factors make a successful sale?
2. What factors enter into the pricing of a sale item like these coats?

Case 49

SANDINI'S CORPORATE IMAGE

Janice Ellinwood, Marymount University

Antonio Sandini, corporate king of the global fashion empire Sandini, is thinking of changing his corporation's promotional image. The Italy-based apparel business has been gaining notoriety for an advertising campaign that uses shock-tactic themes. Ever since the campaign started, it seems as if Sandini is constantly being barraged by individuals and/or groups that oppose this style of advertising. There have also been lawsuits and threatening letters to corporate officers and their families. Perhaps life would be easier if a new image were adopted (and the socio-cultural "waves" were stilled). Antonio does know that his life would certainly be calmer if the company were to forgo its controversial campaign. He must also consider the other employees that have suffered as a result of the backlash from the publicity. Sandini wonders, however, how much of their successful sales history can be attributed to the publicity that the company gets from its non-traditional advertising.

Such themes have nothing to do with the origin of the company. Sandini began as a knitting business; handmade sweaters were sold directly to Italian shops using no middleman. Antonio offered discounts to retailers who paid cash on delivery. As the business grew, he bought knitting machines to make the sweaters. Out of that purchase, factories developed, first in Europe, then others in the United States, South America, South Korea, and Japan. Foreign factories meant Antonio could avoid import taxes and cut transport time and costs. He also used subcontractors to do some of the manufacturing, which limited the necessity for employees and helped circumvent union and government controls.

As in the case of the advertising campaign that brought public attention, Sandini attempts to be at the cutting edge in all aspects of its business. At the business's headquarters, designers work with the most up-to-date computer and knitting technology to develop the samples. Even the packing and circulation of goods inside the warehouse is computerized. Technology aids in the adjustment to sudden changes in production and mid-season reordering.

Sandini has several thousand licensed stores in over 100 countries, including Japan, China, Russia, Czechoslovakia, Poland, Turkey, Egypt, as well as the United States. The company sells its goods at wholesale prices to stores that agree to sell Sandini's merchandise exclusively. The product line is extending into menswear, children's wear, infant apparel, shoes, underwear, perfumes, watches, and sunglasses. Any financial risk rests entirely on the shop owners. They pay no fees or royalties to the Sandini corporation and do not share their profits. Sandini therefore is not limited by regulatory franchise laws. The shop owners are selected by several worldwide agents who are often part owners of the shops in their region. Most of these agents are Italian. They also book orders and monitor standards.

Sandini does not actually make up a garment until it is ordered. It takes 80 percent of the orders nine months before the season starts for its two yearly collections—Fall/Winter and Spring/Summer. Their most important target market is 15- to 25-year-old females with considerable disposable income. But this market is expanding to include many 30- to 50-year-olds. Because of its first priority market, Sandini began to advertise in teen and rock magazines, and then in career and fashion magazines.

Sandini uses a Paris firm to develop its advertising. The first campaign highlighted models of various skin colors, emphasizing society's multiethnicity. At that time, the firm decided to omit copy in the ads, except for the corporate name Sandini. That campaign received a lot of praise from the public. There was also an increase in the quantity and quality of editorials featuring Sandini's merchandise in the leading magazines.

Then the Paris advertising firm tried another approach. It chose to run productless ads, a method meant to market company philosophy or designer image. Without emphasis on product characteristics, the ads attempted to predispose the consumer to what makes one manufacturer distinctive from another. Without any merchandise or copy, the impact of the ads rested solely on the unexplained visual image.

What followed was a series of artistically composed ad layouts, featuring images meant to reflect problems in contemporary society in regard to perceived equality between peoples. These images touched on race, religion, birth, illness, death, among other relevant aspects of life. These were met with negative reactions from some minority, religious, and parents' groups—confirmation that the campaign attracted attention.

The first ad pictured two male arms, one white and one black, handcuffed together at the wrists, both garbed in light-blue, denim workshirts. American civil rights groups complained that handcuffs do not convey brotherhood. The United Kingdom would not run the ad.

Another ad was rejected by some U.S. publications. It featured a black woman nursing a white infant. The rejection partially came from an American awareness of conditions before the Civil War when black women were forced to nurse white children while their own went hungry. The other negative reactions were in response to the woman's bare breast being shown in the ad.

In the midst of a Persian Gulf conflict, another ad pictured a cemetery with one white star of David among a field of white crosses. In Italy, a Milan jury deemed it offensive to religion.

Another ad made use of a photograph that earned an international journalism award. It portrayed a family grieving at the bedside of a young man who has just died of AIDS. The public wondered whether the ad raised awareness of the disease or exploited it. As a result of other ads that referred to the same illness, a French court found Sandini guilty of exploiting the illness and ordered the company to pay damages to a national AIDS organization, which was responsible for the suit.

A subsequent ad pictured the actual image of a newborn baby with its placenta and umbilical cord still attached. The ad was rejected in the United States by several fashion magazines. The editor of one parenting magazine said that Americans view childbirth as a very personal and private subject, and she was afraid of offending her readers.

Perhaps the biggest reaction was caused by an ad picturing a nun and priest kissing on the mouth. This ad was rejected by all American publications except one. A religious association made the public statement that Antonio Sandini's company had offended religious values and trivialized the Catholic Church.

Antonio believed that, in developing advertising campaigns that made social comment, his company was freeing the product from the world of merchandising. By capitalizing solely on an image, the ads were an effort to communicate beyond the consumer to the individual. This meant that the campaigns did not aim at the company's target market, but rather at individuals who shared similar views.

Regardless of the controversy, Antonio is generally pleased with the attention the ads received. Despite economic problems and lawsuits during the campaign, the corporation's net earnings increased 21 percent, largely because of licenses for new merchandise in the product line and expansion into new countries. Sales in Italy, France, and the United Kingdom (two regions) account for nearly 70 percent of Sandini's

TABLE 8.4 Sandini's Sales by Region

France and the United Kingdom	38%
Italy	31%
Japan, Korea, and China	15%
United States	6%
Russia, Czechoslovakia, Poland, Turkey, Egypt	6%
South American Countries	4%

total volume. Two other regions contribute 6 percent each to the total sales and the sixth region constitutes the lowest amount—4 percent. Sandini's sales by region appear in Table 8.4.

Major Question

Should Antonio Sandini change his corporation's promotional image? How might he accomplish the task?

Study Questions

1. Has the existing ad campaign attracted the company's target market?

2. Examine corporation sales by region. Could the advertising campaign have hindered sales in some locations? What else might influence quantity of sales volume?

3. Is political or social comment appropriate within the scope of a fashion ad campaign?

Exercises

1. Bring to class examples of recent advertising campaigns you identify as the most effective. What attributes make them successful—humor, entertainment, effective imagery, and so on? Present your thoughts to the class.

2. Visit the Web site for a company currently making social comment in its advertising campaign in order to report to the class on the company's stated motivation.

3. Evaluate print ads from international fashion magazines with those of American ones. What are the similarities and differences?

Case 50

THE CO-OP ADVERTISING FIASCO

Nancy J. Rabolt, San Francisco State University
Judy K. Miler, Florida State University

Howard Peterson, the moderate dress buyer for Perkins Apparel, was having his weekly meeting with Paul Jacobs, the ready-to-wear merchandise manager. Perkins is a large, privately owned specialty store located in New York City. They have been successful for over 50 years, but competition from the large chains makes it tougher and tougher each year to make the profit that they require.

This particular meeting took place at the beginning of the month. Paul, while reviewing the department's figures, remarked to

Howard, "Say, you'll have to come up with a big promotion to meet and hopefully beat your last year's figures for the last week of this month. Last year you were lucky and latched on to an item that was hot, and it was responsible for last year's tremendous figures. I don't see any strong trends in sight at this time, so you better go out and find one."

Howard replied glumly, "You're right, there's nothing really hot that I'm aware of. And, to tell you the truth, I've been worrying about those figures for awhile now myself. My key resources do not seem to be in a position to even give me a promotional buy, so I'm not sure what to do."

All of a sudden, Paul's face lit up. He had an idea of how to help Howard. "Tell you what—the way I figure it, you need to get 3,000 dresses to sell for about $69.99 each to make your figures. To meet your last year's record, you should pay about $34, no more. I'll get you about $105,000 in open-to-buy for the event and also arrange for extra advertising money for a full-page ad in two papers. That ought to do the trick; but, Howard, you better get some good merchandise at a price. . . . The ads have to generate a sellout for us if we're to come out all right."

The next day, Howard went to Goodman Dresses, a dress manufacturer who had been after him for a long time and who was very eager to get his foot into Perkins's door. Previously, Howard had made several unimportant purchases from Goodman Dresses and had found the dresses to be nicely made. Thinking (and hoping) that this was his big chance to become a key resource with Perkins, Sam Goodman went all out in

shaving his prices and ensuring delivery well in advance of the promotion.

Shortly after the purchase was made, Paul called Howard and told him that a small problem had arisen. "Howard, I hate to tell you that the general merchandise manager was not able to come across with the whole $12,800 we need for the ads. We can't cut the ads—we need all the ad space we can buy to make the ad scream PRICE! I was only able to get half the ad money; we'll need $6,400 from the vendor to pay for the rest."

Howard was incredulous because the inference was unmistakable. Paul wanted him to get a $6,400 co-op ad contribution on a promotional purchase, and he knew that was almost impossible. However, he dutifully went to Sam Goodman and asked him for the money to help pay for the ad. Goodman looked at Howard as if he was nuts; he swore that he was losing money on each of the 3,000 dresses he had already sold to Howard. Sam pointed out what Howard already knew: he was taking this deal only because he was hoping to do business later with Perkins on a more profitable basis.

Howard reported back to Paul and informed him of his inability to get the ad money. "There is only one way out," Paul replied. "We'll have to load the invoice. Instead of $35, we'll ask Goodman Dresses to bill us at $37.15 per dress; and then we'll retail them for $74.99 instead of the $69.99 we originally planned. Also, ask Goodman to throw in some dresses that can genuinely be sold at retail for $125 so that we can legitimately advertise 'VALUES UP TO $125 FOR $74.99.' We'll then charge the manufacturer back $2.15 for each garment to cover the $6,400 we need for the ad money. In the final analysis, we'll get the volume and sacrifice a little markup."

And so it went. The merchandise arrived at the store in time and was ticketed at $74.99. The ad was to appear on Wednesday evening, for the big Thursday to Saturday sale.

After dinner on Wednesday evening, Howard went to buy the morning paper. He found his full-page ad and was quite pleased with the way it looked. But, to his horror, he discovered that on the page following his big promotion there was one from Sommers Specialty Store, their chief competitor. The Sommers ad appeared to feature the identical merchandise, but the dresses were priced at $69.95 each. Both ads had photographs illustrating what appeared to be very similar merchandise.

Howard ran to the phone and called his merchandise manager at home, exclaiming, "Paul, we've been killed—did you see the ads?"

Paul replied, "Howard, you selected the merchandise. Who told you to buy from someone who could not be trusted to not sell the same dresses to another store in our market?"

The next morning Howard stopped at Sommers Department Store on the way to work and looked at the merchandise on sale. Of course, it was the same—style numbers, colors, sizes. No customer in her right mind could fail to see that it was the same merchandise at $5 lower than it was at Perkins across the street. It is well known in the trade that the moderate dress customer is a very smart shopper who does not impulse-buy, but shops around before purchasing.

When Howard arrived at his desk there was the expected message to see Jacobs at once. Paul went right to work on Howard.

"You, as a seasoned buyer, should have known how to select a resource, negotiate your needs, and then buy a promotional purchase. I don't see how this happened!"

Major Question

If you were Howard Peterson, how would you reply to this criticism, and how would you propose to remedy this situation?

Study Questions

1. When do manufacturers offer cooperative advertising money? In what situation should a retailer accept it?

2. Why did the retailer end up in this situation? Should he deal with this vendor in the future?

3. How will customers view this price war?

4. Is it ethical to "load" the invoice as was done in this case? Is that standard business practice?

5. Is Paul Jacobs culpable in this situation?

Case 51

ANTHROPOLOGIE: DISPLAY AND STORE IMAGE

Janice Ellinwood, Marymount University

Anthropologie, the Philadelphia-based chain store group owned by Urban Outfitters Inc., along with the wholesale and retail brand Free People and a store group known by the corporate name, does not operate with the conventions of most retailers. It doesn't interpret its fashion research fastidiously and stock vast numbers of a few trends. It doesn't run major advertising campaigns and establish policies at the top level until they trickle down to store personnel. The appearance of each store is not standardized. Compared to most other retailers, Anthropologie's unique approach buoyed the company in the wake of the poor economy that followed the September 11 terrorist attacks.

Its target market evolved as the Urban Outfitters store's customer grew up. She is 30 to 45 years of age, college or post-graduate educated, and married or in a committed relationship. More than 50 percent of her peer group have children. She is suburban or ex-urban, but she is also well-traveled, well-read, with a host of avocations, such as cooking, gardening, movie-going, and wine-tasting. Anthropologie's merchandising policy is an outgrowth of its

understanding of the target customer; this understanding is learned from focus groups and customer surveys. The store's success originates from identifying trends for this customer and showcasing them in its stores. Consequently, the approach has been to set a mood in the store each season by creating a unique and varied store mix of apparel, linens, books, and furniture.

This operation's buyers, equipped with their own unique buying style, are primarily responsible for pulling off this task. Buyers, who call their shopping trips "digs," scour the world to find unique items, operating in an almost entrepreneurial fashion. Fifty percent of the stock is private label, and 50 percent is market driven. The result is an extremely eclectic product mix reflecting a range of product categories, each one edited in a unique way for the season. Retail prices range from $4 for a bar of soap to $30,000 for an antique. The apparel is priced at the better range. Stores are densely and artfully presented.

The loyal customer can spend hours looking at the stock, seduced by an implied narrative that pulls her through a space that easily holds the interest of the worldly female. It is ripe with appeals to the customer's senses of sound, sight, touch, and smell. The company tries to provide a setting in which the customer can experience feelings of discovery and escape. In keeping with this approach, Anthropologie does not encourage its sales personnel to come up to the customer directly and suggest merchandise for purchase. It is assumed that she is educated and caught up in the store

Sales Promotion, Advertising, and Visual Merchandising

263

experience enough to make her own confident selection.

Each season Anthropologie's president, design staff, merchant staff, and visual team develop concepts together. There are usually several simultaneous fashion themes or stories. Some of these have focused on 1960s-inspired silhouettes, bohemian styles, starlet glamour of the 1950s, and holiday looks. Displays are changed several times during a 12-week cycle in order to keep the stores looking fresh. The inventory turns six times per year and new products appear four days per week.

Every Anthropologie store employs two full-time display people, although most retailers would consider this excessive. The company takes the 2 percent of sales normally spent on advertising and puts it into store execution. However, there is concern that the customized visual merchandising approach may be difficult to manage across many units as the store group size increases. Although the unique merchandising approach is thought to have been a worthwhile method for holding off competitors, the current retail environment is fraught with strong competing store chains, newcomers, and attractive print and television ad campaigns, all vying for the attention of the Anthropologie customer.

Major Question

Would Anthropologie benefit from cutting display persons in each store and putting more budget toward advertising?

Study Questions

1. What methods of buying are used in other chain and department stores?

2. What is the relationship between the jobs of the visual merchandiser and the buyer?

3. What publications might Anthropologie's target customer read?

Exercises

1. Create a hypothetical print ad campaign for Anthropologie based on a celebrity. Which celebrity might appeal to the company's target market? How might you arrange the print ads and what message might they convey?

2. Create a hypothetical print ad campaign for Anthropologie's furniture and linens. In what publications might they run? What message should they convey?

3. Create a theme for a spring season's merchandise at Anthropologie. What might appeal to the target customer? What implications for merchandise arrangement might arise from the theme?

Bibliography

Edelson, S. (2003, July 28). Anthropologie's customer-focused culture. *Women's Wear Daily,* p. 27.

Palmieri, J. E. (2004, November 17). A lesson in Anthropologie. *Women's Wear Daily,* p. 31.

Case 52

PROMOTING A SALE[1]

David Ehrlich, Marymount University

A consumer electronic chain in the Washington, D.C., area is planning a big sale in its suburban Virginia warehouse over the three-day President's Day weekend (Saturday through Monday). On sale will be nearly $2 million worth of consumer electronic products, 50 percent of the merchandise sold in the store. The company hopes to realize at least $900,000 in sales during the three days. In the retailer's past experience, the first day's sales were 50 percent of the total. The second day's were 35 percent, and the last day's, 15 percent. One of every two customers who came made a purchase.

It's known that large numbers of people always flock to such sales, some driving as far as 50 miles. They come from all economic levels, but all are confirmed bargain hunters. You're the assistant to the general merchandise manager, who has asked you to plan the event's marketing campaign. You have the following information:

1. A full-page *Washington Post* ad costs $10,000, a half page ad costs $6,000, and a quarter-page ad costs $3,500. To get the maximum value from a newspaper campaign, it's company

policy to always run two ads (not necessarily the same size) for such events.

2. The local northern Virginia paper is printed weekly and distributed free to some 15,000 households. It costs $700 for a full-page and $400 for a half-page ad.

3. To get adequate TV coverage, at least three channels must be used, with a minimum of eight 30-second spots on each at $500 per spot, spread over three or more days. Producing a TV spot costs $3,000.

4. The store has contracts with three radio stations. One appeals to a broad general audience aged 25 to 34 years. One is popular with the 18-to-25 group. A classical music station has a small but wealthy audience. Minimum costs for a saturation radio campaign, including production, on the three stations are $8,000, $5,000, and $3,000, respectively.

5. To produce and mail a full-color flyer to the store's 80,000 charge customers costs $10,000. When the company used such a mailing piece before, about three percent responded.

Major Question*

The company wants a mixed-media ad campaign to support this event. How would you prepare an ad plan for the general merchandise manager that costs no more than $40,000?

*Do not use the alternative solutions format for this case.

[1]Levy and Weitz, *Retailing Management*, 6th ed., The McGraw-Hill Companies. Reproduced with permission of The McGraw-Hill Companies.

Exercises

1. Work out the daily scheduling of all advertising.

2. Work out the dollars to be devoted to each medium.

3. Justify your plan.

CHAPTER DISCUSSION QUESTIONS

1. Compare types of promotion and advertising of well-known retailers. What media is used? What image is presented to the public? Explain what methods might be more effective for different types of retailers. Use case examples from the chapter to reinforce your decisions.

2. Compare institutional and product ads, and institutional and product displays at various stores. Which stores use mostly institutional? Which use mostly product? How does this relate to fashion leadership and the type of retailer?

3. What type of promotion is used by manufacturers, catalog companies, and other Internet retailers? How is this different from stored retailers?

4. How can a retailer be assured that a particular promotion will be successful?

5. Discuss promotional mix and how it relates to media selection. Why is it important for companies to have a promotional mix?

6. Compare and contrast the various types of interior display, and suggest what types of merchandise might be best suited for each.

nine

Personal Selling and Customer Relations

CHAPTER OBJECTIVES

- Emphasize the importance of customer service and the role of personal selling at retail.
- Examine the various aspects of customer service relations, compensation, and selling incentives.
- Define product knowledge and explain its importance in the selling process.
- Discuss the methods and importance of effective sales training and evaluation of retail sales personnel.

*T*oday's retail customers are highly educated and sophisticated. Because they often shop with only their needs in mind, without time to waste, they are looking for good service to help them obtain what they want—when they want it. The retailers and manufacturers that address the issue of customer service can help make the sales experience a positive one that brings the customer back to shop again and again. After all, service is often at the crux of sales. More and more today, vendors are playing an active role in attracting and keeping retail customers. In many cases, they are partnering with retailers through training, to work cooperatively toward the same goal: selling merchandise. Selling skills are crucial to retail *success. Effective selling is reliant on a number of factors. For example, having a good, effective sales force to motivate customers not only to buy but to come back to a retailer is paramount. Sales associates—who are courteous, knowledgeable, and ready to serve and sell to the customer—can do the job they were hired to do with confidence. This can be achieved through the proper hiring and training of the sales force. Most experts agree that the relationship between a satisfied employee and customer is closely linked, so both the customer and the retailer benefit when a well-trained sales associate performs well.*

SALES AND PROFIT

Sales lie at the base of retailing, because without sales, there would be no resulting profit and no point in being a retailer. Sales are affected by many factors, many of which are discussed in this book. These include proper positioning of merchandise, having the right merchandise, atmospherics, and an inviting store appearance (i.e., getting the customer in the mood to buy, see *Case 53, Dollars and Scents*), having great customer service, and effective promotion.

Most authorities agree that service and selling must be combined in an effort to run a successful, integrative, customer-driven business. *Case 54, Best Buy's Customer Centricity Business Model* illustrates how successful that company's experimental stores with a customer-centric approach were compared with an earlier one. Eighty percent of the new business model is directly related to customer service and the Best Buy experience.

Improving sales and customer relations at retail should be an ongoing process that is attempted by retailers and manufacturers alike through various means. New technology, merchandising techniques, and customer service policies, in combination with pricing, have all been used by retailers to gain the competitive advantage in building good customer relations.

More and more retailers and manufacturers are marketing and promoting their products online directly to consumers, engaging and encouraging them to play an active role, and giving feedback in real time to their questions and concerns about service and products. Companies are even letting customers create their ads. See *Case 55, Online Clothes Reviews Give "Love That Dress" New Clout,* for a discussion of how some online retailers are inviting consumers to review products. This is one way to engage the customer and at the same time give the company valuable feedback, maybe even better than formal focus groups. The technological marketplace is certainly changing direct selling.

Sales often rely on promotion (as discussed in Chapter 8), and personal selling is a major component of sales promotion. Because of its importance, personal selling warrants separate attention in this chapter.

PERSONAL SELLING

Selling is the person-to-person (most often face-to-face) contact between the retailer and customer, or between the manufacturer and customer, which results in a purchase by a customer. Personal **direct selling** involves direct sales contact with the customer. This includes two major kinds of selling: (1) wholesale selling and (2) retail selling. **Wholesale** (or **contact**) **selling** involves the customer purchasing directly from the manufacturer. **Retail selling** often involves using an actual physical location, for example, a store for the customer and retailer to conduct business. Retail selling can be one of three types: (1) **over-the-counter,** (2) **mail** and (3) **electronic** (e.g., telephone, television, and computer). Today, the majority of retail sales still occur over-the-counter, but the Internet is the fastest-growing method of selling in the United States, and online sales of apparel and fashion goods is the fastest growing of all categories sold online. Stored retailers rely on **sales personnel (sales associates)** at a store location to sell merchandise to the customer. Non-stored retailers rely on various other types of personnel to service the customer (although there may be sales representatives at some level in the marketing channel, and often there are guest hosts and telemarketer/order takers instead of traditional salespeople).

Retail selling has always been an interactive and communicative process between buyer (customer) and seller (retailer). In its early days, shopping at a department store was a form of entertainment that included listening to concerts, attending art exhibits, and enjoying a fine meal at the store itself; therefore, visiting a department store was not done only to shop and buy but was a social occasion. Today, the interactive nature of television and electronic retail (**e-tailing**) has elevated shopping once again to a new level of entertainment—one of fun, in which virtual window shopping can be done without purchasing. (See Figure 9.1 for Neiman Marcus' electronic shopping home page.) Part of the fun is researching and exploring what there is to buy, as the presentation of merchandise is enjoyable in and of itself for those who have and take the time to do so. The megamalls (for example, Mall of America) have become vacation entertainment destinations with much more to do than purchase goods. From food to fashion, once again, retail has become a form of entertainment for all ages.

Figure 9.1 With online sales increasing, retailers can expand their customer base through their Web sites. Pictured above is the Neiman Marcus electronic (e-tailing) shopping home page site.

At brick and mortar stores, the responsibility of directing the sales staff varies from retailer to retailer. Most large stored retail organizations direct and manage sales at the store level. Merchandising plays both a direct and indirect role in selling. Some large retailers, such as JCPenney, Belk, and Nordstrom, and the majority of small independent merchants clearly integrate the buying and selling functions at the store level. Store merchandisers at these retailers actively participate in the purchasing, presentation, and subsequent sale of merchandise through the supervision and direction of the sales staff and working directly with their buyers. Other retailers—particularly large chains—have their merchandising and selling functions clearly delineated. These retailers have management that is responsible for sales at the store or non-store distribution location and/or operations headquarters. Their buyers are attached to a merchandising division and are

Figure 9.2 Escada Look Book pages. This type of vendor-provided product knowledge helps to educate retailers and their salespeople about Escada's line of merchandise by showing combinations of the various apparel pieces, as well as suggesting display and advertising possibilities.

indirectly responsible for sales, because they do not supervise the sales personnel. (See Chapter 1 for more information on store management and organization.)

To achieve success today, retailers and their suppliers are working together to gain the sales that both desire and require. In some instances, a retailer's selling staff may actually be a part of the manufacturer's payroll. As mentioned earlier, some vendors, for example Liz Claiborne (who was one of the first to do such), may furnish the merchandisers to help sell their goods at the retail establishment. In other situations, the manufacturer will supply informative booklets on their lines, such as the Escada "Look Book" that is shown in Figure 9.2. In doing so, vendors can be assured that the sales staff is trained and knowledgeable about their products.

EXPANDING THE CUSTOMER BASE

Maintaining and expanding a retailer's customer base is necessary for growth. There are many ways for retailers to expand their customer base to ensure positive growth and sales increase. They could open more stores, expand into new markets, such as through the Internet, or diversify their merchandise assortments. However, the major way to expand customer base and stimulate sales at the retail location level without expansion or remerchandising is to encourage sales personnel to meet or exceed established **sales goals** and/or **sales quotas,** which are sales plans that are set by the retailer. Usually, the retailer hopes to either achieve or exceed these sales goal or quota plans.

Incentives

Both the retailer and vendor often create incentives or motivators to stimulate sales at the retail level. Sales associates in *Case 56,* Apropos: *Managing a Multi-Aged Staff* are in desperate need of motivation as a young new manager arrives to find an older staff unmotivated to sell. **Retail-induced incentives** are those motivators that are produced or provided by the retailer to encourage sales personnel to sell, while **vendor-induced incentives** are those furnished by the supplier to the retailer or directly to the sales employee. Retail-induced incentives include compensation and recognition. **Compensation** rewards employees for work they have accomplished and/or goals that they have met or have exceeded. This compensation may be direct or indirect. **Direct compensation** is the awarding of such monetary payment as salaries or wages, **commissions** (monetary reward based on achievement of goals and usually a percentage of sales), **bonuses** (extra rewards), and **prizes** and **awards. Indirect compensation** involves nonmonetary rewards, which include paid vacations, paid insurance, parking, retirement, and other perks. **Perks** are nonmonetary rewards that express gratitude for work done or a position that is held by the employee. Free lunches or the right to use a company-owned vacation home are sometimes given as perks. While recognition could include compensation, it is primarily concerned with emotional well-being. A salesperson being honored as employee of the month, thereby acknowledging that person as an outstanding employee, is an example of employee recognition.

Often, retailers use a combination of compensation methods to reward sales employees. For example, many retailers pay a minimum wage salary but also award a commission if a sales objective for a certain time period is met or exceeded. They may also run sales contests that further compensate personnel by giving rewards such as free trips or free parking to outstanding salespeople. Additionally, some vendors participate in providing incentives for sales. In efforts to strive for high sales, sales associates at Nordstrom are encouraged to compete against each other through contests and high sales goals. The company culture is definitely one of competition within the company and amongst the employees to achieve the sales goals of the company. A settled lawsuit brought against Nordstrom by employees, however, questioned the fair treatment and equitable compensation of the employees for the customer service they rendered off the clock.

What type of monetary compensation to pay sales personnel—whether salary, wages, or commission—is often a difficult decision for retailers to make. Paying only salary or wages often results in complacency and lack of motivation in many salespeople. Commissions, on the other hand, are sometimes just the boost some need to strive harder to generate more sales. They may, however, create a harder selling (i.e., more pushy and aggressive) retail environment than some customers like.

Vendor-induced incentives may also include the same variety of compensation methods as already mentioned, but often they supplement the incentives that the retailer uses. **Spiffs** or **push money** are sometimes provided to retailers by vendors. These are incentives that compensate the salesperson, thereby providing motivation to try to sell particular items. In addition to monetary rewards, various other forms of vendor support and incentives include training, trunk shows, and educational material. Contests to win items or trips may also be vendor provided to help encourage strong sales. Additionally, some of these incentives are promotionally oriented (see Chapter 8).

TRAINING AND EVALUATING THE SALES ASSOCIATE

Having well-trained and knowledgeable salespeople helps ensure that retailers communicate well with their customers. Communicating a retailer's particular message to the customer also relies on training. Periodic reviews of the salesperson's performance evaluates the job being done and helps to rectify any problems that occur, as well as providing rewards for a job well done.

Training

The people who do the selling within an organization are the most important tool a company has with which to run and improve a business. These salespeople, however, must know the goals of the company and receive instruction in what their particular role is in accomplishing these goals. **Goals** are the objectives for which a company and its employees strive. Job descriptions should clarify what is expected of employees, but training is often the means to ensure that goals can be met by teaching employees what to do. Sales personnel should be taught how to perform their jobs in the best, most productive manner according to company policy and procedures. They should also be instructed in particular selling methods and toward a customer-service orientation. Policies and procedures are guides for companies to run their business how they so desire. **Policies** set governance guidelines and rules as to specific ways in which a company wants to accomplish its goals. **Procedures** are the methods—or steps—and therefore the means for a company to reach a goal. A company's procedures should be within the established policy guidelines. Training can be time-consuming and expensive and is a very serious matter to many retailers. Because it is of the utmost importance, however, it can be the basis for success or failure of a business.

The **human resources** (or **personnel**) **department** often plays a major role in training and evaluating the retailer's sales personnel, particularly when the retailer is large enough to have a separate division or department for this function. The specific role human resources plays within a retailer varies depending on the size of the company and staff, but in general, it is involved with employee matters. A small retailing operation might employ a single individual who handles all personnel tasks. Conversely, a large, multi-unit department store chain might have a large human resources staff in which the various functions are divided amongst the personnel of that department. Four major functions are usually allocated to the human resource department no matter who does the job or how many people are in the department: recruiting, training, evaluating, and rewarding. Hiring and firing may also be done centrally by this department, or it may be done at the retail outlet level, depending on the policy of the retailing establishment. If help in sales training (or any of the other personnel functions) is not available within an organization, professional training assistance can usually be found outside the company.

Sales training varies in type and style and from retailer to retailer but is always concerned with readying salespeople to sell products and/or services that are being offered. Some organizations realize the importance of sales training; others do not.

Types of training, along with methods and levels of training, differ depending on the mission and goals of the retailer. The retailer's image and the types of services offered should also play a role in determining what type and level of training that employees receive. Training may be formal or informal, on-the-job or in the classroom, or even a combination of types. These types of training methods are explored in the following sections.

Formal Training

Structured training that involves teaching specific tasks, methods, and/or other objectives is called **formal training**. This method of training relies on a person or persons and/or written instructions, which are used to relay the information to be taught. Sometimes formal training may be taught in a classroom in much the same way as school. Another example is a salesperson learning from a sales manual with instructions on how the job is to be performed.

Major formal methods of training salespeople include the following:

- Lecture (and/or oral presentation)
- Demonstration (a showing of capabilities of a product)
- Videos (or films)
- Meetings, seminars, and conferences
- Role playing (i.e., acting out situations and simulations)
- Case analysis

Sales manuals are used by numerous retailers to convey the expectations of the company to the sales associates. Sales manuals are written procedures or directions and policies that a company wants to ensure their employees follow. Sometimes, salespeople are tested on the material found in a sales manual, which they are expected to know after training is completed. Additionally, some sales manuals are written specifically for a retail operation and incorporate all policies and procedures; these are called **store manuals.**

Informal Training

The **informal training** approach relies on employees learning skills as they work (i.e., **on-the-job training**) and as they need to learn specific skills. In this type of training—more popular with small independent retailers than larger ones—employees are often solely responsible for learning what they believe they need, rather than what their employer thinks is necessary. This method of training can often present problems because how can new employees know what is expected, or how their jobs should be performed?

Many retailers today find that a combination of both formal and informal training methods works best. This combination of training methods helps ensure that the company policies and procedures are relayed; at the same time, the employee can get a "feel" for the job and learn it while actually practicing it. The degree and mix of methods depends on the type of retailer and its philosophy or mission.

Whatever the method of training, effective selling is usually the major emphasis in training sales associates. They are trained on the mechanics of selling as well as the techniques. Some stores use sequential steps to complete a sale:

1. Approaching and greeting the customer
2. Determining the needs and wants of the customer
3. Presenting the merchandise and/or service to the customer
4. Relaying product information and answering questions
5. Suggestive selling of merchandise that may be related to that which the customer is already interested in, or stimulating interest in another product or service
6. Closing the sale

While some stores have a two-minute rule (i.e., an associate should approach the customer within two minutes of entering the store), others have the philosophy of letting customers discover the merchandise on their own and do not approach them right away. See *Case 51, Anthropologie: Display and Store Image* in Chapter 8 for Anthropologie's practices.

In addition to selling, salespeople usually have other duties tied to their job that may also have to be taught, for example, housekeeping, display, stock, pricing, and merchandise handling. These tasks may also be taught formally or informally.

Training should be considered an investment in people for a better return on financial investment (i.e., profit). Employee turnover, particularly at the sales and entry-level management positions, is an unfortunate major financial problem for retailers, which is always being examined by retailers in order to improve it. **Employee turnover** is the percentage of employees who begin with a company at a certain time period but do not remain employed at the end of that set time period. This percentage figure is usually calculated on an annual basis. Hiring and training the right people can help improve a company's employee retention level and return on investment.

As mentioned previously, partnerships are sometimes made between the retailer and supplier for training sales staff and management about merchandise. Traditionally, this was done for products that needed special instructions or fit. Today, however, it is important to relay product knowledge from sales to customer no matter what the category of merchandise. The variety and quantity of goods available today have created competition among both manufacturers and retailers that requires a higher level of product knowledge than ever before in order to win the customer's patronage. For example, if a salesperson can knowledgeably answer a customer's question about a product at one store, while at another store the salesperson cannot answer the query, the customer is more likely to purchase at the store where the question was answered.

Sales training should not only communicate exactly what the job is, but it should also motivate salespeople to do the best job they can toward improving sales and customer service. When salespeople understand what is expected of them and feel confident and happy about doing their jobs, their positive attitude is usually relayed to customers. Some retailers train sales help only once, after they are hired. Others believe that training should be ongoing, because business and the customers change and the salespeople should be prepared to meet those changes. It may also be necessary to change procedures and policies to meet the changes that a particular business encounters, and this must be relayed to employees through training.

Evaluation of the Sales Associate

The **evaluation** of sales associates helps monitor their work and also informs the employee of job performance. Additionally, the evaluation of salespeople's performance can aid in bettering the work that is done, and this contributes to the improvement of the retailer's performance.

Evaluating salespeople should include a **performance review** on a regular basis. Reviewing work performance can be formal or informal, and some retailers use both methods. **Formal reviews** use time set aside on a periodic basis for supervisors to meet one-on-one with the salesperson to go over their accomplished work. Additionally, feedback can be given on performance at these formal reviews. **Informal reviews,** however, consist of feedback given at any time it is needed. Some experts believe that this is the more effective means of evaluation, because it is given at the same time as the incident that warrants the feedback. The performance of salespeople is measured primarily on the **sales goals** and quotas they have been given, along with their customer service behavior. **Evaluations,** whether formal or informal, should be used to provide performance feedback and to reward, help, and/or promote that employee—if warranted. In *Case 3, Learning to Document Performance at Gap,* in Chapter 1, an employee is surprised by his poor evaluation. Earlier feedback may have been warranted.

Sometimes a sales associate's poor performance or problematic behavior requires evaluation by a supervisor in order to find a resolution. In *Case 57, Jeremy's Problem: A Possible Drug Situation,* a department manager tries to determine just what lies at the root of a problem with a sales associate who performs quite well but has personality problems with other staff members, who refuse to work with him.

PRODUCT KNOWLEDGE

Some say a good salesperson can sell anything. Others say that a salesperson must know and believe in the product in order to sell it. No matter what the truth is, the more knowledgeable a salesperson is about a product, the easier it is to explain it to others, who may then more readily purchase that product. **Product knowledge** educates sales associates, which enables them to educate their customers, help interpret their needs, and in turn (through the sale of that product), provide for those needs. Information about a product often sells the merchandise. Retailers and vendors both supply information to the salespeople about merchandise that helps them answer questions and resolve problems knowledgeably.

Some products require more selling and product knowledge than others, and often a vendor must help provide information for a salesperson to relay to the customer. Additionally, warranties and guarantees may help convince the customer that the product is what it should be and therefore will help to close a sale. A **warranty** ensures the integrity and life of a product for a specific period of time usually in writing, while a **guarantee** ensures that a product will perform as it is supposed to or the customer will be compensated.

CUSTOMER SERVICE

Many retail experts say that **customer service** is an overused and misused term. Simply stated, it is assisting customers by providing retail activities. Prompt and courteous service is what most customers look for from retailers today because this type of effective customer service supplements the value received from a retailer. Some retailers and customers say service beyond a customer's expectations is what "good service" is all about (Kennedy, 1996). Therefore, knowing what the customer wants in regard to customer service is vital when trying to provide it. Nordstrom has a reputation for superior-quality customer service, to which they partially attribute their overall success. Employees are given the empowerment and the freedom to do almost anything it takes to satisfy customers—from delivering merchandise to accepting any product return without question. See *Case 58, Customer Service and Relationship Management at Nordstrom* for a discussion of Nordstrom's philosophy and practice, and *Case 59, Story of Target Guest Service* for Target's policies.

Customer service should supplement and facilitate sales. The service given and offered to customers plays a very real role in creating their perception of the store and the image they have of the retailer. It also contributes greatly in making the shopping experience positive or negative. Convincing customers to return to a store

TABLE 9.1 Customer Service Practices

1. Greet, smile, and acknowledge customers, even walking through the store.
2. Listen to customers' needs.
3. Satisfy customers' needs and offer more—suggest merchandise.
4. Go out of our way to appease unhappy customers so they will always want to come back!
5. Mention their last name.
6. Offer extra services if needed such as deliveries, gift wrap, alterations, etc.
7. Always make customers feel important as if they are the only one.
8. Being ready and willing to help every customer, being cheerful and helpful. Call other stores for additional merchandise.
9. Be willing to transfer merchandise or send something out to customer.
10. Say "Thank you" and "Have a good day."
11. Say "Hello, how are you?" not just "May I help you?"
12. Always smile and be excited, which will make the customer feel good.
13. Do not point to the customer where to go, show them.
14. Follow through!
15. Take the time to meet the customer's needs.
16. You should be able to help a customer find what they want, which means knowing your merchandise.
17. Start talking about what the customer is looking at to get conversation going and draw the customer to you.
18. LISTEN to the customer.
19. Ask questions that will help you make suggestions.
20. Give benefits that the customer will receive from the purchase.
21. Treat each customer as though he or she is special.
22. Do move around departments to assure customers you want to service them.
23. Follow up whenever possible; call or ask if you see them again how they are enjoying their purchase.
24. Smiles and a positive attitude will be a plus for any customer.

Source: Adapted from "Castner Knott Customer Service Definitions."

to purchase again is key to the success of a retailer. It is often not just dependent on having the merchandise a customer wants but is also directly related to how the customer is served. Some customer service practices are listed in Table 9.1.

Levels of Service

The manner in which a retailer sells (stored and/or non-stored) helps determine what level of customer service the merchant should provide. Self service, limited service, or full service are terms used to describe the levels of service available to the customer. The next paragraphs briefly describe these different levels and their implications for the retail establishment.

Self service is minimal service, for example, when customers are first expected to find the merchandise they want, then take it to a service desk (cashier) to purchase it. **Limited service** provides a modicum of assistance to the customer beyond the self-serve level, but still in restricted amounts. For example, a store that has hours from 10 to 5, has a small sales staff, takes credit cards, does not gift-wrap or deliver merchandise but has alterations available can be described as having limited service. **Full service** gives the customer the maximum amount of services that can be expected. These services include basic and secondary services, as well as all possible transactional services. A full-service department store today, for example, would provide cash and credit, returns, exchanges, delivery, alterations, private dressing rooms, restrooms, personal shoppers, gift wrap, and probably a restaurant or snack bar; customers would expect all regular department stores to provide these services.

The types of services available are numerous. **Essential services** (also called **primary** or **basic**) are those services that most retailers provide. Some retailers today, however, neglect supplying what is considered basic and essential service by everyone—for example, mirrors, dressing rooms, parking, and someone to ring up your sale pleasantly. **Ancillary services** are also referred to as **support services** or **secondary services**. These ancillary services usually include merchandise transfers between stores, gift wrap, valet parking, alterations, and delivery. What is considered basic service for one store, however, may be considered support services for another—depending on the company. Services may also be tangible or intangible. **Tangible services** are those that provide such concrete assistance as personal shoppers, child-care, and delivery service. **Intangible services** are those abstract activities provided that cannot be touched physically, for example, assistance with decision making and merchandise selection. These intangibles can be product-use displays, convenient store hours, and personal assistance. The purchased merchandise is, of course, tangible, but the aid from the display or the salesperson is not.

Customer-service philosophies and policies vary from retailer to retailer and are often dependent on the type of retailer, although this is not always predictable either. Again, what is full service to one retailer may differ from another and is often defined by company policies and procedures as well. At one time, it was rather predictable as to the kinds and levels of service that could be associated with the type of retailer. Today, it is not as easy to typecast because everyone seems to be concerned with providing service to the customer. An example of this is that at one

Figure 9.3 H&M represents a trendy, fast fashion self-service retailer.

time all factory outlet stores were self-service stores that had only one or two employees to ring up sales and customers were on their own to decide what to buy. There were certainly no services such as gift wrapping or instore restaurants. The first department stores were full service and had everything from lounges, restaurants, libraries, and post offices, in addition to a high ratio of sales personnel to customers. Today, many factory outlets and discount stores may rival the full-service stores of the past, whereas some department stores often provide only limited service and sometimes even seem like self-service outlets.

In addition to helping a customer with a purchase, customer service also includes ways of accommodating the purchase. These are called **transactional services,** for example, credit or charge cards, returns, and exchange adjustments. **Credit** is an alternative to paying cash, allowing the customer to buy on time, getting merchandise now, but paying for it later. Many stores find that issuing their own **charge cards** a successful way to issue credit to their customers and increase sales.

When exchanges and returns are made to a retailer, there are various ways to handle these transactions. Service includes the policies and means by which these

Figure 9.4 In a full service retail environment, customers expect salespeople to assist them with their purchases.

actions are handled. For example, does a store only give credit for merchandise returned or does it give cash as well? Or, is cash only rendered if the customer has a sales receipt that proves that the merchandise was purchased with cash? Today, more and more customers want transactions handled in the manner that is preferable to them, and many times they equate a retailer's level and type of service with this accommodation to their requirements. *Case 59, A Story of Target Guest Service* offers a scenario of a dissatisfied customer due to Target's return policy.

The way in which employees behave toward the customer is also an indicator of the type of customer service a retailer provides. According to customers, customer service often is judged primarily on how the sales associates have treated the customer—it is an emotional response—rather than being reflective of tangible services. Consequently, it is wise for retailers to remember that no matter what type and number of actual services they provide—from delivery to repairs—if the customer is not treated well, these services do not mean much. Consumers today have enough stress in their lives, so eliminating stress from the retail environment certainly helps to make the customer want to stay and shop. So even if a retailer offers full service, it may not be perceived as providing good service, and conversely, if a retailer provides limited service, it may be perceived as providing the highest level of excellent service.

Professionalism is a term used to describe employees utilizing a businesslike manner in their interaction with other employees and/or customers. When one is unprofessional, the actions are usually those not in accordance with company policy and/or procedure. Not only is professional behavior important for sales associates to model for success, but holding the values and beliefs necessary to behave toward customers in a positive manner that is appropriate for types of merchandise, environments, and customers is also important. Sales associates' behavior is said to be the major cause of customer dissatisfaction with a retailer according to a national survey of retail management and sales personnel (Kabachneck, 1996). Results of this survey indicate that such characteristics as friendliness, enthusiasm, and being outgoing (which are usually thought of as being the most important to effective selling) are not effective without "the qualities that indicate a belief and value system aligned with [the] sales and service" (p. 6) of the company for which the salesperson is working. So determining the selling styles of individuals, which reveals their values, attitudes, and strengths, will make a better match of seller to customer from a behavioral perspective, thereby creating more success in sales.

The customer of today is said to be "time-poor" and either does not have extra time or does not want to use it to spend hours and hours shopping. Consequently, speed in the sales transaction is essential. The time involved in completing a sale, along with the manner in which it is accomplished, is very important to the customer. Customers regard standing in line the biggest time waster of all. If help is needed to expedite a purchase, the customer wants that service. Even more disturbing to the customer is when a store that is known and counted on for good customer service fails to provide it. Unhappy customers may result and can be harmful and even devastating to a retailer. *Case 60, Beware of Dissatisfied Customers: They Like to Blab* explores the concept of negative word-of-mouth and dissatisfied customers.

LOYALTY PROGRAMS

Customer **loyalty programs** are effective methods used to encourage customers to return to the company. These programs promote relationships with customers and develop loyal patronage. We are most familiar with frequent flyer program developed by the airlines, but other industries, from credit cards and hotels to grocery and apparel stores, have borrowed the concept. Retailers have developed successful programs through which customers earn discounts and a variety of rewards. InCircle, the loyalty program of Neiman Marcus, offers rewards at different levels. For example, 5,000 points may give you a nice luncheon experience, while the highest level, the Chairman's Circle, can bring you membership in exclusive resorts. *Case 61, SaksFirst Builds Customer Relationships* explores Saks Fifth Avenue's preferred customer program.

SUMMARY

One major outcome of good, effective, courteous customer service is that customers will want to return to a retailer to shop. Building customer loyalty is important if a retailer wants to ensure the return of the customer, and loyalty can be partially built from good customer service. Providing good customer service today involves much more than just having sales associates wait on customers. It also involves learning the skills and product knowledge necessary to sell the merchandise and services offered to the customer. This may be provided to the sales associate through various training methods. Another important aspect of customer service is being attuned to the customer's needs and wants and providing a pleasurable environment in which to shop and purchase. Relaying this through personal selling helps reinforce positive customer relations. Successful retailers must provide the best training, incentives, and evaluations for their sales personnel to stimulate and create customer loyalty and patronage. Retailers must also pay attention and address their customer's needs, wants, and values; if they do not, there are many other retailers that can (and will) satisfy their customer's desires.

KEY TERMS

ancillary service
awards
basic service
bonuses
charge cards
commissions
compensation
contact selling
credit
customer service
direct compensation
direct selling
electronic selling
e-tailing
employee turnover
essential service
evaluation (of sales associates)
formal review
formal training
full service
guarantee

human resources personnel
    department
indirect compensation
informal review
informal training
intangible service
limited service
loyalty programs
mail selling
on-the-job training
over-the-counter selling
performance review
perks
policies
primary service
prizes
procedures
product knowledge
professionalism
push money
retail-induced incentive

retail selling
sales goals
sales manuals
sales personnel/associates
sales quotas
sales training
secondary service
self service
selling

spiffs
store manuals
support services
tangible service
transactional service
vendor-induced incentive
warranty
wholesale (contract) selling

BIBLIOGRAPHY

Calvin, R. J. (2004). *Sales management.* New York: McGraw-Hill.

Elements of good customer service. (2007, June). *Stores.* www.stores.com.

Gschwandtner, G. (2007). *The sales manager's guide to developing a winning sales team.* New York: McGraw-Hill.

Hartley, B., & Starkey, M. W. (1996). *The management of sales and customer relations: Book of readings.* London: International Thomson Business Press.

Kabachneck, T. (1996, May). *DNR, Specialty Stores. The Men's and Boy's Newsletter,* p. 6.

Kennedy, E. (1996, January). Excellent customer service means exceeding expectations. *Women's Wear Daily.* [Special Atlanta Report], p. 57.

Kinkaid, J. W. (2003). *Customer relationship management: Getting it right.* Englewood Cliffs, NJ: Prentice Hall.

National Retail Federation. (2002). *Customer service and sales skill standards.* Washington, DC: National Retail Federation Foundation, Sales & Service Voluntary Partnership, Inc.

Rayport, J. F., & Jaworski, B. J. (2005). *Best face forward: Why companies must improve their service interfaces with customers.* Boston: Harvard Business Publishing.

Sherman, G. J., & Perlman, S. (2007). *The real world guide to fashion selling and management.* New York: Fairchild Books.

Spector, R., & McCarthy, P. D. (2005). *The Nordstrom way to customer service excellence: A handbook for implementing great service in your organization.* Hoboken, NJ: John Wiley & Sons.

Tenser, J., Shim, S., & Burke, M. (2004). *Customer service excellence 2004.* Washington, DC: National Retail Federation Foundation.

Case 53

DOLLARS AND SCENTS[1]

Ylan Q. Mui, "Dollars and Scents: Retailers Use Technology to Get Shoppers by Nose." Washington Post *Staff Writer, December 19, 2006*

Through Christmas, the [Sony Style] chain fill(s) its stores with a designer scent called "Seasons Greetings," which also has undertones of gingerbread, as a way to evoke happy memories in customers and put them in the shopping spirit. Other retailers are following suit with custom fragrances of their own.

. . .

The burgeoning "scent technology" industry has fueled sales at companies such as ScentAir. Since its founding six years ago, the Charlotte firm has developed fragrances for thousands of retailers, including Sony, said chief executive David Van Epps. Many placed their orders for holiday smells over the summer. Popular requests include mulling spices, pine trees and cranberry sauce.

. . .

The product is not just for holiday use, however. Sony fills its stores with a mandarin orange and vanilla fragrance year round, and KB has experimented with scents of Creamsicle, cotton candy and Play-Doh. Upscale men's clothier Thomas

[1]Copyright © 2006 by *The Washington Post.* Reprinted with permission. (The text printed here represents an excerpted portion of a longer article.)

Pink has ordered an ambient version of its signature "line-dried linen" scent from Lake Elmo, Minn.-based AromaSys.

ScentAir's fragrances are dispersed by a small coffee can-shaped device called the ScentWave. At the Sony Style store in Pentagon City recently, the machine was sitting at the front door, emitting waves of "Seasons Greetings" that drove out the smell of chicken stir-fry from the food court below. Customers who spent more than $200 got complimentary sachets of scent beads. Others could buy them for $1.50 if they craved that in-store experience in their own homes. Store manager Frank Kroner said one customer last week bought about 10.

Daniel Lieberman, an associate professor of psychiatry at George Washington University, called smell the most "primitive" of the senses. Odor receptors in the nose are actually brain cells, he said. He cited recent studies that linked increased electrical and metabolic activity in the brain to pleasant odors.

Study Questions*

1. What are retailers doing with scents in their stores?
2. Why are they doing it?

Exercise

Visit local retailers to identify scents that are used. Do you think they are effective in creating a pleasant shopping experience?

*Do not use the alternative solutions format for this case.

Case 54

BEST BUY'S CUSTOMER CENTRICITY BUSINESS MODEL

Denise T. Ogden, Penn State University, Lehigh Valley

The retail environment is very competitive. In order to survive, retailers must continuously look for ways to improve their operations. Often companies will focus on customer service as a way to differentiate themselves from the competition. Although it seems easy to make the customer the center of company decisions, in reality it is difficult and many companies fail to deliver.

Best Buy is a multichannel international retailer of consumer electronics, home office equipment, entertainment software, and appliances. In 2004, in an effort to boost sales and differentiate from the competition, Best Buy initiated a program called "customer centricity" that places emphasis on meeting and exceeding customer needs. The strategy revolves around providing a differentiated experience for customers by understanding them better than the competition does, and training and motivating employees to have rich interactions with customers. At the time the company instituted these changes, Best Buy was the nation's top seller in its category. The company implemented changes, in part, because it saw Wal-Mart and Dell starting to offer similar merchandise, such as high-definition televisions.

The customer centricity program started with 32 lab stores. These lab stores experienced higher comparable store sales gains. Also observed were improvements in customer loyalty, employee retention, and market share. Employees were also contributing more ideas and that helped improve operations. The program was expanded, and as of 2006, 40 percent of U.S. Best Buy Stores (300 stores) had implemented the customer-centric model. All stores were expected to operate under the new model by the end of FY 2007. According to a company spokesperson, 20 percent of the new business model is directly related to merchandise and the other 80 percent is related to customer service and the Best Buy experience.

Under this model the company expanded the number of Geek Squad (computer support) agents by 5,000, brought home theater installation services in-house, and grew membership in their customer loyalty program, Reward Zone, to 7.2 million (a 50 percent increase). The Reward Zone program charges customers a fee to join and is aimed at recruiting more profitable customers. As a result of the customer-centric philosophy, employee retention improved by 15 percent.

The model is not without drawbacks. There are higher expenses associated with the customer-centric program due to its labor-intensive aspects. Training sales associates in the new model alone has a price tag in the millions of dollars. Selling, general, and administrative expenses also increased because the company was still running under the previous product-centric model while trying to implement the newer customer-centric model.

Part of the customer-centric strategy is to get rid of the company's worst customers. Estimated to number as high as 100 million (20 percent of their customers), these "devil" customers buy loss leaders and then post them for sale on Internet auction sites at higher prices. Devil customers find the lowest prices on the Internet and then demand that Best Buy meet those prices. They buy products, apply for rebates, return the purchases, and then buy the same product back at returned-merchandise discounts. These undesirable customers are more likely to take up a salesperson's time without buying anything. "Angel" customers are the best customers because instead of draining profits, they contribute to the company's growth and profitability.

To identify devil customers, Best Buy examined sales data, demographics, and customer databases. Devil customers are then cut from marketing lists. In addition, the company is cutting back on sales promotions that tend to attract the devil consumer. The company did not go so far as to ban customers; they simply engage in "demarketing," or discouraging, these customers, without their direct knowledge, from shopping at Best Buy. A restocking fee of 15 percent of the purchase price for returned items is a policy instituted to deter returns. The company also analyzed other company policies and procedures and made changes so it is not easy to take advantage of the system.

Best Buy also develops profiles for the most desirable customers by shopping preferences and behavior. "Barry" is an affluent, professional male who likes action movies and cameras. "Jill" is an upscale suburban mom. "'Buzz" is an early adopter, who likes technology and is an entertainment enthusiast. Also targeted are small businesses and families that are practical technology adopters. The merchandise mix, staffing, promotions, and store design are determined with these customer profiles in mind.

Major Question

You are a manager at a chain of department stores. Your manager has heard of Best Buy's customer-centric strategy and wants you to pursue a more customer-focused strategy as well. Would you take the same approach as Best Buy? Why or why not?

Study Questions

1. What, if any, are the risks involved with labeling customers as angels and devils?
2. Why is Best Buy's strategy successful?
3. In order to provide the best customer service, what type of environment do employees need?

Bibliography

Best Buy Fiscal 2006 Annual Report.
Carlson, S. (2006, May 28). Gunning for Best Buy: Striving to fend off its rivals, the no. 1 electronics retailer focuses on service, "centricity." *Knight Ridder Tribune Business News,* Washington, DC. Obtained from Proquest database.

Concepts and Cases in Retail and Merchandise Management

Cha, A. E. (2005, August 17). In retailing, pro-filing for profit; Best Buy stores cater to specific customer types. *The Washington Post* (final edition), p. A1. Obtained from Proquest database.

McWilliams, G. (2004, November 8). Minding the store: Analyzing customers, Best Buy decides not all are welcome. *Wall Street Journal* (Eastern edition), p. A1. Obtained from Proquest database.

Case 55

ONLINE CLOTHES REVIEWS GIVE "LOVE THAT DRESS" NEW CLOUT[1]

James Covert, The Wall Street Journal, December 07, 2006

Sears.com and Federated Department Stores Inc.'s Macys.com added reviews . . . as did smaller sites such as Genesco Inc.'s Journeys.com, which sells shoes. Gap Inc.'s new Piperlime shoe site is considering adding reviews next year. And at J.C. Penney Co., customer reviews are "something that our internal teams are looking into," a spokesman says.

The result: Shoppers online are tipping each other off on everything from how the latest fashions fit to who's wearing them.

[1]Reprinted by permission of *The Wall Street Journal,* Copyright © 2007 by Dow Jones & Company, Inc. All Rights Reserved Worldwide. License number 1767800983464. (The text printed here represents an excerpted portion of a longer article.)

Advocates of reviews say the feedback is more useful than focus groups because shoppers tend to be so frank in their emails. Another benefit for retailers: Reviews boost traffic by adding keywords that might not turn up in a retailer's product description, but might be used by shoppers to search for clothing online . . . .

Some apparel retailers say fashion changes too quickly for online reviews to be useful. "Building up a bunch of feedback on products that are designed to sell through seasonally is not necessarily valuable," says Toby Lenk, president of Gap Inc. Direct, which runs Web sites for Gap, Banana Republic, and Old Navy. Reviews are more useful for retailers like Macy's that sell lots of different brands that consumers can discuss, he says.

Luxury retailers also have been wary of reviews. Upscale forums such as Conde Nast Publications's Style.com have flourished, but the commentary comes from highbrow fashion writers rather than shoppers. Having meticulously cultivated their brands, some luxury retailers may be wary of customer postings that might point out lower-priced alternatives to their wares, including knockoffs.

Study Question*

What are the relative merits and problems associated with online clothes reviews from the retailers' perspective and from the customers' perspective?

* Do not use the alternative solutions format for this case.

Case 56

APROPOS: *MANAGING A MULTI-AGED STAFF*

Judith Everett, Northern Arizona University

Apropos is a chain of 25 specialty stores, featuring better and designer merchandise. Several branches are located in Los Angeles, San Francisco, and San Diego, and one branch is out-of-state in Phoenix, Arizona. This company targets an affluent female customer generally between the ages of 35 to 60, who is career-oriented or who is the spouse of a successful professional. She has a relatively high clothing budget—typically spending between $10,000 and $22,000 per year on clothing and accessories.

The buying and merchandising operations for *Apropos* are centralized in Los Angeles. Employees who are interested in an executive or professional career with the company are promoted from within the firm. All personnel start as sales associates. The first executive position is as an assistant store manager, which involves learning the successful operation of a branch store and hands-on training to become a manager. After successfully completing this training, an individual is assigned his or her own store to manage. It is expected that a manager will remain in that position for a minimum of five years. In addition to the supervision duties, store managers are given sales responsibilities. With the

company expansion plans, it is realistic to expect to be a district manager or return to the central offices as a merchandise planner or assistant buyer after working as a store manager. *Apropos* typically asks management personnel to transfer to another branch when they accept promotions. This is done to avoid any problems associated with managing former peer employees.

Janet Hudson has recently been promoted from the assistant manager of the Horton Plaza store in San Diego to the manager of the Biltmore Shopping Center in Phoenix, Arizona. Janet completed a Bachelor of Science degree in Merchandising while she served as the assistant store manager. Sandy Cohen, the district manager, saw excellent executive potential in Janet despite her young age of 25. Normally managers of *Apropos* are 30 years old or older because of the nature of the target customer, who tends to expect service from an older sales associate. Janet's enthusiasm, her ability to finish school with a high grade-point average, in addition to working full-time as the assistant manager in San Diego reminded Sandy of herself at that same age.

The store at the Biltmore Shopping Center has been open for nearly 25 years. It is the only branch of *Apropos* located in the Phoenix market. Two of the full-time sales associates, Blanche Darcy and Elsie Scheiner, and Sophie Rostoff, the assistant manager, are nearing retirement age. They have been with *Apropos* as long as the store has been open in Phoenix. They take pride in the store, their customers, and the fact that several of the previous store managers from that store have been promoted into the executive ranks and now serve as buyers and other merchandise executives. Sophie feels that because of her leadership and training skills as the assistant manager, most of the former Biltmore store managers have been promoted and achieved success as company executives. Because she is close to retirement and wants to spend more time with her grandchildren and hobbies, Sophie wants to cut back on her responsibilities and hours. All three of these older employees enjoy their work at *Apropos,* but are not assertive in sales, nor motivated to rise careerwise within the company. Sandy has asked Sophie to remain as assistant manager, however, during Janet's transition to manager of the Phoenix store.

The remaining sales staff are younger than the senior staff. They are between 35 and 42. Kathy Acres, Andy Wright, and Mickey Malone have bachelor degrees in liberal arts or education. All three of these associates would like to move up in the company as managers, but each is aware of the transfer policy. They are assertive salespeople and are extremely competitive. Kathy, who is 35 years old, has been with the firm for four years and is married with two children. Her husband is a well-respected physician in Phoenix. Because of her family responsibilities, it is impossible for her to leave the area. Mickey has also been with the firm for four years. She started a Master of Business Administration degree on a part-time basis and will complete it in two years. Andy is a single woman with aging parents who live in Sun City—a nearby retirement community. She has been

working at *Apropos* for eight years. This group of employees is resentful and jealous that a young "25-year-old girl" has been given the manager's position. They all feel that the company policy of "asking" employees to transfer after accepting a promotion is unfair and unrealistic in a market such as Phoenix, which has only one branch. Kathy, Andy, and Mickey each feel that they should have been eligible for the manager's position at the Biltmore store.

When Janet arrived in Phoenix, she detected a serious morale problem in the store. The enthusiasm she has seen in all other *Apropos* stores she has visited or worked in seems to be totally absent. The older employees are very friendly, personable, and rather matronly, helping her adjust to the new city. But these women don't seem to have much work enthusiasm, and she feels that she cannot really motivate them. The younger employees seem efficient in their job tasks, but they are not very friendly toward her at all. They are distant and cool, causing Janet to feel somewhat uncomfortable. It seems as if the employees resent Janet, and she is uncertain as to why. Janet is familiar with the *Apropos* policy in regard to promotion and transfer, and she figures that everyone else was told about the policy at the onset of their employment with *Apropos* as well, so she doesn't consider this to be a problem that would contribute to the low morale of her staff. Janet is concerned because she has never had a problem getting along with fellow employees, and she is particularly proud of the way in which she has motivated others to work for the benefit of the total company in the past. Working for *Apropos* has always been fun, and Janet wants it to continue to be. Attitudes have continued to deteriorate, however, during her first few months on the job, regardless of Janet's various attempts to try to build enthusiasm and motivate everyone to work together as a team.

This is the first time that Janet has lived this far from her friends and family. Therefore, she does not have a personal support group to brainstorm in regard to her concerns at work. Although San Diego is only a couple of hours away by plane, Janet never seems to have the time to visit. Because she is so busy learning her job and managing the Phoenix branch, she has had little time to socialize and meet new friends and is therefore very lonely in this new town. This loneliness, along with her frustration at her futile attempts to motivate her staff, is beginning to seriously worry Janet about her capabilities as a store manager.

During a spring trend meeting in Los Angeles, Janet decides that she must discuss her problems of motivating her multi-aged staff with Sandy, because she knows no one else to turn to. Janet is extremely discouraged with her sales associates and their generally poor attitudes, and she hopes that Sandy can give her some insight and recommendations to help her improve morale.

Major Question

What recommendations should Sandy make to Janet in regard to the lack of motivation and poor morale of her staff?

Study Questions

1. How can Janet motivate her multi-aged staff and learn to balance her professional life with some type of social life?
2. Was Janet promoted too quickly?

Case 57

JEREMY'S PROBLEM: A POSSIBLE DRUG SITUATION

Peggy Gorbach, Evergreen Valley College
Nancy J. Rabolt, San Francisco State University

Jeremy Christopher, at the age of 23, has worked for three years in the men's department at a moderate Southern California department store. His job performance rating is excellent because of his high sales records, and he does all the different aspects of his job completely and accurately. Jeremy rarely misses a day when he is scheduled to work, and he always stays for his entire shift. However, at times Jeremy is rude to fellow employees, and he appears to have severe mood swings from time to time. This behavior never shows in his manner with customers, whom he treats courteously and professionally. Lately Jeremy's mood swings have become more extreme, provoking constant conflicts with other sales associates. These conflicts include disagreements over department displays, miscommunication regarding merchandise that has been placed on "hold" by customers, rotation of customers, follow-ups on special orders and store transfers, and the responsibility for markdowns. When Peggy Kerns, the department manager, finally asked him about his behavior, Jeremy had a reason for his actions and blamed the other associates. After a month of conflicts, fellow employees no longer wanted to work with him and asked to be scheduled on opposite days. Suzi Tepper and Claire Morgan, new employees, have gone so far as to call in sick on the days they were scheduled to work with Jeremy.

At first, Peggy thought Jeremy was becoming bored with his job, but because of Jeremy's dramatic mood swings, Peggy suspected he had a drug problem, but she had no proof. She repeatedly tried to find the source of his problem, but Jeremy never came forth with any information, only denial of drug usage or any problem with his private life. Jeremy's answer was always related to other people, not to himself. The store's policy was dismissal of employees—on the spot—if they were found to be using drugs at work. The store had no mandatory drug testing for new or current employees; therefore, there was no chance of physical evidence.

Because Jeremy is an effective salesperson and customers like him, there appeared no reason to dismiss him. But there still was the big problem of the fact that no one wanted to work with him. Peggy approached the store's human resources department about this particular situation. and

consequently a company policy was developed. This new policy stated that if an employee had a drug problem, and if the employee came forward with it, everything possible would be done to assist the employee if he or she would go into a drug rehabilitation program at the company's expense. An employee would be able to take sick leave, vacation time, and any other necessary time off to complete the rehabilitation program and keep his or her job. Upon implementation of the company policy, every employee received a leaflet explaining the program and ensuring complete confidentiality. Also in the flyer was an explanation of the company policy regarding employee drug usage. (If an employee was found to be using drugs and didn't come forward with the problem, he or she would be terminated.) Employees were asked to sign a statement that they understood store policy and the program that was available to them.

After the new program was in place and known throughout the store, Peggy again approached Jeremy. She spoke to him about his continued abusive actions toward the other associates and their complaints about him. She advised him that if he was using drugs, he would lose his job. Again, Jeremy denied any use of drugs. He said "You have a very active imagination," and turned and went back to the sales floor. Peggy was dumbfounded.

Major Question

As a department manager, what should Peggy do about Jeremy's abusive, erratic behavior toward the other employees?

Study Questions

1. What could be the cause of Jeremy's behavior?

2. What types of activities and conflicts can lower the morale of employees in the workplace?

3. What criteria should the human resources department use when firing an employee with a problem like Jeremy's?

Case 58

CUSTOMER SERVICE AND RELATIONSHIP MANAGEMENT AT NORDSTROM[1]

Alicia Lueddemann, the Management Mind Group
Sunil Erevelles, University of North Carolina, Charlotte

Nordstrom's unwavering customer-focused philosophy traces its roots to founder Johan Nordstrom's values. Johan Nordstrom believed in people and realized that consistently exceeding their expectations led to success and a good conscience. He built his organization around a customer-oriented philosophy. The organization focuses on people, and its policies and merchandise selections are designed to satisfy its cus-

[1]Levy and Weitz, *Retailing Management*, 6th ed., The McGraw-Hill Companies. Reproduced with permission of The McGraw-Hill Companies.

tomers. As simple as this philosophy sounds, few of Nordstrom's competitors have truly been able to grasp it.

A Focus on People

Nordstrom employees treat customers like royalty. Employees are instructed to do whatever is in the customer's best interest. Customer delight drives the values of the company. Customers are taken seriously and are at the heart of the business. Customers are even at the top of the Nordstrom's so-called organization chart, which is an inverted pyramid. Following customers from the top of the inverted pyramid are the salespeople, department managers, and general managers. Finally, at the bottom is the board of directors. All lower levels work toward supporting the salespeople, who in turn work to serve the customer.

Employee incentives are tied to customer service. Salespeople are given personalized business cards to help them build relationships with customers. Uniquely, salespeople are not tied to their respective departments but to the customer. Salespeople can travel from department to department within the store to assist their customer, if that is needed. For example, a Nordstrom salesperson assisting a woman shopping for business apparel helps her shop for suits, blouses, shoes, hosiery, and accessories. The salesperson becomes the "personal shopper" of the customer to show her merchandise and provide fashion expertise. This is also conducive to the building of a long-term relationship with the customer, as over time, the salesperson understands the customer's fashion sense and personality.

The opportunity to sell across departments enables salespeople to maximize sales and commissions while providing superior customer service. As noted on a *60 Minutes* segment, "[Nordstrom's service is] not service like it used to be, but service that never was."

Despite the obsession with customer service at Nordstrom, ironically, the "customer comes second." Nordstrom understands that customers will be treated well by its employees only if the employees themselves are treated well by the company. Nordstrom employees are treated almost like the extended Nordstrom family, and employee satisfaction is a closely watched business variable.

Nordstrom is known for promoting employees from within its ranks. The fundamental traits of a successful Nordstrom salesperson (such as a commitment to excellence and customer service) are the same traits emphasized in successful Nordstrom executives.

Nordstrom hires people with a positive attitude, a sense of ownership, initiative, heroism, and the ability to handle high expectations. This sense of ownership is reflected in Nordstrom's low rate of shrinkage. Shrinkage, or loss due to theft and record-keeping errors, at Nordstrom is under 1.5 percent of sales, roughly half the industry average. The low shrinkage can be attributed in large part to the diligence of salespeople caring for the merchandise as if it were their own.

Employees at all levels are treated like businesspeople and empowered to make independent decisions. They are given the latitude to do whatever they believe is the right thing, with the customers' best interests at heart. All employees are given the tools and authority to do whatever is necessary to satisfy customers, and management almost always backs subordinates' decisions.

In summary, Nordstrom's product is its people. The loyal Nordstrom shopper goes to Nordstrom for the service received—not necessarily the products. Of course, Nordstrom does offer quality merchandise, but that is secondary for many customers.

Customer-Focused Policies

One of the most famous examples of Nordstrom's customer service occurred in 1975 when a Nordstrom salesperson gladly took back a set of used automobile tires and gave the customer a refund, even though Nordstrom had never sold tires! The customer had purchased the tires from a Northern Commercial Company store, whose retail space Nordstrom had since acquired. Not wanting the customer to leave the Nordstrom store unhappy, the salesperson refunded the price of the tires.

Nordstrom's policies focus on the concept of the "Lifetime Value of the Customer." Although little money is made on the first sale, when the lifetime value of a customer is calculated, the positive dollar amount of a loyal customer is staggering. The lifetime value of a customer is the sum of all sales generated from that customer, directly or indirectly. To keep its customers for a "lifetime," Nordstrom employees go to incredible lengths. In a Nordstrom store in Seattle, a customer wanted to buy a pair of brand-name slacks that had gone on sale. The store was out of her size, and the salesperson was unable to locate a pair at other Nordstrom stores. Knowing that the same slacks were available at a competitor nearby, the sales clerk went to the rival, purchased the slacks at full price using petty cash from her department, and sold the slacks to the customer at Nordstrom's sale price. Although this sale resulted in an immediate loss for the store, the investment in promoting the loyalty of the happy customer went a long way.

Nordstrom's employees try to "Never Say No" to the customer. Nordstrom has an unconditional return policy. If a customer is not completely satisfied, he or she can return the new and generally even heavily used merchandise at any time for a full refund. Ironically, this is not a company policy; rather, it is implemented at the discretion of the salesperson to maximize customer satisfaction. Nordstrom's advice to its employees is simply, "Use good judgment in all situations." Employees are given the freedom, support, and resources to make the best decisions to enhance customer satisfaction. The cost of Nordstrom's high service, such as its return policy, coupled with its competitive pricing would, on the surface, seem to cut into profit margins. This cost, however, is recouped through increased sales from repeat customers, rare markdowns, and, if necessary, the "squeezing" of suppliers.

Nordstrom's up-channel policies (related to suppliers) also focus on maximizing customer satisfaction. According to former CEO Bruce Nordstrom, "[Vendors] know that we are liberal with our customers. And if you're going to do business with us, then there should be a liberal influence on their return policies. If somebody has worn a shoe and it doesn't wear satisfactorily for them, and we think that person is being honest about it, then we will send it back." Nordstrom realizes some customers will abuse the unconditional return policy, but Nordstrom refuses to impose that abuse back onto its vendors. Here again, the rule of "doing what is right" comes into play.

Nordstrom's merchandising and purchasing policies are also extremely customer focused. A full selection of merchandise in a wide variety of sizes is seen as a measure of customer service. An average Nordstrom store carries roughly 150,000 pairs of shoes with a variety of sizes, widths, colors, and models. Typical shoe sizes for women range from 2 1/2 to 14, in widths of A to EEE. Nordstrom is fanatical about stocking only high-quality merchandise. Once when the upper parts of some women's shoes were separating from the soles, every shoe from that delivery was shipped back to the manufacturer.

Study Questions*

1. What steps does Nordstrom take to implement its strategy of providing outstanding customer service?

2. How do these activities enable Nordstrom to reduce the gaps between perceived service and customer expectations?

3. What are the pros and cons of Nordstrom's approach to developing a competitive advantage through customer service?

*Do not use the alternative solutions format for this case.

Case 59

A STORY OF TARGET GUEST SERVICE

Joseph H. Hancock, II, Drexel University

Paul is a brand new executive guest services team leader (GSTL) for a Target store in Portland, Oregon. His responsibilities include managing the front lanes, guest services, returns, the cash office, and store sales contests. Paul is a people pleaser, very upbeat, and he likes to get to know each of his customers. He feels his excellent interpersonal skills allow him to maintain Target's level of "Fast, Fun, and Friendly" service with all customers, or "guests," as they are referred to by Target.

Many of the guests who come into the store know and ask for Paul when shopping because of his excellent service. Most of the guests who visit this store come from local wealthy suburbs located in the northwest hills of Portland. Some of these customers are stay-at-home moms; however, a majority are young business professionals who are not used to taking "no" for an answer.

Target's Return Policy

New and unused merchandise can be returned to Target within 90 days. Target store personnel are required to follow this procedure. When guests make purchases, their receipts are printed with the date of an item's "last day to return." The actual return policy is printed on the back of each receipt. After 90 days, guests are no longer allowed to return merchandise. If guests do not have a receipt when they return an item, the guest services representative gives them instore credit for the lowest sale price of the item. If a guest paid with a credit card, the guest services team member can do what is called a "credit card lookup." When the correct credit card is identified, the Target employee can return the purchase to the credit card. When guests paid in cash, they are required to show a Target guest services team representative their driver's license or state ID. This allows the employee to check the computer, verifying whether or not the guest returning the item habitually abuses Target's return policy. When a guest comes up as a "habitual returnee," someone who brings back too many items without receipts, the guest services team member is prompted by an error message and a special slip of paper prints from the POS system that the customer receives. At that moment, the customer is required to call the number on the slip of paper. When the customer calls the 800 number, a Target Corporate Assets Protection

Representative usually tells the customer that he or she is no longer allowed to return items at Target store locations without receipts.

Sometimes guests become angry or frustrated. However, many of these guests are those who abuse the return policy. While the return policy at Target seems strict, it has saved the company millions of dollars of phony returns. Before this policy was initiated, some of Target's guests would return used, worn, and broken items that had been owned for years.

The Scenario

Marsha is a frequent guest at Target. She usually visits the store at least once or twice a week. Marsha is a retail buyer who works for Nordstrom. She is based out of the Nordstrom store that is located next to the Target store. Marsha loves shopping at Target and buys all her home furnishings and bath products at this store. Since she works for a retailer as well, she knows just how fashion and design savvy Target has become.

One day on her lunch hour Marsha returns a set of towels that she decides do not really match her guest bathroom. Marsha bought Target's most expensive brand of Fieldcrest towels. She paid full price for these $200 towels because she really liked the color. She hung them in her guest bathroom for a month and had to wash one since it had gotten dusty while it was on the towel bar.

Because her job has been so hectic and crazy, Marsha keeps forgetting to bring the towels back to the Target store. She has kept them for over four months. Noticing the last day to return on her receipt has expired, she decides to be a little sneaky. Marsha takes the towels back to Target without her receipt. At the guest services counter, the Target team member informs Marsha that the entire set of her towels are currently selling for $35. The color has gone on clearance and is no longer full price. The team member tells Marsha that she can only give her $35 worth of store credit. Marsha is furious. She demands to speak with a manager on duty. The employee uses her walkie-talkie and calls Paul to come to the guest services desk.

When Paul arrives, he notices Marsha looks mad; however, he smiles at her. Once at the desk, the employee explains the situation to Paul, who then explains the policy to Marsha and asks her how she paid for the purchase. She tells him that cash was used for the towels because she had just received a bonus from work. Marsha states she is a very loyal Target customer, spending approximately $2,500 a year at the store. Paul states he will try to "override the system" and give her credit for the $200 she paid, but he needs to see her driver's license.

Paul notices one of the towels has all the tags removed and smells of fabric softener. He asks Marsha if she used one of the towels. She tells him "no." Marsha hands Paul her driver's license, and he begins to key in her information. Once he is finished, a notice appears on his screen to print a guest services message. Paul prints the message and hands it to Marsha so she can call the 800 guest services phone number. Paul informs Marsha that he is unable to accommodate her and that she will need to call the number. Marsha's anger grows and she becomes hostile. She grabs the receipt and begins to dial the number on her cell phone.

An assets protection team member answers the call and informs Marsha that she has returned too many items in the store without receipts. The Target assets protection member also tells her that she will need receipts for all future returns. Marsha yells at the person on the phone, telling her she wants her supervisor's contact information. She then looks at Paul and tells him she wants his store team leader's contact information as well as that of the district manager. After she writes down the assets team leader's information, she snatches Paul's information from him. She tells Paul how horribly he has treated her and tells him she will *never* shop at Target again. She takes her towels and storms out of the store. Paul and the Target employee are very upset and feel bad for Marsha. However, they both know they have followed procedure.

Major Question

If you were the manager what would you have done?

Study Question

Should the guest services team leader inform anyone of this episode or just leave it alone?

Case 60

BEWARE OF DISSATISFIED CONSUMERS: THEY LIKE TO BLAB[1]

Knowledge@Wharton, March 8, 2006

Results of [a] Retail Customer Dissatisfaction Study . . . show that only 6% of shoppers who experienced a problem with a retailer contacted the company, but 31% went on to tell friends, family or colleagues what happened. Of those, 8% told one person, another 8% told two people, but 6% told six or more people.

. . .

Overall, if 100 people have a bad experience, a retailer stands to lose between 32 and 36 current or potential customers, according to the study. The complaints have an even greater impact on shoppers who were not directly involved as the story spreads and is embellished, researchers found. Almost half those surveyed, 48%, reported they have avoided a store in the past because of someone else's negative experience. For those who had encountered a problem themselves, 33% said they would "definitely not" or "probably not" return.

. . .

Parking was a major source of aggravation for shoppers, according to the survey. It topped the list of problems, with 40% of those surveyed reporting dissatisfaction in the parking lot . . . In addition to parking problems, shoppers surveyed complained that it took a long time for them to be waited on (24%) or to pay (33%).

. . .

Retailers . . . need to find ways to get customers to share complaints with management, not friends and family. One way is for retailers to ask customers to check a box on their credit card slip indicating they had a problem at the store. Retailers could then attempt to follow up, or give the customer a phone number or web address to make their complaints directly. If nothing else . . . it would give the customer a chance to blow off steam. That could prevent them from spouting off to others who might then embellish the experience and make matters that much worse for the retailer.

Study Questions*

1. Why should retailers be careful not to have dissatisfied customers?

2. What are some reasons that customers become dissatisfied?

3. What specific actions can retailers take to curb customer dissatisfaction?

*Do not use the alternative solutions format for this case.

Case 61

SAKSFIRST BUILDS CUSTOMER RELATIONSHIPS[1]

Teresa Scott, University of Florida

It's Wednesday afternoon, and as usual, Gwendolyn has a fitting room ready for Mrs. Johnson. She has picked out some of the new items in Mrs. Johnson's size that came in the previous week. She has everything from scarves to jewelry to shoes ready to go along with the outfits.

"Good evening, Mrs. Johnson. So how was your birthday?" Gwen asked.

"It was wonderful. My husband took me to Italy. Thank you for the card."

"I pulled some new items for you to try on," Gwendolyn said.

"Thank you, Gwen. You are the best!" replied Mrs. Johnson.

The reason Mrs. Johnson has such a friendly relationship with Gwen is because Mrs. Johnson is a regular customer and a SaksFirst member.

Saks Fifth Avenue started in the early twentieth century. Saks is considered the epitome of class, style, and luxury. When customers go to Saks, they receive excellent customer service; when they join SaksFirst—started in 1994—they also receive a

[1]Levy and Weitz, *Retailing Management*, 6th ed., The McGraw-Hill Companies. Reproduced with permission of The McGraw-Hill Companies.

lot of additional benefits. SaksFirst is a preferred customer program that helps facilitate more personal customer–sales associate relationships.

To become a member, a customer has to have a Saks Fifth Avenue credit card, and once she or he spends at least $1,000 a year, the customer is automatically enrolled. For every dollar spent, the customer will receive a reward point. At the end of the year, preferred customers receive 2, 4, or 6 percent in bonus points based on how much they charged that year above $5,000 at Saks.

SaksFirst customers receive many exclusive benefits. The tangible benefits include the points, rewards, and discounts. Customers also receive complimentary shipping and delivery for catalog and online orders, advance notice of sale events, the SaksFirst newsletter, catalogs, promotions and giveaways, double- and triple-point events, and double points on their birthdays. The intangible benefits include recognition and preferential treatment.

For the retailer, the main purpose of the SaksFirst program is to promote excellent customer service. The better the relationship between the customer and the sales associates, the more money loyal customers will spend. Every year there is a triple-point event in the first week of November. That one-day event accounts for the highest-volume sales day of the year, higher than the day after Thanksgiving or Christmas Eve. Knowing this, the company understands the importance of the preferred program.

The SaksFirst program can also be used by sales associates as a selling tool. If a customer is uneasy about purchasing large-ticket items, the sales associate can remind the member of the bonus certificate that will return a percentage of the cost. Sales associates are motivated to enroll as many of their customers as they can because they are given incentives such as "lottery tickets" that are redeemed for cash.

Study Questions*

1. How effective do you think the Saks-First program is in developing customer loyalty?

2. Whom should Saks target the Saks-First program toward?

3. Is the SaksFirst program worth what it spends giving back to customers?

Exercise

Compare loyalty programs for other retailers.

*Do not use the alternative solutions format for this case.

CHAPTER DISCUSSION QUESTIONS

1. How can personal selling be directly related to providing good customer service? What roles do training and evaluations of sales personnel play toward the goal of good customer service?

2. Why is it imperative that apparel retailers and resources partner for the benefit of good customer service? Explain some methods of doing such, in addition to those described in the chapter cases.

3. Compare and contrast formal and informal sales training. What are the benefits and shortcomings of both methods? Case examples may support your discussion.

4. Explain why product knowledge is important for sales. How is it related to customer service?

5. Discuss the relationship between employee compensation, sales incentives, and customer service. How do these relate to good and/or poor customer service? Cite case, examples and specific methods to support your arguments.

6. Discuss how new technologies have changed customer service and the way retailers communicate with customers.

ten

Entrepreneurship and Small Business Ownership

CHAPTER OBJECTIVES

- Describe entrepreneurship and present the characteristics of successful entrepreneurs.
- Relate leadership to entrepreneurship.
- Explain the process and challenges of starting your own business.
- Distinguish between an entrepreneurial and a nonentrepreneurial small business.

*T*he U.S. business base was founded on entrepreneurism and small businesses. Today we see developing countries following in these footsteps, with many new successful businesses, particularly in the apparel and textiles fields, bringing continual competition to established American companies. Entrepreneurs are future-oriented risk takers who have shown leadership in developing new businesses. Many large, successful companies started out small—with a single creative leader. However, not all small business owners are entrepreneurs, nor are they leaders. Starting your own business takes a great deal of time, energy, planning, and self-sacrifice, and is not for everyone; but it can be a rewarding undertaking *that leads to success. Careful consideration and decisions must be made along with self-analysis of strengths and weaknesses to determine one's entrepreneurial aptitude and direction relative to small business ownership.*

THE REALITIES OF ENTREPRENEURSHIP

Starting your own business is the dream of many people, but how many are really prepared for the realities of business ownership? More small businesses fail in the first year than survive. Entrepreneurs often fail in their first attempt, but the successful ones do not give up even in the face of several failures. Successful entrepreneurs have a vision for their business that is carried through to completion. Consider the case of Allen Breed, who developed the air bag and waited 20 years to convince the automobile industry of its usefulness; or Sam Walton and Rowland H. Macy, whose first attempts at retail businesses failed.

There are many definitions of **entrepreneur.** He or she can be considered as a person who is a leader, is a visionary, and has the ability to see and evaluate business opportunities, bringing together the factors of production in such a way that new wealth is created as the business grows. Some feel an entrepreneur also must possess a certain inventive genius.

Many of today's successful retail and manufacturing giants started out as small businesses. Today the majority of U.S. retailers and apparel manufacturers are small businesses, and many of these may be tomorrow's successful entrepreneurs. Table 10.1 profiles leading retail entrepreneurs, the originators of some of today's leading companies, all of whom started with small businesses.

Being an entrepreneur means combining personal characteristics, knowledge, financial means, and resources. Entrepreneurs are all unique, and each has an individual style; therefore, it is difficult to list all the personal characteristics required to be successful. What works for one person may not work for another. However, one trait they all have in common is that they are visionary: they perceive what others have not seen and act upon that perception. Some personal characteristics that frequently surface in successful entrepreneurs include the following:

- Ability to make their own decisions
- Ability to organize
- Ability to lead
- Ability to get along with people
- Acceptance of responsibility

TABLE 10.1 Profiles of Leading Retail and Apparel Entrepreneurs

Sam Walton	He opened his first retail store shortly after World War II; his first Wal-Mart discount department store was opened in 1962. In 2007, Wal-Mart had $374.5 billion in sales, more than 7,200 facilities around the world that included 4,100 stores in the United States and 3,100 international units, and more than 2 million associates, or employees, worldwide. Sam Walton was the richest man in America before his death in 1992.
Leslie Wexner	He borrowed $5,000 from an aunt to start a ladies' clothing store in the early 1960s. In 1994 his firm, The Limited, Inc., had almost 5,000 stores, but by the late 1990s, it began downsizing its extensive holdings, which included Express, Structure, Lerners New York, Henri Bendel, and others. In 2002, the company changed its name to Limited Brands, and by 2005, the firm promoted six brands: The Limited, Victoria's Secret, Express, White Barn Candle Company, C.O. Bigelow, and Bath & Body Works, accounting for more than 4,000 stores across the United States. Today Limited Brands employs more than 100,000 people.
Gary Comer	In 1963, he founded Lands' End, a mail-order company. Prior to that, Comer was an advertising copywriter for Young & Rubicam. Lands' End became a publicly held corporation in 1986 with circulation of 200 million catalogs. It is the second largest apparel-only mail-order business and the world's largest clothing Web site. In 2002 Sears purchased Lands' End for $1.9 billion. The Comers gave more than $40 million to the new University of Chicago Comer Children's Hospital.
Susie Tompkins Buell	She cofounded Esprit in 1968 with Doug Tompkins. Esprit grew into one of the most recognized global brands with more than $800 million in annual sales. Esprit was known for its revolutionary fusion of corporate mission with social responsibility. The Esprit Foundation was created in 1990 to support at-risk youth, AIDS awareness, women's issues, and the environment. It has since been renamed the Susie Tompkins Buell Foundation and continues to carry the original spirit of innovation and social responsibility by focusing on empowering, educating, and promoting leadership among women.

TABLE 10.1 *(continued)*

Dov Charney	He opened the first T-shirt company in 1989 and was in bankruptcy in 1996. Two years later he started American Apparel with a partner in Los Angeles and opened the first store in 2003. He built American Apparel into a $250 million company selling T-shirts and casual clothes, all made in Los Angeles plants. His sweatshop-free, pro-labor philosophy, paying employees higher than industry wages with generous benefits, is rare in the U.S. apparel industry, where most apparel is imported.
Renzo Rosso	He owns the Diesel brand which was originally created to get rid of leftover fabrics and closeouts. The name was chosen to say "cheap, a slow car that smells bad." Renzo Rosso became the sole owner of the $7 million label in the 1980s and made it into a $1.4 billion brand after acquiring Martin Margiela in 2002 and adding manufacturing and distribution acquisitions. In the 1990s Diesel launched tongue-in-cheek ad campaigns that spoofed fashion advertising. Rosso says his goal is to be the "coolest of the biggest."

- Possession of willpower, self discipline, good time management skills, self-confidence
- Possession of originality and flexibility
- Physical stamina and the capacity for hard work and long hours
- Enjoyment of competition
- Being task-result oriented
- Being a risk taker
- Being future-oriented
- Having a strong desire to be independent and to succeed

Knowledge or technical information needed for success might include the following:

- Knowledge about products or services sold
- Finding the target market, selling techniques, and how to promote the product or service
- Knowledge of personnel management, record keeping, and inventory controls
- Experience or formal training, depending on the area

It is important to remember, however, that not all entrepreneurs possess these characteristics.

The **entrepreneurial process** can be seen in several ways: (1) introduction of a new product or of improved quality, (2) introduction of a new method of production, (3) opening of a new market, (4) conquest of a new source of supply of materials, and (5) carrying out a new organization of an industry. Advice often given to would-be entrepreneurs includes:

- Avoid businesses that are oversaturated.
- Originality isn't always necessary; improving on a well-established business type can be successful.
- Concentrate your research on filling a need or niche.
- Start a business cautiously with sufficient capital. And don't expect to get rich overnight.

WHAT AN ENTREPRENEUR IS NOT

A person who merely owns a company or gives orders is not necessarily an entrepreneur. A **venture capitalist** or **financier** is a person who supplies money and takes a financial risk, but this person is not necessarily an entrepreneur—he or she can be merely an investor. These roles have often been confused. A person who creates in the literary or artistic sense is not an entrepreneur; that person would need to recognize an innovative idea or creation and capitalize on it to be an entrepreneur. Merely being self-employed also is not necessarily being an entrepreneur because an element of growth is required that leads to innovation, job creation, and economic expansion. Not all small firms are entrepreneurial, but most entrepreneurs start out in small firms. In this chapter, *Case 62, When a Small Business Has a Chance to Become Large; Case 63, Weighing the Options: Should Kristen Buy a Struggling Business?; Case 64, Katie's Kloset in Cedar Spring Grove: Sales, Smoke, and Small-Town Business; Case 65, A Case of Poor Planning; Case 66, Part I, Many Tasks, Few People: Lullaby Begins, and Part II, Out of Control: Lullaby, Fifteen Years Later; and Case 67, Amber's Wave* all discuss retailers and manufacturers that are small businesses or started out as such, but all may not be thought of as entrepreneurs.

THE OWNER AS LEADER

Being a leader is a prerequisite to entrepreneurship. **Leadership** is the process of moving a group in a direction that is in their long-term best interests. The leader must demonstrate strength and the ability to carry the followers. Common

TABLE 10.2 Recommended Entrepreneurial Skills

1. Keep your perspective.
2. Know why you want to lead.
3. Identify your targets (dream); know when to shoot.
4. Be clear and fixed.
5. Observe when people listen to you.
6. Leverage your small successes.
7. Be tough, not mean; use carrots, not sticks.
8. Let them see you err.
9. Show you are willing to pay the price.
10. Create positive-sum games. (Create something.)
11. Withstand temptations.
12. Study your opportunities.
13. Select the right followers.
14. Take responsibility for their mistakes.
15. Select the birds you flock with.
16. Give.
17. Keep your goal in sight.
18. One-to-one is the same as 1-million-to-1-million (some people won't take risks).
19. Trust.
20. Communicate to inspire.
21. Be a cheerleader.
22. Remember what they wish they were.
23. Do windows, but not details. (Do anything to make the dream happen, but know your strengths and weaknesses.)

Source: Shefsky (1994).

characteristics of a leader include having a realistic, clear vision of a goal; the means to accomplish it; and the ability and means to communicate the vision to inspire others. Most believe that people are not born leaders; leadership skills can be learned. Shefsky (1994) developed a list of 23 recommended skills to help develop entrepreneurial leadership, as shown in Table 10.2. In addition to these 23 skills, number 24 should be "caring." Perhaps Sam Walton is one of the best examples of this, as he visited hourly employees at the stores showing how important the business was to him while undergoing chemotherapy for bone cancer. They knew he cared, and they responded in kind.

Leaders are not always managers. Some people are both, but many managers are devoid of leadership. Managers instruct people on what to do, but leaders help them decide what to do. (For more on managers, see Chapter 1.) A leader is not necessarily the best at doing what needs to be done, but he or she motivates others. As small companies grow large, the originators often find they are not good managers.

Companies often find they have outgrown their founder's skills and their ability to integrate other talented people. This happened when Banana Republic's originators sold to Gap. Initially, this was also the case with Apple Computer as Steve Jobs and Steve Wozniak went on to other ventures; however Steve Jobs returned to Apple and as a true entrepreneur led the company to develop the iPod, iTunes, and the iPhone. On the other hand, Bill Gates, owner of Microsoft, and Sam Walton, owner of Wal-Mart, stayed with their companies as they grew large and successful. Most attribute the success of Wal-Mart to the entrepreneurial spirit of Sam Walton, which he maintained throughout his life. Sometimes the resources and capacity of a small business cannot handle too much growth, such as in *Case 62, When a Small Business Has a Chance to Become Large,* where a small knitwear company has to decide if they can handle a large order from JCPenney.

Entrepreneurial leaders have a dream. They start without followers and proclaim their beliefs publicly, risking being wrong. They are inspirational. If they believe wholeheartedly and can demonstrate that to others, followers will join in the dream. People want to associate with those who can give them a positive experience.

STARTING YOUR OWN BUSINESS

As previously mentioned, not all small businesses are entrepreneurial, but most entrepreneurs start out in small businesses. Who knows which small enterprise will be the next Levi Strauss or Wal-Mart? With today's large businesses downsizing, we are seeing an increase in the creation of small companies. The **Small Business Administration (SBA)** defines a small business differently depending on the industry; however, for retailing it is sales of less than $5 million and for manufacturing it is defined as fewer than 500 employees. Small businesses have advantages and disadvantages over larger companies and corporations. Advantages include being your own boss and decision maker, the freedom to do what you want when you want, and the satisfaction of knowing you were responsible for your success and the employment of other people. Disadvantages include not being able to be all things or possess all the skills necessary to run your business, limited capital, time and energy, and being responsible for the things that go wrong, which perhaps result in the loss of the livelihood of others. The positive aspects of business ownership may be a detriment to others. For example, being the sole decision maker may be stressful to some, which could result in poor decision-making at times.

Small business owners have other options besides starting a new business. They may buy an existing business as in *Case 63, Weighing the Options: Should Kristen Buy a Struggling Business,* and *Case 64, Katie's Kloset in Cedar Spring Grove: Sales, Smoke, and*

Small-Town Business, or they could buy into an independent or corporate business and become a partner with another person already in that business, or they could buy a franchise. Of course, there are dangers in these options too. *Case 7, Corporate-Owned Stores versus Franchising for Comfort Cloud Shoes,* in Chapter 2, looks at the pros and cons of franchises.

New small business owners may need assistance, as usually no one holds all the skills and knowledge necessary to run a successful business. The legal aspects of starting or buying a business may necessitate the services of a lawyer for assistance in complying with local laws and ordinances. Accountants may be necessary to develop a system of record keeping, including payroll, sales, and tax reports. First-time apparel store owners may need help developing merchandise plans or even shopping the market. In *Case 64,* Katie went to market for the first time with no idea of how much merchandise to order or how much money to spend.

It takes an incredible amount of time and personal sacrifice to start a business. Putting all of your time into a business very often leaves little time for a personal life. Going into a new venture with your eyes wide open will help to increase your chance of success.

Planning

Planning is the anticipation and organization of what tasks need to be done to reach an objective or goal. A business plan is an important part of the overall strategy for a new business. It should include a marketing plan, financial plan, and legal considerations. Additionally, a merchandise plan may be necessary if goods are to be sold (Chapter 5 explains merchandise planning and its importance). A **marketing plan** includes an analysis of the business environment that should support the definition of the designated target market. Generally, small businesses need to find a niche market that is not completely filled.

A **financial plan** includes an estimate of startup costs and the amount of financing required. It should include performance objectives, estimated sales, and cash flow. Legal requirements include a basic understanding of the laws affecting the business such as permits, licenses, and regulations. This information can be procured from the SBA, local chamber of commerce, or department of economic development. *Case 65, A Case of Poor Planning* explores problems with a growing business without a good plan.

Access to Capital

While many businesses can be started with little money, most businesses need some capital to get started. Access to capital—a perpetual problem for the entrepreneur and new business owner—can take several forms. Having your own money is the easiest way of financing your business, but that is not always possible. Some borrow from family and other personal sources who may want to invest. *Case 66, Part 1, Many Tasks, Few People: Lullaby Begins* illustrates a situation with a young couple starting a business using personal and family funds to get started.

If small business owners can prove credit worthiness, generally through a proven track record, they may be able to secure a loan to start their business. Loans are possible through the SBA, a federal agency with special programs for minority business development and for the economically disadvantaged. Another source of income is through venture capitalists, individuals who invest money in someone else's business. For a substantial part of the profits, the venture capitalist provides financial backing for the company to get started. Many well-known designers have such financial backing. It can be risky business for both the backer and the designer. If profits are not as anticipated, the financial backer may pull out of the deal, leaving the designer no way to continue in business. Designers have been known to even lose their trademarked name when their business went bankrupt. Entering into a partnership is another way of procuring funds for a small business. A partner contributes financial support and shares in the profits or losses.

Most new businesses need startup costs. These vary, of course, from business to business. Stores often require interior and/or exterior remodeling that can take considerable funds unless one is creative and can "beg or borrow" to get started. A direct-mail or Internet retail business does not require such investment; however, startup costs would be required for the paper or online catalogs and distribution. Part of startup costs goes toward procuring inventory (if merchandise is sold). Some retail companies can start out with **consignment** or "on memorandum" merchandise in which the supplier is paid for only those items that are sold. Some retailers refer to these as "goods on wheels." The owner does not take title to the goods and, hence, does not need to have funds up front to purchase the merchandise as most retail does. Other costs incurred for a new business include rent, supplies, employee wages, advertising, utilities, insurance, taxes, delivery costs, and so forth.

Environmental Influences

The economic and political environments play crucial roles in the survival and growth of new and small businesses. High inflation and interest rates can be devastating to a new, struggling business. The effect of most governmental regulation is generally most severe on small businesses. For example, the small pharmaceutical company has all but disappeared due to the high costs of testing requirements imposed by the Food and Drug Administration (FDA). The FDA also monitors the cosmetics industry, which has come under attack for claims that cosmetics affect the functioning of the body, thus defining the product as a drug. Small companies may not be able to survive such legal battles. The Federal Trade Commission (FTC) regulates unfair competition including deceptive advertising and has the power to remove products from the market if suspected of trademark infringement or to effect changes in advertisement claims if warranted. Additionally, the Consumer Product Safety Commission (CPSC) has the power to recall products in the marketplace if they have been proven to be a safety risk or hazard. (U.S. governmental regulatory agencies are discussed further in Chapter 11.)

The competitive environment can also be difficult for a new small business. With tight resources and many roles to occupy, new owners may not find time to evaluate their competition and keep on top of fashion and/or business trends as they should. The owner described in *Case 67, Amber's Wave* considers selling on the Internet, an environment which she doesn't know much about and is outside her mission.

Small Business Performance

Many people can start a business if they possess the desire to do so. Achieving success, however, is another story. Individuals wanting to own their own businesses should possess similar personal characteristics as entrepreneurs, for example, sufficient knowledge, skills, interest, and financial means; however, as mentioned earlier, not all owners are necessarily entrepreneurs. Many small businesses fail for many reasons. *US News & World Report* ("Checklist for small business," 1989) cited ten major reasons for small business failures, which still hold true today:

1. Insufficient profits
2. Poor growth
3. Too much debt or too little equity
4. Inexperience
5. Heavy operating expenses
6. Industry weaknesses
7. Internal factors such as high interest rates, poor location, or competition
8. Neglect
9. Fraud
10. Poor planning

Case 64, Katie's Kloset in Cedar Springs Grove: Sales, Smoke, and Small-Town Business is an example of a small business owner with several of the above problems, not the least of which was a fire that destroyed all the stock in her store. She has to decide whether or not to start up the business again after the fire. On the other hand, some small companies with good ideas and new niches can be phenomenally successful, as illustrated in Table 10.1.

SUMMARY

Most businesses in the United States and around the world are small, and there are many success stories of small companies becoming leaders in the economy. Such is the American dream. These small businesses often were started by entrepreneurial leaders who may or may not have been successful in their first venture. Entrepreneurs are risk takers and visionaries who are dedicated to long hours of work to realize their dreams as they create something new. Not all small business owners are entrepreneurs, but they are the backbone of our economy. Starting a new, successful business takes careful research, analysis, and planning, in addition to sufficient capital.

KEY TERMS

consignment	leadership
entrepreneur/entrepreneurial leader	marketing plan
entrepreneurial process	Small Business Administration (SBA)
financial plan	venture capitalist
financier	

BIBLIOGRAPHY

Checklist for small business. (1989, October). *US News & World Report,* pp. 72–80.

Larenaudie, S. R. (2006, Fall). Who drives Diesel? *Time New York,* p. 84.

Leslie Wexner. (2007). http://www.ohiohistorycentral.org, accessed September 3, 2007.

Palmeri, C. (2005, June 27). Living on the edge at American Apparel. *Business Week,* p. 88.

Reda, S., & Schulz, D. (2008, May). Guiding a retail brand from start-up to smash hit in 10 years (or less) is no small feat. *Stores.* www.stores.com.

Schefsky, L. E. (1994). *Entrepreneurs are made not born.* New York: McGraw-Hill.

Shroeder, C. L. (2007). *Specialty shop retailing: Everything you need to know to run your own store.* Hoboken, NJ: John Wiley & Sons, Inc.

Small Business Administration. http://www.sba.gov/smallbusinessplanner/index.html

Startup Studio: Biweekly podcast showcasing startup stories and inspiring entrepreneurs (2007). (www.startupstudio.com), accessed September 3, 2007.

Zook, M., & Graham, M. (2006). Wal-Mart nation: Mapping the reach of a retail colossus. In S. Brunn, Ed., *Wal-Mart world: The world's biggest corporation in the global economy* (pp. 15–25). New York: Routledge.

Case 62

WHEN A SMALL BUSINESS HAS A CHANCE TO BECOME LARGE

Suzanne G. Marshall, California State University, Long Beach

Vera Campbell began her career in the fashion business as a buyer for retail stores owned by her husband. She had been a history major in college and had dreams of becoming a professor, but the thrill of fashion changed her mind. After she married, her direction changed to retail management.

After a few years her marriage collapsed and she was without a job. Still loving the fashion business, she went into product development for a company, specializing in juniors. She traveled extensively to Asia, sourcing products, working with contractors, and learning the import/export business.

Vera later decided she was well versed in the business, having worked both sides—retail and wholesale—and wanted a business of her own. Having skills and know-how but no money, she sought the route of many business ventures and found a financial partner. She sold her new partner 49 percent of her business and worked with

him for several years. When she discovered he was cheating her out of profits, she dissolved the partnership and took control of the business, knowing that the threat of exposure would make her former partner extremely amenable to her plan.

With complete ownership and control of her own business, Vera began to produce women's knitwear and named her company Knitworks. Located in Los Angeles, she produced domestically and grew the business to 17 employees. She built a headquarters in close proximity to the California Mart so that she had quick access. She frequently went to her showroom to close deals with large clients. She found she was content as a small manufacturer and earned a salary that allowed her to live a life of ease and travel frequently, a perk she really enjoyed.

As the company grew, Vera found she needed to hire an additional salesperson. She hired Jerry North, who had been a rep in the juniors business and was well connected with buyers who worked for many large retailers. Jerry's dream was to sell Knitworks' products to JCPenney. He had worked with Penney's for many years and had a solid relationship with the buyers. However, because Penney's worked with a vendor matrix and Knitworks could not get on the matrix, he was consistently denied a sale. Not giving up, he repeatedly called the buyers he formerly worked with, urging them to give Knitworks a chance. After

18 months of effort, the Penney's buyer offered to allow him a test in one of her stores. The product tested well, and Penney's bought some additional items to test further.

In the meantime, Vera was doing a test of her own—children's wear. She had wanted to develop a sub-brand of her Knitworks brand for children. Her reasoning was that she already had staff that was familiar with knits, which were the perfect choice of fabrication for children. She also already had established relationships with knit contractors. So she began to develop some products for knits under the label Knitworks for Kids.

As Knitworks began to enjoy positive sell-through at Penney's, additional locations picked up the label. When the new Knitworks for Kids became available for sale, Jerry immediately took it to his Penney's buyer, who introduced him to the Penney's children's buyer. The children's buyer agreed to give the new brand a test mainly because of the positive results of the junior line. The sell-through was positive for the test, and the buyer ordered more. Jerry and Vera were very pleased.

After selling to JCPenney for a year, the Knitworks for Kids line had a particularly cute T-shirt that the buyer really liked. She decided that she would show the shirt to the corporate buyers in Penney's headquarters in Plano, Texas. The centralized buying group for kids loved the shirt and decided to buy it for all JCPenney stores in the United States. The order totaled 10,000 units. It was by far the largest order Knitworks had ever received.

Although immediate excitement welled through the company, a quick feeling of panic seized the team when they began to access the situation. They listed the facts as follows:

1. They had never taken such a large order.
2. They used only local, domestic suppliers that did not have the capacity to produce in such large quantities.
3. Even if they used several domestic suppliers, they could not meet the Penney's deadline.

Ultimately the largest issue was that if they were successful in producing and delivering this order by the deadline and if it sold well at retail, their business as they had always known it could change dramatically.

Major Question

Considering all the ramifications of the situation, what should Knitworks decide?

Study Question

If they are successful and Penney's places additional orders, what will happen to Knitworks' other business? Will they have to discontinue selling to others?

Case 63

WEIGHING THE OPTIONS: SHOULD KRISTEN BUY A STRUGGLING BUSINESS?

Joy M. Kozar, Kansas State University
Sara B. Marcketti, Iowa State University

Jill Ross opened In the Name of Fashion, a trendy retail boutique targeting women ages 15 to 35. Owning a boutique had been a goal of Jill's since high school when she was voted the "best dressed" among her peers. Nearing her college graduation, Jill decided that the time was right to pursue her dream. With the assistance of her parents in securing a financial loan, Jill signed a three-year lease for a 1,800-square-foot retail space in a newly constructed strip center. The location was perfect. The strip center, located about a mile from the university where Jill graduated was in an area with other businesses targeting college students. Although young and somewhat inexperienced, Jill was confident in her abilities to identify popular fashion trends and styles. She knew that her business of offering an assortment of apparel items and accessories not found in other retail stores would meet the demand by the college students for trendy looks at affordable prices.

Jill's business quickly achieved financial success. She regularly attended two different apparel markets and stayed current with fashions, selecting only trendy, unique merchandise. A loyal customer base was quickly established, and the store had a good reputation for excellent customer service and reasonable price points. Jill was beginning to earn a profit from her store and she enjoyed the excitement of owning her own business and being her own boss. During the second year of business, the demand that she experienced at the initial startup slowed, so she worked diligently to bring in different brands of merchandise exclusive to the area. Customers were excited about the store's offerings, and they stopped by on a regular basis to survey the latest arrivals of clothing and accessories. Toward the end of the second year, Jill and her long-time boyfriend decided to get married. After the wedding, they moved to a town three hours away from the store to be closer to his place of employment. No longer living in the same town as the business, Jill quickly realized that she could no longer manage it from a distance. Consequently, in the third year of ownership, as the time approached to renew the lease, Jill decided to sell the business.

Kristen Harding, an assistant manager at a local department store and recent graduate of the university's fashion merchandising program, learned about the sale of the business through a mutual acquaintance. Interested in finding out more about the business, she called Jill to schedule a meeting. Jill provided her financial documents to Kristen, including monthly and yearly profit and loss statements. Kristen also had the opportunity to meet with several of Jill's part-time employees.

While learning about the history of the business, Kristen discovered that although Jill was no longer at the store on a regular basis during the last year of ownership, she never relinquished much control to her employees. Despite Jill's prolonged absences from the store, a full-time manager was never hired and employee turnover was high. Each employee was provided with a key to open and close the store and was instructed to call Jill on her cell phone if a problem occurred. The employees informed Kristen that Jill would stop in once a month to price new merchandise, rearrange the sales floor, change the display windows, and create the next month's work schedule. Overall, the employees were disinterested in the store's operations and frustrated by the lack of supervision by Jill. The employees expressed concern to Kristen that unless some drastic changes occurred, the store would soon go out of business.

Indeed, as evidenced in the financial statements, Jill's profits had been declining during much of the third year in business. Kristen believed that these losses were attributed to a number of reasons. Jill had stopped attending market and had become out of touch with her clientele. Because she had moved away from the store's general locale, she was less familiar with the fashions and styles popular with the target market. Most of the merchandise was purchased on the Internet from readily accessible vendors and was marked up higher than normal to compensate for the lack of inventory. During the third year, Jill had stopped seeking out new and different brands to carry in the store. Meanwhile, her competitors, other small locally owned boutiques, started carrying some of the same brands as In the Name of Fashion and advertised them at lower prices. Because of the price sensitivity of her target market, the store was beginning to be perceived by customers as too expensive and out of touch.

After the meeting, Kristen believed that the original image of the business as a unique, trendy, affordable place to shop could likely be restored. Yet she also knew that making the business profitable again would be challenging. She would have to quit her job at the department store to be able to devote her energy full-time to the business. She loved working in retail and was enthusiastic about the prospect of owning a small fashion boutique. However, the risks involved in taking over Jill's business were many and required careful consideration before a final decision would be made.

Major Question

Should Kristen buy the business or stay in her current job at the department store? What are the factors that led you to your decision?

Study Questions

1. If Kristen bought the business, what strategies should she use in making the business profitable again?

2. What are the advantages and disadvantages of buying an already established business versus starting one from the ground up?

Case 64

KATIE'S KLOSET IN CEDAR SPRING GROVE: SALES, SMOKE, AND SMALL-TOWN BUSINESS

LuAnn R. Gaskill, Virginia Tech

Cedar Spring Grove is a quaint, family-oriented community of about 7,500 residents located in southwest Virginia. It sits in a gently sloping valley surrounded by the dogwood- and redbud-covered mountains of the New River Valley. Like many small communities in Virginia, the town offers area residents a variety of locally managed small business venues from which to shop, including several specialty clothing stores, as an alternative to major shopping malls and metropolitan areas some 45 miles away.

Katie Glenn, a long-time resident of Cedar Spring Grove, grew up in a close-knit, well-respected, business-oriented family. Her college years were spent at a small school in northern Virginia pursuing a four-year degree in Environmental Studies with a minor in Public Communications. She was able to help with her educational expenses by working several part-time jobs, including sales work at a major department store located near the university. In her senior year, she interned in Washington, D.C., with the Environmental Protection Agency; this was an invaluable learning experience for her. After her summer in D.C., however, Katie realized she wasn't cut out for life in the world of politics or corporate competition, and she returned to Cedar Spring Grove after graduation.

Hoffman's, located on Main Street in downtown Cedar Spring Grove, was a small retail business that offered a broad assortment of moderately priced plus-sized women's clothing. The 25-year-old business was owned and operated by sisters Loretta Dravillas and Louisa Shiban, two sisters nearing their 70s. Their health failing, they offered to sell Katie their 2,000-square-foot store including its existing fixtures, current inventory, and outstanding orders, which would complete her merchandise needs for the coming season. It was a turnkey setup, and Katie did enjoy her part-time department store sales experience. Ownership of Hoffman's would also allow her to remain close to her family in Cedar Spring Grove, and that was something that delighted her parents.

Katie and her parents reviewed the current financial records for Hoffman's and noted that the initial financial investment would be fairly modest. With the blessing of her parents, as well as their financial backing, Katie purchased the business. After all, the timing was right; she has just finished her college education and it was time to begin a career. Hoffman's offered an opportunity to establish herself as a successful business owner in her hometown of Cedar Spring Grove.

Loretta and Louisa stayed on for several months to orient Katie to the store, and

Katie's mother voluntarily assisted her full-time at the store, where she kept busy handling the accounting paperwork at Hoffman's. Although Katie had hired three part-time salespeople, she spent much of her time on the selling floor.

Within six months, it was apparent that sales were not at the level Katie had expected, and she determined that a new merchandising strategy was necessary. She decided to refocus Hoffman's from primarily plus-sized merchandise to moderately priced misses sportswear. She would also be offering a limited line of misses' petites.

The Spring market was Katie's first real experience at the Atlanta Apparel Mart. Having no knowledge as to how much merchandise to order for the upcoming fall/winter season, she conferred with several small retailers she met at market and learned that they had placed orders in the range of $40,000 to $45,000 (cost) during their market trip.

Because Katie owned and operated her retail establishment under its original name of Hoffman's, she was not able to establish credit lines with any of the vendors at market. Katie learned that Hoffman's had been associated with a bad credit history, since Loretta and Louisa had been negligent in paying their invoices on time in the past. Market vendors wanted all purchases sent to Hoffman's shipped C.O.D.

Immediately after the Spring market credit experience, Katie had the store name legally changed to Katie's Kloset. She also sent out credit applications to her vendors, and given her family's strong credit rating,

she had no further problems placing orders on credit. She followed the other retailers' example and subsequently placed Spring/Summer orders in the range of $40,000 to $45,000. She would continue this practice of ordering around $45,000 of merchandise at both spring/summer and fall/winter markets for the next two years.

During her slower summer months, Katie frequently worked the sales floor, making mental notes of what was and was not selling. She had established a suggestion box for her customers to let her know what merchandise they were particularly interested in purchasing. While working the sales floor, she recognized a growing trend of an older customer clientele, although she offered only a narrow merchandise selection that appealed to them. By fall, Katie determined that she needed to start targeting a revised market. She reestablished her new market as an older customer (60 plus) who valued active, comfortable, easy-care clothing. Orders placed during the fall market were placed with this market modification in mind. Katie even had the store remodeled to reflect the new, more mature woman's focus.

Fall/Winter shipments arrived offering new, moderately priced sportswear for the mature, older customer in misses and petite sizes. Although Katie's Kloset was still heavily inventoried with Spring/Summer merchandise, the newly arriving items added some excitement. Clearing out the old season goods took top priority so that room could be made for the newly arriving orders.

Based on the limited space available on the main floor, there was no alternative but to clear out some of the unused spaced in the basement and establish a bargain-basement sales area for dated merchandise that remained from the previous seasons. Years of broken inventories and seasonal merchandise were relocated to the basement and marked 40 to 90 percent below the original retail price.

Katie took out local ads promoting her bargain-basement and sale prices, and this resulted in a welcome increase in traffic flow. It appeared that most everyone entering Katie's Kloset headed directly to her bargain basement. Consequently, very little exposure was given to the main selling floor, where the current, regular-priced inventory was located.

While the promotional strategy was indeed effective in generating interest and moving out dated inventory, overall profit margins were negligible, if any at all. By the next spring, customer interest in the remaining basement inventory had declined significantly and visitors to the store frequently asked Katie when her next big sale would be taking place. Although no formal merchandise planning or control system was in place and record keeping was minimal, Katie knew that her business was losing money, and lots of it.

No one knows what time the fire started, but it probably was around 11:00 p.m. The local fire chief determined that it started as a result of a faulty furnace. Smoke, water, and fire damage to Katie's Kloset resulted in a complete loss of inventory and records.

Katie's insurance company, Statewide Mutual, settled with her by reimbursing the cost value of all the merchandise existing in the store. Katie was able to salvage most of the fixtures, but renovating the interior of the store would require some work.

It was not an easy decision for Katie and her family to make; but after considerable debate and with the encouragement of her parents, Katie decided to reopen the business, but help was sought. With advice from small-business support groups, Katie made the following changes to her business.

She continued with the 60-plus age market but purchased a turnkey POS computer software package that allows her to track her sales and inventory. It is a simple, effective record-keeping system, so she now knows when merchandise (by specific style number) arrives, how long it is on the selling floor before it sells, what the final selling price is, and so forth. With this information, she has a much clearer picture of what is selling and is able to develop assortment plans that reflect sales trends. Purchases are based on sales plans, existing inventory, and open-to-buy. Now Katie says she wouldn't think of going to market without her computer-generated merchandise plan. With her commitment to record keeping and inventory documentation, Katie now spends much more of her time off the selling floor. She also relies much more on her mother and the part-time salespeople to work with the customers.

Although customer service was always important, Katie has become increasingly committed to letting the community know how much she values their patronage. Thank-you letters are sent to customers after each purchase. She makes a more conscientious effort to involve herself in community events and to make herself visible in town, if for no other reason than to remind people that she's a business owner in Cedar Spring Grove.

Advertising has continued using the same media (radio and newspaper) as before the fire, but the focus of the ads has changed. She is now promoting the image of the store and merchandise quality rather than low prices.

Katie has hired an accountant who supplies her with monthly profit and loss statements. The accountant is teaching her how to develop these statements. Katie and her mother are also now paying themselves full-time salaries.

When asked what her biggest mistakes were before the fire, Katie replied, "Not paying close enough attention to what was selling and not better researching the store. We didn't look at any information other than the current books at Hoffman's. We have since learned that the owners had been losing money for years and were continuously infusing family funds into the store to keep it in operation. They also paid themselves no salaries."

Katie knows very well that continuous improvements must be made, but she is not certain what specific undertakings should be initiated. Because she had success previously with the consultants from the Small Business Administration, she decides to seek them once again.

Major Questions

1. What recommendations would you make to Katie to improve her business to achieve profit?

2. What advice do you think the Small Business Administration should give Katie in regard to recommendations to help ensure business success?

Study Questions

1. What is the best way to determine the amount of merchandise to buy at market for a small store?

2. What guidelines could Katie have used for promotional campaigns?

3. What mistakes did Katie make in determining her market? How should she have determined her market?

4. What are reasons for the store's loss of profit?

5. How typical is this actual business owner's experience compared to other small business owners?

6. In light of the existing revised business strategies, what are her chances of small business success?

Case 65

A CASE OF POOR PLANNING

Jaya Halepete, Marymount University

Mary had worked as a merchandiser for an apparel manufacturing company for two years. While working for that company, she dealt with buyers who demanded exclusive lines, quicker turnaround time for product lines, and on-time delivery. She constantly dealt with production problems when the fabric did not arrive on time, or the accessories ordered by assistant merchandisers turned out to be the wrong ones. She had learned to deal with difficult situations very well. After having experienced the manufacturing environment, Mary was ready to move on to a position of senior buyer in a retail chain.

Being a buyer was more challenging and allowed her to use the skills that she had developed in her manufacturing position. She was aware of what kind of problems she could expect from her vendors, as she had been in that situation herself. She timed her orders well so that there would be no delays due to mistakes made by vendors. She was highly successful as a buyer and was soon promoted to the position of divisional head. After being in that position for two years, she decided that she was ready for a bigger challenge and decided to quit. She had always dreamed of owning her own apparel export house.

Mary got some funding from friends, who were sure of her success, and set up her office. She invested all the money in setting up a production house with sewing machines, embroidery machines, and a showroom to showcase her lines. She then used her contacts from her earlier jobs and managed to get her first order from Tara of SM Stores, a retailer in Saudi Arabia that sold a large number of heavily embroidered tops. Tara provided the designs, and Mary met the wholesale prices that she was looking for. Mary was able to meet all the requirements, and she fulfilled the order exceptionally well. She got several repeat orders from Tara and developed a very good relationship with the retailer. The only problem was that the orders were not continuous. There would be two consecutive big orders and then no orders for the next few months. To overcome the problem of keeping her production unit running, Mary decided to look for other buyers.

She then met Betsy, who was an agent for several boutiques in London. Betsy promised Mary that she would get her large orders on a regular basis. Mary produced a line of garments for Betsy and waited for the orders to come in. Betsy, as promised, came up with a large order. Mary was thrilled and immediately started production. Since the designs were Mary's own, she could mark them up higher and made better margins. She developed a very good relationship with Betsy, and they started doing mutually successful business.

Since Mary was used to bigger challenges, after a few months into her export business, she decided that while she was making the lines for exports, she could produce some extra quantity and sell in the domestic market. She decided to convert the showroom into a store and started selling from there. Since her production facilities were not located in the main shopping area, the business was slow, but it did generate some additional revenue for her.

Everything was set up and doing well until she received a large order from both Betsy and Tara. Considering that Mary made more profit on order from Betsy, she was partial toward Betsy's order and completed her order on time. This resulted in a delay on Tara's order, however. Tara was very upset and threatened to not place any more orders.

Meanwhile, the boutiques that Betsy had received orders from decided to cancel the orders at the last minute due to a slowdown in sales. The garments had already been shipped to London, but the boutiques refused to accept them. At the same time, having to deal with all the problems that had developed, Mary neglected her retail store and lost sales from many of those customers. She was now in a fix, as she had money tied up in Betsy's order and was not getting any revenue from any other source. In addition Mary did not have any money to fill Tara's orders.

Major Question

What should Mary do to overcome the problem she has gotten herself into?

Study Questions

1. Do you think that Mary was well equipped to start her own business?

2. What could Mary have done to ensure that she would never be in a similar problem situation?

Case 66, Part 1

MANY TASKS, FEW PEOPLE: LULLABY BEGINS

Marcia Morgado, University of Hawaii

John Chang is a graduate of the University of Hawaii, where he majored in accounting. For five years he worked in the central accounting office of the Honolulu Sears store, and then became the assistant manager of his division. John's wife, Jennifer, received a degree in fashion merchandising from the University of Hawaii three years ago. She completed an internship at Liberty House (a Hawaii-based specialty store) while in college, and continued with the firm for a time after graduation. Since then, Jennifer has held various positions, including buying office clerical, assistant department manager, and assistant buyer.

Recently, John and Jenny decided to give up the security of their respective positions and open their own small fashion retail store. Their market research indicated that upscale maternity wear was not readily available in Honolulu, and that both the resident and tourist markets for this merchandise were rapidly expanding. John and Jenny found space for a shop on the ground floor of Ward Center, a small, centrally located, upscale destination mall. Although the space was expensive, the location was in high demand, and the couple determined they should move quickly to secure it.

The Changs signed a five-year lease and named the new shop "Lullaby." Jenny's mother, Martha, an experienced interior designer, provided 30 percent of the funds they required for the business venture, and they were able to secure the balance with a bank loan. They purchased merchandise fixtures and a cash register; selected a tropical green and warm peach color scheme to use throughout the store; placed an order for stationery, gift wrap, and paper bags; and flew off to New York to review merchandise lines and to place orders for the opening inventory.

Martha served as a silent partner in the business, which normally means that she would participate in 30 percent of the profits or losses without further input. However, she offered to help out by overseeing the refurbishing of the shop during the Changs' market visit. She offered, as well, to continue working in the store on a casual basis without compensation. Although John was not enthusiastic about working with Martha (he finds her domineering and overly critical), he was willing to accept her offer. After taking all costs into account, the Changs determined they would be able to afford only

two full-time, minimum-wage employees to help them with all the activities necessary to merchandise, manage, and operate the store. Upon Jenny's insistence, John realized Martha's offer was an opportunity to acquire additional help and expertise—without extra expense.

Their first market trip was a frustrating experience. Although they agreed that the merchandise offerings were exciting, John and Jenny found themselves in continuous disagreement over which lines to select and what quantities to order. John insisted on purchasing only from vendors who offered cash discounts or allowances or who would accept small or random assortment orders. Jenny was not insensitive to economic advantages but was strongly committed to developing shallow assortments with an emphasis on lines that offered unique and unusual styling details. John felt it essential that the shop carry nationally advertised goods, arguing that Lullaby's upscale market would want—and would expect to find—these represented in the inventory. Jenny was adamant about avoiding nationally advertised lines, arguing that such merchandise was widely available and would detract from the shop's unique, upscale image. Although shaky compromises were reached, neither looked forward to receiving the goods, nor to the grueling tasks of unpacking, counting, tagging, pressing, hanging, and displaying the merchandise.

The Changs returned to find other problems awaiting them. In their absence, Martha had ordered a change in the color scheme. The walls were painted and the carpet installed, but the sophisticated green and peach palette had been replaced with pastel yellow and deep blue. A strange young woman, who introduced herself as the "assistant manager" and who apparently had a key, was inside the store drinking coffee and eating a fast-food, carry-out meal on an obviously new, unfamiliar, brocade sofa. A note from United Parcel Service informed the couple that repeated attempts to deliver C.O.D. packages were unsuccessful and that those parcels had been returned to senders. Excess lumber and empty paint cans were piled in the delivery lane behind the rear security door, and a warning notice from the mall management admonished the Changs for defaulting on their obligation to keep access lanes free from obstruction.

Jenny took the circumstances in stride. Although the color scheme was not as they intended, it did "work," and the couple could now concentrate on developing inventory control and financial accounting systems. Jenny was also hopeful that the "assistant manager" would work out, and that if Martha stayed on, they could escape the costs of an additional employee. Quietly, she hoped the returned parcels contained merchandise that John had selected, and that the trash blocking the delivery lane was simply an oversight on the part of the contractor. But John was furious. Although he admitted the color scheme "wasn't bad," he argued that Martha had no right to make independent decisions affecting the business, that she was not authorized to hire employees, and that she should have had the common sense to accept the C.O.D. deliveries and to arrange for removal of the trash. Martha's efforts, John said, were simply complicating what was obviously becoming an overwhelming venture.

Jenny and John are exhausted and concerned about the future of their business. Because both are equal partners in the business, neither has final decision-making authority. Because they have comparable educational backgrounds and professional experience, neither outranks the other. Because personal as well as financial relationships are involved, it is important that solutions be amicably reached—soon.

Major Question

How would you diagnose the problem at Lullaby? What measures would you suggest to ensure against similar circumstances in the future?

Study Questions

1. What are the problems of working with relatives in a business venture?

2. What are the differences between the demands of running a small private business and the owners' previous job experience? Did it prepare them for their present situation? Why or why not?

3. How can large-store policies/procedures work in a small store?

Exercises

1. The Chang's business venture is set up as an equal partnership.

(a) Identify the strengths and weaknesses of partnership arrangements such as the one at Lullaby.

(b) Describe other forms of business arrangements under which Lullaby could operate, pointing out the strengths and weaknesses of each.

(c) Recommend an appropriate business structure for the Lullaby operation. Explain the bases on which your recommendation was made.

2. Like the Chang's, students in merchandising, retailing, and management classes often hope to open their own retail stores in the future. What is the nature of the competitive environment for stores such as Lullaby in your trading area? To answer this question, conduct an assessment of brick-and-mortar outlets for infants' and children's wear, nursery furniture, and related baby toys and accessories in your area.

(a) Name and identify the types of outlets available for these products (e.g., national specialty chains, department stores, discount stores, mass merchandisers, family-owned businesses).

(b) Compare and contrast the merchandise categories in each store or department relative to diversity, price zones, depth and breadth of inventory.

(c) Compare and contrast the floor arrangements, merchandise displays, and signage in each of the stores or departments.

(d) Compare the selling techniques in each location in terms of customer greeting, speed of approach, help with customer questions, and/or other aspects of ease of purchase.

(e) The Changs are considering opening a branch of Lullaby in your trading area. Prepare a recommendation for them based on your research. Should they bring Lullaby to your trading area? Address the factors that lead to your recommendation.

Case 66, Part 2

OUT OF CONTROL: LULLABY, FIFTEEN YEARS LATER

Marcia Morgado, University of Hawaii

When John and Jenny Chang opened their first small retail maternity shop in the Ward Center destination mall in Honolulu, little did they imagine what growth they would realize 15 years later. They now have a moderately sized specialty store in the island's gigantic Ala Moana Shopping Center, a small branch store on each of the three largest neighboring islands, and a staff of almost 80 people on the payroll.

Jenny now serves as the general merchandise manager and the vice president in charge of advertising and public relations. Three merchandise buyers report to her: one who is responsible for buying and managing the sale of maternity wear and infants' and toddler clothing, another who is in charge of buying and managing the sale of nursery furniture and related accessory items, and a third who is responsible for purchasing and managing the sale of toys and soft animals. These buyers are directly responsible for the sales volume in the neighboring island shops as well as in the main store.

In addition to the buyers, Jenny has two line assistants who report directly to her; both are assistant merchandisers. One works with the selling and display staff in the parent store. She merchandises the main store selling floor and handles other visual merchandising activities, such as selecting merchandise for window and interior displays, designing the displays, and moving merchandise between and around departments as she sees fit. Salespeople are responsible for assisting her with merchandise transfers and interior merchandise arrangements.

Jenny's second assistant is responsible for the same activities in all the neighboring island branches. Additionally, because she visits each of the branch stores every week, she is responsible for pulling merchandise from the parent store and sending it to the branches whenever she judges it necessary. In addition to shifting merchandise between the branches, she is also authorized to return merchandise to the parent store if she believes it will sell better there.

Jenny needs to spend much of her time in public relations activities. She is active in the local chapter of the National Retail Federation, is on the Board of Directors of Small Business—Hawaii, and is involved in activities with the Hawaii Visitors Bureau. She also participates in weekly meetings of the shopping center Retailers' Board, oversees the newspaper advertising for the shops, and periodically arranges and serves as commentator for mother–toddler fashion shows.

John is vice president in charge of finance and control and store operations. The people who report directly to him include four store managers (one for each of the island branches, as well as one for the parent store), an alterations room manager, a receiving and marking manager, an accounts payable and receivable manager, and a cleaning crew manager. The four store managers work on a "salary plus bonus" basis: each earns a minimum base salary, to which is added a bonus based directly on the sales volume of the store for which they are responsible.

There are three area managers in each store. The area managers are responsible for sales volume, customer service, and inventory control in their respective areas of the store. They are also responsible for scheduling the workdays, hours, lunchtimes, and breaks for the sales staff assigned to their areas. Area managers report to store managers and are directly responsible, as well, to the buyer or buyers whose merchandise is housed in their areas. The selling staff in each store is responsible to an area manager and to the store manager, as well as to the buyer or buyers of the area to which they are assigned.

Jenny's mother, Martha, is vice president in charge of personnel. She recruits, trains, evaluates, hires, and fires employees. She has two assistants. One handles all the clerical and paperwork. The other is Martha's assistant director of personnel. Because Martha has a 30 percent financial interest in the store, she is anxious to see that sales volume is high and customers are happy. Martha's assistant director holds sales training classes and periodically patrols the selling floor, making sure that customers are properly attended to, that the merchandise looks fresh and interesting, and that salespeople are keeping busy. When necessary, she directs the selling staff to stock keeping and/or facility cleanup; she may also shift salespeople from one area of the store to another on an as-needed basis to accommodate changes in customer traffic throughout the day.

All Lullaby management are paid salary. Benefits include group medical and life insurance, of which employees pay a contribution based on salary and tenure with the company. Sales personnel are paid more than minimum wage, but bonuses or commissions are not given. There are no other benefits or incentives.

Martha approves all hiring, including salespeople. Sometimes John and Jenny also participate in the hiring, firing, and disciplining of employees. Everyone knows Lullaby is a family-owned and family-operated company. Morale throughout the organization is low, and employee turnover at all levels is considerably higher than industry averages.

Major Question

How would you change the organizational structure of Lullaby to help alleviate the high turnover and morale problems?

Study Questions

1. What are possible reasons for morale and employee retention issues?

2. What changes to the benefits/bonus system would you make in order to reduce employee turnover and to raise morale? What would you establish as an incentive program?

Exercises

1. Visit the online information site of a national specialty chain that specializes in infants' and children's wear, or make an appointment to visit the personnel offices of a brick-and-mortar store in your area that sells merchandise similar to that carried by Lullaby. Ask for information about the organizational structure and/or lines of authority and reporting relationships that govern that store's operations. Compare and contrast with the structure that characterizes the Lullaby operation.

2. Design and conduct a study of wage and benefits packages offered to beginning-level salespeople, department or area managers, and/or to merchandise buyers employed in bricks-and-mortar outlets for infants' and children's wear in your trading area.

3. Conduct a state-by-state or region-by-region study of average wage and benefits packages for retail sales, management, and merchandise buyers. Use federal and state government sources, trade papers and business magazine sources, electronic search engines, and the career placement or career advising services on your campus as resources for your study.

Case 67

AMBER'S WAVE

Nancy A. Oliver, Northern Arizona University

Amber Marcel has a multimillion-dollar accessory manufacturing business and a problem. Amber started making her accessories in high school when she couldn't find the perfect belt to wear with a dress for the prom. She went to a fabric store; bought fabric, trim, and binding; and made a belt that was the highlight of her outfit. With the success of her first belt, Amber started making more accessories. By the time she was in college she had expanded to designing and making her belts, earrings, and vests.

Amber was a good student and during college received a scholarship from the local Women's Business League. The organization enjoyed meeting the young women to whom they awarded scholarships and invited each recipient to a luncheon in September.

Because of the uniqueness of her accessories, Amber continuously received compliments and inquires about items she was wearing, and it was no different at the Women's Business luncheon. Two women inquired if she made accessories for other people. Amber had not considered expanding beyond her own personal production and hesitated with her answer. Before she could reply, one woman suggested she would pay Amber $55 to make a belt like the one Amber was wearing. Amber quickly made a mental calculation of the cost of materials and time and realized she could make a 50 percent profit. She readily agreed.

So began the visual advertising of her belt. Soon other women were requesting belts and other accessories. Between nights and weekends Amber started a cottage accessory business. During peak periods, the demand became so great that she hired several friends to form assembly-line production of belts and earrings. Amber quickly realized she needed to establish her part-time hobby into an official business. She went to the U.S. Small Business Administration Web site (www.sba.gov) and read about business licenses, tax registration, trade name registration, and regulations for employees. Once she obtained the information for the federal requirements in the United States, she checked with her state and city offices for any additional requirements in order to set up a small business. After the paperwork was complete, Amber had officially and legally established a small business. She had obtained a license and tax ID number, registered her business name, and opened a bank account for the business. Amber also set up communication aids including phone number, fax number, and business cards.

As the popularity of the accessories continued, she decided to market the products to a larger area. With samples of belts, earrings, and vests, Amber visited five towns within a 200-mile radius of her location. She had researched the best specialty shop in each town and, acting as her own sales representative, presented the items to the owners. Many of the owners selected several designs, and some requested designs exclusively for their stores. Again the appeal of her accessories resulted in a growth surge in the business.

Two years after her college graduation, Amber's Wave was subcontracting with a manufacturing plant in Mexico to produce the accessories based on her samples and specifications.

Amber had hired several employees to help with the research, sourcing, and marketing of her products, although she tried to stay involved in all aspects of the business. Often she would attend market weeks and operate the showroom herself in order to interact with potential clients. Amber also attended markets that were indirectly related to her products in order to anticipate as many trends as possible. Sales representatives received samples of her line and regularly showed them to small specialty stores that could not attend the national markets.

Part of Amber's original intent was to produce accessories that were unique and did not portray the mass-production stigma that dominated most of the accessories in department stores. Therefore, as the business expanded, she marketed most of her lines to specialty stores and upscale department stores. She developed accessory lines that correlated with the apparel products of her customers, thereby increasing her costs and the cost of the product because she was not mass-producing just one line. So far this strategy had succeeded, as her target market expected product differentiation.

Amber's Wave uses technology for as much of the decision-making process as possible. Because the actual production of the garments is outsourced, efficiency is paramount. An automated computer system installed at corporate headquarters itemizes all the materials used in the accessories. Previous sales data, current projections, and weekly orders are charted to compare current trends with past records. Amber has the ability, in a visual format, to compare each daily, weekly, and monthly production and sales performance since she first started her business. Amber and her in-house team meet weekly to discuss trends, observations, and ideas. In a recent weekly meeting the newest employee, hired for her technology skills, indicated that the company needed to expand into selling on the Internet.

Amber had been thinking about Internet sales for some time, but the mission of the company was as a producer of fashion accessories, a vendor that provided the products to retail establishments but did not work directly with the consumer. When Amber first started her business over ten years ago, the Internet was not the massive communication and information source it had become today. Amber decided to revisit her business plan, which she had updated during the years, and to do some research on Internet sales.

Major Question

As an entrepreneur who owns her own successful business, what direction should Amber consider for rethinking or expanding her business?

Concepts and Cases in Retail and Merchandise Management

Study Questions

1. How should Amber go about deciding on changes to be made, if any?

2. Is the company growing too fast?

Exercises

1. Go to the United States Small Business Administration at www.sba.gov. Click on Small Business Planner, and go to Plan Your Business. Click on (a) Write a Business Plan and look at Writing the Business Plan ("examples of real business plans"), and (b) Finding a Niche. Develop a business plan outline for a fashion accessory manufacturing business.

2. Go to the United States Small Business Administration at www.sba.gov. Click on Small Business Planner, and go to Start Your Business. In this topic, look at the following (a) Finance Start Up, (b) Choose a Structure, and (c) Get Licenses and Permits. List the advantages and disadvantages of the different business structures. Check with your state and city, and list the regulations for starting a small business.

3. Using a search engine (such as Google), type in fashion accessories and analyze some of the Web pages available under this topic. Links will be available for manufacturers, retailers, and trade associations. Using the Web sites as a guide, determine what would be the competitive challenges of starting a business manufacturing accessories.

CHAPTER DISCUSSION QUESTIONS

1. Describe the characteristics of successful small business owners.

2. What extra qualities does a small business owner need to be thought of as an entrepreneur?

3. What are the challenges and opportunities for starting your own small business?

4. Explain how planning is a vital part of the process of starting a business. Cite case examples to support your position.

eleven

Ethical and Legal Behavior in Retail Management

CHAPTER OBJECTIVES

- Explain ethics and social responsibility of retailers and manufacturers.
- Discuss the ethics involved with sourcing and selling.
- Identify and examine legal considerations within which retailers and manufacturers operate.

A wareness of ethical and socially responsible business behavior has increased today as consumer advocacy has become more prevalent and also because there are more methods available to do business. With increased affluence to meet our basic needs, we expect more socially responsible behavior from business and industry. For example, we can now afford to have a clean environment, and society is demanding that businesses contribute toward that goal. Laws explicitly outline appropriate business conduct to protect the consumer and maintain fairness, while ethical and socially responsible behavior go beyond the law to include the further expectations of society. Globalization has introduced increasingly complex issues regarding cross-cultural values, such as intellectual property and use of labor. Also, the highly *sophisticated and competitive nature of retail today raises new potential ethical issues. There-fore, strong personal and business codes of ethics applicable to many situations may be more important today than ever before.*

WHAT ARE ETHICS?

Ethics are rules or standards based on moral duties and obligations by which society evaluates conduct. They furnish criteria for distinguishing between right and wrong. Some people use the terms ethics and morals interchangeably; however, morals most often are referred to as personal beliefs that are more closely tied to religious tenets, whereas ethics deal with living up to society principles. In either sense, ethics are forms of "dos and don'ts." Table 11.1 lists ten core values central to ethical choices and interpersonal behavior.

Most of us have both personal and business ethics, which are the basis for business decisions. An individual may have different standards for personal ethics and business ethics, which can cause conflicts for that person. Others may share personal and business ethics. **Business ethics** deal with what is right or wrong for the company, while **personal ethics** deal with an individual's own personal beliefs and principles. In some instances, corporate standards may be higher than an individual's own. In other instances, company goals of growth and profit may conflict with personal ethical standards. For example, in *Case 68, To Go or to Stay: Ethics in the Workplace,* a young buyer wrestles with her personal ethics as she considers corporate requests to cancel merchandise orders, which she knows have already been produced for her company, and which will result in financial hardship and possible bankruptcy for the vendor.

A business may have a written **code of ethics** that states what that company has decided is ethical and unethical behavior. Similarly, associations have a written code of **professional ethics.** For example, The American Marketing Association has set forth a clear and extensive statement of its professional code of ethics that deals with responsibilities of the marketer, honesty and fairness, and the rights and duties of those in the exchange process, which include promotion, distribution, pricing and market research, and organizational relationships. An example of an explicit code of **corporate ethics** is the public notice run in

TABLE 11.1 Ten Core Values

Caring
Honesty
Accountability
Promise Keeping
Pursuit of Excellence
Loyalty
Fairness
Integrity
Respect for Others
Responsible Citizenship

Source: Guy (1990).

apparel trade papers during the holidays by such retailers as TJX Companies to their suppliers, as shown in Figure 11.1. Their public notice was in regard to their policy of prohibiting employees to accept any gifts—without exception. Written codes of corporate ethics should refer to practices specific to the company, for example, accepting gifts, kickbacks, or false record keeping, and should be supported by top management. Sometimes a company's statement of philosophy incorporates their code of ethics. James Cash Penney, the founder of JCPenney, was a religious man and used the "Golden Rule" in his philosophy statement for his company, merging personal and corporate ethics. See Table 11.2 for the "Penney Idea."

Other companies have an implicit code of ethics, which is an unwritten but understood set of standards of moral and ethical responsibility. Whether implicit or explicit, corporate ethics are important guidelines in decision making, especially for those issues that are not clearly defined by law.

Ethical decision-making can be viewed in four ways:

1. *Prima facie* **duties** (or moral obligations), which some feel are universal, include such things as keeping promises, telling the truth, honoring warranties and abiding by agreements or understood guidelines (see *Case 19, "With It," or Without,* in Chapter 4), not taking abnormal credit extensions or making unjust retail cancellations (see *Case 68*), and ensuring product safety. Pricing policies fall under this concept, for example, the setting of unfair prices, maintaining the same price after a lowering of quality of the products that

TABLE 11.2 The "Penney Idea"—JCPenney's Philosophy Incorporating an Ethical Stand

1. To serve the public, as nearly as we can, to its complete satisfaction.
2. To expect for the service we render a fair remuneration and not all the profit the traffic will bear.
3. To do all in our power to pack the customer's dollar full of value, quality and satisfaction.
4. To continue to train ourselves and our associates so that the service we give will be more and more intelligently performed.
5. To improve constantly the human factor in our business.
6. To reward men and women in our organization through participation in what the business produces.
7. To test our every policy, method, and act in this wise: "Does it square with what is right and just?"

To Our Manufacturers and Suppliers: Statement of Policy Concerning Gifts

We are taking this opportunity to restate our policy concerning gift-giving, not only during the forthcoming holiday season, but at all times of the year. On any occasion, gifts, no matter how well-intentioned by the donor, tend to shake the moral structure of the firmest business foundations by substituting subjective emotions and motives for objective judgment based on service, quality and price.

Accordingly, for the mutual protection of our suppliers, our associates and the Company, we prohibit our associates from accepting gifts, gratuities, payments or favors. Gifts received by our associates will be returned to the donor or donated to charitable organizations. Our associates are advised that violation of our policy is considered to be a grievous matter.

We call upon you to assist us and our associates by refraining from giving or offering such gifts. Your awareness of and cooperation with this policy will foster the continuation of fair business practices that favor our close association.

Best wishes for a happy holiday season and a prosperous New Year.

Bernard Cammarata
Chairman and Acting CEO

Carol Meyrowitz
President of The TJX Companies, Inc.

The Marmaxx Group/T.J.Maxx/Marshalls • HG Buying, Inc./HomeGoods
Winners Merchants International LP/Winners/HomeSense
Concord Buying Group Inc./A.J.Wright • T.K.Maxx • Bob's Stores

770 Cochituate Rd., Framingham, MA 01701

Figure 11.1 An example from TJX Companies of an explicit code of corporate ethics regarding a no-gift policy. TJX prohibits any gift-giving from suppliers to employees, while other companies do permit such gifts as lunches or dinners.

were previously ordered, taking excessive markups, and gaining unfair advantage because of a retailer's or manufacturer's size and/or power.

2. **Proportionality framework** relates to decisions that focus on actions rather than consequences—that is, the ends do not justify the means. For example, high profits should not be achieved by deceiving customers or by exploiting employees. Employees have been known to steal the ideas of their colleagues under the pressure of coming up with new lines each season.

3. **Social justice framework** means everyone should be treated equally and no group should be taken advantage of, for example, the dumping of unsafe products in third world countries. Discrimination in hiring practices on the basis of age, gender, race, or ethnicity is illegal and explored in *Case 69, Abercrombie & Fitch: Hiring for Looks.*

4. **Utilitarianism** can be thought of as doing "the greatest good for the greatest number." A cost-benefit analysis can assess the viability of this and is generally used in business and governmental decision making. For example, an improvement to a process will only be made if the benefits are greater than the cost of making that improvement. Therefore, those who may have benefitted will not if the cost is too high.

ETHICS IN SOURCING AND WORKING WITH VENDORS

Global sourcing and international retailing today have stimulated much interest and concern for humanitarian rights. These concerns often cause dilemmas because of the differences between cultures. Should one country impose its ethical standards on another? For example, should a manufacturer hire a third world contractor that uses child labor? In the extremely price-competitive apparel business, some companies use such contractors to keep labor expenses down. It is an ethical issue that more and more companies are facing, especially with increased public awareness of apparel assembly locations and conditions around the world.

The International Labor Organization (ILO) estimated that 211 million children aged 5 to 14 were working around the world in industries such as textiles, apparel, and footwear (Ellis, 2003). The U.S. Department of Labor has spent millions of dollars on child labor education programs. However, there are barriers to the elimination of child labor; the greatest is poverty. Some families in developing countries need the income from their children to survive. Western countries have felt outrage at their clothing being made by children and have loudly protested companies that have been shown to use overseas contractors using child labor.

Activists and fair-trade organizations have pressured companies, notably Nike (Kletter, 2005), into disclosing lists of their supplier/contractors, and have raised significant awareness of sweatshop conditions around the world. Ironically Nike has become one of the "good guys" with a strong record of social responsibility.

Many apparel companies today have developed **codes of conduct,** statements of principles and standards by which business decisions are made. Levi Strauss & Co. set standard guidelines, also referred to as values, when choosing business partners, which many apparel manufacturing companies have used as a basis for developing their own. These business partners are defined as contractors and subcontractors that manufacture or finish Levi Strauss products, and as suppliers that provide material utilized in the manufacture and finishing of their products (see Table 11.3). Through its guidelines, called Terms of Engagement, Levi Strauss & Co. implemented an agreement with contractors in Bangladesh to initiate child labor standards that identified an individual under 15 years of age as an "underage worker." This initiative resulted in requiring children to submit a school certificate stating that they are 15 years or older to the contractors that the company uses in Bangladesh. In *Case 70, To Work, Study, or Starve: Bangladesh Child Labor,* an employee searching for appropriate sources of apparel production finds himself in conflict over whether he should or should not engage a contractor that employs children.

The Fair Labor Association (www.fairlabor.org) and Worldwide Responsible Apparel Production (WRAP) (www.wrapapparel.org) have compiled similar principles of codes of conduct. Their Web sites are good sources of information of innovative and sustainable solutions to abusive labor conditions and guidelines for factories interested in becoming WRAP-certified and monitors seeking WRAP accreditation.

Sometimes large companies that have such strict policies are caught in a "catch-22" situation when they cancel a contract because of labor abuses and consequently put many people out of work. Some wonder how ethical that is. Monitoring human rights at foreign contractors is complex, to say the least.

A **kickback** is the return of part of monies received, which has been prompted by a threat or secret agreement, and is illegal in the United States. Some people say this type of corrupt behavior is happening more and more today and on a larger and larger scale. It also happens in smaller related ways, for example, suppliers that offer meals or gifts to buyers in efforts to secure orders. Because of these variations, it is hard to know where the line is between ethical and unethical behavior in regard to kickback-type favors. Additionally, kickbacks, or inducements, are legal and sometimes expected in many countries; therefore, these standards and expectations vary around the world. This can be a real problem because so many buyers now

TABLE 11.3 Levi Strauss's Business Partner Terms of Engagement

1. *Ethical Standards:* We will seek to identify and utilize business partners who aspire as individuals and in the conduct of all their businesses to a set of ethical standards not incompatible with our own.
2. *Legal Requirements:* We expect our business partners to be law abiding as individuals and to comply with legal requirements relevant to the conduct of all their businesses.
3. *Environmental Requirements:* We will only do business with partners who share our commitment to the environment and who conduct their business in a way that is consistent with Levi Strauss & Co.'s Environmental Philosophy and Guiding Principles.
4. *Community Betterment:* We will favor business partners who share our commitment to contribute to the betterment of community conditions.
5. *Employment Standards:* We will only do business with partners whose workers are in all cases present voluntarily, not put at risk of physical harm, fairly compensated, allowed the right of free association and not exploited in any way. In addition, the following specific guidelines will be followed.
   - *Wages and Benefits:* We will only do business with partners who provide wages and benefits that comply with any applicable law and match the prevailing local manufacturing or finishing industry practices.
   - *Working Hours:* While permitting flexibility in scheduling, we will identify prevailing local work hours and seek business partners who do not exceed them except for appropriately compensated overtime. While we favor partners who utilize less than sixty-hour work weeks, we will not use contractors who, on a regularly scheduled basis, require in excess of a sixty-hour week. Employees should be allowed at least one day off in seven.
   - *Child Labor:* Use of child labor is not permissible. Workers can be no less than 14 years of age and not younger than the compulsory age to be in school. We will not utilize partners who use child labor in any of their facilities. We support the development of legitimate workplace apprenticeship programs for the educational benefit of younger people.
   - *Prison Labor/Forced Labor:* We will not utilize prison or forced labor in contracting relationships in the manufacture and finishing of our products. We will not utilize or purchase materials from a business partner utilizing prison or forced labor.
   - *Health & Safety:* We will only utilize business partners who provide workers with a safe and healthy work environment. Business partners who provide residential facilities for their workers must provide safe and healthy facilities.
   - *Discrimination:* While we recognize and respect cultural differences, we believe that workers should be employed on the basis of their ability to do the job, rather than on the basis of personal characteristics or beliefs. We will favor business partners who share this value.
   - *Disciplinary Practices:* We will not utilize business partners who use corporal punishment or other forms of mental or physical coercion.

Source: Levi Strauss & Co.

source internationally and deal with people from different cultures who hold different values, morals, and ethics. Some retailers explicitly prohibit employees from accepting anything from a supplier; others allow a few such items as meals. Wal-Mart, the largest U.S. retailer, may have the strictest standards, as they do not allow their employees to accept anything from a vendor—not even a cup of coffee. *Case 71, Today's Woman: The Buyer's Personal Decision* explores the conflict of interest—or the illusion of a conflict—of giving an order to a personal friend.

ETHICS IN SELLING AND MANAGEMENT

Should a salesperson withhold information about a product from customers, sell them merchandise (or a service) that does not meet their needs, or use high-pressure, manipulative sales techniques to secure a commission? Some industry analysts feel that if sales associates are paid commission or have high sales quotas, this type of selling behavior, which is seen as unethical by some, will continue. As an example, consider the stereotypical reputation of the used car salesperson.

Sharing responsibilities on the sales floor is considered appropriate conduct for sales associates; however, with several generations working together today, value systems and individual work ethics can clash. Also, sales associates have been known to "steal" customers from cohorts when commission is involved. Some sales associates can become pretty aggressive on the sales floor. Departments generally develop a system of fairness regarding who should approach which customer.

The misuse of company assets by employees is unethical, but there are certainly different degrees and interpretations of what is right or wrong behavior. Stealing merchandise or money from an employer is illegal, but what about taking a pen? Or an extra break? Or making long-distance personal calls on the company telephone? These are all forms of employee theft and may be considered by some companies as unethical behavior. A new employee who uses confidential information from a previous employer is considered unethical. Is it also unethical for a company to lay off employees because they make high salaries and replace them with younger, lower-salaried employees or to lay off an employee before pension benefits become available? This appears to happen in some companies when they downsize or in an economic recession when companies are worried about their bottom line. Thus, potential unethical behavior can originate from both employee and employer behavior.

Saks Fifth Avenue has set forth its core values that underscore its ethics:

- Quality: Do things right.
- Integrity: Do the right things.
- Service: Be responsive to others' needs and goals.

- Teamwork: Work is a team process. Success is a team result.
- Responsibility: One can be counted on to deliver. Period.
- Winning: Consistent, winning results are a requirement.

SOCIAL RESPONSIBILITY

Closely related to ethics is **social responsibility,** that is, a company's duties and obligations to society that extend beyond ethics and legalities. Robin and Reidenbach (1989) differentiate between ethics and social responsibility based on the level of structure. As social responsibility is related to a loose social contract between business and society, ethics requires more structured rules of moral behavior. Often the two concepts lead to the same decision, but sometimes they do not. Retailing and manufacturing often suffer from a consumer perception of being profit-oriented and not particularly caring about the individual or community. However, there is a trend toward returning to an increased business involvement in society as the early retail pioneers did. Actually, the public expects business to be part of the community and to act responsibly. Because of this sentiment, many companies have found that ethics and social responsibility are good business.

Some tangible responses to the needs of society are the giving and partnership programs conducted by many retailers and manufacturers, as well as their involvement in educational and environmental programs and assistance to the disadvantaged. WWD Exec Tech Community Service Awards in 2007 were given to the best examples of this: to Giorgio Armani, Converse, and Gap, each having a first-of-its-kind cross-branding campaign called (Product) Red to raise money for the Global Fund to fight AIDS in Africa; Nike's Homeless World Cup soccer tournament, which raised millions of dollars for the homeless and refugees around the world; Wal-Mart's remarkable efforts to aid victims of Hurricane Katrina and subsequent grants to continue the recovery work; New Balance's effort to help fight childhood obesity; and Life is Good, which demonstrates that small apparel companies can make an impact as they brought awareness and raised funds for children's causes. These activities are examples of **cause marketing** in which activities are linked to charitable causes. See Figure 11.2 for an example.

Esprit, in the 1980s, was one of the best known companies for having a corporate social conscience by supporting programs that promoted the protection of the environment. Notably their E-collection line of **environmentally friendly** apparel attempted to incorporate only environmentally safe methods and materials in its production. Today more and more retail buyers are seeking out vendors who specialize in "green" products, which do not harm the environment when they are

Figure 11.2 Gap is one company exploring cause marketing.

produced. Products using Sally Fox's FOXFIBRE, a naturally colored cotton fiber that eliminates the need for toxic dyeing processes, and organic cotton are examples of green products. As more consumers gain a social conscience about the environment, these products will be in higher demand.

In England, the concept of "ethical fashion" is growing, with such things as events sponsored by U.K.'s Ethical Fashion Forum, which supports fair-trade production and other environmental issues. The concept of free trade, probably first heard of in the coffee production industry, includes:

- human rights such as fair wages and no child labor
- fair business relationships, including accountability and fair prices
- environmental protection and sustainability

Meanwhile, some companies find fair trade can be expensive, and although consumers have an interest in buying environmentally sound products that are produced "fairly," they also want style, fashion, and a reasonable price. It can be difficult for a company striving to balance social responsibility with profits.

Today, more and more consumers are holding companies accountable for their behavior and are acting as watchdogs in pressuring businesses to be more socially responsible. The day after Thanksgiving—traditionally one of the busiest retail days of the year—seems to be a designated day for animal rights protests and boycotts against retailers that sell furs as fashion. For years, both Europeans and Americans have lodged loud complaints against the slaughter of animals for the beautification of consumers. See Figure 11.3 for an ad by the Humane Society. Because of consumer pressures and the resulting decrease in consumer demand (which go hand in hand), many retailers have closed their fur salons. However, the popularity of furs appears to cycle, as other retailers have reopened their fur salons or have added fur pieces to their offerings.

GOVERNMENT REGULATION

In addition to ethics and social responsibility, retailers and manufacturers cannot make decisions without regard to the laws of their resident country if they want to stay in business. Laws represent the formalized set of ethical standards of a country, region, or population center. However, legal and ethical behavior are not necessarily the same, and some unethical behavior may very well be legal. Often, laws do not change as quickly as they should to meet the needs of the times. The legal environment includes federal, state, and local laws and ordinances. Because the latter two can vary widely from area to area, companies must become familiar with

Figure 11.3 Protests against the killing of animals for the production of fur coats are becoming more and more common, causing the apparel industry to reconsider the use of fur in garments.

them to be in compliance. At the federal level, independent regulatory and other government agencies monitor such unfair business practices as price fixing, bait and switch, misleading advertising, and discrimination in hiring practices as explored in *Case 69, Abercrombie & Fitch: Hiring for Looks*. Table 11.4 lists the legislation that impacts the manufacture, distribution, and retailing of merchandise, and provides other consumer protection provisions. Regulatory laws can be complicated and very confusing for non-lawyers—and most retailers are not lawyers.

Legalities of Pricing

Price discrimination occurs when two retailers buy identical merchandise from the same supplier but pay different prices. The purpose of the law against price discrimination is to protect competition by ensuring that retailers are treated fairly by suppliers. However, a U.S. Supreme Court ruling in 2007 struck down a 96-year-old ban on minimum pricing agreements, giving brands the potential to enforce the lowest price at which their products could be sold (Clark & Ellis, 2007). The ruling gives lower courts the leeway to determine, on a case-by-case basis, whether minimum pricing is anticompetitive.

Price fixing creates monopolies and has been considered illegal and a restraint of trade. It occurs when a group of competing retailers (considered horizontal price fixing) or a retailer and manufacturer (considered vertical price fixing) agree to maintain the price of merchandise. Vertical price fixing is called price maintenance, which is a violation of the Sherman Antitrust Act. However, until 1975 with the passage of the Consumer Goods Pricing Act, **fair-trade laws** were in effect. These laws formerly had protected the small retailer from larger retailers as they both sold the same goods at the same price, since large retailers were not allowed to receive a discount for quantity purchases. The Consumer Goods Pricing Act repealed all resale **price maintenance laws** and enabled retailers to sell products below the suggested retail prices that were set by manufacturers. Although this ended protection for the small retailer, it allowed consumers to buy at the lowest possible free-market price. Price maintenance laws and rules, however, change with the sentiment of the U.S. Congress, the justice system, and presidential administration. For example, in 1988, the U.S. Supreme Court ruled that manufacturers can refuse to sell to retailers that sell below the manufacturer's suggested retail price, to protect the manufacturer's reputation. And in 2007, as mentioned above, the Supreme Court has allowed brands to set retail prices.

Predatory pricing, a situation in which a retailer prices a product below cost with the intent to drive out any competition, is illegal. Not all below-cost selling is

TABLE 11.4 Selected Federal Legislation Affecting the Manufacturing, Retailing, and Distribution of Merchandise

Sherman Antitrust Act (1890): Banned "monopolies or attempts to monopolize" and "contracts, combinations, or conspiracies in restraint of trade" in interstate and foreign commerce.

Federal Trade Commission Act (1914): Established the Federal Trade Commission with broad powers to investigate and to issue cease-and-desist orders to enforce Section 5, which declares that "unfair methods of competition" in commerce are unlawful.

Clayton Act (1914): Adds to the Sherman Act by prohibiting specific practices (e.g.. certain types of price discrimination, tying clauses) "where the effect . . . may be to substantially lessen competition or tend to create a monopoly in any line of commerce."

Resale Price Agreement (1931): Legalized resale price maintenance between manufacturers and retailers.

Unfair Practices Act (1935): Prohibited sales below cost.

Robinson-Patman Act (1936): Amends the Clayton Act. Adds the phrase "to injure, destroy, or prevent competition." Defines price discrimination as unlawful and provides the FTC with the right to establish limits on quantity discounts, to forbid brokerage allowances except to independent brokers, and to ban promotional allowances or the furnishing of services or facilities except where made available to all "on proportionately equal terms."

Miller-Tydings Act (1937): Legalized certain resale price maintenance contracts.

Food, Drug and Cosmetic Act (1938): Expanded the responsibility of the Food and Drug Administration to include cosmetics and therapeutic devices, by amending the 1906 act.

Wheeler-Lea Amendment of the FTC Act (1938): Prohibits unfair and deceptive acts and practices regardless of whether competition is to the injured.

Fair Labor Standards (1938): Established minimum wages.

Wool Products Labeling Act (1939): Required that products containing wool carry labels showing the fiber content.

Antimerger Act (1950): Amends Section 7 of the Clayton act by broadening the power to prevent intercorporate acquisitions where the acquisition may lessen competition.

Fur Products Labeling Act (1951): Required that all fur products carry labels correctly describing their contents.

McGuire Act (1952): Validated specific price maintenance contracts.

Flammable Fabrics Act (1953): Prohibited the manufacture or sale of fabrics or wearing apparel that were dangerously flammable.

Textile Fiber Product Identification Act (1960): Required fiber content identification on all apparel.

Kefauver-Harris Amendment to Food, Drug and Cosmetic Act (1962): Required that all drugs be tested for safety and efficacy.

TABLE 11.4 *(continued)*

Child Protection Act (1966): Amended the Hazardous Substances Labeling Act (1960) to ban all hazardous substances and prohibit sales of potentially harmful toys and other articles used by children.

Fair Packaging and Labeling Act (1966): Makes provision for the regulation of the packaging and labeling of consumer goods. Permits industries' voluntary adoption of uniform packaging standards.

Flammable Fabrics Act (1967): Amended the 1953 act and expanded textile legislation to include the Department of Commerce Flammability Standards for additional products.

Truth-In-Lending Act (1968): Requires lenders to state the true costs of a credit transaction. Established a National Commission on Consumer Finance.

Fair Credit Reporting Act (1970): Regulated credit information reporting and use.

Care Labeling Act (1971): Required all apparel selling for over $3 to carry labels with washing or dry-cleaning instructions.

Consumer Product Safety Act (1972): Established the Consumer Product Safety Commission and empowered it to set safety standards for a broad range of consumer products and to impose penalties for failure to meet these standards (includes flammable fabrics regulations).

Equal Credit Opportunity Act (1974): Insured that financial institutions engaged in the extension of credit make credit available without discrimination on the basis of sex or marital status.

Magnuson-Moss Warranty/FTC Improvement Act (1975): Empowers the FTC to determine rules concerning consumer warranties and provides for consumer access to means of redress, such as the "class action" suit. Expands FTC regulatory powers over unfair or deceptive acts or practices.

Consumer Goods Pricing Act (1975): Outlawed legalized resale price maintenance. (Fair trade laws)

Fair Debt Collection Practice Act (1978): Made illegal to harass or abuse any person and make false statements or use unfair methods when collecting a debt.

Amendment to the Wool Products Labeling Act (1980): Required that products containing recycled wool carry labels showing the content.

Amendment to the Care Labeling Act (1984): Expanded requirements on apparel labels to include water temperature, bleaching, ironing requirements.

Amendment to the Textile Fiber Product Identification Act (1984): Required apparel labels to indicate country of origin to include Made in the USA.

Price maintenance ban repealed by U.S. Supreme Court (2007). Allows brands to set minimum retail prices.

Source: Dunne and Lusch, 2007; Bohlinger, 1993.

illegal or considered predatory pricing, as some end-of-season goods are sold at a loss to clear out old merchandise. Wal-Mart has been accused and acquitted in court of predatory pricing, as they have driven small retailers out of business. Wal-Mart claims the intent of its pricing is to provide low prices for consumers, not to hurt competition. There appears to be a gray area here, as that certainly was not the interpretation of the situation by the bankrupt small retailers.

Legalities of Distribution

Retailers and manufacturers are also subject to laws that affect the distribution of goods. **Tying contracts,** a situation in which suppliers force retailers to buy unwanted merchandise in order to purchase other desired merchandise, is illegal. Collusion between manufacturers and retailers to exclude competition is also illegal if this collusion restrains trade. *Case 72, Collusion to Catch Anti-Trust Offenders* explores this type of illegal activity in which a supplier sold only to one large retailer, the result of which pushed out several smaller stores.

The Legal Aspects of Advertising

The **Federal Trade Commission (FTC)** monitors the legal aspects of business advertising. **Bait and switch** is a form of deceptive advertising in which a product is promoted at an unrealistically low price to serve as bait. After a consumer arrives to buy an advertised product, the retailer attempts to switch the customer to a higher-priced item. A retailer must have the stock on hand that is advertised and in sufficient quantity. For example, an advertised item with a stock of one piece stored in an inaccessible place would be suspect of a bait and switch scheme. **Misleading advertising** is another form of consumer deception that is illegal. If a manufacturer's claims are untrue or misleading, a cease and desist order can be issued, putting a halt to such claims.

Special Apparel Regulations

The FTC and the **Consumer Product Safety Commission (CPSC)** are independent regulatory agencies charged with overseeing the area of consumer protection and restraint of trade and have the specific responsibility of apparel regulation. Within the purview of the FTC are labeling requirements for apparel. These include the Textile Fiber Products Identification Act, which requires generic fiber identification, manufacturer identification, and country of origin; the Permanent

Care Labeling Act, which requires care labels to be placed in most apparel items; and legislation covering fur and wool products labeling. Even though there has been no new legislation related to care labeling since 1984, the FTC has considered adding alternative care labeling to the current recommended care labeling requirement. *Case 73, The Flannel Organic Fiber Fiasco* presents a circumstance in which a supplier provides fabric that has a different fiber content than that which had been contracted. This was done without notifying the manufacturer, who, unknowingly, had been labeling garments incorrectly. When the deception was discovered, the manufacturer knew it was not in compliance with the law and something had to be done to rectify the situation.

The CPSC regulates flammability requirements of both apparel and home furnishings. Strict requirements for children's sleepwear decrease the risk of young children being burned from highly flammable fabrics. From time to time, this agency has also considered more stringent requirements for adult sleepwear. All apparel must meet basic standards for flammability, and no dangerous fabrications are allowed to be sold or imported into the United States for sale. Occasionally, apparel is recalled for safety purposes. An example of this is when there was a recall of a popular, sheer-cotton skirt that had been made in India.

The CPSC also monitors other product safety, such as children's toys, which from time to time are recalled after instances of young children who died as the result of inhaling or swallowing small objects or using dangerous products. A major recall was due to lead paint that was found to be used on toys produced in China.

Intellectual Property Protection

Patents, copyrights, and trademarks are considered a company's **intellectual property**. Infringement of any of these is illegal. A U.S. **patent** grants to the inventor the right for 20 years to exclude others from making, using, or selling that invention. The applicant makes a complete disclosure of the invention, which is published and which moves into the public domain when the patent expires.

There are few patents granted to developers of fashion because one small alteration in a design can negate its originality; however, patents are granted if a unique process or material is developed in textiles or special purposes in apparel. For example, Ultrasuede, a simulated suede developed in Japan, was patented. Because the patent has expired, it is now copied by other companies. In apparel there have been patent applications for such functional items as devices to alleviate back strain, safety vests with lighting and tear-away features, forced-air cooling vests, wetsuits with inner and outer layers, and apparel with other protective devices.

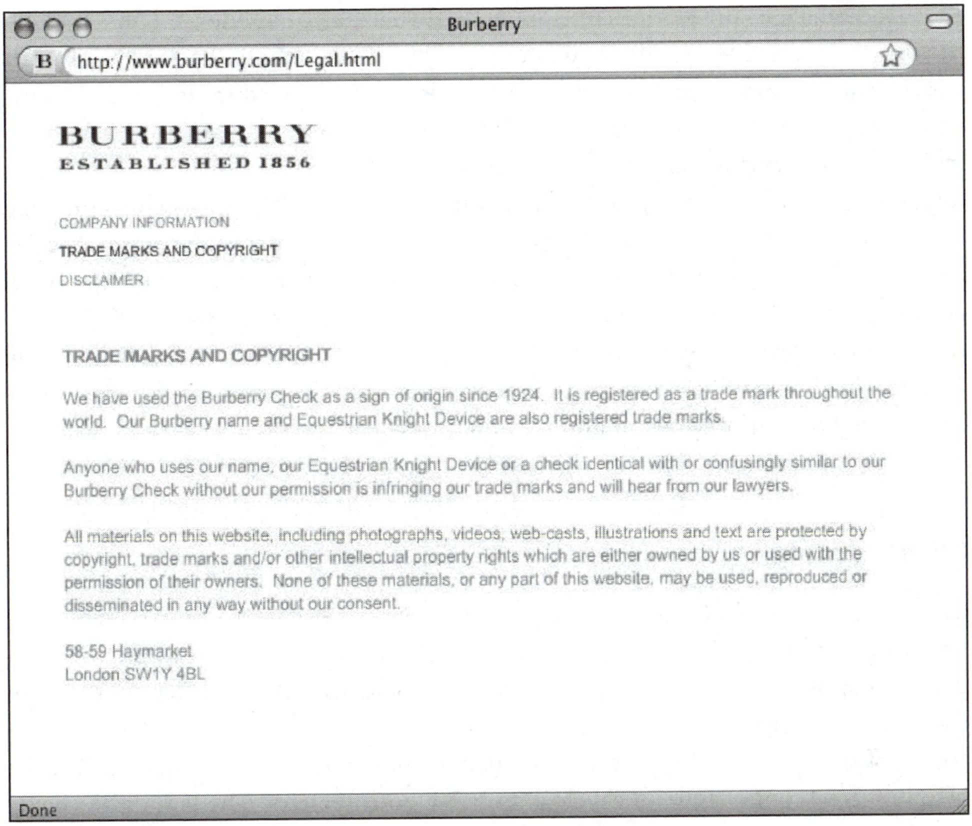

Figure 11.4 Burberry, like many companies, reminds the public of the company's intellectual property rights, including relevant trademarks and copyrights, by way of statements on their Web sites.

A **copyright** is protection for original creative writings or works of art. Since fashion is mostly reinterpreted and not considered original, copyrights on apparel are rare. From time to time, an apparel designer will procure a copyright on a design, which is designated on the label by the copyright symbol. For example, Karen Alexander copyrighted her sleeve design. She published notices in the trade papers warning would-be copiers that she would prosecute those who infringed upon the copyright. Designers often copyright their logo designs. Most copyright infringement today is on videos, audiotapes, and computer software. There has been a bill proposed by Representative Goodlatte from Virginia to extend copyright protection to fashion designs for a limited three-year period. This would be a departure from current copyright law, which affords no copyright protection to "useful articles." Some feel it might take more than three years to get through the legal channels before the fashion is gone, so we await the effect on this effort to protect apparel designers.

A **trademark** is any word, name, or symbol that has been adopted and used by the owner to identify a product and distinguish it from others. The first person to use the trademark in conjunction with a product has ownership of the trademark and can exclude others from using it. This is not the case, however, in other countries, where often it is the person who registers it who holds the trademark; therefore, companies trading overseas may not have rights to use the trademark they use in the United States. Knowing the local laws is extremely important. Also, if consumers cannot separate a specific trademarked product (such as Levi's) from a generic product (such as jeans), the company can lose the exclusive rights to its trademarked terminology. Therefore, companies use a generic name with their trademark to remind consumers that theirs is a special type of that product. So even though it seems awkward and redundant, we see the use of Kleenex facial tissue, Xerox photocopies, Jacuzzi whirlpool baths, and Levi's jeans.

Counterfeiting

Counterfeited merchandise violates a company's intellectual property rights. The Anti-Counterfeiting Coalition, which is strongly supported by many apparel companies, was instrumental in gaining the federal legislation in 1984 that makes trademark infringement a crime. As discussed in Chapter 4, knockoffs, or close copies of designs, are common in the fashion industry. Some companies' knockoffs, however, come dangerously close to being **counterfeits.** The law states that a protected trademark or copyright cannot be copied and offered for sale by another company. One person's idea of a knockoff can be another's idea of a counterfeit, and therefore we see many cases of designers fighting in court over whose idea was first. One classic case involves Yves Saint Laurent, who sued Ralph Lauren for copying his tuxedo dress, which was then claimed to have been designed by Bernard Perris five years earlier, which had already been copied by the "king of copycats"—Victor Costa! As fashion is interpretation and often is inspired by earlier designs, many times it is hard to know who is the originator of a particular design. And sometimes the offender is unaware that he or she is purchasing counterfeits. Normally buyers know and trust their vendors and know if they are getting the "real thing," but there may be times when they don't, and take a risk. *Case 74, The Denim Dilemma at Velvet Moon Boutique* may be a case of a small owner not knowing that she is breaking the law.

Levi Strauss has been actively involved for years in the pursuit of protecting its trademarks, many of which are counterfeited and sold mostly overseas. They were one of the first to use technology to ensure authenticity for their retailers. For example, a tracking system has been developed that codes the inside label of the jeans with a serial number; through a computer-generated light beam, it can detect whether the merchandise is legitimate or counterfeit. Kathrine Baumann actually did her own research and went after her counterfeiters, something that might be dangerous. *Case 75, Kathrine Baumann's Crusade Against Counterfeiting* describes her relentless battle against them. *Case 76, When Is Imitation Not the Highest Form of Flattery?*, another example of a recent counterfeiting case, describes Pottery Barn's case against Target, which is claimed to have copied a Christmas stocking. A great deal of money is involved with knockoff and counterfeit profits and companies fighting cases in court.

Luxury apparel designers and retailers, which were once the major companies targeted by counterfeiters, are fighting in efforts to curtail counterfeiting. The problem, however, has become so rampant that it is now prevalent in every sector of our global economy, from all price lines of apparel and other fashion items, to CDs, movies, appliances, textiles, and technology. The movement of counterfeit products has become big business on the Internet as well, where the problem is extremely difficult to address because of the sheer magnitude of the trading area. Educating the consumer through the media is one method being widely used by the fashion industry to help fight the manufacturing and selling of illegal goods.

Gray market goods also plague both the cosmetics and apparel industry. These are not illegal but are imports that are unauthorized by the company owning the trade name. Often such goods are sold at discounters with no warranty or with older dates than those through authorized channels. Fragrances, for example, may have been on shelves for longer than the recommended product life. The prices, however, are lower, which benefits the consumer. There is an ongoing campaign to make gray goods illegal. *Case 74* involves a possible situation of buying gray goods from an overstock supplier at significantly lower prices than regular retail—or were these good counterfeits? The manufacturer threatened a lawsuit if these goods were continued to be sold without its authorization.

Other Regulations

The **Food and Drug Administration (FDA)** is responsible for regulating the food, drug, and cosmetics industries in regard to the safety of and disclosure of ingredients of products. Cosmetics claiming to have effects that permanently change the skin have come under fire by the FDA because such claims define the product as a drug, which would also carry the requirement of effectiveness in addition to safety. If the FDA didn't become involved over such claims, the FTC would then intervene with a misleading advertising charge as the permanent change claims had not been proven.

SUMMARY

Successful businesses conduct themselves in a legal, ethical, and socially responsible manner. As retailing and manufacturing expand globally, this type of behavior becomes more complicated as laws and standards vary from country to country. Much attention and public awareness has been focused on the use of labor throughout the world to produce products that we buy at low prices. Some companies formulate strict ethical standards and policies; others stay within the letter of the law. At the same time, government action mandating certain behavior has been considered by many as excessive regulation. So, whatever a company's ethical standards may be now, ethics and socially responsible behavior will continue to grow as issues for businesses. The challenge is for companies to find a way to comply with both the law and with society's dictates, and still offer their customers a good product at a good price.

KEY TERMS

bait and switch	kickback
business ethics	misleading advertising
cause marketing	patent
code of ethics	personal ethics
codes of conduct	predatory pricing
Consumer Product Safety Commission (CPSC)	price discrimination
copyright	price fixing
corporate ethics	price maintenance laws
counterfeit	*prima facie* duties
environmentally friendly	professional ethics
ethics	proportionality framework
fair-trade laws	social justice framework
Federal Trade Commission (FTC)	social responsibility
Food and Drug Administration (FDA)	trademark
gray market goods	tying contract
intellectual property	utilitarianism

BIBLIOGRAPHY

Apparel industry and codes of conduct: A solution to the international child labor problem? (1996). Washington, DC: U.S. Department of Labor.

Bohlinger, M. S. (1993). *Merchandise buying.* Boston: Allyn and Bacon.

Casabona, L. (2007, January 31). Panel: Web, demand aiding counterfeiters. *Women's Wear Daily,* p. 3.

Clark, E., & Ellis, K. (2007, June 29). Power to set prices: Supreme Court backs brands over retailers. *Women's Wear Daily,* pp. 1, 14.

Corcoran, C. T. (2007, April 7). Brands fight online deluge of counterfeit goods. *Women's Wear Daily,* p. 10.

Corcoran, C. T., & Power, D. (2007, January 10). Designs on good deeds earn WWD awards. *Women's Wear Daily,* p. 14.

DesJardins, J. (2007). *Business, ethics, and the environment: Imagining a sustainable future.* Upper Saddle River, NJ: Prentice Hall.

Dunne, P. M., & Lusch, R. F. (2007). *Retailing.* Norman, OK: South-Western College Publishing.

Ellis, K. (2003, June 3). DOL report: Child labor still abounds. *Women's Wear Daily,* pp. 2, 4.

Ellis, K. (2007, May 1). Report sees China counterfeiting worsening. *Women's Wear Daily,* p. 3.

Esbenshade, J. (2004). *Monitoring sweatshops: Workers, consumers, and the global apparel industry.* Philadelphia: Temple University Press.

Fair Labor Association (www.fairlabor.org).

Groves, E. (2006, October 31). Ethical fashion goes mainstream. *Women's Wear Daily,* p. 12.

Guy, M. E. (1990). *Ethical decision making in everyday work situations.* New York: Quorum Books.

Hartman, L. P. (2001). *Perspectives in business ethics.* New York: McGraw-Hill/Irwin.

Hethorn, J., & Ulasewicz, C. (2008). *Sustainable fashion: Why now?* New York: Fairchild Books.

Kletter, M. (2005, April 14). Labor cites Nike study as model. *Women's Wear Daily,* p. 14.

Kunz, F. I., & Garner, M. B. (2007). *Going global: The textile and apparel industry.* New York: Fairchild Books.

Levi Strauss & Co. (n.d.) *Case study: Child labor in Bangladesh.* Retrieved September 12, 2007, from www.levistrauss.com/Downloads/CaseStudyBangladesh.pdf.

Littrell, M. A., & Dickson, M. A. (1999). *Social responsibility in the global market: Fair trade of cultural products.* Thousand Oaks, CA.: Sage Publications.

Office of Textiles and Apparel (www.otexa.ita.doc.gov).

Ottman, J. A. (1994). *Green marketing: Challenges and opportunities for the new marketing age.* Lincolnwood, IL: NTC Business Books.

Robin, D. P., & Reidenbach, R. E. (1989). *Business ethics: Where profits meet value systems.* Englewood Cliffs, NJ: Prentice Hall.

Ross, R. J. S. (2004). *Slaves to fashion: Poverty and abuse in the new sweatshops.* Ann Arbor, MI: University of Michigan Press.

Socha, M., & Edelson, S. (2007, June 7). Attaching counterfeits: Wal-Mart unit settles with Fendi over fakes. *Women's Wear Daily,* pp. 1, 11.

U.S. Customs and Border Control (www.cbp.gov).

U.S. Patent and Trademark Office (www.uspto.gov).

Wolf, J. H., & Dickson, M. A. (2002). Apparel manufacturer and retailer efforts to reduce child labor: An ethics of virtue perspective on codes of conduct. *Clothing and Textiles Research Journal,* *20*(4), 183–195.

Worldwide Responsible Apparel Production (www.apparel.org).

Case 68

TO GO OR TO STAY: ETHICS IN THE WORKPLACE

Kitty Dickerson, University of Missouri

When Janice Heitler landed a job after graduation in the buyer training program at retailer BuyBest, she believed her career dreams were close to being fulfilled. Although she had limited experience with the company through an internship, she was particularly fortunate to be hired immediately into the BuyBest's buying office. Typically, potential buyers spend at least two years in a BuyBest store before having an opportunity to go to the headquarter's buying offices.

Janice plunged quickly into her work as a buyer trainee at BuyBest. Although she was given a relatively limited amount of training and guidance in her new job, Janice learned quickly. She soon earned the respect of her colleagues and the vendors with whom she worked. Before long, Janice was given limited opportunities to do some of the actual buying for her area. As her experience increased, so did her responsibilities for buying. In what was a relatively short period of time for a buyer in training, she was made buyer of her own area. Although this first buying area was relatively low profile, the multiple stores represented in the chain meant that the dollar volume for which she bought was fairly significant.

As Janice continued her successful performance, she was rewarded with higher-dollar-volume areas for which to buy. Within less than three years, she was buyer for two merchandise areas and was responsible for a staggering dollar volume for a person of her age and experience. Although somewhat uneasy at times because of her fast promotion, Janice continued to perform well. Her areas were successful, and she was a valued employee of BuyBest.

As the economy changed and consumer apparel expenditures declined, Janice's satisfaction with her job began to wane. Although her own buying areas were doing reasonably well, the company as a whole was less profitable than in prior years. Many of BuyBest's buyers had merchandise on order with manufacturers and found that consumer demand was not adequate to sell all the merchandise ordered. Many of Janice's buyer peers canceled their orders with manufacturers.

As Janice's buying areas began to show lackluster performance, she began to be pressured from her superiors to cancel orders for merchandise not yet shipped. She understood why her superiors wanted her to cancel the orders; however, she felt it was unethical treatment of the manufacturers with whom she had developed trusted relationships. Because Janice was buying a substantial volume of merchandise for the multiple stores in the

BuyBest organization, she was sensitive to what this meant to those vendors. For many small suppliers, in particular, the volume she ordered could make or break the manufacturer. For those companies with whom she had placed orders, the fabrics and others supplies would have been purchased by the manufacturers, and in several cases, production was already in progress. This also would mean the manufacturer would have incurred labor costs at that point. In short, the losses associated with canceled orders from BuyBest could put some of her vendors out of business or seriously cripple them.

Janice found herself torn between her conscience and the expectations of her employer. To stay in her job, she must cancel orders to meet BuyBest's financial expectations for her area. To do so, Janice knew she would be seriously hurting vendors with whom she had developed good relationships, and she had become friends with several. Additionally, she knew that she might need to place orders again with those companies—if they were still in business—and she was uncertain if they would sell to her again if she treated them in this manner.

Janice's superiors were very much aware of the implications of canceled orders on vendors. They, too, were responding to pressure from their superiors. Janice could not be sure how high in the corporate structure the decisions were being made.

Janice saw some of her buyer peers leaving BuyBest. Although she was troubled by her dilemma, she knew she would not likely find another job with comparable opportunities at this stage in her career.

Major Question

What should Janice do?

Study Questions

1. What other factors, besides an economic downturn, would cause a retailer to cancel orders so close to delivery dates?

2. What are the retailers' rights regarding cancellations?

3. What can the vendor do to protect itself against last-minute retail cancellations?

Case 69

ABERCROMBIE & FITCH: HIRING FOR LOOKS[1]

Hope Bober Corrigan, Loyola College in Maryland

Clothing retailer Abercrombie & Fitch often recruited on college campuses and in the mall to find attractive young people and then urge them to apply for jobs. This company, known for building an attractive workforce, did so by aggressively hiring pretty young women and handsome young men to match their all-American brand image. Abercrombie & Fitch refers to these great-looking sales associates as brand ambassadors. They project the retailer's brand and make the store a better experience for customers.

[1]Levy and Weitz, *Retailing Management*, 6th ed., The McGraw-Hill Companies. Reproduced with permission of The McGraw-Hill Companies.

Is seeking only good-looking employees a necessary trend in the retail industry? Is hiring an attractive sales force a smart and necessary practice to differentiate the store in the competitive retail environment? Do salespeople need to mirror the images seen in the retailer's catalog and home page? Does all-American mean thin, tall, and white with blonde hair and blue eyes? If the store has great-looking college students working in the store, will others want to shop there? How important are retail experience and ability versus a pretty face?

In seeking good-looking employees, companies are risking lawsuits for discriminatory hiring practices. Hiring attractive people is not illegal, but discrimination on the basis of age, gender, race, national origin, disability, or ethnicity is. Employers may establish and enforce grooming and appearance standards. Exceptions to Title VII are possible if the employer can prove that one of the protected characteristics is a bona fide occupational qualification.

In 2003, Abercrombie & Fitch was named in two class-action lawsuits alleging discriminatory hiring practices. Black, Asian, and Latino plaintiffs alleged that they were denied sales associate positions. These workers were directed to low-visibility jobs in the stockroom or maintenance department.

Abercrombie & Fitch did not admit guilt and denies that it engaged in any discriminatory practices but settled these cases for $40 million distributed to several thousand minority and female plaintiffs. The company agreed to appoint a vice president for diversity, use benchmarks, train all hiring managers, and hire 25 diversity recruits in an attempt to alter its white, all-American image and more accurately reflect the applicant pool in its stores. The settlement also calls for Abercrombie & Fitch to increase diversity in its promotional materials.

Major Question*

If you were responsible for hiring today at A&F, what qualifications would you look for?

Study Questions

1. Why would Abercrombie & Fitch want to hire employees with a certain look?

2. From a business perspective, do you think this is a good idea? What about from an ethical perspective or a legal perspective?

*Do not use the alternative solutions format for this case.

Case 70

TO WORK, STUDY, OR STARVE: BANGLADESH CHILD LABOR

Kitty Dickerson, University of Missouri

Ted Jonas is involved in global sourcing for a major retail chain, Dazzlemore. He travels a good portion of the time, going from country to country to find good potential contractors to produce the lines developed in his company's product development department.

Ted has found many of his prospects for contractors in less-developed countries. Many of these countries offer good quality and will produce apparel at costs that are attractive to Dazzlemore. One of the countries Ted often visits is Bangladesh, one of the poorest countries in the world. When he has visited factories there, he has noticed that some of the workers looked more like children than adults. At least when he has been present, he has seen no evidence that these young people were held against their will or abused. He suspected, however, that the youngsters probably worked very long days, just as the older operators did.

At the same time, Ted is aware of the poverty, the malnutrition, and the poor health conditions of many—both old and young—in Bangladesh. In Dhaka, the capitol of Bangladesh, he has also noticed the number of children who were running in the streets, often in physical danger as they peddled trinkets and gum. He has seen few schools to accommodate the large number of children who seem to be everywhere.

When Ted was back in the United States for a meeting, he happened to see an exposé on television about a major U.S. retailer doing business with a Bangladesh supplier who appeared to be using child laborers. In the weeks that followed, Ted followed the repercussions of this exposé about child workers. He learned that members of the U.S. Congress are sensitized to the issue, and bills have been introduced to regulate the importation of products made by children. Senator

Tom Harkin from Iowa has introduced several bills to combat the worst forms of child labor, including the Child Labor Deterrence Act, the most comprehensive legislation in the United States to curb abusive child labor overseas (http://harkin.senate.gov). And through his position on the Senate Appropriations Committee, Senator Harkin has allocated more than $200 million for the International Program on the Elimination of Child Labor (www.ilo.org/ipec/lang—en/index.htm), a division of the International Labor Organization that removes children from abusive labor situations around the world.

When visiting with European colleagues, Ted learned that the issue of child labor in developing countries had also been featured in the media there. As in the United States, some European policy makers were launching an effort to place a ban on products made with child labor. But banning child labor entirely was doing a disservice to starving children in some of the poorest developing nations. Some feel that factory work is far safer for children than running in the streets, and that earning a wage was better than starving—even if the wage earner happened to be younger than developed country standards for minimum age workers.

Meanwhile, back in the United States, a group called the Child Labor Coalition developed plans for a boycott of Bangladesh apparel unless Bangladesh manufacturers agreed to eliminate child labor. UNICEF and the International Labor Organization also supported the boycott.

Finally, the Bangladesh Garment Manufacturers and Exporters Association agreed to ban workers under 14 in apparel factories. Estimates of the number of children under 14 in the country's large industry were as low as 8,000 and as high as 50,000. The agreement required that schooling be provided for the children who would be dismissed because of the agreement. Coalition leaders heralded the agreement as a breakthrough for the child labor issue in the third world.

Ted followed the results with interest. He pondered his own position on this issue. He agrees that abusive child labor conditions should be eliminated. He knows that children generally have no advocates in those situations and are therefore easily exploited. He also knows the dire poverty in Bangladesh and the alternative activities for children. He agrees that the safe confines of a factory, as unacceptable as that may be to many westerners, might also be safer than dodging in and out of traffic. He also knows that far too few schools exist in Bangladesh to believe that all the children denied factory work would be sent off cheerily by their mothers to school each day.

Ted searched his heart for an answer to what he expected to confront in future visits to potential contractors in developing countries.

Major Question

What should Ted do when he sees children at work in the factories he contracts from?

Study Questions

1. How can apparel and retail companies stay competitive when some companies utilize contractors with employment practices less than ethical (using Western standards)?

2. Does a buyer have the power to decide what contractors a large retailer uses for their private-label merchandise?

Exercise

Investigate the status of child labor bills in the U.S. Congress and in Europe.

Case 71

TODAY'S WOMAN: THE BUYER'S PERSONAL DECISION

Judith Everett, Northern Arizona University

Diane Mather has recently accepted the position of buyer of denim for Today's Woman, a women's specialty chain. Previously Diane was the regional manager for the Southwest division. This promotion required relocating to New York City, where the corporate headquarters is situated.

Diane had a strong record as a hard worker and had been promoted regularly since graduating with a degree in fashion merchandising eight years ago. Diane set high standards for her personal and ethical performance. She expected no less from her staff. She always met or exceeded her sales and performance goals, and moved quickly up the ranks from assistant manager to branch store manager. Her next promotion was to Southwest regional manager. This job included training store managers, providing budget and inventory information to the personnel in her region and to the buyers at corporate headquarters, and completing product and consumer demand analysis. She watched the changing consumer demands in her region and reported the trends in consumer behavior to the buying offices. The merchandise demands for the Southwest region emphasized casual yet updated merchandise. Demand was growing for less rigid and traditional denim; consumers wanted fashionable denim that could be worn for day as well as evening. When Diane took over the buyer's job, it was clear that the trend occurring in her homebase of the Southwest region was a national trend.

Today's Woman is a national chain store with nearly 300 branches. It targets an audience of working women between the ages of 25 and 45. The company has aggressive growth plans, opening several new branches each year. The denim buyer has a significant position in the firm because nearly 35 percent of annual sales are denim. The company sells coordinated separates, tops, and such accessories as belts, handbags, totes, shoes, and jewelry. The company has traditionally purchased 90 percent of their denim from one manufacturer, Ben Ross.

Ben Ross is a manufacturer of good-quality denim in the moderate to better price range. The company has been producing denim for nearly 50 years. The owner of the firm has provided excellent service through fair pricing and reliable delivery. The styling of the merchandise is quite traditional and conservative, serving the traditional woman very well for the past 50 years.

After arriving in New York, Diane has been invited to many social events sponsored by the senior executives at Today's Woman, her college alumni association, and the Fashion Group International, a professional organization for women executives in the fashion industry. She has learned to love living in the "big city." At Diane's college alumni association annual banquet, she met George Robinson, a sales representative for Hunting Brothers, a men's apparel manufacturer" with retail outlets on the East Coast. Diane and George were immediately attracted to each other and began dating. They have attended several Broadway shows together and have enjoyed dining at some of the great restaurants in New York.

Hunting Brothers has a reputation for innovative men's apparel and has recently expanded into manufacturing women's denim. The women's market is a very small part of the company at this point, but the firm's products have tested very well in the East Coast retail stores owned by Hunting Brothers. The firm does not plan on opening retail stores in other parts of the United States at this time. Hunting Brothers plans to expand the market share of the women's denim by selling to other retailers.

George has given Diane several denim garments as gifts. She thought that the items had a nice, up-to-date fashion appearance. They fit well and are of excellent quality.

The fabric and styling would fit the growing casual yet updated merchandise segment.

After several months of dating, George suggests that Diane drop Ben Ross as the primary denim vendor and purchase most of her merchandise from Hunting Brothers. Diane recognizes the quality of the product and the more fashionable styling but fears that her supervisor will question why she is buying denim from her "boyfriend."

Major Question

What should Diane do?

Study Questions

1. What are the ethical considerations in this situation?

2. What should be the criteria for vendor selection?

Case 72

COLLUSION TO CATCH ANTI-TRUST OFFENDERS

Nancy J. Rabolt, San Francisco State University
Judy K. Miler, Florida State University

Guido Paolluci Knitwear Company is a very successful manufacturer of medium to better knit garments. They feature knit jacquard design motifs that are produced on Italian knitting machines in Mexico. The two principals of the firm are Irving Copeland, who is "inside" handling production, purchasing, and so forth, and Bill Samuels, who is "outside" in charge of marketing and sales functions. The firm's merchandise is well known in its field as a result of years of regular advertising in a variety of fashion magazines as well as in repeated store (cooperative) ads. The company has also received "good press" from the excellent work of its public relations agency. Guido, as the company is frequently called, is sold in many large department and specialty stores and in hundreds of better independent stores throughout the country. They have over 2,000 accounts and an annual sales volume approaching $20 million.

Meryl Alexander is the misses sportswear buyer for Benson's, a prestigious retailer in Spokane, Washington. Meryl came to Benson's from a fine specialty store in the Midwest because her husband had been transferred to his firm's new offices in Spokane. Benson's felt extremely fortunate to get someone like Meryl, who was known in her market as a fashion innovator, as well as a good promotions authority.

On one of her early buying trips to New York, Meryl went to the Guido Paolluci showroom and had a reunion with Bill Samuels. After exchanging hearty greetings and nostalgic reminiscences, Meryl got down to business and went over the line with Bill.

Benson's, in addition to its main store, has nine branches in the surrounding suburban areas. Many of the branch stores were in upper-middle class sections of the metropolitan area.

Guido had never sold to Benson's before, but Meryl, an old customer, knew the firm well and had done an excellent job with its merchandise in the past. Her first thoughts were possibilities of exclusivity of the Paolluci knits. Large retailers frequently seek to control the distribution policies of manufacturers in an effort to eliminate as much competition as possible. This is in exchange for the opportunity granted by the large store to permit the manufacturer to use the order to influence other stores in purchasing the line. When a store is not sure about carrying a line, the success of a well-regarded retailer with the line helps reinforce to the unsure store that "what is good enough for so and so is good enough for me."

When she had reviewed the line, Meryl turned to Bill and asked a simple question: "Bill, who do you sell to in my area, and who do you intend to sell to in the immediate future?" In reply to her question, Bill told Meryl that there were six independent stores in her area that were currently carrying the Guido line. Meryl indicated that her opening order for Benson's and its branches would be much greater than those six stores' total annual purchases combined.

Overcome by the probable size of the forthcoming Benson's business, Bill rapidly lost his sense of loyalty to the six independent stores. After doing some rapid mental arithmetic, Bill came to an understanding that Benson's with its branches probably would buy about 2,000 pieces for the sea-

son, whereas the six smaller stores would each wind up with an average of 60 to 100 pieces for the same period. Although Bill would like to continue to sell to the six independent stores as well, he knew that he could not have his cake and eat it, too!

He and Meryl agreed that he could not cancel the independent stores' orders because this would be a direct violation of federal anti-trust statutes, and it was still fresh in his memory that three of the most prestigious fashion stores in the country had recently been found guilty of just such a violation. Accordingly, he agreed to kick their orders around until they "got lost" for the current season. In the future, he promised, he would dream up further measures designed to discourage the local stores from ordering the Guido line.

Soon after, the merchandise began to arrive at Benson's, and, as expected, it did very well. About this time, Jerry Peters, owner of Peter's Fashions, and Harold Tillman of Milady's accidentally met in the bar at Rudi's, a well-known eating establishment. Being friendly noncompetitors (Peter's Fashions was located in a nearby suburb, while Milady's was a downtown competitor of Benson's main store), they had a drink and decided to dine together.

During the course of the meal, Harold asked Jerry how business was and particularly how the new Guido Paolucci merchandise was moving.

"How could I know? I never received one piece of it," Jerry replied.

"Neither did I," mused Harold. "I wonder what's going on?"

"Hey, wait a minute, Hal," interjected Jerry. "Did you see that Benson ad on the Guido merchandise? I'll bet that's the answer—they're trying to squeeze us little guys out."

To avoid any semblance of collusion, before they parted company that evening, Harold and Jerry decided to begin simultaneous but independent action to rescue their Guido merchandise orders. They agreed to call Bill at separate intervals and, if they received no satisfaction, to have their attorneys threaten him with civil, as well as criminal, action. They also agreed to check the other four independent stores to see if they were in the same boat.

When Jerry reached Bill in New York, he accused Guido of giving Benson's preferential treatment, which, of course, Bill denied. Bill professed ignorance of the order and said he would look into the matter. Jerry then reported this conversation to Harold.

Another call to New York from Harold brought a similar response—ignorance of the order and the promise of investigation. Both men agreed that there must be collusion between Benson's and Guido's and now was the time for action.

Major Question

If you were advising Jerry and Harold, how would you go about handling this situation?

Study Questions

1. Do you think the actions of the knitwear company and retailer were illegal? Unethical?

2. What is more profitable for the manufacturer: selling to one large retail account or several smaller ones? Which is safest for the manufacturer relative to any of the companies going out of business?

3. Can you cite a recent example of small retailers being squeezed out of the market by a large retailer?

4. How can the law protect against collusion between a manufacturer and retailer to discriminate against a small retailer?

Case 73

THE FLANNEL ORGANIC FIBER FIASCO

Connie Ulasewicz, San Francisco State University

Lewis & Lee is a contemporary domestic clothing manufacturer of a line of whimsical layette items and accessories for the infant to 4T set. The line includes hats, booties, blankets, and bibs offered in bright novelty stripes, prints, and solids. The Lewis & Lee layette collection is marketed as a 100 percent organic cotton, gift-packaged, flannel program. The layette items are continually available for stores to reorder 12 months of the year. Lewis & Lee products are available in a variety of department stores including Macy's and Saks, independent specialty stores, hospital gift shops, and through its Web site. The manufacturer is successful because it delivers a high-quality, domestically manufactured, well-priced, organic fiber product.

One of the fabrics with wide customer acceptance in the layette line is a 100 percent organic cotton flannel. Moms seem to love the softness next to their babies' skin and are willing to pay a higher price for an organic cotton receiving blanket, cap, and booties from Lewis & Lee versus a nonorganic or blended flannel from their competition. Based on the success of their flannels, the company offered a second product line this past year: corduroy hats and booties lined in flannel. The products are quite sturdy and still have the softness of organic flannel next to the infant's head and toes.

Finding a consistent quality of 100 percent organic cotton flannel available year-round in solids, prints, and matching yarn dyes at an affordable price is a real challenge. The responsibility of the Lewis & Lee fabric merchandiser, Kayla Woolsey, is to swatch, sample, and test fabrics from many different resources. The fabric tests performed are for shrinkage and colorfastness. Both finished garments and fabric squares are tested. When Kayla approves a quality, an order is placed. Most of the solids and basic prints are ordered three to five months in advance through a fabric distributor in Oregon. The lead times are long because the flannels are manufactured in China. This requires long-range planning, but it has been worth it for the ability to reorder the same color and prints throughout the year and the great price received when purchasing in large quantities.

One day while taking the fabric inventory of a recent shipment, Kayla discovered a fiber content label reading 60 percent organic cotton/40 percent polyester stuck inside one of the rolls of fabric. The fabric and color number on the tag was the same as the flannel she had been ordering for four seasons. After looking inside several more tubes, she discovered three more of these 60/40 content labels. She was shocked. Was there an error? She had order confirmations for 100 percent organic cotton flannel. Had she been sold 60 percent organic cotton/40 percent polyester goods all along with the assumption she would not know it was not 100 percent organic cotton? She immediately telephoned her fabric manufacturer in Portland to find out what was going on.

After a sleepless week of investigation, the situation became more complicated. Indeed, Lewis & Lee had been shipped from Oregon some 60/40 flannel on this and past orders. The fabric supplier had contracted for 100 percent organic cotton flannel from China and was unaware of the switch. Unfortunately, all current available solid red flannel would need to be the 60/40 blend. At this time, another concern was raised regarding the cotton: was it really organic? As there are no standards for labeling or international standards for methods of growing organic cotton, the owners of Lewis and Lee began to question if the cotton in their fabric was organic. They no longer trusted their fabric distributor and questioned the company's integrity.

The owners of Lewis & Lee were outraged. Their company's image was based on delivering an organic fiber product, not a blend like their competition. Also, all the garment labels sewn in the products and in the warehouse clearly stated 100 percent organic cotton. The owners knew that legally all textile products must be correctly labeled with the percentage of each fiber present listed in order of greatest percentage. With the new knowledge of the actual fiber content, all garments containing red and blue flannel in production and in stores were incorrectly labeled.

Major Question

If you were a business consultant to Lewis & Lee, what would you advise it to do about this situation?

Study Questions

1. What are the legal ramifications of mislabeling garments?

2. What other government regulations apply to labeling apparel besides fiber content?

3. Does Lewis & Lee have a legal case against their fabric manufacturer for shipping a different fabric quality from that which was contracted?

4. What type of tests could the manufacturer perform on the fabric before production?

5. How do manufacturers test if a cotton fabric is produced from organic or nonorganically grown cotton?

6. Generally polyester/cotton flannels are less expensive than 100 percent cotton flannels. Would they receive money back to compensate for the difference?

Exercises

1. Go to a store that carries similar merchandise and speak to the sales associate. State that you are doing some research for class, and ask if customers read fiber content labels and ask for organic cotton. Note the manager's answers, and include your reflection.

2. View the Federal Trade Commission Web site, www.ftc.org, investigate label requirements, and write about three requirements that are new to you.

3. Visit several organic cotton company Web sites, and search how they label their products organic. Do they use a unique logo?

Case 74

THE DENIM DILEMMA AT VELVET MOON BOUTIQUE

Joy M. Kozar and Cristiana Piccinni, Kansas State University

Melia Turner established Velvet Moon Boutique, a woman's apparel and accessory store located in a Midwest college town. During the first five years of ownership, Melia created many solid relationships with vendors and clientele. She identified specific characteristics of her target market, including customers' purchasing behaviors. She kept in constant contact with her vendors as new merchandise was introduced, bringing in the latest styles and trends on a continual basis. Melia also got involved with the local small business owner's association, forming friendships with several other area business owners.

As Velvet Moon Boutique grew and store traffic increased, Melia was able to identify her primary customers as girls and women between the ages of 16 and 30. Over time, she identified the brands and product categories that sold best. She included a product assortment of low- to moderately priced tops, denim, and accessories. Given the price sensitivity of the target market, Melia quickly learned that in order to sell merchandise within the same selling season, thus reducing the need for markdowns later, the average price for tops should remain around $50, denim jeans could sell for $75 to $100, and accessories should be kept at $20 to $40.

During Velvet Moon's third year of operation, Melia initiated what she believed to be a strategic marketing move. Through a vendor that sold overstock merchandise, Melia was able to obtain high-end denim brands at a fraction of the original wholesale price. Although the jeans were overruns from previous seasons, the styles were basic enough that they could be worn year after year. Given the reduced wholesale cost, Melia could sell the jeans for a quarter of the suggested retail price. In a relatively short period of time, the jeans became a popular item in the store, attracting additional clientele. Whenever customers inquired about the discounted prices, Melia simply explained that they were last year's overstock from large department stores such as Macy's and Saks Fifth Avenue. Customers overlooked the simple styling differences and were eager to take advantage of Velvet Moon's bargain prices.

During the summer just one month prior to the city's annual sidewalk sale, a new store opened one block away from Velvet Moon. Through some inquiring, Melia learned that the new owner, Laura Burns, had successfully established several other fashion boutiques in the area. Understandably, Melia was somewhat uneasy about the new competing business but felt content in knowing that she had already established a loyal customer base.

After the grand opening of Mania, Laura's store, Melia stopped by to welcome Laura to the community. The conversation was cordial, but it left Melia disappointed, as Laura had not been nearly as friendly as the other local small business owners. During the visit, Melia noticed that Laura's price points were much higher than her own at Velvet Moon. Although the merchandise mix was trendy and would appeal to the same clientele, Melia also knew that most local customers would be deterred by the higher prices.

While preparing for the annual sidewalk sale, Melia's focus quickly shifted away from the new competition. In previous years, she had been quite successful during the sale, as it was an effective way of selling any remaining summer merchandise while introducing new fashions for the upcoming fall season. One day into the sale, everything at Velvet Moon was operating smoothly and sales were up from the previous year. Melia was receiving positive feedback about the new fall arrivals from many of her customers. However, on the second day of the sale, an incident occurred that left Melia frustrated and angry. That afternoon, as Melia was at the register closing a sale with a customer, she noticed Laura walk in and begin to examine the display of new denim arrivals. She then selected two pairs of jeans off the rack, walked up to the counter and started accusing Melia of selling counterfeit goods. Flustered by the occurrence, Melia tried to calmly explain that the jeans were from the previous fall/winter season purchased from an overstock vendor. Laura responded by saying the jeans were not authentic; otherwise, Melia would not have obtained them at such a low cost. She also threatened to contact the brand owner of the jeans and alert them to the situation. Laura then demanded that Melia ring up the two pairs of jeans. Melia complied, anxious for Laura to leave and stop making a scene in her store.

The conflict elevated the following week when an ad for Mania appeared in the local newspaper stating: "Tired of people scamming you by selling fake brand name jeans? Come into Mania and we'll show you the difference between what's fake and real." Melia could not believe what she had read. She knew she had to act before Laura could do anything else to damage Velvet Moon's image. Consequently, the next morning after Mania opened, Melia went in to confront Laura about the ad. A sales associate informed her that Laura was spending the day at one of her other businesses. As Melia left the store, a display near the entrance caught her attention. Laura had displayed the two pairs of jeans purchased the previous week at Velvet Moon next to a blow-up of the same ad that had been in the newspaper the day before.

Distraught, Melia went back to Velvet Moon and called Laura. As soon as she heard Laura pick up the receiver, Melia went into a tirade and started accusing Laura of slandering her business. She continued by emphasizing that this was a tightly knit community, that she was very involved with the local small business owner's association, and that she would not allow Laura to sabotage all of her hard work in creating a loyal customer base. Laura, apparently unaffected by the accusations, told Melia that the jeans were not authentic since they were not purchased directly from the manufacturer and it was her intent to make sure Melia could not sell the jeans at such low prices. After all, Laura continued, she couldn't sell this year's jeans at higher prices if customers could save money buying them at Velvet Moon the following year. The conversation ended as Laura abruptly hung up.

A few weeks passed and Melia continually grew more concerned about the situation. One day a letter arrived from one of the manufacturers whose jeans Melia was selling at discounted prices at Velvet Moon. The letter explained that Melia must stop selling the jeans immediately including all counterfeits and overstocks. The manufacturer concluded with the threat of a lawsuit if a percentage of all Melia's sales of the jeans were not paid. Melia was perplexed as to how to handle the situation. She pulled the jeans off the sales floor and hung them in the stock room.

Major Question

How should Melia handle the situation with the brand owner of the denim line who threatened the lawsuit?

Study Questions

1. How should Melia handle the situation with Laura?

2. Was Melia illegally selling the overstock jeans by not purchasing them from the original brand owner?

3. Do you agree or disagree with the way Laura conducted herself? Was she right to contact the brand owners whose jeans Melia was selling at discounted prices? Explain your answer.

KATHRINE BAUMANN'S CRUSADE AGAINST COUNTERFEITING

Karen Marchione, Bowling Green State University
Sara Marcketti, Bowling Green State University

Artist Kathrine Baumann is an American entrepreneur. Founding her company with a mere $130 unemployment check, she quickly built her company into a multimillion-dollar business. She prides herself for being part of the country's small business force, credited as the backbone of the American economy. Baumann designs and manufactures exclusive, limited edition, haute-couture miniaudieres and complementary ladies' accessories. A miniaudiere is a small ornamental purse. The collectibles are numbered and registered with certificates of authenticity personally signed by Kathrine Baumann ("About Kathrine," n.d.). These works are protected by copyright laws that state that other artists and designers cannot legally reproduce her works.

During a Henri Bendel trunk show in 2001, a customer told Baumann that Manhattan retailers were selling unauthorized copies of her work. Baumann believed her works to be protected under copyright; however, after touring several Manhattan stores, she realized counterfeits of her designs have

Figure 11.5 Kathrine Baumann and her creations.

products are dropped, they would keep their shape and form because of the thickness of the metal used (Baumann, 2007). Each miniaudiere contains a chain strap that can be worn over the shoulder or tucked inside so that the wearer can have a stylish clutch. The retail price for most bags ranges from $800 to $2,700. Some specially commissioned pieces containing semiprecious or precious stones were valued at more than $250,000 ("Baumann's Baubles," 1998).

Counterfeit copies were often finished with inexpensive glass, a "clip" closure and a process known as a "flash" (a light gold color that quickly wears off), rather than the elegant plating of the original. Inferior in quality, these bags are made of thin metal, are easily dented, and do not keep their shape. Sometimes the counterfeiters use the Kathrine Baumann name on their copies but do not have the distinctive Kathrine Baumann logo; the italicized "KB" initials with the words "BEVERLY HILLS" in capital Arial font through the center. Many selling these counterfeit goods would try to "market" their products by stating their miniaudieres were made in the same factory as the originals. These claims proved untrue, as Baumann's frames are made by skilled old-world craftsmen in Italy, while the counterfeit copies are usually made in China under sweatshop conditions (Baumann, 2007).

In order to protect the reputation of her brand, her name, and her collectors' investments, Baumann decided to personally go undercover to expose and halt the counterfeiting of her designs. Baumann believed this was critical to protect their value and

been made available to unsuspecting customers (Tucker, 2005). These counterfeit copies look strikingly similar to Baumann's work, using similarly colored motifs and crystals. Yet the copies were not as sophisticated as Baumann's, and definite distinctions could be made between them.

Baumann's work is handcrafted by skilled artisans. She uses the world's finest Swarovski crystals, carefully hand-attached to metal miniaudieres using an exclusive water-resistant adhesive. Baumann's products feature a spring-loaded clasp and are plated with an elegant gold finish, equivalent to that used by Cartier. If Baumann's the substantial investment her collectors made in her originals. Baumann also took action because the counterfeiting violated the stability and security of her staff, many of whom have worked with her for more than 18 years and are considered "family." Having experienced the birth and development of many of their children, she became incensed when her ability to provide an income for them was threatened. That's when the gloves came off. Baumann stated, "If the counterfeiters came after me that is one thing, but they crossed the line when they affected their children and those dependent on me" (Baumann, 2007).

Baumann was also infuriated with the infringement of a particularly noteworthy design idea: the Stars and Stripes Collection originating in 1993. Heralding from Independence, Ohio, Baumann's family has served the United States in uniform since the Civil War. As first runner-up in the Miss America pageant and having traveled with Bob Hope to entertain the troops in Vietnam, Baumann felt a special reverence for the American flag. After the 9/11 attacks, this collection had more significance. Therefore, to support the relief efforts for the families of those lost on that tragic day, Baumann donated a substantial portion of the Stars and Stripes Collection proceeds to the Fire Fighters Fund, and sales for this collection during that quarter exceeded those of all designs in the history of her company. Of course, insult soon added to injury, and Chinese copies of Baumann's Stars and Stripes design immediately flooded the New York market; counterfeiters even had the

audacity to place an ad for their copies in Town & Country, where Baumann had previously invested $20,000 for advertisement of the collection (Baumann, 2007).

Baumann remained positive and stayed active by painting designs on apparel and adorned them with pearls, crystals, and beads, marketing them to specialty stores and boutiques. Inspired by Judith Leiber, an upscale handbag designer, Baumann began to make miniaudieres. When sales for the miniaudieres surpassed the clothing sales, Baumann decided to specialize in this artistic arena ("About Kathrine," n.d.).

K. Baumann Design, now known as Kathrine Baumann Beverly Hills, was founded in 1988. Baumann has created custom apparel items worn by celebrities such as Madonna and Cher and purchased by discriminating international collectors. Baumann has national and international licensing agreements with mega-companies such as Coca-Cola, Disney, NFL, NBA, Mattel, and McDonalds. She has re-created American icons and transformed these accessories into "wearable art." Some of her best sellers include the Mickey and Minnie Mouse Bag featured in People and the Coca-Cola Bag featured in Time. CNN named Baumann "The Female Andy Warhol." Baumann's casual and contemporary designs have attracted the young-at-heart consumer and have outsold many competitors. Her designs have been carried in boutiques, department stores, and specialty stores nationwide and internationally, including F.A.O. Schwarz, Estée Lauder, Disney Attractions, Saks, Neiman Marcus, Marshall Field's, and fine jewelry stores throughout the country ("About Kathrine," n.d.).

Baumann began her fight against counterfeiting in 2001. A small business owner, she did not have the funds available to hire a lawyer, so she made the decision to personally investigate these counterfeits. Baumann used hidden cameras and placed herself in potentially dangerous situations, gathering evidence in order to determine the connections between stores and suppliers (Tucker, 2005). "Your life is truly in jeopardy when you try to stop these people. Counterfeiters can earn 10 to 20 million in nontaxable income, so they will think nothing of killing you," stated Baumann. During her undercover investigation, she wore wigs to disguise herself. Even close friends did not recognize her when she walked past them on city streets (Baumann, 2007).

Baumann posed as a customer and conversed with store managers and owners who carried copies of her designs. They did not recognize Baumann when she was dressed in disguise; they did not even recognize her when she was not dressed in disguise. "They did not know or actually care who I was or care to know me as a person. All that mattered was that I supplied them with the means to make substantial revenue. Their sole objective was to make money off of my efforts and that of my staff," explained Baumann. This illegal income and profit was considerable, since goods were marked up to 200 to 400 percent and produced very cheaply (Baumann, 2007).

Much time and energy has been spent investigating the fakes. This has taken time away from her business, and that has meant a decrease in sales of her collections and the unfortunate unemployment of employees. Baumann states that the counterfeiting has cost her company millions in potential revenue and growth (Tucker, 2005). However, if Baumann did not invest that time, energy, and money fighting the counterfeiters, she would not have a company today. Baumann acknowledged that there really was not any option but to stop them because the counterfeiters would have totally destroyed her business. Baumann occasionally hired private investigators to accompany her, and she personally guided them in the investigation even though she knew it was dangerous. Armed with more knowledge of her work than the detectives, she knew the questions that needed to be asked such as processes, the type of crystals used, and the brilliance of the stones (Baumann, 2007).

When performing her investigation, Baumann carried over her shoulder a camera inside a camera bag that had a hole in the side of the bag. She put her hand over the hole when the counterfeiters were looking toward her and would take her hand off when they looked away so that she could scan the entire store with her camera. Baumann got very good at using her camera while walking in front of the copies and pausing so she could get a good close-up shot (Baumann, 2007).

Baumann uses the analogy of David versus Goliath when discussing her crusade against counterfeiters. Even though she is a mature woman, Baumann still feels like the little girl from Independence, Ohio, standing up to the town bully. As a child, when someone picked on her kid brother, she told them, "If you are going to hit him, you are going to go through me first."

Baumann explained, "You have to stand up to these bullies because if you don't they are going to take advantage of you. Counterfeiters in China never met a girl from Independence, Ohio, before and I was ready to get down in the trenches and fight" (Baumann, 2007).

Baumann even traveled to China to further investigate the manufacturers of the counterfeit goods and to take photos and videos in offending stores. Baumann stated, "This was the most dangerous venture, as the U.S. Customs had confiscated millions of dollars in counterfeit goods; therefore, the Chinese were very unhappy with me. Had they realized who I was, I might have disappeared. Human life has no value there and I was an obstacle they would like to permanently eradicate!" She added, "The prices they quoted us were phenomenal." The counterfeiters thought they were going to make a profit, so they even allowed Baumann to take pictures, which were turned over to the Hong Kong Strike Force. If anyone tries to copy Baumann's designs again, the Strike Force is armed with photographs, product samples, and the ammunition to fight the infringers. Baumann stated that Hong Kong takes counterfeiting very seriously. They publish magazine articles discussing counterfeiting, and raids are seen practically on a daily basis (Baumann, 2007).

When Baumann originally began filing her copyrights with the Office of Patents and Copyrights in Washington, D.C., in 1993, she was told that copyrights were only necessary if you would need to sue someone to protect your product and that your products were automatically copyrighted as soon as an image of the product was published. What she was not told, however, was that if your designs are copied and you haven't filed within three months of "publishing," you cannot sue for triple damages and attorney fees. If you do have your copyright filed and someone copies your designs, the counterfeiters have to pay three times the damages and all attorney fees. Baumann now believes that the $33 that it costs to file a copyright is well worth the protection (Baumann, 2007).

When Baumann realized her products were being copied, she halted her business and focused on filing her copyrights. After six months of working on them, she told her staff, "We are not leaving the office tonight until all copyrights have been sent to Washington." They finally left at 11:30 that night. The next morning Baumann's secretary came in to the office stating, "Kathrine, there's someone really upset calling from Washington. She is really furious and I don't know what to say to her." Baumann took the call and said, "This is Kathrine Baumann." Then the woman said, "Oh, you're her? I just want to know, what's your problem? I got two reams two inches thick of e-mails from you. All of our paper is running out. The computers are jammed and it's all from you. What is your problem?" Baumann laughed and said, "Problem, I have a few problems. Which one do you want to hear about first?" That broke the ice and the woman laughed but stressed that Baumann reached the wrong division; the liaison between the FBI and customs, the enforcement division. Baumann replied, "No, I didn't reach the wrong department. Somehow I reached the right one. I don't know actually how I did it, but I need to talk to you because I have been knocked off." The woman responded, "Ninety-five percent of people think they are being copied and you are part of the 95 percent." "No, I am part of the 5 percent," refuted Baumann. The woman said, "Trust me, you're not." Baumann pursued, "Could I please send you some documents to read and review and then call me back tomorrow." The woman agreed and Baumann sent overnight 700 pages of paperwork, with everything backed up on CDs for easy access and reference via computer, including comparison photos of her products and of the counterfeit copies so that within seconds, information could be accessed and referenced. The next day the woman called from Washington, D.C., and said, "Kathrine, you are part of the 5 percent. How quickly can you get to Washington? We are having a conference next week with all the people you need in attendance. If you have to walk, get here!" Because of limited cash flow, Baumann called the President's Office at Continental Airlines and worked out a ticket for a pending flight to D.C. with a two-day stop over in New York (Baumann, 2007).

In New York, Baumann worked once more with her private detective to establish more current information. She was informed that once she handed her case over to Washington, she was no longer allowed to be part of the investigation. One last time Baumann donned her disguise by stuffing her long brunette hair under a synthetic blond wig. Wearing rhinestone sandals, rhinestone sunglasses, and a white linen outfit adorned with rhinestones on the sleeves and bottom of the pant, Baumann visited counterfeiters' stores in New York and filmed current footage (Baumann, 2007).

Baumann then went to the intellectual properties meeting in Washington, D.C., Baumann commented about the meeting, "I was sitting there by myself. All the [movie] studios were there concerned about the massive DVD counterfeiting. Microsoft, Fila, Nike, Disney, and numerous multimillion dollar companies with major brands were in attendance with private detectives and attorneys in tow. Hundreds of companies were represented with their associates, and I was there by myself." The official welcomed and introduced the major firms. Then she stopped and introduced Baumann saying, "We have someone who is here alone; no detectives, and no attorneys. We care about her as much as we care about you. She represents the small business owner, the backbone of our American economy. Kathrine Baumann, will you please stand?" The official then stated, "Kathrine Baumann is the 'role model' for the way a case should be assembled and if everyone provided as much info as she did, then we would be able to help people much more." Baumann was shocked that they introduced her and so touched that she teared up when they referenced and credited her efforts. During the meeting Baumann met with law enforcement, and they were very supportive and interested in her case (Baumann, 2007).

These government officials arrested and convicted retailers on criminal charges of copyright infringement; Baumann's lawyer filed additional civil lawsuits against store owners for selling the counterfeit goods. Unspecified monetary settlements have been reached, and permanent injunctions have been imposed. Baumann estimated that through litigation, as much as 85 percent of the fakes of her designs have been removed from the streets (Tucker, 2005).

One of Baumann's goals is to educate consumers on the negative ramifications of counterfeit products and to get the attention of government enforcement officials. She has attended numerous conferences and met with many authorities in Washington, D.C., to discuss the counterfeiting problem. Baumann has become a defender of intellectual property rights and plans to use her knowledge and experience to serve as a spokesperson and role model for designers and manufacturers (Beres, 2005). According to Baumann, "Our 'American Dream' is very vulnerable because of the damage counterfeits have caused to our small business owners, the backbone of the American economy. This dream could become extinct by the time our children are ready to pursue it for themselves. It is imperative that the public understand the damage they are creating for us and our children. There comes a time for us to 'just say no' and 'walk on by.' These copies have no guarantees, no serv-ice, and no residual value. Buying counter-feits destroys jobs for Americans and causes the American Public to incur additional expenses, in addition to jeopardizing the moral core of our people and country" (Baumann, 2007).

Major Question

If you were Kathrine Baumann, would you crusade against the counterfeiting of your products?

Study Question

What are the ramifications of counterfeiting?

Bibliography

About Kathrine Baumann. (n.d.). Retrieved March 12, 2007, from www.kbaumann .com/kbweb_2000/aboutkb/about1.html

Baumann's baubles. (1998, October). *Women's Wear Daily Accessories Supplement,* p. 40+.

Baumann, K. (2007, March 25). Phone Interview. Entrepreneur and miniaudiere designer, Kathrine Baumann Beverly Hills, CA.

Beres, G.A. (2005). Kathrine Baumann wages war against counterfeiters. *IDEX Magazine.* Retrieved March 12, 2007, from www.kbaumann.com/kbweb_2000/news/ fashion.html

International anti-counterfeiting coalition. (2004). *Facts on fakes.* Retrieved July 9, 2004, from www.iacc.org

LaRocca, J. (2006, May). Fighting back against fraud. *Stores,* p. LPI 4.

Tucker, R. (2004, October 19). Designer Kathrine Baumann wins lawsuit over knockoffs. *Women's Wear Daily,* p. 2.

Tucker, R. (2005, March 14). Designer Baumann's undercover war on knockoffs. *Women's Wear Daily*. Retrieved March 12, 2007, from www.kbaumann.com/kbweb_2000/news/fashion.html

The White House. (2005). *U.S.-EU working together to fight against global piracy and counterfeiting*. Retrieved June 11, 2007, from www.whitehouse.gov/news/releases/2005/06/20050620-6.html

Wood, S. (2003, July 27–29). Buying knockoffs is a slippery slope, *USA Weekend*, p. 17.

Case 76

WHEN IS IMITATION NOT THE HIGHEST FORM OF FLATTERY?

Jongeun Rhee, University of Wisconsin-Stout
Kim K. P. Johnson, University of Minnesota

Williams-Sonoma, Inc. is a premier specialty retailer based in San Francisco, California. The company operates Williams-Sonoma stores, as well as Pottery Barn stores. Products offered include furniture, home furnishings, and products for bedrooms, bathrooms, kitchens, as well as decorative accessories for the home. Williams-Sonoma puts significant resources into the development of creative and distinctive products to appeal to its upscale customers.

Over the years, Williams-Sonoma developed a series of signature patterns. One pattern was used in the development of a line of holiday items including stockings, tree skirt, and table linens. The stockings featured a red and white gingham fabric used in both the toe and top areas. A band of white quilted fabric was also used in the top and in the ankle areas of the stocking, along with a light blue fabric featuring appliquéd snowflakes. The snow scene was connected to a band of corduroy fabric. Highlighted on the stocking was a Santa Claus. This distinctive combination of fabrics and motif was also used on other types of holiday decorations. The stockings were retailed through Pottery Barn outlets and had been available since 2002. Williams-Sonoma sold more than 5 million of the holiday stockings between 2002 and 2005.

Target is a Minneapolis, Minnesota-based discounter and one of the biggest retailers in the United States. Target offers customers a wide variety of products including home furnishings and bed and bath items. Target is positioned as a fashion discounter with the strategy of design for everyone, and it offers well-designed items with a reasonable price point. To this end, Target has partnered with well-known designers including Isaac Mizrahi, Todd Oldham, and Michael Graves.

Several years after Pottery Barn first offered its unique holiday stockings, Target introduced a holiday stocking that contained several design elements that were similar to the Williams-Sonoma stocking. The Target stocking featured the use of red and white gingham as well as a light blue fabric appliquéd with snowflakes. The stocking

Figure 11.6 Do you think this is a knockoff or an example of copyright infringement?

featured a Santa Claus motif, and the stocking was also topped by a band of quilted white fabric, followed by gingham fabric.

Toward the end of that same year (December 9, 2006), Williams-Sonoma filed a federal lawsuit that accused Target of copyright and trademark infringements. The suit charged that the quilted holiday stocking sold at Target stores contained several distinctive elements of the Williams-Sonoma holiday stocking. Williams-Sonoma also claimed Target copied its reindeer sculpture in a line of reindeer ornaments, candle holders, and a wire-tree votive candle holder Williams-Sonoma referred to as Scary Tree. Williams-Sonoma began to sell their Scary Tree in the Halloween season of 2002.

In 2004, Target introduced a similar Halloween tree-shaped votive holder. Target even placed a testimonial on its Web site from a consumer that noted her friends could not tell the difference between the Target and William-Sonoma votive holders.

The lawsuit suggested that Target made indemnity agreements from vendors who offered the Scary Tree, Spiral Votive Holder, and reindeer products to Target. Williams-Sonoma believes that Target requested these knowing exactly what the products looked like and those agreements were made on condition of continuing business with Target.

This was not the first time Target had been accused of copying the designs of others. Lucky Brand Dungarees, which sells jeans that retail for more than $100 and have been worn by celebrities such as Salma Hayek, also filed a lawsuit in federal court in New York. Target was sued over copying Lucky Brand's distinctive floral design jeans and its rear-pocket stitching. In a response to the lawsuit, Target and its vendor denied the accusations. Target claimed its embroidered floral pattern "represents a mere trivial variation of public designs."

Major Question

Merchandisers and designers constantly look at products developed by their competitors. Would you have knocked off the stocking? Why or why not?

Study Questions

1. Williams-Sonoma believes that Target has intentionally copied Williams-Sonoma's products. Does making an imitation of products originated by the upscale retailer harm the reputation of Williams-Sonoma and its affiliated brands?

2. As competition between retailers intensifies, copyright infringement lawsuits among retailers and designers have increased. If your employer were a major retailer and you were asked to contact a vendor and order a product using the same approach as described (i.e., identical design details to that of a competitor), what would you do?

Bibliography

Scafidi, S. (2007). *On the naughty list*. Retrieved from http://www.counterfeitchic .com/2006/12/on_the_naughty_list.php

Serres, C., & Lundegaard, K. (2006, December 19). Target, known for trendy goods, accused of copying product designs. *Buffalo News,* p. B 9.

CHAPTER DISCUSSION QUESTIONS

1. Discuss why ethics are important issues today in retail management. How is this related to global retailing and manufacturing? How can a company adapt to the ethics of different cultures when doing business with many countries around the world?

2. How can legal behavior and ethics be tied together in retailing and manufacturing? Cite some examples of laws that exemplify this interdependence.

Concepts and Cases in Retail and Merchandise Management

3. Distinguish between morals and ethics. How do they relate to business decision-making? Also, discuss how personal and professional ethics work together and/or separately. Support your rationale with case examples.

4. Discuss how personal and business ethics can be similar or different for various individuals.

5. What is social responsibility for businesses? Why is it important in today's society?

Glossary of Key Terms

A

adjustments are reductions in the cost of goods to the retailer because of problems with the merchandise or because the items were returned. (See Chapter Seven.)

Ad valorem **tariff** is a rate of duty that is based on a percentage of dutiable value. (See Chapter Six. Also see *tariff.*)

advance orders commit the retailer to a long-term delivery. Often imported goods require advance orders, as do seasonal merchandise. (See Chapter Six.)

advertising is any form of paid/impersonal communication from a company. (See Chapter Eight.)

agile manufacturing is a technology that incorporates modular production rather than the traditional piece goods line method and allows for special orders at the last minute without disruption. (See Chapter Six.)

aisle display is a display in which merchandise might be layered and accessorized and then hung at the end of the display case. (See Chapter Eight.)

allocators and *planners* are often included in the merchandising staffs of larger businesses. They work with buyers and their assistants to ensure that the right merchandise gets to the right place at the right time. (See Chapter Five and *Case 26, Planning and Allocation of a Basic Business.*)

allowances are price concessions given by a vendor to a retailer in return for certain actions that the retailer is taking. (See Chapter Seven.)

anchor store is a large retailing establishment that attracts considerable numbers of people to a mall and is usually located at the end of the mall (hence the term "anchor"). (See Chapter Two.)

ancillary services (support services/secondary services) usually include such services as merchandise transfers between stores, gift wrap, valet parking, alterations, and delivery. What is basic service for one store, however, may be ancillary services for another. (See Chapter Nine. Also see *essential services.*)

assortment is the selection of merchandise offered in a store at any given time. Descriptions of assortments are often presented in terms of breadth (i.e., number of styles) and depth (i.e., number of sizes and colors available for each style). (See Chapter Five.)

assortment planning is the plan for mixture of merchandise found in a store. It regards not only what vendors to carry, but the number of units and stock levels, price ranges, styles, sizes, colors, fabrics, and even the level of fashion. (See Chapter Five.)

atmospherics refers to the use of space—virtual or real—to evoke certain effects in a target audience. (See Chapter 3 and *Case 17, A Hunka-Hunka of Burnin' Hot! A Case of Abercrombie & Fitch's Brand and Store Positioning.*)

automatic replenishment describes a quick response in which the retail sales data gathered by computer automatically arranges for stock to be replaced when stock levels are low. (See Chapter Six.)

awards are given as a type of direct compensation, which is based on recognition of a employee's meeting or exceeding a company's goal. In retail organizations, awards are usually given to sales people for exceeding *sales goals.* (See Chapter Nine. Also see *compensation.*)

B

baby boomers are those 76 million Americans born after World War II between the years 1946 and 1964. (See Chapter Three.)

back orders are either full or partial orders that are still outstanding (i.e., not shipped) from the manufacturer, but will be completed when the merchandise (or the balance of the merchandise) is available. (See Chapter Six.)

backward integration is a form of *vertical integration* in which a company acquires another or develops a function that serves as its supplier. As an example of backward integration, The Limited acquired Mast Industries, which manufactures The Limited's apparel. (See Chapter Two.)

bait and switch is a form of deceptive advertising in which a product is promoted at an unrealistically low price to serve as bait to the consumer. After a consumer arrives to buy this advertised product, the retailer attempts to switch the customer to a higher-priced item. (See Chapter Eleven.)

basic service (See *essential service.*)

basics (staples) are products that generally have a stable customer demand. Some examples of basics are pencils, shoelaces, jeans, T-shirts, and hosiery. (See Chapter Four.)

basic stock method is a merchandising method that relies on having a minimum level of stock, as a reserve stock level and also enough stock to meet projected sales each month. Basic stock is equal to the average stock for the season minus the average monthly sales. (See Chapter Five.)

basic stock planning is a system of developing assortment plans that involves staple merchandise. (See Chapter Five.)

better goods are merchandise offerings at price points between *bridge* and *moderate goods.* (See Chapter Four.)

big box store (See *category killer.*)

blanket orders are those that do not have specific information spelled out, but which commit the retailer to a certain number of units or dollars that will be detailed at a later date. (See Chapter Six.)

bonus is an extra monetary reward given to an employee, which is a type of *direct compensation* that is based on recognition of a employee's meeting or exceeding a company's goal. (See Chapter Nine.)

bottom-up planning involves goal setting at the lowest levels of management—and even sometimes non-management—which then filters plans up the organizational structure to the highest management level. (See Chapter Five. Also see *top-down planning.*)

boutique is a small specialty store, often owned or franchised by designers. Boutiques can offer both accessories and apparel. (See Chapter Two.)

brand is a known name associated with a specific product or group of products carrying with it an expectation of such perceived values as style and image, quality, price, fit, reliability, and consistency. (See Chapter Four.)

breadth is a term used to refer to the number of different product lines, styles, or brands that are carried in a retailing establishment. (See Chapter Five.)

bridge lines is a merchandise pricing level between *designer* or couture and *better goods*. (See Chapter Four.)

broad assortment is a term that describes a merchandise assortment featuring numerous styles. (See Chapter Five.)

broadcast media is a type of media that includes television and radio. Broadcast media is used by retailers and manufacturers for advertising and promotion. (See Chapter Eight.)

brokers are *middlemen* who help negotiate business between the buyer (retailer) and seller (manufacturer). (See Chapter Six.)

budget goods are products sold at the most inexpensive price point, usually at discount department stores and mass merchandisers. (See Chapter Four. Also see *opening price point.*)

business ethics are policies (both written and unwritten) that deal with what is right or wrong for a company. These can be part of a company's mission statement or management philosophy. (See Chapter Eleven. Also see *code of ethics* and *corporate ethics.*)

buyer is an individual given formal authority to undertake the purchasing for a retailer. (See Chapter Five.)

buying is the purchasing of goods and/or services for the retailer to sell to the consumer. This function can be separated out as a division, as is most often the case in large organizations, or it may be combined with the operations function, as it often is in smaller companies. (See Chapter Five.)

C

career ladder (See *progressive management advancement.*)

career path (See *progressive management advancement.*)

category is a major grouping of merchandise that includes all types of *departments, classifications,* and *sub-classifications* that a particular type of customer would shop for—for example, women's or men's apparel. (See Chapter Five.)

category killer is a specialty discounter that focuses on one product and has the best selection at the best price. This effectively "kills" the competition. (See Chapter Two.)

cause marketing, or social marketing, refers to a type of marketing where a company publicly supports a socially positive cause in an attempt to widen the company's consumer appeal. (See Chapter Three.)

centralized buying entails focusing all the purchasing activities in one place, where it is initiated and overseen by one individual or a group. Many large retailing chains use centralized buying exclusively. (See Chapter Six. Also see *decentralized buying.*)

chains can be defined as multiple retail units, which are under common ownership and usually have centralized buying and management. (See Chapter Two.)

chain of command (See *organizational charts.*)

charge card is a store credit account that is established in a customer's name and purchases are billed to their address. (See Chapter Nine.)

class (See *classification.*)

classification (class) is a group of items (or the same general type of merchandise that is housed within a department), for example, sportswear or eveningwear. (See Chapter Five.)

closed/closed-back window display is a traditional store window display or enclosure with solid backings that isolate the merchandise to be presented. (See Chapter Eight.)

closed-island display is a type of display in which the merchandise is enclosed (and sometimes locked) behind glass. It provides less customer access, which results in fewer thefts, but also possibly fewer sales because of an intimidation factor. (See Chapter Eight. Also see *showcase display.*)

closeout is an assortment of merchandise that is left over from a seasonal line. Usually closeouts include all remaining items and are sold at a discount. (See Chapter Six.)

code of ethics is a written policy that states what a company has decided is ethical and unethical behavior. (See Chapter Eleven.)

commissions are monetary *awards* based on achievement of goals. These are usually given to salespeople as an incentive to achieve a *sales goal* or to increase sales. Commissions are generally based on a percentage of sales. (See Chapter Nine.)

company rep (corporate rep) is a *sales representative* who works exclusively for a supplier and is a company employee. (See Chapter Seven.)

compensation rewards employees for work they have accomplished and/or goals that they have met or have exceeded. This compensation may be direct or indirect. (See Chapter Nine.)

computer-aided design (CAD) is a computer technology that enables products (e.g., apparel) to be designed and augmented on a computer. This technology can significantly decrease production time for a company. (See Chapter Six.)

computer-aided manufacturing (CAM) is a computer technology that enables manufacturers to significantly decrease production time by using computers to do formerly labor-intensive work. (See Chapter Six.)

consignment is a term used for merchandise not paid for by a retailer until it is sold. Usually the retailer will keep a percentage of the price and the consignee retains the remainder. (See Chapter Ten.)

Consumer Product Safety Commission (CPSC) is an independent regulatory agency charged with overseeing consumer protection. The CPSC regulates flammability requirements of both apparel and home furnishings and monitors other product safety. (See Chapter Eleven.)

contact selling (See *wholesale selling*.)

continuing (ongoing) education can be in the form of seminars or classes, which teach specific job skills or product knowledge. Usually, this type of ongoing training is done as the need arises. (See Chapter One.)

contractor is an independent producer who performs specific aspects of manufacturing, such as sewing, cutting, and finishing. (See Chapter Six.)

controls are the methods employed to help a retailer track the business to see how it is doing and how effective the merchandising strategies are. (See Chapter Five. Also see *Mazur plan*.)

convenience goods are products that are purchased with relatively little evaluation as compared to *shopping goods* and *specialty goods*. (See Chapter Four.)

cooperative advertising normally involves retailers and suppliers sharing the costs of advertising. (See Chapter Eight.)

copyright is protection for original creative writings or works of art. Because fashion is mostly reinterpreted and not considered original, copyrights on apparel are rare. From time to time, an apparel designer will procure a copyright on a design, which is designated on the label by the copyright (©) symbol. (See Chapter Eleven. Also see *patents, trademark* and *intellectual property*.)

corporate ethics refer to practices specific to the company, for example, accepting gifts, kickbacks, or false record-keeping. Sometimes a company's statement of philosophy incorporates its *code of ethics*. (See Chapter Eleven. See also *business ethics*.)

corporate rep (See *company rep*.)

corporation is a firm owned by one or more persons, each of whom has a financial interest. A corporation allows capital to be raised through the sale of company stock and does not allow legal claims against individuals, as is the case with sole proprietorships and partnerships. (See Chapter Two.)

counterfeit is a type of merchandise that violates a company's intellectual property rights. The law states that a protected trademark or copyright cannot be copied and offered for sale by another company. (See Chapter Eleven.)

countertop display is a merchandise display in which the merchandise can be touched and self-selected by the customer. (See Chapter Eight.)

credit is an alternative to paying cash. It allows the customer to buy merchandise now, and pay for it later. There are many national and regional credit companies that issue credit cards that are widely accepted by retailers. (See Chapter Nine.)

customer service is assisting customers by providing retail activities. Prompt and courteous service is what most customers look for from retailers today because this type of effective customer service supplements the value received from a retailer. (See Chapter Nine.)

Customs and Border Protection (CBP), a part of the U.S. Department of Homeland Security, oversees imports to the United States involving *quota safeguards, tariffs,* and *counterfeits*. Its major roles are to collect revenue and to ensure that the trade laws and sanctions that the U.S. government legislates are upheld. (See Chapter Six.)

D

data mining entails electronically tracking product, sales, and customer information to use in a business. (See Chapter Seven.)

dating refers to setting a predetermined amount of time during which discounts can be taken and the invoice is to be paid; for example 8/10 EOM means the retailers can take an eight percent discount if the invoice is paid by the 10th day of the month. (See Chapter Seven.)

decentralized buying centers the purchasing activities at the local or retail-store level. (See Chapter Six. Also see *centralized buying*.)

deep assortment is a term that refers to a merchandise assortment of many colors and sizes. (See Chapter Five.)

demographics are used to identify and count groups of people, including population factors of age, gender, income, education, marital status, religion, family size, life-cycle stage, ethnicity, and mobility, among others. Demographics are used by retailers because they are often linked to market place needs and are relatively easy to access. (See Chapter Three.)

department is a segment of a retailing establishment that groups *classifications* of merchandise together that are complementary to one another, such as a junior department or a men's department. (See Chapter Five.)

department store is a large retailer that carries an extensive assortment of merchandise organized into separate departments. The U.S. Bureau of Census uses three criteria to define department stores: (1) at least 25 employees; (2) must carry dry goods and household items, family apparel, and furniture and home furnishings; and (3) $10 million in sales with some stipulations. Both a traditional department store such as Macy's and a full-line discount store, such as Kmart, qualify for this definition. However, today we often refer to other specialty stores such as Nordstrom and Saks Fifth Avenue as department stores—even though they don't carry furniture. (See Chapter Two.)

depth refers to the number of units within a product line, style, or brand. (See Chapter Five.)

designer collection is the most expensive, high-end line produced by a designer. (See Chapter Four.)

destination store is a type of retailer that a customer frequents because only it can provide the product or service that the customer wants. *Discount Store News* defines this as a "magnet" for customers, distinguishing it from other retailers that customers also patronize. Customers make special efforts to go to destination stores. (See Chapter Two.)

direct compensation (See *compensation.*)

direct mail is used by both retailers and manufacturers to send flyers, catalogs, or other literature to target customers. (See Chapter Eight.)

direct marketing is a broad term that includes many forms of non-personal communication—for example, mailed catalogs, flyers, radio, magazine, and newspapers. It also includes forms of personal communication, such as telemarketing and TV home shopping, in which customers call "800" numbers to order merchandise. (See Chapters Two and Eight.)

direct selling involves direct sales contact with the customer. This includes two major kinds of selling: (1) *wholesale selling;* and (2) *retail selling.* (See Chapter Nine.)

discounts lower the retail price for a consumer. At retail establishments, discounts are commonly given to employees and special customers. (See Chapter Five.)

discount stores sell merchandise at prices lower than other traditional department and specialty stores due to lower operating costs. Generally, they offer self-service and large quantity purchases to lower costs. Kmart and Wal-Mart are considered discount stores. (See Chapter Two.)

division is the largest breakdown of merchandise for a retailer. It contains *categories, departments, classifications,* and *sub-classifications.* Examples of divisions are: soft goods, hard goods, women's and children's. (See Chapter Five.)

dollar plans forecast the merchandising activities for a department or store for a specific period of time. Dollar planning is regarded as the money budget preparation of retail dollars to meet sales plans. (See Chapter Five.)

domestic market refers to a market in the continental U.S., such as New York City. (See Chapter Six. Also see *international market* and *regional market.*)

domestic source/sourcing is the purchasing of merchandise within the borders of the U.S. (See Chapter Six. Also see *international source/sourcing, sourcing.*)

drop shippers take title for merchandise, but do not take actual possession of the goods. A drop shipper merely arranges shipment of the goods to the retailer. (See Chapter Six.)

duty (See *tariff*.)

E

e-commerce includes individual retail Web sites, such as www.macys.com and www.landsend.com, and Internet portals, such as www.fashionmall.com, which tie together a large variety of sites. (See Chapter Two. Also see *non-stored retailers*.)

electronic data interchange (EDI) is a communications system that electronically transfers information from one point to another via computer. An important application is the transfer of purchase orders between manufacturers and retailers. This is one way that vendors and retailers can respond instantaneously to quickly changing consumer demands. (See Chapter Five.)

electronic retailing (e-tailing) offers products through such electronic media as the Internet and television. (See Chapter Nine.)

embargos are legal bans on trade with certain countries that may prevent a company from importing exactly the products that they need or want. (See Chapter Six.)

employee turnover describes the percentage of employees that begin with a company at a certain time period but do not remain employed at the end of that set time period. This percentage figure is usually calculated on an annual basis. (See Chapter Nine.)

entrepreneur/entrepreneurial leader is a person who is a leader, is a visionary, and has the ability to see and evaluate business opportunities, bringing together the factors of production in such a way that new wealth is created as their business grows. (See Chapter Ten. Also see *leaders* and *leadership*.)

entrepreneurial process can be seen in one of five ways: (1) introduction of a new product or of improved quality; (2) introduction of a new method of production; (3) opening of a new market; (4) conquest of a new source of supply of materials; and (5) carrying out a new organization of an industry. (See Chapter Ten.)

environmental factors come from both an internal (inside) and external (outside) perspective. External environmental factors include aspects of technology, the economy, society, and culture, along with political and legal issues that impact the business and the customer being considered. Internal environmental factors include information from store records to the store's particular culture and vendors. (See Chapter Five.)

environmentally friendly is a term that refers to products that are made with an attempt to incorporate only environmentally safe methods and materials in its production. (See Chapter Eleven.)

essential services (primary services/basic services) are those services that most retailers provide—for example, dressing rooms, parking, and someone to ring up your sale pleasantly. (See Chapter Nine. Also see *ancillary services*.)

ethics are rules or standards based on moral duties and obligations by which society evaluates conduct. They provide criteria for distinguishing between right and wrong. (See Chapter Eleven. Also see *business ethics, code of ethics, corporate ethics,* and *personal ethics*.)

evaluations (of sales associates) help to monitor their work and also informs the employee of job performance. Additionally, the evaluation of a salesperson's performance can aid in bettering the work that is done and this contributes to the improvement of the retailer's performance. Evaluating salespeople should include a performance review on a regular basis. (See Chapter Nine. Also see *formal reviews* and *informal reviews*.)

even priced is a term used for prices ending with numbers that can be divided evenly. Odd price point endings, such as .95 or .99, often reflect sale merchandise, while .00 or evenly divisible numbers usually indicate non-sale prices. (See Chapter Five.)

exclusive contractor is a supplier that only works for a particular company. (See Chapter Six.)

exclusive orders are those orders that are placed for merchandise that can only be sold to one particular store or buyer. Exclusive merchandise is usually a special arrangement between vendor and retailer. (See Chapter Six.)

expenses are the costs incurred by a business to generate sales. (See Chapter Five.)

extrinsic rewards are those tied to material gain—for example, raises, promotions, and recognition within a company. (See Chapter One. Also see *intrinsic rewards*.)

F

factory outlet is a manufacturer-owned store that sells the manufacturer's close-outs, overruns, canceled orders, discontinued items, and irregulars. (See Chapter Two.)

factory outlet mall is a mall composed of several *factory outlet* stores. (See Chapter Two.)

fair trade laws formerly protected the small retailer from larger retailers when both were selling the same goods at the same price, since large retailers were not allowed to receive a discount for quantity purchases. In 1975, the Consumer Goods Pricing Act repealed all resale price maintenance laws and enabled retailers to sell products below the suggested retail prices that were set by manufacturers. Although this ended protection for the small retailer, it allowed consumers to buy at the lowest possible free-market price. (See Chapter Eleven.)

fashion cycle (product life cycle) represents the stages of a product's life cycle and the adoption level of consumers of a particular style at each stage. (See Chapter Three.)

fashion followers are consumers who adopt a new fashion after the *fashion leaders* do; they are also sometimes called emulators. (See Chapter Three.)

fashion forward is a term used to describe designers, retailers, consumers, and merchandise that represent the newest, latest styles. (See Chapter Three.)

fashion goods are thought of as something new, in demand, or popular—at any particular time. They are less stable, have a short life span, and therefore are more risky (financially) than basics. (See Chapter Four.)

fashion leaders are the first group of consumers to adopt new fashions. (See Chapter Three. Also see *fashion followers* and *fashion forward.*)

fashion seminars involve discussions of new fashions in order to attract audiences into stores and malls, and to promote new, seasonal merchandise. (See Chapter Eight.)

fashion shows are live presentations of new, seasonal merchandise. (See Chapter Eight.)

fast fashion is a term used in the retail industry that refers to low-priced, fashionable items that are expected to have a short life span.

Federal Trade Commission (FTC) is an independent regulatory agency charged with overseeing the area of consumer protection and restraint of trade. Within the purview of the FTC are labeling requirements for apparel. (See Chapter Eleven.)

financial plans are part of merchandising plans that include estimates of start-up costs and the amount of financing required. A financial plan should include performance objectives, estimated sales, and cash flow. (See Chapter Ten.)

financier (See *venture capitalist.*)

first-line, entry level managers are the lowest level of management and include supervisors and assistant managers. (See Chapter One.)

Food and Drug Administration (FDA) is a federal agency that is responsible for regulating the food, drug, and cosmetics industries in regard to the safety and disclosure of product ingredients. (See Chapter Eleven.)

forecasting is a term used to describe the prediction of styles and trends. These predictions assist retailers in making both long- and short-term merchandising decisions. (See Chapter Five.)

formal management training is usually supervised or directed, and follows a program that involves the accomplishment of certain set goals. Training can involve working with new employees or can entail working with established employees who may be changing positions. (See Chapter One. Also see *informal management training.*)

formal reviews involve time set aside on a periodic basis to meet one-on-one with a salesperson to review his or her job performance and accomplishments. (See Chapter Nine. Also see *evaluation [of sales associate]* and *informal reviews.*)

formal (structured) evaluation (See *management evaluation/review.*)

formal training is structured training that involves teaching specific tasks, methods, and/or other objectives. This method of training relies on a person(s) and/or written instructions, which is used to relay the information to be taught. (See Chapter Nine. Also see *informal training.*)

forward integration is a form of *vertical integration* in which a company acquires another company or develops a function that serves as its customer. Examples include manufacturers that have retail outlets for their products. (See Chapter Two.)

franchise is a contractual arrangement between a franchisor (the entity selling its name) and a franchisee (the owner). A franchise combines independent ownership with franchisor-management assistance, which includes a well-known name and image. The franchisee pays royalties for the privilege of using the company name. (See Chapter Two.)

free trade is a concept subscribed to, in varying degrees, by most business and government officials and describes a form of trade without significant restrictions or barriers. (See Chapter Six.)

full service is a type of overall customer service that is provided to the customer by a retail establishment. Full service implies the maximum amount of services that can be expected. These services include *essential* and *ancillary services,* as well as all possible *transactional services.* (See Chapter Nine.)

G

General Agreement on Tariffs and Trade (GATT) is a multinational agreement regarding global trade policies. In international trade of textiles and apparel, GATT allows for the use of *tariffs* to protect domestic industries and for quantitative limits *(quotas)* on the entry of certain textile and apparel merchandise into the United States from specified countries during a specified period of time. (See Chapter Six.)

generation X (Gen X) is a term used to describe the population group born following the *baby boomers.* (See Chapter Three.)

generation Y (Gen Y) is a term used to describe the population group born immediately following Generation X. (See Chapter Three.)

gray market goods describes merchandise that is not illegal, but is an unauthorized import. Often such goods are sold at discounters with no warranty or with older dates than those through authorized channels. (See Chapter Eleven.)

gross margin is the difference between the net sales and the cost of goods sold and usually is an indicator of profit. (See Chapter Five.)

guarantee is issued by a manufacturer and ensures that a product will perform as it is supposed to or the customer will be compensated. (See Chapter Nine. Also see *warranty.*)

H

hard goods include home furnishings, appliances, electronics, and so forth. (See Chapter Four. Also see *soft goods.*)

hierarchical structure (See *organizational charts.*)

high fashion is apparel that is produced and priced for the small percentage of the population who want something new and different from mass fashion, with the added panache of exclusivity. High fashion products are generally high-priced because of these factors. (See Chapter Four.)

home party is a non-stored retailing format consisting of merchandise showings in the home to guests or customers. (See Chapter Two.)

horizontal integration is one company buying, merging, or forming another company that is different from its customer or supplier. (See Chapter Two.)

human resources department (personnel department) often plays a major role in training and evaluating the retailer's sales personnel, particularly when the retailer is large enough to have a separate division or department for this function. Four major areas are usually allocated to the human resource function: recruiting, training, evaluating, and rewarding. Hiring and firing may also be done centrally by this department. (See Chapter Nine.)

I

identity is a consistent, well-articulated company mission, including the nature, purpose, and direction of the company. (See Chapter Three.)

image is a term used to describe the perception customers have of a company or a product. (See Chapter Three.)

imports are goods and services that are purchased from other countries. (See Chapter Six.)

impulse goods are goods that are purchased with little or no planning on the part of the consumer. (See Chapter Four.)

income statement (See *profit and loss statement.*)

independent buying offices are owned and operated separately from their client retailers. Their functions can also include forecasting, finance, personnel, advertising and promotion, as well as providing consultation services and the manufacture of private-label merchandise. (See Chapter Six. Also see *resident buying office, store owned buying office.*)

independent rep is a *sales representative* who may be under contract to a specific company as their sales agent, but who may also represent other firms and is paid a commission on sales. (See Chapter Seven.)

independent store is a single retailing unit owned by an individual or a group of individuals, but is not connected to any chain of stores. (See Chapter Two.)

indirect compensation involves non-monetary rewards given to employees, which can include paid vacations, paid insurance, parking, retirement, and other *perks*. (See Chapter Nine. Also see *direct compensation*.)

informal management training is a type of training in which managers are expected to learn "on-the-job," and to take the initiative themselves for learning how to perform successfully. (See Chapter One. Also see *formal management training*.)

informal reviews consist of feedback given at any time it is needed. Some experts believe that this is the more effective means of evaluation, because it is given at the same time as the incident that warrants the feedback. (See Chapter Nine. Also see *management evaluation* and *formal reviews*.)

informal training relies on employees learning skills as they work (i.e., on-the-job training) and as they need to learn specific skills. In this type of training, employees are often solely responsible for learning what they believe they need, rather than what their employer thinks is necessary. (See Chapter Nine. Also see *formal training*.)

informal (unstructured) evaluation (See *management evaluation*.)

information technology (IT) is a general term that describes all data and facts that may be captured electronically. (See Chapter One.)

institutional advertising is concerned with building a company's reputation or *image* rather than selling a product. Institutional advertising may illustrate the good deeds a company is doing in the community, the services it offers, or the prestige it maintains or desires. (See Chapter Eight.)

intangible services are those abstract activities provided by a retail establishment that cannot be touched physically—for example, assistance with decision-making and merchandise selection. (See Chapter Nine. Also see *tangible services*.)

intellectual property includes *patents, copyrights,* and *trademarks*. Infringement of any of these is illegal. (See Chapter Eleven.)

interior product displays help customers locate merchandise and can illustrate how the merchandise is used or worn. They include *counter top* or *point-of-purchase* *displays, showcase displays, wall* or *ledge displays, aisle displays, open selling displays,* and *closed-island displays.* (See Chapter Eight.)

international market is a market that could be located anywhere in the world and that draws buyers from around the world. Paris, London, Milan, and Tokyo are just a few of the larger international markets. (See Chapter Six. Also see *domestic market* and *regional market.*)

international source/sourcing is the process of buying of goods *offshore,* from countries other than the United States. (See Chapter Six. Also see *import, domestic source/sourcing, sourcing.*)

internships are structured methods of training employees to become managers while students are still enrolled in college. Management/executive training and internship training can be classroom and/or on-the-job, at headquarters and/or at the retail store level. (See Chapter One.)

intrinsic rewards are those personal rewards that are given to employees and which fill that individual's needs such as self-esteem. (See Chapter One. Also see *extrinsic rewards.*)

inventory (stock) planning entails the determination of the stock levels necessary to meet the sales plan. Note: the terms inventory and stock are used interchangeably. (See Chapter Five. Also see *basic stock planning* and *model stock planning.*)

J

jobber is a resource that sells *closeouts* and *job lots.* (See Chapter Six.)

job description (See *job roles.*)

job lot is a group of merchandise that includes the odds and ends of remaining styles that a manufacturer wants to sell. Often it consists of broken sizes, colors, and/or styles and is sold at a considerable discount as a group. (See Chapter Six.)

job promotion occurs when an employee is advanced into a higher level position. (See Chapter One. Also see *progressive management advancement.*)

job roles designate the part an employee plays for an employer, while job descriptions spell out these roles and clarify them. Job titles may also help to identify those roles and responsibilities a particular position denotes. (See Chapter One.)

job title (See *job roles.*)

joint venture describes an arrangement between an international and a domestic company that join together to form a new company. Join ventures are often instigated by the laws of some countries, such as China and India, where international retailers are allowed to own only a percentage of any domestic company. (See Chapter Two and *Case 12, To Commit or Not: The Indian Retail Affair.*)

just-in-time (JIT) is a concept used in manufacturing to lessen costly inventories. On-line communications and partnerships with suppliers enable fabric and other supplies to be delivered to the manufacturing site "just-in-time" for production. (See Chapter Six.)

K

key resource list (See *vendor matrix.*)

keystone markup is a *markup* that doubles the cost of the merchandise. Essentially, it is a 50 percent retail markup. (See Chapter Five.)

kickback is an illegal return of a portion of monies received in a business deal that has been prompted by a threat or secret agreement. (See Chapter Eleven.)

kiosk is a small stationary facility used as advertising venue or sometimes has the capability of customers ordering merchandise via computer. (See Chapter Two. Also see *interactive kiosk.*)

knockoff is a copy of a new (or *fashion forward*) style that has been accepted by consumers. It is usually made with less-expensive fabrication and detailing and is produced and sold at lower-price points. (See Chapter Three.)

L

leaders are people who have qualities and/or abilities that emerge to influence and direct others. Common characteristics of a leader include having a realistic, clear vision of a goal, the means to accomplish it, and the ability and means to communicate the vision to inspire others. (See Chapter One.)

leadership is the process of moving a group in a direction that is in their long-term best interests. Leaders must demonstrate strength and the ability to carry followers. (See Chapter Ten. Also see *entrepreneur/entrepreneurial leader.*)

lead time refers to the amount of time that lapses between the placement of an order and the arrival of the merchandise at the retail establishment. (See Chapter Six.)

ledge display utilizes dead or unused store ledge space to display merchandise. (See Chapter Eight.)

licensed goods carry the name of a famous person, character, or company. In this arrangement, a company allows a marketer to sell a product with its registered trademark or logo (for example, Mickey Mouse nightshirts). (See Chapter Four.)

lifestyle brand describes complementary products that fit into every part of a consumer's life. (See Chapter Four.)

limited assortment store (See *specialty store*.)

limited service provides a modicum of assistance to the customer beyond the *self-service* level, but still in restricted amounts. For example, a store that has hours from 10 to 5, has a small sales staff, takes credit cards, does not gift wrap or deliver merchandise but has alterations available can be described as having limited service. (See Chapter Nine. Also see *full service*.)

line (See *organizational charts*.)

long-range planning entails looking toward the future for a business and projects goals of five or more years. (See Chapter Five.)

loss leader is a term used to describe merchandise that is priced at or below cost in order to attract customers. (See Chapter Five.)

loyalty programs encourage customers to continue to patronize a company by offering incentives. An example of a well-known type of loyalty program would be an airline's frequent-flyer program. (See Chapter Nine.)

M

magazines are publications that are generally geared to a national audience and provide good-quality, expensive print and color for ads. Many national magazines produce regional editions in which an ad can be targeted to local retailers. (See Chapter Eight.)

mail order is a form of non-store retailing in which customers typically purchase products from a catalog. Mail order can be an extension of a store's business. (See Chapter Two.)

mail selling (See *retail selling*.)

management is the process of getting activities completed efficiently and effectively with and through other people. A business usually has at least three management aspects: (1) the business; (2) the employees; and (3) the operations. (See Chapter One.)

management by objectives (MBO) is a method of *management evaluation* that is a way of involving managers in monitoring their own progress and success on the job. In this method, *managers* play an active part in setting their own *management* goals. (See Chapter One.)

management by walking around is a *management* technique that places the *manager* in the work site, interacting directly with employees. (See Chapter One.)

management evaluation/review should be conducted by the manager's immediate supervisor as a means to communicate how that manager is performing. These evaluations can be formal evaluations and/or informal evaluations and should provide feedback on the work that is being completed. (See Chapter One.)

management information systems (MIS) are software programs utilized to plan, organize, and monitor a business and its employees. (See Chapter One.)

managers are the people who have been given formal authority and power to direct, supervise, and motivate employees to complete those activities that ensure that a company's needs are met. (See Chapter One.)

manufacturers offer goods for sale that they have produced. Manufacturers are also referred to as vendors, suppliers, or resources, and these terms often are used interchangeably. (See Chapter Six.)

markdown is a lowering of a retail price. This can be either promotional or permanent and will either adjust the initial retail price downward temporarily or set a new retail price, respectively. (See Chapter Five.)

market is the actual physical place where the retail buyer and seller come together to purchase or sell goods and services. This marketplace may be at a *merchandise mart* or *trade show*, or even a specific city site as in New York City. A market may also refer to a time when buyers and manufacturers come together, such as the Spring market. (See Chapter Six.)

market calendar publicizes the dates (called market weeks) and locations of trade shows and markets that are available. (See Chapter Six.)

marketing plan is a part of a business plan that includes an analysis of the business environment that should support the definition of the designated target market. (See Chapter Ten.)

market week (See *market calendar.*)

markon (See *markup.*)

markup cancellations adjust the amount of *markup* that was put on an item originally, thereby lowering the retail price. (See Chapter Five.)

markup (markon) is the difference between the manufacturer's cost and the retail price offered to the customer. To realize profit, a retailer must sell merchandise for more than it costs. (See Chapter Five.)

mass customization allows for individualized sizing to be incorporated into regular mass production. (See Chapter Six.)

mass fashion appeals to the majority of consumers and is produced and distributed at moderate or *opening price points* at both discount and department stores. Consumers who buy mass fashion are not *fashion leaders,* but still want to be in fashion. (See Chapter Four.)

mass merchandiser is a large discount store that serves the mass market. (See Chapter Two.)

Mazur plan divides retail activities into four divisional areas. Descriptions of the responsibilities of the four major retail divisions are: (1) merchandising, which is the buying and selling of goods and services for a profit. This includes the planning, pricing, and control of sales and inventory; (2) publicity, which is concerned with promotion and advertising, display, special events, and public relations; (3) store (operations) management, which involves the operations of the retail store, selling, customer service, and all such physical concerns for the store as maintenance and security; (4) accounting and control (finance), which is concerned with all the financial aspects of the business, including credit, collection, budgets, control, and bookkeeping. (See Chapter One.)

merchandise budget is a monetary plan that forecasts the merchandising activities for a department or store for a specific period of time. (See Chapter Five.)

merchandise mart is a trade center built to house manufacturer's representatives and provide a center for retailers and manufacturers to come together to do business. Major marts are located in such metropolitan areas as Dallas, Atlanta, and Chicago. Secondary marts are located in such smaller cities as Charlotte, Pittsburgh, and Seattle. (See Chapter Six.)

merchandise mix (See *assortment.*)

merchandise planning is a broad term that describes those retailing activities that are based in planning. It directly involves the five "rights" of merchandising that Mazur brought to our attention. These are: purchasing the right merchandise, at the right time, at the right place, in the right quantities, and at the right price. (See Chapter Five.)

merchandiser (See *purchasing agent.*)

merchandising is the buying and selling of goods and/or services for the purpose of making a profit. (See Chapter Five. Also see *Mazur plan.*)

middleman is a term used to describe an agent who processes goods in one way or another from the manufacturer to the retail distributor. For example, a manufacturer produces a garment and does not do the finishing or packaging but sends the garment to another company (the middleman) for these steps. (See Chapter Six.)

middle manager is a management position that includes department heads, managers, and buyers. (See Chapter One.)

minimum orders designate a specific amount of merchandise that must be purchased from a vendor in order to place an order. (See Chapter Seven.)

misleading advertising is a form of consumer deception and is illegal. If a manufacturer's claims are untrue or misleading, a cease and desist order can be issued by the *Federal Trade Commission,* putting a halt to such claims. (See Chapter Eleven.)

model stock planning sets a determination of merchandise levels according to factors important to the buyer—for example, fabric, price, style, and so forth. A model stock plan is for fashion and/or seasonal merchandise within a particular merchandise category. (See Chapter Five.)

moderate goods are lower in price and quality than better goods and are sold at many department stores. (See Chapter Four.)

mom-and-pop store is a small, privately owned, independent store that is owned and operated by the proprietor with perhaps a few employees. Often these stores are run by a husband and wife, hence "mom and pop." (See Chapter Two.)

morale refers to the state of enthusiasm and happiness of employees. It is often very difficult—if not impossible—to keep all employees happy, because of the nature of individuality. (See Chapter One.)

moral obligations (See *prima facie duties.*)

motivation is the drive to stimulate action. *Managers* are usually responsible for motivating others, based on the needs or goals of the company. Often motivation is tied to rewarding the employee. (See Chapter One. Also see *extrinsic rewards* and *intrinsic rewards.*)

Multifiber Arrangement (MFA) was the general framework for international textile trade that originally operated under the authority of *General Agreement on Tariffs and Trade* and allowed for the establishment of bilateral agreements between trading partners. (See Chapter Six.)

N

narrow assortment refers to a type of assortment plan characterized by offering relatively few different styles. (See Chapter Five.)

national advertising refers to manufacturers advertising directly to consumers. (See Chapter Eight. Also see *retail advertising* and *trade advertising*).

negotiations can result in a settlement and mutual agreement between two or more parties on any matter. This settlement is based on communication and the satisfaction of a goal of one or more of the parties. From a retailer's or manufacturer's perspective, negotiations are often undertaken to solve problems, resolve conflicts, reduce costs, and/or improve profit. (See Chapter Seven.)

niche is a term used to describe a narrowly defined customer segment. Because niches have very specific needs, niche retailers offer deep assortments of one particular type of merchandise. (See Chapter Three.)

nonseasonal goods are products that sell steadily year-round. (See Chapter Four.)

non-stored retailers include such nontraditional ways of selling merchandise as e-commerce, television shopping, mail order, direct marketing, home parties, kiosks, and temporary retailers. (See Chapter Two.)

O

odd priced goods have prices ending with an odd number. Odd price point endings, such as .95 or .99, often reflect sale merchandise, while .00 or evenly divisible numbers usually indicate non-sale prices. (See Chapter Five.)

off-price orders are orders that are placed for merchandise that is purchased at a price below the regular line price. Usually, this is regular merchandise being sold later in the season, or is surplus merchandise. (See Chapter Six.)

off-price store sells *brand* merchandise at lower than department store prices due to low overhead and such special purchases as overruns or end-of-the-season merchandise. (See Chapter Two.)

offshore is a term used to describe buying or manufacturing goods in countries other than the United States. (See Chapter Six. Also see *international source/sourcing* and *imports.*)

ongoing education (See *continuing education.*)

online advertising is advertising that is accessed via the Internet. (See Chapter Eight.)

on order refers to goods that have been ordered but have not yet arrived. (See Chapter Five.)

on-the-job training (See *informal management training* and *informal training.*)

open-door policy is a practice in which a superior (manager) allows employees to interact with him or her—as the need arises—as if his or her office door was always open. (See Chapter One.)

opening price point is the most inexpensive, low-end price point. (See Chapter Four. Also see *budget goods.*)

open orders allow a manufacturer the discretion of shipping merchandise when deemed necessary, rather than locking into a set delivery date. Open orders may also specify a dollar amount that must be purchased, but not always the specific styles, sizes, or colors. (See Chapter Six.)

open-selling displays are those that enable customer self-service. They do, however, create a greater risk of merchandise being shoplifted. (See Chapter Eight.)

open-to-buy (OTB) is an adjustment to the planned purchases that takes into account what is already *on order* (i.e., what is due in). It is calculated on a frequent basis and aids the buyer in making necessary adjustments throughout the season to help control inventories and profitability. (See Chapter Five.)

open window displays enable the viewer to see directly into the store through the street window display. (See Chapter Eight.)

organizational charts are used by many retailers to model the structure of their companies. These charts depict the hierarchical structure (pecking order), chain of command (who reports to whom), and the relationship between the parts of the company and the whole through line (direct authority and responsibility) and staff (advisory and support) components. Usually the divisions, departments, and even positions within an organization are pictured on a company's organizational chart along with who reports to whom. (See Chapter One. Also see *Mazur plan*.)

organizational structure describes how a company is set up and directed. The organizational structure aids in monitoring and managing work to be done by assigning accountability for that work. This, in turn, facilitates companies to reach their objectives and goals. To aid in this, *organizational charts* are used by many retailers to model the structure of their companies. (See Chapter One.)

outdoor advertising includes billboards, the roving billboard, and posters at train and bus stations, and on the buses, trains, and subways. In larger cities, *kiosks* are also used to advertise retailers, manufacturers, banks, performances, and other city events. (See Chapter Eight.)

over-the-counter selling (See *retail selling*.)

P

partnership is a term that can refer a firm owned by two or more persons, each of whom has a financial interest. A partnership is also a working relationship that is formed to achieve a goal, which is mutually beneficial. Today, vendor and retail planning is often part of a partner relationship, because managing merchandise is no longer just the retailer's job. (See Chapters Two and Seven.)

patents grant to the inventor of a product or process the right for 17 years to exclude others from making, using, or selling that invention. The patent applicant makes a complete disclosure of the invention, which is published and which moves into the public domain when the patent expires. (See Chapter Eleven.)

percentage variation method is a stock method that determines stock for a high turnover rate (six or more per year). This method allows for stock fluctuation and is based on the premise that the variation of monthly stock from average stock should be half as much as the percentage variation in monthly sales from average sales. (See Chapter Five.)

performance review (See *evaluation*.)

periodic inventory is a method of stock control in which the retailer physically counts merchandise at designated time periods. Many apparel retailers take periodic inventories twice a year, in July and January. (See Chapter Five.)

perk is a non-monetary reward that expresses gratitude for work done or a position that is held by the employee. Free lunches or the right to use a company-owned vacation home are sometimes given as perks. (See Chapter Nine. Also see *indirect compensation.*)

permanent markdowns refer to permanent lowering of the initial retail price, setting a new retail price. (See Chapter Five.)

perpetual inventory is a term that describes a type of stock control method that provides a continuous record of the movement of incoming and outgoing merchandise. (See Chapter Five.)

personal ethics deal with an individual's own personal beliefs and principles, as opposed to the company's *code of ethics.* (See Chapter Eleven. Also see *business ethics* and *corporate ethics.*)

personnel department (See *human resources department.*)

planned purchases are the difference between what is needed and what is on hand. The amount of planned purchases that is projected is based on the planned sales, beginning of month (BOM) and end of month (EOM) inventory levels desired, and the amount of reductions that are being planned. (See Chapter Five.)

planners (See *allocators.*)

planning is a means of control that helps to provide the buyer with information to make the best decisions in purchasing, which generally results in a profit. (See Chapter Five.)

point-of-purchase displays are displays in which the merchandise can be touched and self-selected by the customer. (See Chapter Eight.)

point of sale (POS) is technology that retailers use to track inventory and sales by the use of computer software programs that are implemented at the point of sale (i.e., traditionally the cash register). These information systems and communications technologies have improved retail productivity and profits. (See Chapter Five.)

policies set governance guidelines and rules as to specific ways in which a company wants to accomplish its goals. (See Chapter Nine. Also see *procedures.*)

pop-up retail describes a form of temporary store often utilized by larger retailers. (See Chapter Two.)

positioning refers to the image of a company relative to its competition in the marketplace. (See Chapter Three.)

predatory pricing is a situation in which a retailer prices a product below cost with the intent to drive out any competition, which is illegal. Not all below-cost selling is illegal or considered predatory pricing, as some end-of-season goods are sold at a loss to clear out old merchandise. (See Chapter Eleven.)

prepack is an assortment of merchandise that is chosen according to a manufacturer's or retailer's direction. This predetermined choice directs that a certain amount of sizes and/or colors of a style or styles are shipped to the retailer. (See Chapter Six.)

preprints (See *tabloid inserts.*)

price discrimination occurs when two retailers buy identical merchandise from the same supplier but pay different prices. The purpose of the law against price discrimination is to protect competition by ensuring that retailers are treated fairly by suppliers. (See Chapter Eleven.)

price fixing creates monopolies, is illegal, and is a restraint of trade. It occurs when a group of competing retailers (horizontal price fixing) or a retailer and manufacturer (vertical price fixing) agree to maintain the price of merchandise. Vertical price fixing is called price maintenance, which is a violation of the Sherman Antitrust Act. (See Chapter Eleven.)

price maintenance laws (See *fair trade laws.*)

pricing strategy is the determination of the type of pricing policy a buyer or retailer will use along with the practices the buyer or retailer will employ. It involves understanding not only who the target customer is and what their needs and/or wants are, but also a number of other such factors as the image and identity that a retailer wants to project. (See Chapter Five.)

***prima facie* duties (moral obligations)** include such responsibilities as keeping promises, telling the truth, honoring warranties, abiding by agreements or understood guidelines, not taking abnormal credit extensions or making unjust retail cancellations, and ensuring product safety. (See Chapter Eleven. Also see *business ethics, code of ethics, corporate ethics,* and *personal ethics.*)

primary service (See *essential service.*)

primary trading area is the area in which a retailer can serve its customers better in terms of convenience and location than its competitors. A primary trading area usually extends three to five miles from the site, while a *secondary trading area can* be seven or more miles away. (See Chapter Eight.)

print media includes newspapers, magazines, flyers, and direct mail. (See Chapter Eight.)

private label is a term used to describe goods that are produced and named by the retailer that sells them. Private labels may carry names other than the store's name, however, unlike *store brands*. (See Chapter Four.)

prizes (See *awards* and *compensation*.)

procedures are the methods—or steps—and therefore the means for a company to reach a goal. A company's procedures should be within the established policy guidelines. (See Chapter Nine. Also see *policies*.)

product advertising promotes immediate consumer action—that is, the ad urges the consumer to come into the store and buy that product. Product ads are designed to sell products rather than promote a company's *image*. (See Chapter Eight. Also see *institutional advertising*.)

product differentiation distinguishes a product from a competitor's in order to avoid competing for the same customer. (See Chapter Three.)

product knowledge educates sales associates, which enables them to educate their customers, help interpret customer's needs, and, in turn (through the sale of that product), provide for those needs. Information about a product often sells the merchandise. (See Chapter Nine.)

product life cycle (See *fashion cycle*.)

product manager is one of the titles that can be given to an individual who has been granted buying authority at the manufacturing level. (See Chapter Five. Also see *buyer, merchandiser, purchasing agent,* and *sourcing agent*.)

professional ethics identify what is ethical and unethical behavior within a particular industry. Trade associations often have a written code of professional ethics. (See Chapter Eleven. Also see *business ethics, code of ethics, corporate ethics,* and *personal ethics*.)

profit results when operating expenses are less than the *gross margin*. (See Chapter Five.)

profit and loss statement (P&L) summarizes the financial workings of a business during a certain period of time and documents whether or not there is a profit or loss. (See Chapter Five.)

progressive management advancement is the most common way for employees to be promoted within a company. An employee moves through the management level ranks of a company to higher levels by phases and structured management training programs. (See Chapter One.)

promotional campaigns attempt to communicate a message to consumers in various ways. These can include: television, online, radio and print advertising, store and/or mall signage, and articles written in local newspapers about an event. (See Chapter Eight.)

promotional markdowns are temporary reductions in the initial retail price. (See Chapter Five.)

promotional mix is a term used to describe a company's use of the various advertising and promotional venues. It can also include personal selling, advertising, displays, publicity, and/or special events. (See Chapter Eight.)

promotional orders are orders that are placed for goods at a better-than-regular manufacturer's cost. These are often special purchases from vendors that can be promoted by the retailer at a savings to the customer. (See Chapter Six.)

promotional plan is a determination of what percent of the budget will be spent on various types of promotion in the appropriate media. Often a percentage of sales is used to determine the amount to be spent on promotion. That amount would be divided among television, magazine, and newspaper ads, special events, publicity, displays, and other general promotion items. (See Chapter Eight.)

promotional pricing means offering goods at sale prices. (See Chapter Five.)

proportionality framework describes an area of ethical decision-making relating to decisions that focus on actions rather than consequences, that is, the ends do not justify the means. For example, high profits should not be achieved by deceiving, customers or by exploiting employees. (See Chapter Eleven.)

proprietary software refers to systems that are designed specifically for a company and its needs. (See Chapter One.)

psychographics is a term used to describe data that is related to the activities, interests, and opinions of the target consumer. (See Chapter Three.)

publicity is information reported in the media by a source outside the company with no vested interest. This is the primary method of generating unpaid communications. (See Chapter Eight.)

public relations is a part of a corporate structure that is responsible for creating public impressions about the company. They are responsible for press releases and press conferences to release facts about a company. (See Chapter Eight.)

purchase order (PO) is the legal contract that binds the buyer and seller. All pertinent information that must be relayed between the two parties for the purchasing of merchandise should be contained on this document. Purchase orders ensure that what the retailer wants is being requested, and they also verify any special requests that have been negotiated. (See Chapter Seven.)

purchasing refers to *buying* at the manufacturing level—i.e., obtaining the materials to make the end product. (See Chapter Five.)

purchasing agent is the individual given buying authority at the manufacturing level. Sometimes this position is called a merchandiser or sourcing agent. (See Chapter Five.)

push money (See *spiffs.*)

Q

quality is often thought of as "degree of excellence." In apparel, quality is determined by many aspects and is comprised of many aesthetic and functional features. Aesthetics include appearance, fit, design, fabrication, construction, and details or decoration. Functional features include such attributes as durability and serviceability. (See Chapter Four.)

quality control is done at the fabric manufacture, garment manufacture, and retail levels. Normally, the manufacturer is responsible for checking the quality of materials before production. (See Chapter Four.)

quick response (QR) shortens the pipeline of getting a product from its conception to the consumer by capitalizing on *electronic data interchange*. Quick response was developed as a strategy to fight imports because domestic manufacturers have the advantage of proximity to the marketplace over the offshore manufacturer. (See Chapter Six.)

quota is the limit to the number of units of specified merchandise permitted to be brought into a country for consumption during a specific period of time. (See Chapter Six. Also see *safeguards/safeguard quotas.*)

R

records are documents or electronic data that help management to follow and guide businesses to success. Retailers generate various reports to help monitor their businesses, which may include many types of planning reports and records. Reports on units, dollars, assortment, pricing, fast or slow sellers, sell-through analysis, vendors, and other information desired are frequently used methods of retail control. (See Chapter Five.)

reductions are a provision used by retailers to reduce the retail price of merchandise and to encourage the sale of stock so that it can be replaced with fresh, new goods. *Markdowns, markup cancellations,* and *discounts* are all types of reductions that a retailer should plan to incur. (See Chapter Five.)

regional market is a smaller type of market that serves U.S. retailers as a geographical convenience. Atlanta, Dallas, and Los Angeles are examples of regional markets. (See Chapter Six.)

regular pricing refers to prices on merchandise that is not on sale and are not promotionally priced. (See Chapter Five.)

remote displays are product displays that are not located at the actual store. These free-standing units can target tourists because they are often placed in hotels. A department store that is located at one end of a mall might also use a remote display at the other end to alert customers of its presence. (See Chapter Eight.)

reorders are orders that are placed on merchandise that has purchased at least once before by the retailer. Reorders are more common with basics than with *fashion goods.* (See Chapter Six.)

resident buying office (RBO) is an organization located in a given fashion market that serves as a retailer's market representative for the procurement of merchandise. The two major types of resident buying offices are independent and store-owned. (See Chapter Six. Also see *independent buying office* and *store owned buying office.*)

resource (See *manufacturer.*)

retail advertising is advertising by retailers directed at consumers. (See Chapter Eight. Also see *trade advertising* and *national advertising*.)

retail divisions (See *Mazur plan*.)

retail-induced incentives are those motivators that are produced or provided by the retailer to encourage sales personnel to sell. Retail-induced incentives include *compensation* and recognition. (See Chapter Nine.)

retail selling can be accomplished via several channels, including mail and electronic (e.g., telephone, television, and the Internet) or over-the-counter. (See Chapter Nine.)

returns to vendor (RTV) occur when a retailer returns goods to a manufacturer for any reason, for instance not liking the merchandise or inherent problems (e.g., poor quality) in the product. (See Chapter Seven.)

run of press/newspaper (ROP) advertisements are ads in daily newspapers, usually used to promote weekly specials. (See Chapter Eight.)

S

safeguards/safeguard quotas are trade-related terms that have been in use since 2005. Safeguards are additional quotas if certain quota categories are disrupted. WTO members sometimes initiate safeguards. (See Chapter Six. Also see *World Trade Organization*.)

sales goals (sales quotas) are sales plans that are set by the retailer. Usually, the retailer hopes to either achieve or exceed these sales goals or sales quotas. (See Chapter Nine.)

sales manuals are used by retailers to convey the expectations of the company to the sales associates. Sales manuals are written procedures or directions and policies that a company wants their employees to follow. (See Chapter Nine.)

sales planning is the first step in developing the merchandise budget and is the estimation of the sales that a retailer will make over a period of time. (See Chapter Five.)

sales promotion is thought of, in the broadest sense, as all the efforts that attract consumers, build customer loyalty, and overall contribute to generating sales. The purpose of sales promotion is to inform, persuade, or remind customers about the business and its product. (See Chapter Eight.)

sales quotas (See *sales goals.*)

sales training varies in type and style and from retailer to retailer but is always concerned with readying salespeople to sell products and/or services that are being offered. (See Chapter Nine.)

seasonal goods are merchandise that sell best during either the Spring or Fall season. (See Chapter Four.)

secondary line is a similar version of a company's own popular item produced in a lower-cost fabrication and generally with lower-cost construction techniques, but keeping the "flavor" of the original design. These products are sold in a different market, at different stores, and to different consumers. (See Chapter Four.)

secondary service (See *ancillary service.*)

secondary trading area is the area beyond a store's *primary trading area* that yields customers despite a competitor's location advantage. A primary trading area usually extends three to five miles from the site, while a secondary trading area can be seven or more miles away. (See Chapter Eight.)

self service is minimal service, for example, when customers are first expected to find the merchandise they want, then take it to a service desk (cashier) to purchase it. (See Chapter Nine. Also see *limited service* and *full service.*)

selling is the person-to-person (most often face-to-face) contact between the retailer and customer, or between the manufacturer and customer, which results in a purchase by a customer. (See Chapter Nine. Also see *direct selling.*)

sell-through is the percentage of merchandise sold during a specific time period. It is also a type of sales plan that sets a certain percentage of the amount of merchandise sold as a goal to achieve. (See Chapter Five.)

shallow assortment refers to a merchandise assortment with relatively few sizes and colors for each style. (See Chapter Five.)

shopping goods is a term used to describe merchandise that is evaluated more by the consumer than *convenience goods* and include most clothing purchases. (See Chapter Four.)

short markup is a markup smaller than a *keystone markup*, i.e., one that creates a retail price that is less than double the cost of the goods to the merchant. (See Chapter Five.)

short-range planning involves looking at the most immediate concerns and setting goals of the business to achieve them. Two examples of short-range planning include such subjects as what to do about a sale that is a week away or how to meet a sales plan for the week. (See Chapter Five.)

showcase displays are often used for small or expensive items. These are usually enclosed and locked. (See Chapter Eight. Also see *closed-island display.*)

six-month plan is a unit and dollar merchandise plan covering six-month time frames within a calendar year, i.e., Spring/Summer (February–July) and Fall/Winter (August–January). (See Chapter Five.)

Small Business Administration (SBA) is a federal agency with special programs for minority business development and for the economically disadvantaged. It can provide financial information to small business owners. (See Chapter Ten.)

social justice framework is an area of ethical decision-making and asserts that everyone should be treated equally and that no group should be taken advantage of. For example, the dumping of unsafe products in third world countries would be considered unethical in a social justice framework. (See Chapter Eleven.)

social responsibility describes a company's duties and obligations to society that extend beyond ethics and legalities. The public expects business to be part of the community and to act responsibly. (See Chapter Eleven.)

soft goods include apparel and linens and generally have higher turnover and profitability than *hard goods,* which include home furnishings, appliances, electronics, and so forth. (See Chapter Four.)

sole proprietorship is a company owned by one person that is fully controlled by the owner, and all benefits and costs accrue to that individual. (See Chapter Two.)

sourcing is the term used to describe the process of determining how and where goods will be procured. (See Chapter Six.)

sourcing agent (See *purchasing agent.*)

special events can be classified as paid/personal communication and can include demonstrations, trunk shows, fashion shows, celebrity appearances, or other events, which are used to gain the interest of consumers and attract them to a retail environment. (See Chapter Eight.)

special orders are orders that are placed with a vendor usually for a specific customer. (See Chapter Seven.)

specialty goods is a term used for merchandise that is a particular brand. (See Chapter Four.)

specialty store (limited assortment store) sells a limited type of merchandise, for example, shoes, electronics, or apparel. Generally this type of store provides the customer with special services not often seen in department or discount stores. (See Chapter Two.)

specific tariff is a rate of duty that is based on a set amount per each unit imported. (See Chapter Six. Also see *ad valorem tariff* and *tariff*.)

spiffs are incentives provided by vendors that compensate the salesperson, thereby providing motivation to try to sell particular items. Sometimes this compensation is money for merchandise that is being pushed and sold. Spiffs are sometimes called push money. (See Chapter Nine.)

staff (See *organizational charts*.)

standards are a means of measuring performance through accepted guidelines that help to monitor performance. (See Chapter Five.)

staples (See *basics*.)

stock keeping unit (SKU) is the smallest unit level of merchandise and includes style, color, size, and any other information that needs to be tracked. (See Chapter Five.)

stock-to-sales ratio method (SSR) is a method of *inventory planning*, which arrives at a planned stock level that is based on what should be on hand at any given time, rather than on an average stock basis. It may be arrived at by multiplying the planned sales for the month by the BOM stock-to-sales ratio. (See Chapter Five.)

stock turn (ST) (See *turnover*.)

store brand is a term used to describe goods that are produced and named by the retailer that sells them. Store brands literally carry the name of the store. (See Chapter Four. Also see *private label*.)

stored retailers include traditional, bricks-and-mortar locations that sell merchandise, such as department stores, boutiques, variety stores, mom-and-pop stores, discount stores, mass merchandisers, and off-price stores. (Chapter Two. Also see *non-stored retailers*.)

store manuals (See *sales manuals*.)

store (operations) management (See *Mazur plan*.)

store-owned buying office is a buying office that is owned and operated by a retail firm or group of retail stores. (See Chapter Six.)

strip center is composed (generally) of a relatively small number of stores set beside each other, with the largest tenant perhaps a grocery store, variety store, or drugstore. Usually the remainder of the stores are convenience stores. These strip malls are not enclosed as are larger malls. (See Chapter Two.)

sub-classification (subclass) is the term used to describe a group of merchandise within a classification that is closely related in styling, such as bottoms or tops under the classification of sportswear. (See Chapter Five.)

supervisor is usually a first-line, entry level manager and is any person who is responsible for the conduct of others in the accomplishment of a task. Supervisors can be managers or vice versa. (See Chapter One.)

supplier (See *manufacturer.*)

support service (See *ancillary service.*)

T

tabloid inserts are printed separately from the regular newspaper and are usually inserted into Saturday or Sunday papers. (See Chapter Eight.)

tangible services are those services that provide such concrete assistance as personal shoppers, childcare, and delivery service. (See Chapter Nine. Also see *intangible services.*)

target market is the group of customers that a company seeks to serve. (See Chapter Three.)

target marketing (customer segmentation) is identifying one's *target market* by such *demographic* variables as age, gender, income, education, marital status, religion, family size, life-cycle stage, ethnicity, and mobility; *psychographic variables* are also used including activities, interests, and opinions. (See Chapter Three.)

tariff is a special tax, paid to the government, placed on imported merchandise that adds to the cost of goods. (See Chapter Six. Also see *ad valorem tariff* and *specific tariff.*)

television shopping is a term used for retailing programs that are broadcast on television, through such networks as the Home Shopping Network and QVC. Customers watch the programs on TV and then phone in (or e-mail) their orders. (See Chapter Two.)

temporary retailers are generally vendors who set up tables or carts and sells goods—often one-of-a-kind—made by a seller or artist. They usually set up on street sidewalks or walkways of malls. Some larger retailers are also experimenting with temporary stores that sell goods related to specific events, such as the Olympics or the Super Bowl. (See Chapter Two. Also see *pop-up retail*.)

terms of sale are conditions in a purchase agreement between retailer and vendor that include *discounts,* delivery, and transportation costs. (See Chapter Seven.)

top-down planning involves goal setting at the highest level of the organizational structure and management, then filtering the goals down to the other levels. (See Chapter Five. Also see *bottom-up planning*.)

top, upper-level manager is a high-level management position that includes officers and top executives—for example the president and vice president of a company. (See Chapter One.)

town centers/lifestyle centers are terms that describe residential and multipurpose structures (work/live/play) near mass transit, often with less parking than normally would be planned because residents have the ability to walk to the stores. (See Chapter Two.)

trade advertising is advertising by manufacturers to retailers, for example in *WWD* or *DNR.* (See Chapter Eight.)

trademark is any word, name, or symbol that has been adopted and used by the owner to identify a product and distinguish it from others. In the U.S., the first person to use the trademark in conjunction with a product has ownership of the trademark and can exclude others from using it. This is not always the case in other countries, however. (See Chapter Eleven. Also see *copyright*.)

trade shows are groups of temporary exhibits of vendors' offerings for a single merchandise category or group of related categories. (See Chapter Six.)

transactional services help to accommodate a purchase being made by a customer—for example, *credit* or *charge cards, layaway,* returns, and exchange adjustments. (See Chapter Nine.)

trunk shows are presentations of apparel lines by designers or vendors to store personnel or to customers. For some designers, trunk shows have provided the bulk of their sales in some stores. (See Chapter Eight.)

turnkey software is ready-made and mass-marketed for use across a range of businesses. (See Chapter One.)

turnover (TO) is a term used to describe how many times stock is sold and re-placed within a period of time. (See Chapter Five.)

tying contract is an illegal situation in which suppliers force retailers to buy un-wanted merchandise in order to purchase other desired merchandise. (See Chapter Eleven.)

U

U.S. Harmonized Tariff Schedule (USHTS) itemizes all products subject to the tariff imported from different countries and lists the rates of tariffs imposed on these products. (See Chapter Six.)

unit plan is a type of plan that involves the actual physical units and refers most often to the *assortment planning* and qualitative aspects on this plan. Unit planning involves decisions about what types of merchandise (or mix) should be bought and stocked by a retailer down to the number of pieces in inventory. (See Chapter Five.)

universal product code (UPC) is a 12-digit number used to track and identify products to the lowest level of merchandise detail. As more vendors use the UPC for item identification, more retailers can reduce their ticketing time and labor, and the stream of merchandise to the selling floor is further accelerated. Because the UPC provides sales data at *point of sale*, retailers are able to make discerning merchandising decisions on-the-spot including quick adjustment and control of inventory composition and levels. (See Chapter Five.)

utilitarianism can be thought of as doing "the greatest good for the greatest number." A cost-benefit analysis can assess the viability of this and is generally used in business and governmental decision-making. (See Chapter Eleven.)

V

value is the relationship between quality and price. (See Chapter Four.)

variety store is a retail store that sells a wide assortment of popularly priced goods. (See Chapter Two.)

vendor (See *manufacturer.*)

vendor-induced incentives are those furnished by the supplier to the retailer or directly to the sales employee. *Spiffs* or push money are sometimes provided to retailers by vendors. These are incentives that compensate the salesperson, thereby providing motivation to try to sell particular items. In addition to monetary rewards, various other forms of vendor support and incentives include: training, trunk shows, educational material, and contests. The vendor may also supply personnel sales training and/or educational materials. (See Chapter Nine.)

vendor matrix (key resource list) incorporates the company-approved key vendors from which a buyer is recommended and/or required to purchase. (See Chapter Five.)

venture capitalist (financier) is a person who supplies money and takes a financial risk as an investor in a business. (See Chapter Ten.)

vertical integration is a form of diversification that involves a company acquiring another company or developing a function that serves as either its supplier or its customer. (See Chapter Two.)

vertical malls are found in urban settings and consist of multiple shopping levels. Examples include Water Tower Place in Chicago and Trump Tower in New York. (See Chapter Two.)

video walls (i.e., many television screens displaying the same visual and/or large screen projections) make a dramatic display and are effective in gaining consumer attention. (See Chapter Eight.)

visa is a document from the exporting country guaranteeing country of origin and is a way for the exporting country to monitor the amount of its exports to the U.S. (See Chapter Six.)

visual merchandising is a general term that is used to describe everything that is seen when a customer enters a store. This includes the exterior appearance of the store, window displays, signage, and all interior displays of merchandise on fixtures and lighting that are used to create an overall effect. (See Chapter Eight.)

W

wall displays utilize dead or unused store wall space to show merchandise. (See Chapter Eight.)

warehouse stores are discounters that offer food and other items in a no-frills setting. They often concentrate on special purchases of brand-name goods. Generally they are characterized by a lack of such customer services as credit card usage or bagging. Warehouse stores often require a "membership fee," which the consumer must pay before being able to shop at the store. (See Chapter Two.)

warranty ensures the integrity and life of a product for a specific period of time, which is usually in writing. (See Chapter Nine. Also see *guarantee*.)

week's supply method of *inventory (stock) planning* is used when calculating a needed stock level by week. With this method, planned stock is equal to the average stock in a week's supply multiplied by the planned weekly sales. (See Chapter Five.)

wholesaler is a reseller of merchandise. Normally, wholesalers buy merchandise in large quantities, which are then broken down and then sold in smaller quantities. (See Chapter Six.)

wholesale selling (contact selling) involves the customer purchasing directly from the manufacturer. (See Chapter Nine.)

window displays are an important part of visual merchandising. Traditional store window displays are enclosures with solid backings that isolate the merchandise to be presented. These *closed displays* perform a selling function even when the store is closed. *Open displays,* common in malls, enable the viewer to see directly into the store through the display. (See Chapter Eight.)

World Trade Organization (WTO) was formed in 1994 as a result of the extended Uruguay Rounds of talks under the GATT (General Agreement on Tariffs and Trade). The WTO facilitates trade agreements and serves as a permanent forum for members to address trade relations. (See Chapter Six.)

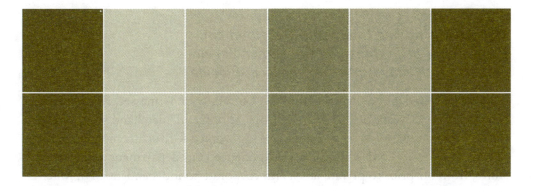

About the Authors

AUTHORS/EDITORS

Nancy J. Rabolt
Professor, Apparel Design & Merchandising
Consumer & Family Studies/Dietetics Department
San Francisco State University

Dr. Rabolt was awarded her Ph.D. from the University of Tennessee. She is coauthor of *Consumer Behavior: In Fashion,* published by Prentice Hall. She is active in the International Textile and Apparel Association and has edited two special publications for ITAA. She is also a member of the American Collegiate Retailing Association. She has published articles in many journals, including *Clothing and Textiles Research Journal,* the *Journal of Fashion Marketing and Management,* and other international journals, in addition to trade and computer journals, and has presented papers at conferences for the past 20 years. Coauthor/editor (with Judy K. Miler) of *Cases 4, 6, 13, 16, 19, 23, 24, 28, 32, 33, 38, 43, 44, 48, 50, 72;* coauthor (with Diane Cantua) of *Case 22;* coauthor (with Peggy Gorbach) of *Case 57.*

Judy K. Miler
Merchandising and Internship Development,
Department of Textiles and Consumer Services
Florida State University, Tallahassee, Florida

Dr. Miler received all her degrees from the University of Tennessee, Knoxville. She brought over 13 years of apparel retail operations and merchandising management experience with her to academia, having worked for such companies as Levi Strauss & Co. and Lord & Taylor. Her experience is in department and specialty stores, from off-price to private label, and corporate to independents. Dr. Miler is a member of the International Textile and Apparel Association, the Costume Society of America, American Collegiate Retailing Association, and the Popular Culture Association. Research interests include women in retail and apparel management, fashion in popular culture, and consumer behavior. She also consults for new business startup ventures. Coauthor/editor (with Nancy J. Rabolt) of *Cases 4, 6, 13, 16, 19, 23, 24, 28, 32, 33, 38, 43, 44, 48, 50, 72*; coauthor (with Janice Ellinwood) of *Case 10.*

CONTRIBUTING AUTHORS

Marina Alexander
Assistant Professor, Interior Design and Merchandising
East Carolina University, North Carolina

Dr. Alexander was awarded her master's and doctorate degrees from Auburn University, Auburn, Alabama. She has been teaching at East Carolina University since 2003. She is an active member of the International Apparel and Textile Association. She conducts research in the areas of application of technology in apparel industry, use of 3D body scan data for shape analysis, consumer behavior, and retail strategies. Coauthor of *Case 12.*

Maryanne Smith Bohlinger
Professor Emeritus, Marketing
Community College of Philadelphia

Professor Bohlinger received her BS in fashion design and MS in Textiles and Clothing from Drexel University and Ed.D. in Marketing and Distribution from Temple University. She is the author of *Merchandise Buying*, published by Allyn and Bacon, and has been a fashion consultant and buyer. Author of *Case 21.*

About the Authors

420

Diane Cantua
Textile Analyst, San Francisco Laboratory
U.S. Customs and Border Protection

Ms. Cantua has her BA and MA from San Francisco State University in textiles. She is a member of the American Association of Textile Chemists and Colorists (AATCC). She has taught textiles at the Fashion Institute of Design & Merchandising and at San Francisco State University. In her current position she analyzes imported textile goods mainly for tariff purposes. Coauthor of *Case 22*.

Billy Christensen
Buyer
JCPenney

Mr. Christensen has worked in the apparel and textile industry for a number of years. He was Sales Manager for the Premiere Neckwear Groupe and a buyer with Harold's Stores, Inc., in Dallas, Texas. He has spent many years on the retail store side of the fashion industry. Currently, Billy is a buyer with JCPenney. Author of *Case 47*.

Courtney Cothren
Instructor, School of Design and Fashion
Stephens College, Columbia, Missouri

Ms. Cothren coordinates the Fashion Marketing Management program at Stephens College. She graduated from Stephens with a BS in Fashion Marketing Management in 2000. After graduation she completed the Neiman Marcus Executive Development Program and worked as an assistant buyer in fashion accessories. She then moved to Harold's Stores, where she worked as the Men's Sportswear buyer and planner prior to moving back to Missouri and teaching at Stephens. Author of *Case 41*.

Kitty Dickerson
Professor and Chair
Department of Textile and Apparel Management
University of Missouri–Columbia

Dr. Dickerson is author of *Textiles and Apparel in the Global Economy* (1999) and *Inside the Fashion Business* (2003), both published by Prentice Hall. She is also author of more than 75 articles in both scholarly and trade journals and has been invited to address industry and academic audiences in the United States and other countries. Dr. Dickerson is a Fellow in the International Textile and Apparel Association and has served as President of that group. She was named to *Textile World's* "Top Ten Leaders" list and was chosen as *Bobbin's* "Educator of the Year." She also serves on the Board of Directors of Kellwood Company, a multinational Fortune 700 apparel firm with annual sales of $2 billion. Author of *Cases 68, 70.*

Lorynn Divita
Assistant Professor, Fashion Merchandising
Department of Family and Consumer Sciences
Baylor University, Waco, Texas

Dr. Divita holds degrees in Fashion Merchandising from California State University Chico, in Apparel Manufacturing Management from University of Missouri, and in Textiles Products Marketing from University of North Carolina at Greensboro. Her research interests include corporate competitiveness, environmental issues in the textile and apparel industry, and textile and apparel economics and trade. Dr. Divita has published in journals including the *Clothing and Textiles Research Journal* and *The Journal of Fashion Marketing and Management,* and has presented her research internationally. She is currently working on a book about the history of West Texas cotton farming in the latter half of the twentieth century with her husband, Dr. David Smith. Author of *Cases 37, 46.*

About the Authors

Molly Eckman
Professor, Department of Design and Merchandising
Colorado State University

After ten years in retailing, Dr. Eckman received her MS from Iowa State University and her Ph.D. from the University of Maryland. She is a past president of the International Textile and Apparel Association. Her research interests include the effect of culture on consumer behavior, internationalization of retailing, and social responsibility in the global apparel and footwear supply chain. Coauthor of *Cases 2, 30, 31.*

Janice Ellinwood
Department Chair, Fashion Design, Fashion Merchandising
Marymount University

Professor Ellinwood was awarded a Master of Fine Arts in Design from The George Washington University. She also studied at the University of Massachusetts and Syracuse University. In addition to having a career in buying women's apparel and accessories, Professor Ellinwood is an artist, professor, and evaluator of fashion design higher education in the United States and abroad. She served as a Fulbright Scholar in Bulgaria during 2001 and 2002. Her research investigates the ethics of fashion advertising, and she worked on the problem of sweatshop labor at the time of the Clinton administration. Coauthor of *Case 10*; author of *Cases 27, 49, 51.*

Judith Everett
Professor
Northern Arizona University

Professor Judith C. Everett is a graduate of Kent State University (BS and MA) and Arizona State University (MBA). Professor Everett was honored with the "Lifetime Achievement Award" from the School of Communication at NAU. She coauthored with Kristen Swanson three books, including *Guide to Producing a Fashion Show, Promotion in the Merchandising Environment,* and *Writing for Fashion* for Fairchild Books. She is a member of the American Collegiate Retailing Association and The Fashion Group International. Author of *Cases 35, 56, 71.*

Tonda K. Fuller
Senior Import Specialist, Port of San Francisco
U.S. Customs and Border Protection

Tonda Fuller specializes in wearing apparel and textile import issues at CBP. Tonda has had a distinguished career with the federal government for over 12 years and is currently assigned to the Wearing Apparel Team with CBP in the Port of San Francisco. She is an active participant in the Textile Production Verification Team (TPVT) program and has worked extensively on both the African Growth and Opportunity Act and Moroccan Free Trade Agreement. Coauthor of *Case 34.*

LuAnn R. Gaskill
Professor and Head, Department of Apparel, Housing, and
*   Resource Management*
Virginia Tech

Dr. Gaskill conducts research on small business management and entrepreneurship and has engaged in a comprehensive research program focused on dimensions of development encompassing business, product, and human resource development leading to business growth and sustainability. She has published in a variety of journals including the *Journal of Business Research, Business Case Study Journal, Clothing and Textiles Research Journal, Journal of Small Business Management, Journal of Small Business and Entrepreneurship, International Review of Retail Distribution and Consumer Research, Journal of Small Business Management,* and *The Journal of Excellence in Higher Education.* As a Fellow of the Price-Babson College Program in Wellesley, Massachusetts, she has worked extensively with the numerous Small Business Development Centers as a consultant and engaged in program development for the U.S. Small Business Administration. Author of *Case 64.*

Peggy Gorbach
Professor, Family and Consumer Studies
Evergreen Valley College, San Jose, CA

Peggy Gorbach received her BA degree in Family and Consumer Sciences at California State University, Long Beach, and her MA degree in Family and Consumer Sciences from San Francisco State University. She is currently a professor in Family and Consumer Studies at Evergreen Valley College in San Jose California. She and her family live in the San Francisco Bay Area. Coauthor of *Case 57.*

About the Authors

424

Jenny Greene
Technical Designer
Harold's Stores, Inc.

Ms. Green has been with Harold's for five years. Her background is in patternmaking and retail. She resides and works in Dallas, Texas. Author of *Case 25*.

Jaya Halepete
Assistant Professor, Fashion Merchandising
Marymount University, Arlington, Virginia

Dr. Jaya Halepete received her MS in Fashion Merchandising from the University of Georgia, and Ph.D. in Textiles and Clothing from Iowa State University. She worked as a buyer for a major retail chain in India before coming to the United States for further studies. Her research interests include international retailing and international consumer behavior. Coauthor of *Case 12*; author of *Case 65*.

Joseph H. Hancock, II
Assistant Professor
Drexel University

Dr. Hancock received his Ph.D. from the Ohio State University. He has a 20-year management, retailing, and product merchandising background, having worked for such U.S. companies as Gap, Limited, Inc., and Target Corporation. He conducts research and lectures internationally in the areas of fashion branding, product merchandising, popular culture, and contemporary men's style. Currently he is authoring a book on fashion brands for Fairchild Books. Author of *Cases 3, 17, 59*.

Abigail Johnson
Assistant Buyer
Friedman's Jewelers

After graduating from the University of Texas, Austin, with a BS in Textiles and Apparel, Abby moved to Florida to start her career in retailing as a Walt Disney World Intern in Merchandising. She then worked in the Parks and Resorts Merchandising office as an Advanced Intern in Planning. Her career brought her back to Texas, working at Harold's stores in Allocation and Planning, and then to Friedman's Jewelers as an Assistant Buyer. In her spare time she enjoys sewing, making patterns, and drawing. Author of *Case 26*.

Kim K. P. Johnson
Professor, Design, Housing, and Apparel
University of Minnesota

Dr. Johnson's research interests include non-normative consumption and issues relating to the social psychology of dress. She has coedited three books: *Fashion Foundations, Appearance and Power,* and *Dress and Identity,* and has coauthored over 60 publications in various journals. Coauthor of *Case 76.*

Dee K. Knight
Associate Professor, Apparel Merchandising
University of North Texas

Prior to joining the ranks of academia, Dr. Knight was owner and President of an upscale apparel specialty store for professional women. She teaches courses in merchandising, promotions, and global fashion retailing. Since 2003, she has codirected an interdisciplinary study abroad program to Asia (Malaysia, Hong Kong, China), with a focus on international sourcing and retailing of apparel and related goods. Her research interests are in two primary areas, professional development of retail employees and retail internationalization. Coauthor of *Case 5;* author of *Case 45.*

Antigone Kotsiopulos
Professor, Department Head and Associate Dean Emeritus
Colorado State University

Dr. Kotsiopulos is a past President and Fellow of the International Textile and Apparel Association and a 2006 recipient of the Oliver P. Pennock Distinguished Service Award. Antigone's industry experience led to several initiatives related to technology applications in the classroom including authorship of *Merchandising Mathematics* published by Fairchild Books. She is currently a private consultant and serves as a CSU Mediation Officer. Coauthor of *Cases 2, 30, 31.*

Joy M. Kozar
Assistant Professor, Department of Apparel, Textiles and Interior Design
Kansas State University

Dr. Kozar received both her bachelor's and master's degrees in apparel and textile marketing from Kansas State University. She received her Ph.D. in textiles and clothing from Iowa State University, where she also received a minor in gerontology as part of her scholarship focus on older consumers. In addition to her academic endeavors, Dr. Kozar has experience working in the fashion retail industry, including co-owning and operating a small apparel retail business. Coauthor of *Cases 63, 74*.

Rebecca A. Lucas
Operations Specialist, San Francisco Field Office
U.S. Customs and Border Protection

Rebecca has worked with CBP for over five years, beginning her career as an intern while receiving her BA at San Francisco State University. As an Operations Specialist, she is responsible for managing several trade enforcement programs, which include quota, free trade agreements, and textile enforcement. Prior to her current position at CBP Field Office, Becky worked as an Import Specialist Team Leader for the textile team at the Port of San Francisco and was active in the Textile Production Verification Team (TPVT) program. Coauthor of *Case 34*.

Karen S. Marchione
Assistant Professor
Bowling Green State University

Dr. Marchione received her Ph.D. from Oklahoma State University, MS from Virginia Tech, and BS from West Virginia University. Her research area pertains to investigating individual factors that relate to consumer ethical decision making. Coauthor of *Case 75*.

Sara B. Marcketti
Assistant Professor, Textiles and Clothing
Iowa State University

Dr. Marcketti's research interests include design piracy, the history of the ready-to-wear apparel industry, and learning strategies for students. Her work has appeared in journals such as *Clothing and Textiles Research Journal, Family and Consumer Sciences Research Journal,* and *Collections: A Journal for Museum and Archives Professionals.* Coauthor of *Cases 63, 75.*

Suzanne G. Marshall
Fashion Merchandising and Design
California State University, Long Beach

Dr. Marshall received her BS from the University of Georgia, MS from Oklahoma State University, and MA and Ph.D. from UCLA. She was an educational representative for Unique Zipper Company and an assistant buyer for The Lullabye Shop in North Carolina. She is lead author of *Individuality in Clothing Selection and Personal Appearance,* 5th through 7th editions, and coauthor of *Merchandising Mathematics for Retailing,* 3rd edition, published by Prentice Hall. She serves on the ITAA Curriculum Committee and has been a reviewer of abstracts for annual conferences. Author of *Cases 39, 42, 62.*

Nancy Anabel Mason
Senior Port Process Specialist
U.S. Customs & Border Protection

Nancy Anabel Mason obtained both a BA and MA in Clothing and Textiles from San Francisco State University. As a graduate student she received the Distinguished Achievement Award. She has worked for the federal government for 16 years. During this time she was the recipient of the National EEO Federal Women's Program Manager Award and a recent graduate of the Federal Executive Board Executive Development Program. Her research on Mexico's *maquiladoras* is published in an *International Textile & Apparel Association monograph* and *Twin Plant News.* Coauthor of *Case 34.*

Ellen McKinney
Instructor, Fashion Design
Art Institute of Dallas

Ellen McKinney received her Ph.D. from the University of Minnesota where she was the lead research assistant in the Human Dimensioning Lab. Her research relates to 3D body scan data for women's pant patterns. She holds an MA in Fashion Design from Texas Woman's University and a BS in Fashion Design from Texas Christian University. She has taught fashion design and merchandising courses at the Art Institute of Dallas, University of Minnesota, Texas Christian University, Tarrant County College, and Texas Woman's University. She has industry experience in apparel manufacturing and retail, as well as fashion support areas. Coauthor of *Case 40.*

Steven McKinney
Retail Consultant

Steven McKinney holds an MBA with a Supply Chain certificate and a BBA in Marketing from Texas Christian University. He is a retail industry consultant and has experience in store operation; merchandising; and strategic and financial analysis. He has helped clients improve profitability by implementing projects that improve margin, reduce expense structure, and make better use of merchandise inventory. He has worked with various retailers including Macy's, Neiman Marcus, Army & Air Force Exchange Services, Saks, and Best Buy. Coauthor of *Case 40.*

Marcia Morgado
Associate Professor, Program in Apparel Product Design
& Merchandising
University of Hawaii-Manoa

Dr. Morgado's interests include fashion and culture studies and semiotics of appearance. She served as the Associate Editor of *Clothing & Textiles Research Journal* from 1997 to 2004. Author of *Case 66.*

Denise T. Ogden
Assistant Professor, Business Administration
Penn State University-Lehigh Valley

Dr. Ogden previously worked at the D&B Corporation, where she was recognized for the training programs she developed. She is currently the President of the Doctors Ogden Group, LLC. Her research interests are in retailing and cultural aspects of marketing. She has authored two books and has articles in several academic journals. Currently she is the editor of *Retail Education Today*. Dr. Ogden holds a Ph.D. in Marketing from Temple University, an MBA from De Sales University, and a BS degree from Adams State College. Coauthor of *Case 7*; author of *Cases 15, 54*.

James R. (Doc) Ogden
Professor, Marketing
Kutztown University of Pennsylvania

Dr. Ogden has published six books in the area of marketing and advertising. Doc is also CEO of the Doctors Ogden Group, LLC. In addition, Doc sits on the board of directors for two corporations and has worked for an array of other corporations including General Motors, Meijer, and D&B. He has consulted for many others in the areas of advertising and marketing. Doc's academic training includes a Ph.D. from the University of Northern Colorado, a master's in Marketing, and a bachelor's in General Business and Business Education with minors in English, Language, and Literature. Coauthor of *Case 7*.

Nancy A. Oliver
Assistant Professor, Fashion Merchandising and Design
North Carolina A&T State University

Dr. Oliver received her Doctor of Philosophy in Social Psychology of Clothing from the University of Tennessee. She has been a clothing specialist for the agricultural extension agency, marketing researcher, and university educator. Author of *Case 67*.

Cristiana Piccinni
Ph.D. Student
Kansas State University

Ms. Piccinni received her MS in Exercise Science from Appalachian State University. She has served over 12 years on active military duty in the U.S. Army and as an officer in the U.S. Air Force and in civil service. Ms. Piccinni has also worked as an Exercise Physiologist and a Health Promotion Director. She was recognized as a distinguished Graduate at the Air Force Officer Training School and is a member of Kappa Omicron Nu and Alpha Chi. Coauthor of *Case 74*.

Jongeun Rhee
Assistant Professor, Apparel Design and Development
University of Wisconsin–Stout

Dr. Rhee teaches courses in functional clothing design, CAD for apparel images, fashion industry, and quality assurance. Her research interests include apparel consumption, apparel shopping behaviors, sustainable apparel consumption, as well as sustainable design. Coauthor of *Case 76*.

Dong Shen
Associate Professor, Department of Family and Consumer Sciences
California State University, Sacramento

Dr. Shen's research interests are cross-cultural studies on consumer behavior and consumer psychology. Her doctoral degree is from the Ohio State University. She is a reviewer of the *Clothing and Textiles Research Journal*. Author of *Case 36*.

Berkeley K. Stone
Student, School of Merchandising and Hospitality Management
University of North Texas

While attending the University of North Texas, Berkeley Stone has achieved academic excellence as a UNT School of Merchandising and Hospitality Management Scholar and Dean's List student. She is an Ambassador of the School and a member of Young Conservatives of Texas. Berkeley has several years of retail experience in both specialty and department stores. In addition to merchandising, her other academic interests include market research, business finance, and political science. Coauthor of *Case 5*.

Connie Ulasewicz
Assistant professor, Apparel Design and Merchandising
Consumer & Family Studies/Dietetics Department
San Francisco State University

Dr. Ulasewicz is an international consultant in the areas of sustainable fashion and socially responsible business practices. She is coauthor of *Sustainable Fashion: Why Now?*, published by Fairchild Books, and *Made In America: The Business of Sewn Products Manufacturing*, published by GarmentoSpeak. Author of *Cases 11, 73.*

About the Authors

Credits

Chapter 1

1.1 Courtesy of Belk
1.2 Courtesy of Macy's, Inc.
1.4 Courtesy of Belk
1.5 Courtesy of Belk

Chapter 2

2.2 Courtesy of Fairchild Publications, Inc.
2.3 Courtesy of L.L.Bean
2.4 Courtesy of The Dubai Mall
2.5 Stephen Chernin/Getty Images
2.6 Courtesy of Fairchild Publications, Inc.

Chapter 3

3.5 Courtesy of Adidas
3.6 Courtesy of Joseph Hancock
3.7 Courtesy of Joseph Hancock
3.8 Courtesy of Joseph Hancock

Chapter 4

4.1 Matt Peyton/Getty Images for American Express
4.2 Courtesy of Fairchild Publications, Inc.
4.3 Courtesy of Fairchild Publications, Inc.
4.6a Courtesy Forever21.com
4.6b Courtesy of Fairchild Publications, Inc.
4.7 MN Chan/Getty Images
4.8 Courtesy of Fairchild Publications, Inc.

Chapter 5

5.1 Courtesy of Fairchild Publications, Inc.
5.2 Courtesy The Doneger Group

Chapter 6

6.1 Courtesy of Gerber Technology
6.4 Courtesy of Fairchild Publications, Inc.
6.5 Courtesy of Fairchild Publications, Inc.
6.6 Courtesy of Fairchild Publications, Inc.
6.7 Courtesy of Fairchild Publications, Inc.

Chapter 7

7.2 Courtesy of Fairchild Publications, Inc.
7.3 Courtesy of Pepper's
7.4 Courtesy of Retail Pro

Chapter 8

8.1 Courtesy of Macy's, Inc.
8.2 Courtesy of Fairchild Publications, Inc.
8.3 Courtesy of OshKosh
8.4 Courtesy of OshKosh
8.5 Courtesy of Fairchild Publications, Inc.
8.6 Courtesy of Fairchild Publications, Inc.
8.7 Courtesy of The Advertising Archives
8.9 Courtesy of Judy Miler

8.10 Courtesy of Fairchild Publications, Inc.
8.11 Scott Wintrow/Getty Images
8.12 Courtesy of Fairchild Publications, Inc.
8.13 Courtesy of Fairchild Publications, Inc.
8.14 Courtesy of Fairchild Publications, Inc.

Chapter 9

9.1 Courtesy of Fairchild Publications, Inc.
9.2 Courtesy of Escada
9.3 Courtesy of Fairchild Publications, Inc.
9.4 Getty Images

Chapter 11

11.1 Courtesy of TJX
11.2 Courtesy of the Gap
11.3 Courtesy of The Humane Society of the United States
11.4 Courtesy of Burberry
11.5 Courtesy of Kathrine Baumann

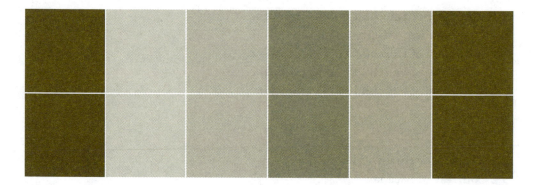

Index

Index